TAMING THE STREET

RANDOM HOUSE
NEW YORK

TAMING THE STREET

THE OLD GUARD,
THE NEW DEAL,
AND FDR'S FIGHT
TO REGULATE
AMERICAN CAPITALISM

DIANA B. HENRIQUES

Published in the United States by Random House,
an imprint and division of
Penguin Random House LLC, New York.

Random House and the House colophon are
registered trademarks of Penguin Random House LLC.

Library of Congress Cataloging-in-Publication Data
Names: Henriques, Diana B., author.
Title: Taming the Street: the old guard, the New Deal, and FDR's
fight to regulate American capitalism / by Diana B. Henriques.
Description: New York: Random House, 2023 | Includes index.
Identifiers: LCCN 2023002524 (print) | LCCN 2023002525 (ebook) |
ISBN 9780593132647 (hardcover) | ISBN 9780593132654 (ebook)
Subjects: LCSH: New York Stock Exchange—History. | Stock
Market Crash, 1929. | Depressions—1929. | New Deal, 1933–1939. |
United States—Economic conditions—1918–1945. | United
States—Social conditions—1933–1945. | Roosevelt, Franklin D.
(Franklin Delano), 1882–1945.
Classification: LCC HB3717 1929 .H46 2023 (print) |
LCC HB3717 1929 (ebook) | DDC 330.973/0916—dc23/eng/20230626
LC record available at https://lccn.loc.gov/2023002524
LC ebook record available at https://lccn.loc.gov/2023002525

Printed in the United States of America on acid-free paper

randomhousebooks.com

9 8 7 6 5 4 3 2 1

FIRST EDITION

Book design by Barbara M. Bachman

For the brilliant Jane Isay,
who never lost faith in this book—
or in its author.

The merchandising of securities is really traffic in the economic and social welfare of our people. Such traffic demands the utmost good faith and fair dealing. . . . Without such an ethical foundation, economic well-being cannot be achieved.

—President Franklin D. Roosevelt, on signing the Securities Act on May 27, 1933

To know what has come before is to be armed against despair.

—Jon Meacham in *The Soul of America: The Battle for Our Better Angels*

CONTENTS

PREFACE

THE JAZZ AGE. THE ROARING TWENTIES.

As America moves into the "twenties" of the twenty-first century, those labels glow like the smoky lights of a speakeasy. The Jazz Age conjures up scenes of bootleg cocktails and raccoon coats, heroic aviators and long-limbed showgirls, the folksiness of comic Will Rogers and the classiness of Broadway's Fred Astaire. Above all, the era brought America a plethora of new things: tabletop radios, Model T cars, electric refrigerators, rayon underwear, cellophane tape, paper tissues, vacuum cleaners, frozen fish, electric fans, canned fruits, telephones. The last century's "twenties" certainly seem, in hindsight, a lot more glamorous than our own version.

But for some Americans—the free market purists who are becoming more influential with every passing year—the Jazz Age is more than a cultural time capsule. It is a template for a future America: an America of limited government, tiny taxes, unregulated financial markets, and unfettered capitalism. For them, the Jazz Age was a capitalist Eden destroyed by a radical left-wing president who tried but failed to fix the Great Depression of the 1930s. As the 1920s and the 1930s sink below the horizon of history, this mythology of a free market paradise destroyed by Washington gets easier to sell and harder to dispute.

A diligent reader can set the record straight, of course. The New Deal, the recovery and reform program set up by President Franklin D. Roosevelt after his landslide election victory in 1932, has been deeply and broadly studied and debated by some of the past century's

most respected historians and economists. But it has also been brazenly distorted, since its earliest days, by adversaries who dispute
Roosevelt's bedrock belief that the federal government should serve
the general welfare, not just the interests of the powerful few.

To dispute what Roosevelt tried to do, then, one must first distort
what Roosevelt tried to change: the selfish plutocratic culture of the
1920s.

In the 1920s, government policy was shaped almost entirely by the
demands and desires of the very rich, regardless of the consequences
for ordinary Americans. Most wealthy Americans condemned regulation of business as socialism, communism, and tyranny—and the
conservative political leaders of the era overwhelmingly agreed. To
them, any effort to curb business and help workers was a call for
"class warfare." Perhaps inevitably, given the temptations of unbridled power, the decade of business domination was a decade of destructive practices that inflicted real harm on millions of Americans.
Of course, nostalgic free marketeers of today generally deny that
their favorite era was beset by any of these sins. To do so would beg
the question of how today's America could keep the same serpents
out of the new unregulated Eden they want to create.

As for the claims that FDR's New Deal failed to fix anything, the
historical record provides ample evidence to the contrary. It is not
my mission here to document the entire constructive legacy of the
New Deal; others have ably done that. I highly recommend *Why the
New Deal Matters,* by historian Eric Rauchway, which briefly but
beautifully describes how Roosevelt left his mark on everyday life in
today's America—with Social Security, unemployment insurance,
new public parks and libraries, power-generating dams, land reclaimed from floods, and priceless murals and cultural archives. My
mission, rather, is to describe just one of the New Deal's most significant achievements: clearing out the vicious jungle that was the
nation's financial landscape in the 1920s and replacing it with a well-
tended terrain where ordinary Americans could save and invest with
confidence.

That this particular New Deal experiment largely succeeded is
proven by the postwar flourishing of an American middle class that

did not fear losing its savings to crooked banks or being swindled by dishonest brokers. Freed of those fears, millions of Americans could save, invest their savings, buy homes, pay tuition for their children, and retire in comfort. By reforming Wall Street, Roosevelt enabled future generations of average Americans to participate in capitalism themselves and share directly in its rewards. We are an immensely richer nation because of this specific legacy of the New Deal.

Roosevelt's primary tool for this transformation was the Securities and Exchange Commission, a watchdog agency initially considered so radical and threatening that the titans of Wall Street fought tooth and claw to kill it before it was born in 1934. The fight to set up the SEC, to make it work, and then to make it work *better* in its early years is the heart of this story.

My narrative opens on the eve of the great stock market crash of 1929, the prelude to the Great Depression. But to understand why FDR was so determined to reform Wall Street in the 1930s, let's march quickly back through the previous decade—the decade Roosevelt lived through before he entered the White House, the decade that showed him what unregulated capitalism looked like.

THE MOST OBVIOUS STAIN on the morality of the Roaring Twenties was Prohibition, the nationwide constitutional ban on the sale of alcoholic beverages that went into effect in 1920, the year that saw the election of Republican president Warren G. Harding. By the end of the decade, the wildly unpopular "dry laws" had created a nation of scofflaws and a subculture of organized crime that plagued the nation for decades. But a close cousin to the gangsters running illegal booze were the respectable lawbreakers running corporate America and corrupting official Washington, where Jazz Age appointees were eager to stuff the business world's bribes into their pockets.

Too harsh? No. The corruption of the Harding administration was not equaled until President Nixon's Watergate scandal in the 1970s, and has not been trumped until our current era.

The decade we call the Roaring Twenties didn't start with a

roar—it started with a whimper. The sudden cuts in defense spending after the end of World War I in 1918 helped trigger one of the
sharpest recessions the nation had experienced to that time. That
downturn didn't end until 1922, and shorter, gentler recessions hit in
1924 and 1927. Unemployment persisted at levels that would be
alarming today. "At any given moment in the 'golden twenties' from
7 to 12 percent were jobless," according to William E. Leuchtenburg,
a leading historian of the era. The prosperity that indisputably
emerged in the decade's good years bypassed millions of formerly
secure American workers; for them, life became increasingly precarious.

In *Anxious Decades: America in Prosperity and Depression, 1920–
1941,* historian Michael Parrish catalogued the plight of those left
behind: "Machines displaced some three million workers; one-third
of them could not find new jobs. Conditions in a number of industries remained depressed throughout the twenties. Cars reduced the
demand for new boots and shoes, bruising the leather goods industry; new building materials put pressure on the lumber industry
across the country." Coal mining saw devastating declines in this
decade. Mining vied with the textile industry for sheer misery. Cotton and wool products were facing market competition from more
affordable silk and the newly invented rayon. "Output in these cutthroat [textile] industries remained high, and prices tumbled between 1923 and 1929," Parrish tells us. "Wages, of course, remained
depressed and because this industry employed more workers than
any other sector of the industrial economy, the drag on purchasing
power was enormous."

While millions of workers struggled, the wealthy grew more
prosperous. "Returns to industry as a whole increased 72 percent,
[and] dividends in rails and industrials went up 285 percent," one
Hoover biographer has noted. By 1930, the richest 10 percent of
Americans owned nearly 90 percent of the private property in the
country.

In 1925, Florida banks and construction firms were battered when
a red-hot real estate bubble there suddenly burst. By 1927, ominous
cracks were showing up in the nation's most important industries;

consumer spending slowed down, and wages in some sectors actually shrank. If reckless lending had not produced a last spasm of stock market speculation in 1928, the crash that came in late 1929 would likely have hit two years earlier.

In April of 1929, in the last days of the Jazz Age, desperate textile workers in North Carolina—many of them teenaged girls who worked fifty-six hours a week for less than 19 cents an hour—reached their limit. When they were ordered to tend to more than twice as many mechanized looms as before with no increase in pay, they went on strike. The strikers were attacked by anti-union mobs and local law enforcement officers; several workers were killed. The strike was broken, the killers went free, and the misery continued.

A decade of seamless, golden prosperity? Not exactly.

The Jazz Age was a time of unchallenged conservative control in Washington; while progressive Republicans still existed in that era, the GOP's conservative ranks were augmented by conservative pro-business Democrats to produce a strong right-wing majority. Three conservative presidents, one ultraconservative Treasury secretary, a host of conservative judges and justices, and countless conservative business executives put their indelible stamp on this decade.

President Harding, an amiable but weak man with too many crooked friends, was sworn in on March 4, 1921. By then, American business had grown impatient with government restraints imposed during the war and business leaders cheered Harding's promise of a "return to normalcy." For most industrial leaders, a return to "normal" required two things: an immediate reduction in taxes on the wealthy and the destruction of labor unions by any means necessary. The Harding administration obediently cut high-end taxes substantially and simply got out of the way while American business waged war on American unions.

There were laws that supposedly protected workers' rights to organize; the Constitution supposedly protected labor organizers' civil rights. Neither deterred corporate executives in their relentless, bloody, decade-long illegal war against organized labor. They used strikebreakers, spies, trumped-up injunctions, company goons, blacklists, secret violence, and public defamation. Their implacable goal was to eliminate the "communistic" threat posed by workers banding together to protest working conditions that were inhuman and almost unendurable. In this war against America's workforce, industry could count on support from the federal government and state and local law enforcement.

Examined today, the brazen illegality of that campaign is breathtaking. Unions had made some gains in the urban building trades, especially in New York City. In December 1920, Eugene G. Grace, the president of Bethlehem Steel, admitted to a New York state legislative committee that his company would not sell its fabricated steel to any builder in New York who used only union labor. Grilled by the committee's counsel, Grace angrily said he did not care if his blacklist shut down every construction project in the city—if it helped to annihilate union labor, it would be worth it. Although this blacklist of builders was surely illegal under the nation's antitrust and fair-trade laws, Grace was not deterred.

Grace had little to fear from the federal government when his outrageous blacklist was exposed to the public. After World War I, little effort was made by the federal government to enforce the antitrust laws adopted in more progressive years—except, occasionally, against labor organizations. American companies were even allowed to engage in price-fixing cartels, as long as they did so offshore. Even that restriction seems to have been rarely enforced: in 1928, General Electric joined with Krupp Industries in Germany to fix the price of tungsten carbide sold in the United States. Before the deal, tungsten carbide cost $50 a pound; afterward, it cost $453 a pound. Similar corporate-suite cartels during the decade fixed the prices of magnesium, titanium, soda ash, electric lamps, radio tubes, copper, lead, zinc, and steel rails.

The world of banking and finance—which I will examine more fully in the coming chapters—had its own deadly sins. As with the price-fixing and antitrust violations of other industries, these financial abuses were committed with impunity by highly respected executives at some of the most prominent, most admired firms on Wall Street.

President Harding saw little wrong with the way American business operated. A shocking number of his appointees operated the same way. While history remembers the Harding administration as a cesspool of official corruption, America's business operators were willing conspirators—paying bribes, accepting corrupt favors, keeping silent about ongoing crimes.

A few examples will suffice.

Charles R. Forbes, the crony Harding tapped in 1921 to head the new Veterans Bureau, went to prison for embezzling an estimated $2 million from the bureau's budget. One way he did that was by selling supplies meant for veterans, from splints to bedsheets, at fire-sale prices to businessmen who retailed the goods at full price and kicked some of their profits back to Forbes.

Albert B. Fall, the rancher and former senator named as Harding's Interior secretary, was convicted at the end of the decade for taking bribes from two oil tycoons, Edward L. Doheny and Henry F. Sinclair, to whom he awarded low-cost leases to some immensely valuable oil fields kept in reserve for the U.S. Navy. (One of the fields was near Teapot Dome, the rock formation in Wyoming that gave the scandal its name.) In this case, Doheny and Sinclair actually cooked up the scam and bribed their friend Albert Fall to go along with it; Fall went to prison for taking a bribe, but Sinclair and Doheny were paradoxically acquitted after claiming that the bribe was just a loan to a friend.

Harding's secretary of the Treasury was Andrew W. Mellon, one of the richest men in the country with vast holdings in banking, oil, and aluminum. Fiercely opposed to organized labor at home and abroad, Mellon interests had run roughshod over Mexican laws in exploiting that nation's oil reserves; the companies "refused to abide by Mexican governmental decrees, refused to pay taxes, fought the new Mexican labor unions." As Treasury secretary, Andrew Mellon managed to keep his trouser cuffs clean in the Harding mire—but just barely.

In one instance, Harding's new appointees to the Federal Trade Commission killed a pending investigation of Alcoa, controlled by

Mellon interests, for allegedly violating both the antitrust laws and a federal court decree. In another case, Mellon personally refused to participate in a messy money-laundering scandal, but failed to report it to anyone.

That money-laundering scandal painted an even darker picture of the era's business morality than the Teapot Dome bribery case did. In 1921, a handful of leading oil executives—including Harry Sinclair and Robert W. Stewart, the chairman of Standard Oil of Indiana, originally part of the Rockefeller family's empire—secretly set up a shell company called the Continental Trading Company. Through it, they bought 33.3 million barrels of oil for $1.50 a barrel, resold the oil to their own corporations for $1.75 a barrel, and thereby picked up an $8.3 million profit that came out of the pockets of their own shareholders. The cash went into a secret slush fund, part of which was invested in government bonds. Some of those bonds were used to bribe Albert Fall, the Interior secretary; others were distributed to wealthy Republican donors in Chicago and New York, who laundered them into cash donations to help pay off the Republican National Committee's campaign debts. Andrew Mellon was one of the big GOP donors asked to launder $50,000 of these slush fund bonds. He declined the bonds and simply made a $50,000 donation from his own great wealth. But he did not tell anyone about the elaborate fraud scheme. When the bond incident later became public, Mellon told a Senate panel he had just been too busy to worry about the matter.

Harding's choice for Commerce secretary was Herbert C. Hoover, a wealthy civil engineer with a sterling reputation who made a wide swerve around the Harding scandals. The ambitious Hoover—Washington wits joked that his title was "Secretary of Commerce and Undersecretary of Everything Else"—devoted his energy to expanding his department and encouraging cooperation among American businesses. Despite his broad self-assigned portfolio, he always insisted he had known nothing about the Harding scandals until they became public.

The Hoovers accompanied President Harding and the First Lady on a western speaking tour in mid-1923 and, therefore, were on hand when the president suffered a fatal heart attack on August 2 in San Francisco. His death opened the Oval Office to his vice president, former Massachusetts governor Calvin Coolidge.

Coolidge had made his national name by breaking a strike called by the Boston police force. He was unalterably opposed to organized labor, big government, high taxes, business regulation, and deficit spending. But Coolidge was selectively stingy. "Coolidge's tendency was to resist proposals for governmental expenditure of kinds that business did not want, or for social reform, and thus to minimize the role of the federal government while business was growing in wealth and power," according to an economic history of the decade. "Nevertheless, a considerable increase in federal expenditures occurred in the decade."

Spending on law enforcement soared as the federal government waged its losing fight to sustain Prohibition. The government freely subsidized the shipping industry, an enormous boon to business. The budget at Hoover's Commerce Department grew sharply to pay for the new services it provided to American business—promoting Wall Street loans and American exports in foreign countries, producing "elaborate statistical publications" to serve business needs, and encouraging standardization to streamline manufacturing. Adding to these benefits, Andrew Mellon privately approved tax refunds, credits, and abatements for wealthy individuals and corporations that would total $3.5 billion during his eight years at the Treasury—the equivalent of nearly $61 billion today.

What Coolidge did not want to spend money on was any program designed to promote public health and the general welfare. "Those on the political left came quickly to the realization that with his rigid devotion to an unfettered capitalist economy, he represented a far greater threat to the progressive legacy than Harding and all his corrupt minions," wrote historian Michael Parrish. Parrish credits author and reformer Lincoln Steffens with what is perhaps the best summation of the Coolidge era. Steffens "observed wryly that Calvin Coolidge had put to rest the idea that the federal government was simply the mistress of business. Under Coolidge, he said, they got married."

The GOP bosses who maneuvered Harding into office and operated with little interference from Coolidge were wary of Herbert Hoover, who seemed too stubborn and puritanical for the party's tastes. But in 1928, when Coolidge announced he would not run again, Hoover quickly sewed up the Republican nomination for president. As Hoover saw it, his mission was to prolong the Coolidge prosperity that American business was producing, and to preserve the American culture of "rugged individualism" that he believed was the basis for both the nation's prosperity and its liberty.

One of Hoover's biographers summarized the state of America in 1928, as Hoover waged his successful campaign for the presidency: "The Republicans, unrepentant after the Harding scandals, ignored the indictment of outraged citizens, ignored the millions of bankrupt farmers, denied labor's reasonable demands for justice . . . Prohibition was a farce, a failure, a nightmare. Banking practices had undermined basic foundations, and stock and commodity exchanges had become gigantic casinos . . . Monopolies through consolidations had proliferated with reckless disregard for federal laws, and the oligarchy of concentrated wealth had expanded."

Herbert Claiborne Pell, a progressive Democratic Party leader whose Hudson River estate was near the Roosevelt home in Hyde Park, later had an even more scathing verdict for the business leaders who came to power in the Jazz Age: "The destinies of the world were handed to them on a plate in 1920. Their piglike rush for immediate profits knocked over the whole feast in nine years . . . They have shown no realization that what they call free enterprise means anything but greed."

That is the unregulated capitalist paradise some conservatives are trying to reimpose in America—apparently certain that in their new jungle economy, they would always be the predators, not the prey.

I BELIEVE THAT DEMOCRATIC capitalism, wisely regulated, is the healthiest way to preserve individual liberty and promote the general welfare. But I know our current regulatory scheme is far from perfect. Over five decades as an author and financial journalist, I have engaged in serious debates about how to regulate the world of finance. In *Fidelity's World*, I examined how mutual funds were regulated. In *The White Sharks of Wall Street*, I tackled the regulatory challenges of hostile takeovers. Writing about the historic Ponzi scheme run by Bernie Madoff in *The Wizard of Lies* and the equally historic market crash in 1987 in *A First-Class Catastrophe*, I wrestled with the best ways to regulate investment advisors and financial derivatives, and exposed the consequences of an increasingly fragmented regulatory system. How we regulate finance must evolve as the nature of finance evolves, and America has fallen dangerously behind in that essential evolution.

But I never dreamed that I would ever find myself arguing with serious, powerful people not about *how* to regulate finance but about *whether* to regulate finance.

Some of those who see no reason to regulate finance are ideological zealots and will not be persuaded by logic or historical evidence. To them, I simply say: "Deregulating finance makes as much sense as deregulating traffic." But I hope I can persuade those who simply do not know why the regulations they reflexively oppose were enacted in the first place and what the world would be like if those rules were taken away.

I am hopeful of making my case to people like the young man I encountered on Twitter a few years ago. I had tweeted about the SEC's swift action to shut down a Ponzi scheme before all the assets were gone, adding something like "those victims should bless FDR for creating the SEC."

This young man pushed back with a familiar libertarian complaint. Smart investors had no need for the SEC and all its burdensome rules and red tape, he wrote. He was fully capable of protecting himself just by reading a company's official annual report, called a 10-K, before he invested.

I laughed out loud. He did not know that there were no 10-Ks for investors to read until FDR set up the SEC in 1934. Companies were not required to produce them. He could protect himself today only because, ninety years ago, Franklin Roosevelt had fought to give him the tools to do so.

It was not easy to tame the Street in the 1930s—indeed, sustaining that achievement is a task that freshly confronts each generation. We would be crazy to let finance once again run wild in our economy. In the chapters ahead, I will show not only how FDR put "a cop on Wall Street" but also why he believed the cop should be there, and should stay there. His reasons for regulating the world of finance are just as compelling today as they were when he took office.

TAMING THE STREET

CHAPTER ONE

A QUARTET FOR A CALAMITY

OCTOBER 24–DECEMBER 6, 1929

HOW MANY PEOPLE DOES IT TAKE TO CHANGE THE WORLD? The world of the Roaring Twenties had embraced the idea that American business leaders, largely free of government constraint, could produce and sustain prosperity for the American people. Nowhere was this belief more deeply rooted than on Wall Street, whose leaders were the financial architects of corporate America.

What mere federal bureaucracy would dare question the decisions or restrict the power of such financial titans?

As the summer of 1929 swept into the fall, four men were moving along different paths—in the market, in business, in politics, and in academia—that would require each of them to weigh the power of Wall Street against the obligations of public service. Their paths would cross; their fates would diverge. But over the next decade, they would answer that question.

How many people does it take to change the world?

It can take just four—four people capable of inspiring others in the public arena; four people who, in the last autumn of the Roaring Twenties, were traveling into a new decade with no idea how important their journey would be to Wall Street, to their country, and to the world.

THURSDAY, OCTOBER 24, 1929

ON A CHILLY GRAY MORNING, RICHARD WHITNEY STRODE ONTO the floor of the New York Stock Exchange in lower Manhattan, listening to the nervous chatter before the opening bell.

Dick Whitney had turned forty-one in August, and this had been his world, his realm, for nearly half his life. He had been a governor of the exchange for a decade, its vice president for a year, and its acting president for three weeks as its official leader enjoyed an extended honeymoon.

He was an impressive figure. Tall, a bit beefy but impeccably dressed, he still moved with the grace of the Ivy League athlete he once was. He had the profile and hooded gaze of a hawk; his sleek dark hair was combed almost straight back from a sharply etched hairline. For nearly fifteen years, he had handled bond trades for the august J.P. Morgan firm, where his older brother, George, was a partner. When President Hoover had sought advice during some anxious trading days earlier in the year, it was Dick Whitney he summoned to the White House.

After years of robust gains, the market had shuddered back in the spring when the Federal Reserve Board, concerned that the market was flying too high and too fast, tried to curb the flow of bank credit to Wall Street speculators. New York bankers defied the Fed and continued to make speculative loans, but the resulting summer rally was erratic. In August and September, the financial seas had grown stormier as investors fretted over the Fed's next steps and debated the economy's direction. Contrary opinions generated a surge of buying and selling. Like the veteran yachtsman he was, Whitney had kept the exchange on course as its clerks grappled with the paperwork from that agitated trading. Some on the Street feared a calamity was coming, but the exchange's board trusted Whitney to cope.

Yesterday, it seemed like that calamity had hit. And he had missed it.

Instead of spending Wednesday on the trading floor, Whitney had spent the day far from Wall Street's telephones and stock tickers, in the New Jersey hunt country. It was the day of the elite Essex Fox Hounds race meeting. He was a steward for the event, assessing the condition of the course, debating whether a fallen mount's rider had been fouled, and declaring a dramatic dead heat in one of the day's biggest races.

Thus, he had not been at his post during the most alarming day of stock trading anyone on the NYSE could remember.

The trading floor on Wednesday had been hit by a tidal wave of selling in its final hour. Only the closing bell had halted the nearly perpendicular plunge. "Brokers who have passed all their lives in Wall Street said it was the most hysterical demonstration they ever witnessed," a New York *Daily News* columnist reported. The men on the exchange floor could not know it, but this traumatic day was merely the prologue of the 1929 crash, an historic three-week siege of plunging prices that would scar Wall Street's memories for nearly sixty years. Wednesday's panic had brought "complete chaos" to the trading floor as the stock ticker fell so far behind it was "valueless as an indicator of prices," the columnist complained. He was one of the market pundits who were still uneasy about Thursday's mood, worried that "mob psychology" was not yet through shaking the Street.

If more shocks came today, Dick Whitney would be ready. In a dark brown double-breasted suit, he resembled a mighty tree trunk planted near the stairs to the raised podium where, each day, an exchange official pressed the button of an electric bell that opened and closed trading.

At that moment, the chief of the NYSE mechanical department, responsible for the tickers and the other modern machinery at the exchange, moved across the felt-tiled floor toward the podium steps. Whitney stopped him and briefly told him to stay near the bell throughout the day. He didn't need to explain why. The previous day's crash might have broken some small member firms, requiring their suspension from the exchange. The bell would be rung to halt trading so the acting president could report these insolvencies. The aide nodded and continued up the steps. At the exact point of 10 A.M., he pressed the button. The firehouse clanging of the opening bell overrode all other sounds for a few seconds.

And so another trading day began, the day that would make Dick Whitney famous.

For the keepers of the Manhattan society stud book, Dick and his brother, George, were not "*the* Whitneys," the wealthy, sporty family whose art collections, Thoroughbred horses, and motor yachts defined class for Jazz Age society. George and Richard were "Boston Whitneys," the grandsons of a shipmaster and merchant, the sons of a respected banker; their lifelong pride in their pedigree was obvious to all who knew them, according to one biographer close to the family.

Their father's death in 1904, when they were teenagers, did not interrupt their athletic march through prep school at Groton and college at Harvard. Both were tapped for Harvard's most coveted club, the Porcellian, earning the right to wear its golden pig mascot on their watch chains. Both gravitated to Wall Street after graduation.

George Whitney paved the way. A star squash player in Harvard's Class of 1907, he moved to New York while his uncle, Edward F. Whitney, still had a partner's desk in the offices of J.P. Morgan, the formidable private banking firm housed in a staid fortress at 23 Wall Street. In June 1914, George married the daughter of a former Morgan partner who had been ambassador to France. Dick was his brother's best man at the lavish country wedding, covered by almost every society columnist between Boston and Washington. The following year, George Whitney was hired into the bond department at J.P. Morgan; he now sat at the right hand of Thomas W. Lamont, the decisive managing partner of the firm and one of the most powerful people in American finance. Thinner and more elegant than his brother, George Whitney was also vastly richer, easily commanding all the luxuries of life. Inevitably, George Whitney's success sprinkled pixie dust on his brother's prospects.

Fierce competition defined Dick Whitney's early life. He had played football and baseball at Groton and had a splendid career on the Harvard crew, helping row the team to victory over Yale in 1909. He completed work for his Harvard degree in 1910, but returned to Cambridge to collect his diploma with his beloved Class of 1911.

Years later, he could astound his friends by reciting from memory the full name of every one of his classmates. (This was no trivial feat; his list included American poet Harold Trowbridge Pulsifer, Hawaiian physician Alsoberry Kaumu Hanchett, and a dozen varieties of "Smith.")

Like his brother, Dick relied on helpful Uncle Edward, who loaned him the money he used, on January 12, 1912, to buy a seat on the New York Stock Exchange. And also like his brother, he married into New York society—in a romantic match touched by tragedy. Gertrude Sheldon Sands was the young and strikingly beautiful widow of Samuel Stevens Sands III. Sands died in a car crash in 1913 and left his widow with a young son and namesake. Sands's bereaved mother, born into the Harriman railroad dynasty, later married the fabulously wealthy William K. Vanderbilt. Mrs. Vanderbilt sat with her young grandson during the quiet at-home wedding at which Gertrude Sands married Dick Whitney on May 27, 1916. Two weeks later, he set up his own NYSE member firm, Richard Whitney & Company. The New York Stock Exchange became the cornerstone of Whitney's professional life. There, he pitted his instincts against other bond traders in a clubby culture as steeped in tradition and camaraderie as Harvard had been.

His wartime service was safe and uneventful. From September 1917 until early 1919, he worked in Washington and New Jersey for the U.S. Food Administration and became acquainted with its autocratic chief, Herbert Hoover. The detour into government service did not interrupt Whitney's progress in society or at the exchange. By 1916, he was an active member of the Essex Fox Hounds, whose red-coated outfits would have been familiar to any Victorian country squire. By 1920, he was a member of the Somerset Hills Country Club in Bernardsville, New Jersey, where he played golf with corporate titans and Wall Street notables. He soon added membership in the New York Yacht Club to his sporting society credentials, and now served as the tony club's trusted treasurer. In May 1919, a few months after George Whitney became a partner at J.P. Morgan, Dick Whitney was elected to the board of governors that ruled the exchange. He worked on the necessary committees and, no doubt,

traded discreetly on his brother's rising influence. In 1928, that golden
year when Wall Street could barely count the money that flowed
into its pockets, Whitney was elected vice president of the exchange,
second in command to the well-connected Edward Henry Harriman Simmons, the nephew and namesake of the great railroad baron
and financier, E. H. Harriman.

Whitney's prospects for advancement were good: "Harry" Simmons, Gertrude Whitney's second cousin by marriage, was clearly
tiring after five years in the volunteer role of exchange president. In
early October 1929, with the markets already wildly turbulent, Simmons became the third husband of a somewhat scandalous divorcée
and left immediately on a two-month honeymoon in Hawaii. Whitney had been given a chance to try out for the presidency.

But when the violent storm of chaotic trading had struck the
exchange on Wednesday, October 23, it seemed that Whitney had
bungled his audition for the sake of some foxhunting friends.

The stock market's crash wasn't the only news that glared out
from front pages across the country that Thursday morning. President Harding's former Interior secretary had just gone on trial in
Washington, accused of taking bribes from oilmen in connection
with drilling leases in the Teapot Dome formation in Wyoming and
elsewhere. The trial was an uncomfortable reminder that the Jazz
Age prosperity that had pumped so much cash into the stock market
owed its longevity at least in part to an environment of almost seamless crime and corruption. The general climate of lawlessness was
reflected in the nation's blithe disregard for the National Prohibition
Act, the law adopted a decade earlier to rid America of "intoxicating
liquors." Whether they were at their Manhattan clubs or at their
country estates or their Florida villas, Whitney and all his friends
could get a cocktail or after-dinner brandy whenever they wanted
one.

His social set was pretty much free to do as it pleased on Wall
Street, too. The corruption of the financial world may have seemed
more genteel than the escapades of gangland bootleggers, but it was
just as pervasive and destructive. Stock prices on Whitney's exchange

were routinely manipulated by "pools," which were coveys of rich investors who secretly combined their funds, bought some company's shares, and hired a trader on the NYSE floor to "paint the tape" with an artificial rally that would lure in unknowing public investors, to whom the pool operators could sell their shares at a quick profit. Bribes were paid to willing journalists who wrote glowing stories about the stock to puff up public interest when the pool was ready to sell. As soon as the insiders sold, the rally would usually collapse and ordinary investors would suffer the inevitable losses. Earlier in 1929, just such a cabal had whipped up the price of Radio Corporation of America stock to produce a fast $5 million profit for the pool members. The RCA pool's profits were plucked, of course, from the pockets of unwitting public investors who bought too late. A more recent effort to boost the stock of the Chrysler Corporation, begun on October 16, had been derailed by the recent market turmoil. One wealthy speculator brazenly refused to cover his share of the Chrysler losses on the grounds that the pool agreement was an illegal contract under New York state law and therefore could not be enforced in court!

Of course, like any private club, the NYSE had adopted rules laying out the criteria for membership and the duties of members. Those rules barred behavior that was "detrimental to the interest or welfare of the exchange" or "inconsistent with just and equitable principles of trade." A member who committed one of these vaguely defined sins could be fined, suspended, or expelled from the exchange.

But the rules that governed the stock exchange were far less powerful than the men who governed the stock exchange. They alone decided when, and if, the rules would be enforced against a misbehaving member. They alone decided whether unjust or inequitable trading had occurred and whether a member's behavior had been detrimental to the exchange. Severe discipline was rare; members disliked causing trouble for their friends unless it was simply unavoidable. In one case, a New York court ruled in 1920 that a major firm had committed fraud but, in reply to a complaint letter from an investor in 1928, Dick Whitney explained that no disciplinary action had been taken against the member firm because he, personally, disagreed with the court's decision.

The code of behavior beyond the NYSE was no less self-serving. Powerful bankers like those at J.P. Morgan typically would give dealers less than twenty-four hours to decide if they wanted a piece of a new issue—sight unseen, no details provided. If they said yes, they would have to sell the new securities, no matter how dicey or dubious they turned out to be; if they said no, they would likely be left out of the next hot new issue. Consequently, new issues of stocks and bonds were sold to investors largely on the strength of rumors, bribed journalists' puffery, and false boardroom promises. Corporate financial statements were sometimes unavailable, frequently unreliable, and occasionally fictional. Bankers, still clothed with rectitude in the eyes of the public, had become stock hustlers, regularly plucking bad loans or dubious shares from their own ledgers and selling them to their own naïve depositors. Foreign government bonds were sold to trusting investors and listed on the exchange by bankers who knew the bonds would likely wind up worthless. Bogus stock trades were done for the sole purpose of dodging taxes or evading exchange rules to reap a quick profit.

For the lucky among the era's renegades, then, the 1920s unfolded with enough glamour and gaiety to blur the memories of the Great War and its carnage. For the unlucky, the "prosperity decade" had been a cruel taunt. Far from the prosperous enclaves, farmers struggled against mounting debt and pitiless drought; factory workers, many of them still children, labored seven days a week for meager pay; labor organizers dodged billy clubs and blacklists, while organized criminals ruled the docks, the slums, and the smoky rooms of political clubs across the country. But the sun shone steadily on Wall Street through most of the decade, nurturing the wealth of Dick Whitney and his exchange colleagues.

On this Thursday morning in late October 1929, that prosperity felt very shaky. Before the exchange opened, telegraphed sell orders had hurtled toward the trading floor from across the country. Now, as the clanging of the opening bell died away, those orders hit the floor. The Dow Jones Industrial Average immediately fell more than 10 percent. There were few buyers, even at the depressed opening prices left behind in yesterday's rout. Shares were dumped in such quantities that the first half hour's trading volume eclipsed the normal levels for an entire day. The search for bidders continued frantically through the first hour, with lower and lower prices being offered and ignored. The ticker was more than fifteen minutes behind by 10:30 A.M., and it never caught up. The blue chips were breaking: U.S. Steel fell almost 6 percent. Bethlehem Steel fell 9 percent. General Motors was off nearly 15 percent. Industrial giant Johns Manville plunged 22 percent, and that technology darling RCA, beloved by the pool operators, fell almost 40 percent. The morning seemed far worse than the free fall of yesterday's final hour—if only because the closing bell was so many hours away.

Crowds filled the visitors' gallery overlooking the trading floor until Whitney decided to shut it down, inadvertently sparking rumors that the exchange itself might close. Outside, people seeking any sort of news were filling the intersection of Broad Street and Wall Street. No one knew what was happening; prices were obsolete before they were even printed on the paper ribbons curling out of stock tickers across the country. By 11:30 A.M., a huge clocklike dial hanging at one side of the trading floor showed the ticker was running nearly fifty minutes behind.

Amid this turmoil, Whitney got a message summoning him to the Morgan offices across the street. Entering by a side door around noon, he found the presidents of the city's major banks conferring with his brother's powerful boss, Tom Lamont. The bankers pledged some undisclosed amount—as much as $240 million, by one account—to help support prices on the exchange and then trooped back out onto Wall Street, careful to let their faces betray nothing to the crowds. Whitney stayed behind to discuss how best to deploy the new funds and then pushed his way through the crowd on Broad Street to return to the exchange.

The moment he reached the trading floor, Whitney marched straight toward Post No. 2, a wooden kiosk almost directly in front of the podium where he'd stood at the opening bell. And like a bell, he called out his bid to buy thousands of shares of U.S. Steel at $205 apiece—well above the most recent recorded price. Cheers greeted his order as a clerk scribbled it onto a paper chit. Seeming "debonair and self-confident," Whitney moved on, making generous bids for other sagging stocks. In minutes, he had bid for an estimated $20 million worth of stock. The effect was galvanizing. Others on the floor started to buy. As word spread of a rally, new buy orders arrived over the wires. The day still ended with a loss, but as one chronicle put it: "Black Thursday ended a good deal less black than it might have."

Whitney was just the servant of the banking lords who provided the money to cover his historic bids. Indeed, while Whitney marched from post to post within his world, Tom Lamont held newsmen's attention at a rare impromptu press conference inside the Morgan offices.

"There has been a little distress selling on the stock exchange," Lamont began, with quaint understatement. "We have held a meeting of the heads of several financial institutions to discuss the situation." He calmly explained that no brokerage firms were in financial difficulty, and credit risks had been dealt with. "It is the consensus of the group that many of the quotations on the stock exchange do not fairly represent the situation."

He said nothing of the pooled funds from the bankers, the generous bids by Whitney, or the rally fueled by that bidding.

But the next day, in the multiple pages of newspaper coverage devoted to this new "worst ever" crash, Dick Whitney's pivotal role was detailed. "His bid of 205 for 25,000 shares of Steel electrified the group around the Steel post and communicated buying enthusiasm to other parts of the floor," reported *The New York Times*. "It was assumed that Mr. Whitney, who is frequently spoken of as a 'Morgan broker,' had received the order from the House of Morgan or interests identified with it." An image emerged of "a field general in the bankers' battle for an orderly market." Prices steadied on Friday, October 25, and again during Saturday's two-hour session. Whitney assured reporters there was no plan to close the exchange—although every firm was working through the night on the staggering paper-work from the 12 million shares that were traded on Black Thursday.

The story of Whitney's glorious march across that panic-stricken trading floor grew in the retelling—indeed, his colleagues gave him the old Post No. 2, which he proudly displayed in the lobby of his firm's office suite. He was applauded within the exchange, saluted outside it. Whitney had become famous "quite literally overnight," and the media spotlight that found him on Black Thursday 1929 would follow him for the rest of his Wall Street career. "All that he did henceforth was to have a touch of magic," one journalist wrote a few years later. "The way he smiled, the look in his eyes, his merest wisecrack—all were to be noted and related."

By Monday, October 28, it was obvious that the bankers behind Whitney's triumphal bids were fighting in a hopeless cause. That day, the ticker ran almost three hours behind. Bankers continued to gather and confer at the "Morgan corner," but their own banks' stock prices were plummeting along with all the other shares; prudence barred further cash pledges. There were reassuring headlines in that morning's papers: "Bankers Mobilize for Buying Today," and "Huge Funds Expected in the Market Today for 'Bargain Buying.'" But those predictions were wishful, not real. By nightfall, anyone still trading with money borrowed from a broker had been told to put up more cash or sell their stocks. Some veterans recalled how the ex-change had closed its doors for several months when hostilities broke out in Europe in 1914; this bombardment of selling was surely the financial equivalent of war. Some brokerage firms began to clamor for the NYSE to close again until the storm of "mob psy-chology" blew over. Whitney, now attuned to the impact the closure would have on the very "psychology" the firms were worried about, resisted those demands.

The New York Federal Reserve Bank, after an emergency meet-ing of its board in the predawn hours of Tuesday morning, Octo-ber 29, took extraordinary steps to pump cash into the banks that would have to help steer Wall Street through this storm. The action, taken without the approval of the Fed in Washington, was announced before the market's opening bell. It was the right thing to do and it no doubt kept some banks afloat and functioning, but it did not cure the panic.

When the exchange opened for business that Tuesday, the bottom fell out of the nation's stock market. It was "the most disastrous day in the stock market's history," the normally staid *New York Times* reported. The more theatrical *Daily News* detected "the dark despair of death" stalking through Wall Street. The basic machinery of the exchange was breaking down. With no bids at all, some stocks had not even opened for trading—forestalling any buyers seeking bargains. Printed orders piled up on shelves and desktops, ignored in the mounting chaos. Immense blocks of stock were dumped on the market for whatever they would fetch. Three million shares were traded in the first thirty minutes of Black Tuesday—at prices that reflected an almost vertical decline from the previous day's calamitous numbers.

The pressure on the board of governors to close the exchange became almost overwhelming. Whitney sent an aide out across the floor to discreetly alert the governors to a secret meeting at noon; he knew even a whiff of news about his summons would accelerate the panic. At his direction, board members slipped away from the floor "in twos and threes," heading not to their usual opulent chamber on the sixth floor but to an obscure administrative office directly below the trading floor. Whitney's colleagues crowded into the low-ceiling room; some found seats on tabletops, others slumped against the walls. Two Morgan partners, after a brief hassle with security guards, glided in. Whitney noticed how uneasy everyone was—cigarettes were lit, puffed once or twice, then stubbed out only to be replaced with fresh ones seconds later. The long narrow room was soon "blue with smoke and extremely stuffy," he later recalled.

Whitney continued to oppose the closure of the exchange and somehow, amazingly, there were not enough votes in that crowd of frightened men to overrule him. The governors temporized, deciding to meet again that evening. They also agreed that, at the first sign of a rally, Whitney would announce abbreviated trading hours to give back-office clerks time to catch up with the mounting paperwork. A feeble rally emerged in the afternoon and, at the evening meeting, the group decided to remain open for another day. As the board members started filing out of the smoky room, Whitney told each of them: "Now get your smiles on, boys!'" One journalist later noted that Whitney had always dealt with a challenge "with an absolutely unromantic poker face, save when the situation was so bad that it called for a broad smile." Confidence was the only weapon he had now to fight the panic at the exchange; the bankers were looking out for themselves.

Wall Street could not continue at this abnormal pace. Night after night, the lights of the office towers in lower Manhattan had never gone out. Staffers grabbed quick naps on cots or on the floor or, if they were lucky, in nearby hotels, and then went back to work processing trades. Battalions of uniformed messenger boys, ordered to stay on the job without respite, trudged through the darkened downtown blocks carrying millions of dollars' worth of paper stock certificates from one firm to another. The clerical and administrative workers of Wall Street were exhausted, and there were four trading days left before the closing bell at noon on Saturday. On Black Tuesday alone, more than 16 million shares had changed hands, at prices that represented a loss of about $10 billion—"twice the amount of currency in circulation in the entire country at the time," according to one account.

The hoped-for rally arrived on Wednesday morning, and at 1:40 P.M., Whitney hurried up the podium steps to announce that the exchange would delay opening on Thursday for two hours and would observe "special holidays" on Friday and Saturday to deal with the backlog of paperwork. But in making the announcement, as one account put it, an increasingly savvy Whitney "resorted to one more of the dramatic anti-panic devices for which he was showing such flair." Normally, the tickers fell silent for public announcements like this. But lest anyone should mistakenly think the exchange had closed "even for a matter of seconds, [Whitney] saw to it that the tickers went right on chattering while he spoke."

Within a few days, Dick Whitney had gained national prominence. Not only did he carry the flag of the House of Morgan on the exchange floor, he was calmly and effectively leading the nation's premier marketplace through the worst crisis in its history. He was recognized on the street, consulted at his various clubs, sought out by reporters, treated with greater deference by his peers. "Lives were disintegrating, and he was the man who could hold them together if anyone could," one account noted. He was becoming the confident face of Wall Street, the voice of unfettered capitalism. He embodied the hope of millions that, soon, the good times would roll again.

FRIDAY, NOVEMBER 1, 1929

A MOUNTED POLICEMAN SCANNED THE CROWD OUTSIDE THE Rialto Theatre on Times Square as a gleaming limousine pulled up to the curb. Other uniformed officers quickly formed a human corridor from the car to the Rialto's entrance. The limousine's rear door opened and movie producer Joseph P. Kennedy climbed out, his tuxedo signaling that this was no ordinary night at the movies. Ruddy and slim with a boyish face and neat auburn hair, Joe Kennedy turned and offered his hand to his fellow passenger. The crowd exploded with cheers as actress Gloria Swanson stepped out into the unseasonably warm Manhattan evening.

Her noisy fans surged forward. The police chain seemed to waver. Several of Kennedy's personal aides leapt from the car and quickly surrounded the star, gripping her arms and lifting her several inches off the sidewalk as they hustled her toward the safety of the lobby.

Even while being voluntarily manhandled, she looked magnificent. Her gold lamé evening coat gleamed like a comet. Those close enough caught a glimpse of a pale blue satin gown trimmed with silky brown chinchilla fur. Dark wavy hair, enormous expressive eyes, a petite but womanly frame—Gloria Swanson was every inch the star Joe Kennedy wanted her to be in public, every bit the alluring female he knew her to be in private. They had been lovers for more than a year.

The theater marquee proclaimed why they were together tonight:

it was the New York premiere of *The Trespasser,* a Joseph P. Kennedy production and Gloria Swanson's first talking picture. The family melodrama, in which Swanson not only talked but sang, had opened to rapturous reviews in London and Kennedy was optimistic about its New York success.

Just turned forty-one, Joe Kennedy could add this laurel to a growing stack of achievements. Wherever he landed, he had piled one business coup on top of another, displaying a buccaneering appetite for risk and ignoring complaints about his sharp dealing and broken promises. Barely a month earlier, a New York *Daily News* columnist had hailed him as one of the ambitious young men who were displacing the gray-haired barons of business. His deal-making prowess was admired by some, feared by others, but acknowledged by all as something out of the ordinary. But this—a glittering premiere, with one of Hollywood's most charismatic stars on his arm and in his bed—this was some heady new species of success.

The theater soon filled up with his invited guests, prominent bankers, brokers, and businessmen who had been woven into his life as a Wall Street speculator, financial consultant, and motion picture executive. But some of the guests had known him since his boyhood in the Irish precincts of Boston, where his father had been a successful saloon owner and a cog in the local Democratic Party machinery—and where his wife Rose's father, John "Honey Fitz" Fitzgerald, had stepped down from his second term as mayor in 1914 but remained a prominent and irrepressible Democratic gadfly.

Joe Kennedy had no interest in following in the footsteps of either his father-in-law or his late father, who had died earlier that year. He had attended the elite Boston Latin School, a competitive public school whose alumni included founding father John Hancock and philosopher Ralph Waldo Emerson—and whose sports rivals included Dick Whitney's teams at Groton. Kennedy had been an excellent athlete but his grades were less impressive so he had been held back and squeaked into Harvard a year behind Whitney, as a member of the Class of 1912. The two men had lived in essentially different worlds that overlapped on the Cambridge campus, one a world of pedigree and privilege with doors opening directly into the corridors of power, and the other a world of outsiders, fenced in by the prejudices of Boston's ruling class.

Like Whitney, Kennedy dreamed of getting rich in the world of finance. Boston's anti-Catholic bias put a job at any prominent bank beyond his reach, so he had passed the state test to become a bank examiner, sitting in judgment of bankers who wouldn't hire him. His expertise had been useful when his father bought a stake in a struggling neighborhood trust company and, in January 1914, put his twenty-five-year-old son on the board as president. With a flair for self-promotion, Kennedy had portrayed himself to the media as "the youngest bank president" in Massachusetts.

In October of that year, Kennedy had married Rose Fitzgerald, a darling of the local newspapers through her poised appearances at her father's campaign events and her romps through Irish Boston's whirl of society parties. The Catholic wedding service, held in the private chapel of Boston archbishop William Cardinal O'Connell, had been front-page news in *The Boston Globe,* which described the bride as "the talented and charming daughter" of the former mayor and the groom as "president of a local trust company." The couple had settled into a comfortable life, with his days spent at the bank and her days filled with social engagements and, soon, a growing family. Their first child, Joseph P. Kennedy Jr., had been born in July 1915. In steady succession, baby Joe had been followed by John Fitzgerald in 1917, Rosemary in 1918, Kathleen in 1920, Eunice in 1921, Patricia in 1924, Robert in 1925, and Jean in 1928.

When the United States entered the European war, the Irishman in Joe Kennedy wasn't eager to risk his life to help bail out the British Empire. He had spent the Great War in the shipbuilding business, as assistant manager of a Bethlehem Steel shipyard in Quincy, Massachusetts. He had made sure the workers had housing, food services, reliable transportation, and medical care during the Spanish flu epidemic—and had overseen the shipyard's baseball team, drawing on his prowess on the Harvard team. Decades later, he would claim that, during these years, he had been bested in a naval contract dispute by the tough young assistant secretary of the navy, a patrician New Yorker named Franklin D. Roosevelt, whose political ambitions Kennedy would later support. Newspapers that closely covered the shipbuilding industry in the Boston area did not print a word about the almost certainly apocryphal conflict—which supposedly had climaxed when marines invaded the shipyard, seized two disputed Argentine battleships, and sailed them away in broad daylight. Roosevelt's own papers from those years were silent about the alleged episode. Indeed, nothing ever backed up the claim except Kennedy's word—and that was a weak staff to lean on.

After his experience as a bank president, Kennedy had invaded the booming world of Wall Street bearing the shield of the successful brokerage firm of Hayden, Stone. "It is easy to make money in this market," he said as he dove into it. "We'd better get in before they pass a law against it." He parlayed his contacts at the firm into a stake in the nascent motion picture industry, and through a series of mergers and consulting arrangements, became a millionaire many times over.

His attractive family had grown up in the sheltering arms of that wealth, with homes on Cape Cod and in the expensive enclave of Bronxville, New York, and leased villas in Florida during the northern winters. Rose and the children, frequently with her parents in tow, traveled on luxury liners to Europe. The children attended private schools, pursued expensive hobbies, and rode in chauffeured cars. When Kennedy was home, he quizzed them at meals about current events and their schoolwork. But as his Hollywood interests expanded, those visits had recently become shorter and less frequent.

Kennedy's family did not feel any jolts from the stock market crash in late October 1929. Like dozens of major American corporations, Kennedy's business interests—chiefly RCA and the RKO theater chain—had made money lending spare cash at sky-high rates to finance Wall Street speculation. But Kennedy himself had grown uneasy about what seemed increasingly to be a sucker's market. He had liquidated most of his investments in the spring of 1929 and cashed out of his RCA stock in early October, avoiding the worst of that month's losses. As November arrived, he was flush with cash and fully focused on his lover's film premiere.

Indeed, the market crash almost seemed to be old news on that warm, glittering night. The stock exchange, closed that day to deal with more paperwork, had rallied in an abbreviated session the day before. The Federal Reserve, prominent bankers, Wall Street executives, and Washington officials from President Hoover on down were all expressing confidence that the worst was over. The news was sure to have put Kennedy's wealthy guests into a better mood for the evening's entertainment.

Kennedy settled into his seat at the Rialto as the lights dimmed and *The Trespasser* began.

There were technical difficulties. The voice recording was not precisely synchronized with the flickering black-and-white images on the screen. Luckily, the reviewers had seen the show at an earlier screening when everything had worked perfectly. The film ended with enthusiastic applause that deepened into a standing ovation as Gloria Swanson made her way onto the stage. She said a few graceful words and glided back to Joe Kennedy's side. The rest of the evening was filled with celebratory parties and the ritual wait for the favorable reviews in the early editions of the city's many newspapers.

The next day, Swanson and her entourage packed up for Chicago and the film's premiere there, after which they would travel on to Hollywood. She would later claim that, some weeks before the New York premiere, she had been secretly summoned from her Manhattan hotel room to meet with a senior Catholic Church official from Boston, who had asked her to end her romantic relationship with Kennedy. Her lover "had sought church permission to live separately" from his wife, the cleric had told her. She had refused to discuss the matter and stalked out. Swanson "could talk about how discreet she was," one Hollywood historian noted, but by the time of this New York premiere, "Joe and Gloria's affair had been going on for well over a year and had reached the level of Hollywood common knowledge."

On the day after the premiere, as Swanson prepared to head west, Kennedy settled down to business in New York. He planned to keep an eye on ticket sales at the Rialto and to promote the film to other theater chains across the country. Given the stacks of newspapers he collected for early reviews, he could not have missed the front-page business news on Saturday: the collapse of the giant Foshay utility holding company in Minneapolis. According to the papers, the court-appointed receiver blamed Foshay's sudden failure on "over-expansion" of the conglomerate's business and "contraction of securities sales" on Wall Street.

The sale of securities on Wall Street had become the lifeblood of utility holding companies like Foshay in Minneapolis and, to an even greater extent, Samuel Insull's sprawling utility empire based in Chicago and the burgeoning Associated Gas and Electric combine in New York. As electric power spread into more unlit corners of America in the 1920s, these holding companies had grown and multiplied by selling shares in complex layers of subsidiaries. The results for customers were higher electricity bills, padded by a lot of self-dealing corporate overhead. The results for investors were upside-down pyramids, with millions of shareholders and bondholders depending on revenue from a small base of actual money-making utilities. The results for a small cadre of insiders were breathtaking wealth and almost total management control, obtained with just a sliver of their own cash.

That was the way Wall Street worked, Kennedy knew. As he saw it, the insiders—those who knew the confidential financial details, who were alerted to price manipulations in advance, who used their seats on countless corporate boards to pick up early news and to promote their own interests—were the real players. Everyone else? Just suckers, mostly: sad, failed men whose borrowed dreams had ended in ruin over the past months, or in suicide in the past weeks.

Kennedy was temporarily out of the Wall Street game, but whenever he stepped back in, it would be as an insider. Nobody who knew him doubted that. And almost all the insiders did know him. He had been helping some of them manipulate prices on Dick Whitney's stock exchange since the early 1920s, and when the market settled down, he would be happy to engage in those games again.

By Thursday, November 7, *The Trespasser* had set a record for box office receipts in its first week, and Kennedy was getting the word out to other theater owners to whip up their interest. The stock market was faring less well: after closing for city elections on Tuesday, November 5, it saw its prices continue to fall, putting pressure on many of Kennedy's friends on Wall Street. But that was their problem, not his. As the weekend approached, he prepared for his own return to his Los Angeles life and to his lover and business partner, Gloria Swanson.

FRIDAY, NOVEMBER 8, 1929

THE CHANDELIERS OF THE CROWDED HOTEL ROOSEVELT BALL-room in midtown Manhattan illuminated the beaming face and leonine head of New York governor Franklin D. Roosevelt, a distant Democratic cousin of the Republican president for whom the hotel was named. The governor did not betray any concern about the empty seat at the head table—a seat that should have been filled by former governor and failed Democratic presidential candidate Alfred E. Smith.

Roosevelt was the guest of honor for the annual alumni association dinner for the Columbia University Law School, where he had studied more than twenty years earlier. Hundreds of formally dressed lawyers and judges were chatting and eating before the speeches began. Near the head table, a lectern was equipped with the big boxy microphones that would carry the evening's speeches out to radio listeners across the region. The alumni association president anxiously checked his watch and scanned the ballroom's entrances for a glimpse of Al Smith, who was scheduled to speak just before the governor. In the broad, faintly British accents of his privileged upbringing, Governor Roosevelt traded genial banter with the university's longtime president.

In his remarks, the university leader intended to remind the conservative audience—most of whom had likely voted against Roosevelt in the previous year's gubernatorial election—that "when a man was chosen for public office, he represented all of the people and was entitled to their whole-hearted cooperation"—or, at least, their courtesy during the public radio address to come.

But what could explain the discourtesy of Al Smith? There had been reports of some friction between the two Democratic politicians, but no one dreamed Smith would neither show up at this honorary dinner for Roosevelt nor call to explain his absence. As the moment for the radio broadcast neared, the alumni president quickly adjusted the evening's program—Roosevelt would speak directly after the university president, with a spot left at the end for Smith, if he showed up.

In his remarks, Roosevelt called for a thorough reform of the legal system so that everyone, whether rich and powerful or poor and friendless, would receive evenhanded justice from the police and the courts. He warned his audience not to be lulled into complacency by the fact that two prominent officials—the state's former banking superintendent and President Harding's former Interior secretary—had recently been found guilty of accepting bribes. In his rolling cadences, Roosevelt pointed out that the mere fact that these convictions were seen as remarkable and newsworthy "is in itself a proof that what should be a matter of course is received by the great majority of the people as an extraordinary triumph of right over might."

Roosevelt's call for equal justice may have drawn rueful looks from the city reformers in the audience. That week, New Yorkers had gone to the polls and reelected, by an enormous margin, the dapper Mayor Jimmy Walker, the darling of the Manhattan Democratic machine known as Tammany Hall and the overseer of a notoriously corrupt city government. If anyone seemed well beyond the reach of justice, it was Mayor Walker and his cronies. Roosevelt's uneasy arm's-length alliance with Tammany Hall left the governor constantly at risk of guilt by association whenever some new outrage was uncovered.

After Governor Roosevelt's speech ended, the alumni association president stepped to the podium. "Up to this morning Governor Smith was expected to be here—up to now he is expected," he said. "It is a matter of deep regret that he is not [here], for he is beloved throughout the state. The next move is, I suppose, to declare this dinner adjourned."

Smith had planned to attend the alumni dinner. Indeed, he had been getting into his formal wear at 7:30 P.M. that evening when he got shocking news: James J. Riordan—a popular Democratic donor whose friendships stretched from patrician Franklin Roosevelt to buccaneering Joe Kennedy—had blown his brains out in his Greenwich Village townhouse.

Seized by grief, Smith forgot entirely about the Roosevelt dinner and immediately left for Riordan's home. Smith and Riordan had been close friends and frequent business associates for more than a decade. Less than a week earlier, they had jointly invested in a big Miami hotel. Beyond the searing personal tragedy, the suicide had the potential to become a political calamity for Roosevelt and the state's Democrats. Riordan was the founder of the County Trust Company, a small but politically important bank in Greenwich Village. Al Smith served on its board along with Vincent Astor, one of Franklin Roosevelt's close friends. Several other major Democratic donors were also board members. County Trust had been a reliable lender to many Democratic campaigns; in return, the Democrats elected to state and city offices had been reliable sources of cash deposits for the bank. At this moment, the bank held hundreds of thousands of dollars of public funds entrusted to it by Democratic officeholders. If too many depositors became worried about the bank's safety and withdrew their cash, the bank would be forced to close its doors. Thus, the bank's failure would be a disaster not only for its customers but for taxpayers as well—and, of course, for the Democratic Party's hopes for the gubernatorial and congressional midterm elections that were less than a year away.

When Smith reached Riordan's home on West Twelfth Street, he joined others there in an urgent appeal to the city medical examiner to suppress news of the suicide until noon the next day, when County Trust's doors would close for the weekend. Despite misgivings, the city official agreed. Smith and his fellow board members immediately put together a blitzkrieg plan to publicize the bank's solvency before it reopened on Monday.

Even Franklin Roosevelt was kept in the dark about his friend's death until the next day. He was at a Democratic Party "unity luncheon" to kick off his 1930 reelection campaign when the news of Riordan's death broke "like a bomb," as the *Daily News* put it. The wedges of ripe melon were abandoned as Democrats huddled in shocked clusters around the room. To an inquiring reporter, Roosevelt seemed stunned, saying only, "This is terrible. This is terrible."

The governor surely was as worried as Al Smith about the solvency of Riordan's bank, with its well-known ties to the state's Democrats. In just ten months as governor, Roosevelt had already faced the scandalous failure of another Tammany-linked bank, the City Trust Company; that collapse had led to the recent conviction of his banking superintendent on bribery charges. No one could claim that Governor Roosevelt had handled that politically fraught crisis very well.

Beyond his intimate circle, Franklin Delano Roosevelt had been an easy man to underestimate. Fellow students at the Groton prep school and in Harvard's Class of 1904 knew him as the cheerfully pampered only child of a domineering widowed mother. He struck them as a little puppyish, a bit too eager to please, always trying but never quite managing to fit in with the more confident campus cliques. Those who knew him as a young bachelor recalled an attractive and frivolous fellow whose primary skill was charming the dowagers at debutante parties; Teddy Roosevelt's daughters joked that his initials, F.D., stood for "Feather Duster." During his brief stint as a young Wall Street lawyer, his associates did not see him as a serious rival for the coveted partnership slots at the firm. To them, one biographer noted later, he was just a "harmless bust." Bearing what one early biographer called "perhaps the best trade-name in American politics," he told friends he planned to follow in the footsteps of his idol Theodore Roosevelt, his wife's adoring uncle. But that ambition did not impress his social circle, where politics was generally seen as a tawdry and undignified calling that reeked of tenement saloons and smoky clubhouses. He was an engaging campaigner but his early service in the state legislature in Albany did not attract much attention, except for a few observations that his height and pince-nez glasses made it seem he was always looking down his nose at his peers. "He was like a hothouse plant just set out among the weathered and hardy rivals," one early political associate later recalled.

But Roosevelt's early enthusiastic support for presidential candidate Woodrow Wilson in 1912 had paid off with an appointment as assistant navy secretary in Wilson's administration, and his distinguished wartime service in that position—once held by Teddy Roosevelt—had raised his profile within his party. In 1920, Roosevelt had been tapped as the national vice presidential candidate on the Democratic ticket, and he campaigned tirelessly for Ohio newspaper publisher James M. Cox, the presidential nominee who was defeated by Warren Harding. Roosevelt strode handsomely into the Jazz Age with athletic grace, political ambition, family wealth—and a marriage that had been twisted into a dutiful political partnership by his early infidelities, his wife's implacable resentments, and his mother's refusal to permit a divorce that would have destroyed his political career and social reputation.

Then, in August 1921, the charming and cheerful Roosevelt, just thirty-nine years old, was stricken with a crippling attack of polio. Within days, this robust father of five was in writhing pain, unable to stand or walk on his own, unable to care for his body's most basic needs, unable to endure even the weight of a bedsheet on his legs. Whatever her private injuries, his wife, Eleanor, did not fail him. She knew only one thing could impel her husband to fight back against this catastrophe: his deep hunger for political success. Only that long-nurtured dream could get him to strap on the heavy leg braces, to endure the painful therapies, to accept the daily indignities of wheelchair life in a world that, in the 1920s, saw "cripples" as damaged goods—mentally, physically, and even morally unfit for much of anything.

His wife and his closest political advisor, a gnomish former newspaperman named Louis McHenry Howe, worked together tirelessly to help him cling to the shreds of his political influence as the GOP decade unfolded. As Roosevelt fought for whatever he could salvage from polio's devastation, Howe helped him produce a steady stream of letters, telegrams, and phone calls to maintain his ties with influential Democrats across the country—never out of touch, rarely out of mind.

Indeed, Roosevelt's years in this private medical nightmare produced some of his most memorable public moments. At the Democratic National Convention in Manhattan in 1924, he brought an electrified crowd to its feet when he smilingly steered his crutches and leg braces to the podium to give an upbeat speech in support of Al Smith's first quixotic bid for the presidential nomination. If his public personality seemed as carefree as ever, his charm was now buttressed by both harder and softer virtues: a steely resolve and an eloquent empathy. In September 1926, at his party's state convention in Syracuse, he devastatingly took on Andrew W. Mellon, the Pittsburgh plutocrat who was President Coolidge's Treasury secretary. With Coolidge's backing, Mellon had dismissed pleas for leniency from wartime allies struggling to pay their war debts to America, saying: "Well, they hired the money, didn't they?" It was true, Roosevelt said, that war had made America "the bankers of the world." He continued: "But there are two kinds of bankers: the kindly, understanding, sympathetic man who, by his tact, his wise suggestions, his willingness to help even the humblest creditor solve his troubles, saves many a shaky loan for his bank and is beloved and honored in the community—and the tight-lipped, steely-eyed, close-fisted financier who thinks only in dollars and cents and whose only answer to a discouraged and bewildered borrower is 'Well, you hired the money, didn't you?' This is the kind of a banker Mr. Coolidge and Mr. Mellon have made us in the eyes of the world."

At the 1928 Democratic National Convention in Houston, he was back again cheerfully and successfully nominating Al Smith for president and warning his party against a pro-business myopia that could "turn these United Sovereign States of America into the 'United States, Incorporated,' with a limited and self-perpetuating board of directors and no voting power in the common stockholders." By now, his leg braces were lighter and his crutches had been replaced by a cane—and an iron grip on the strong arm of one of his sons. But the eloquence and the gallant, grinning courage that had touched so many hearts four years earlier were still there, and were still exhilarating to see. There were pundits, including the influential columnist Walter Lippmann, who would persist in seeing Governor Roosevelt as a lightweight—an "amiable boy scout," as Lippmann put it in late 1931, or "somewhat shallow and futile," as the acerbic H. L. Mencken observed in early 1932. But within Roosevelt's intimate circle, no one doubted that the frivolous "feather duster" of his younger years had vanished during his battle with polio.

One powerful politician who saw FDR's usefulness to the Democratic Party was Al Smith, the parochial big-city Catholic who had won the Democratic nomination in 1928. The Republican candidate was Herbert Hoover, Coolidge's capable and well-traveled Commerce secretary. The common wisdom was that 1928 should be a GOP year, given the uneven but apparently indestructible prosperity of that dazzling decade. But Prohibition was the wild card: Smith and many urban and immigrant voters opposed it; Hoover and many rural Protestants supported it. Otherwise, the two men "shared the same fundamental outlook," one of Hoover's biographers noted. Both were economic conservatives, "friendly toward business" and determined "to minimize government intervention in the market."

But to have a prayer of carrying his Republican-leaning home state, Al Smith needed someone with him on the state ballot who had what he himself lacked: distinguished service on the national stage, a Protestant pedigree that stretched back to Dutch settlers in the mid-1600s, and the cachet of family ties to that irrepressible progressive, Teddy Roosevelt. Smith needed Franklin Roosevelt. He pressured Roosevelt to run for the governorship for the good of the party, and Roosevelt agreed, despite his reluctance to cut short the therapy he hoped would someday allow him to walk again unaided.

It proved to be a wise choice for the state's Democrats. Ignoring the ill-disguised contempt of some of Smith's aides, Roosevelt campaigned from one end of the state to the other. He used his robust shoulders and arms to prop himself up on a convertible's backseat or lean with an apparently relaxed grip on a sturdy podium as he made one clarion speech after another. He called himself a "progressive Democrat" and he promised to continue Smith's programs to support labor, small businesses, and upstate farmers. He somehow managed to keep his affliction out of the spotlight, without denying his experience. He met publicly with other polio survivors, including many children, and encouraged them with his cheerful example. When he had to be physically carried to some upper-story venue, he chatted and smiled during the journey as if he were unconscious of his situation.

In one of his finest speeches on the trail, he lashed out at the religious bigotry besetting Al Smith in the presidential race. He recalled the injured soldiers on the battlefields of the Great War. When medics were carrying stretchers of the wounded and dying, he said, "people were not asking to what church these German boys or these American boys belonged." If anyone could remember that and still "cast his ballot in the interest of intolerance," he continued, ". . . then I say solemnly to that man or woman, 'May God have mercy on your miserable soul.'"

On Election Day, November 6, 1928, Al Smith was defeated overwhelmingly by Herbert Hoover, failing even to carry New York State. Hoover trounced Smith by 6 million votes, swept up 444 Electoral College votes to Smith's 87, and helped push the GOP to a 100-seat majority in the House of Representatives. But in the wee hours, as upstate New York results came in, Franklin Roosevelt won the governorship by a margin of just 25,564 votes. Smith had led the national ticket to overwhelming defeat; Roosevelt had led the state ticket to a razor-thin victory.

In his inaugural address in Albany, Roosevelt gave as succinct an expression of his deeply held principles as he had ever offered. He condemned the glorified selfishness and "rugged individualism" of the Coolidge-Hoover tradition. "Our civilization cannot endure unless we, as individuals, realize our personal responsibility to and dependence upon the rest of the world," he said. "For it is literally true that the 'self-supporting' man or woman has become as extinct as the man of the Stone Age. Without the help of thousands of others, any one of us would die, naked and starved." Those thousands "worked in sunlit fields, in dark mines, in the fierce heat of molten metal, and among the looms and wheels in countless factories" to produce the food, clothing, and small luxuries of life enjoyed by others, he continued. In his view, it was simple *fairness,* not charity, that required those who benefited so much from their fellow citizens' labor to pay attention to those citizens' needs.

But when Roosevelt was sworn in for a two-year term on January 1, 1929, he faced not only a solidly Republican legislature—as resistant to safety net programs and business regulation as it had been for years—but also a covey of sneering Smith loyalists who expected him to be a puppet governor, deferring to the defeated Smith's continued backstage control in Albany. Indeed, on one remarkable occasion—a day when four of Roosevelt's campaign initiatives were killed in the state assembly—Smith crashed one of Roosevelt's first press conferences in the statehouse, jokingly claiming to be a journalist and quizzing FDR about how he had rearranged the office furniture. When the new governor finally could field serious questions, Smith "listened in silence but with a look of satisfaction as his successor was compelled to do the answering to questions ranging from water power development to taxation," reported *The New York Times.* The next day's newspapers focused as much on Smith's stunt as on FDR's comments. Confronted with this persistent interference, the new governor instinctively threw up defenses to protect his independence, cloaking his resistance with charming noncommittal nods and good cheer; Smith grew increasingly disgruntled.

Although Roosevelt retained most of Smith's top appointees, including the secretly corrupt banking superintendent, he drew the line at keeping Smith's secretary of state, an able but abrasive autocrat named Robert Moses, explaining simply that the man "rubs me the wrong way." It went deeper than that—the two men had been feuding since 1924 and Moses made no secret of his contempt for Roosevelt, calling him "a pretty poor excuse for a man."

Then in February 1929, the City Trust Company in Manhattan collapsed in a mess of fraudulent bookkeeping and bad loans; its failure wiped out the savings of thousands of people in the city's Italian immigrant community and outraged their fiery young Republican congressman, Fiorello La Guardia. It was a major political embarrassment for New York Democrats, not least because the bank's legal team included Al Smith's young nephew, hired just six

months after he was admitted to the bar. The Smith-appointed
banking superintendent was soon accused of taking bribes to look
the other way as City Trust unraveled. The City Trust crisis peaked
while Roosevelt was on one of his regular therapeutic trips to Warm
Springs, Georgia, which he had patronized since early in his battle
with polio. That left Lieutenant Governor Herbert H. Lehman, a
son of the Lehman dynasty on Wall Street, in charge of naming
someone to head the investigation of the failed bank. Lehman decided the most credible man for this daunting job was Robert Moses.

City Trust proved to be a cesspool of self-dealing, accounting
fraud, bribery, and conflicts of interest, all carried out under the hapless oversight of a board of directors chaired by a sitting municipal
judge firmly aligned with Tammany Hall. The City Trust collapse
was followed in June 1929 by the collapse of a respected private bank,
Clarke Brothers; that failure, while less politically fraught, also led to
fraud indictments and convictions. In July, Moses had delivered a
scathing public report that encompassed both cases. It called for
tighter regulation of all private banks, which at the time fell in the
crack between state and federal oversight; a robust overhaul of the
state banking department to give it more resources, more expertise,
and broader jurisdiction; a ban on bank affiliates formed solely to
speculate on Wall Street with depositors' money; and stiffer penalties for negligent directors, such as those who presided over the City
Trust debacle.

Roosevelt praised the prescient report but did little that Moses
recommended. He set up a toothless Republican-dominated committee that recommended no meaningful reforms.

Was Roosevelt's response merely a by-product of his deep mistrust of Moses? Perhaps. Or perhaps, as one biographer suggested,
it reflected a more fundamental belief "that bankers were possessed
of a morality somewhat higher than that of businessmen in general."
In any case, the City Trust embarrassment had lingered into the
autumn. At least one state GOP luminary had argued publicly that
Al Smith was to blame for the whole mess, and the scandal was sure
to dog Roosevelt in his 1930 reelection campaign.

With that history, it was no wonder that the suicide of Democratic banker Jimmy Riordan on Friday, November 8, 1929, prompted Al Smith and his allies to launch a vigorous media campaign to tout the soundness of County Trust, with Roosevelt contributing the positive assessment of the state banking department. Fortunately, the bank actually was sound and had not been touched by the stock market losses that Riordan supposedly experienced in the weeks before his death. On Sunday, that good news hit the front pages in tandem with the bad news of the suicide.

When County Trust opened on Monday, November 11, every officer was present. Stacks of cash were visible behind the tellers' windows, ready for a rush of withdrawals that never materialized. Instead, Jimmy Riordan's friends lined up to open new accounts or add cash to existing ones, and the bank ended the day stronger than it had been when it had closed on Saturday. A potential bank run had been averted by a brave show of confidence, but Governor Roosevelt could not be sure he would be as lucky the next time.

Perhaps Robert Moses had been right about the folly of trusting bankers to police themselves? The governor's foxhole education in the art of regulating the world of finance had begun.

DECEMBER 6, 1929

THE FEDERAL JUDGE IN NEWARK, NEW JERSEY, LISTENED AS William O. Douglas, a young law professor from Yale, sketched out a proposal to give intelligence tests to all the debtors whose financial failures were being sorted out in the judge's courtroom.

Professor Douglas, rangy and rumpled, had for months been interviewing debtors involved in more than a thousand cases on the judge's docket, holding "clinics" to learn how they had wound up there. Now he wanted to explore whether a lack of intelligence was the bedrock factor behind these failed businesses. Why not establish, once and for all, whether a low IQ was more to blame for business failures than a weak economy, unequal access to credit, or poorly enforced antitrust laws?

"Probably all of us have a hunch that most of these men are quite dumb and perhaps morons," Bill Douglas explained, his western twang tinged with humor. "It is probably a good hunch but it doesn't mean very much unless it is backed up by facts." With the help of a psychology professor at Yale, he had picked out an intelligence test "devised particularly for business institutions," Douglas told the judge, and he wanted to administer it to all the debtors in his study. After all, Douglas reasoned, if a lack of intelligence is a cause—or perhaps, *the* cause—of business failures, "it certainly is significant. No complete analysis of causes would be complete without it."

And a complete analysis of the root causes of business failures was precisely what Bill Douglas was trying to produce with a groundbreaking study of the bankruptcy process that hit its stride in 1929.

His research project was part of a creative revolution called "legal realism," a view of the law that went beyond the formalism of judicial rulings to incorporate the social, psychological, and economic forces shaping legal outcomes in the real world. "The notion that law was a neutral, scientific system, the realists believed, was an elaborate cover for enforcing the preferences of those in power," explained the legal historian Noah Feldman.

The shift to legal realism at Yale Law School was led by Robert Maynard Hutchins, who became acting dean in 1927. A brilliant and persuasive innovator, Hutchins shared the realists' belief that lawyers needed to understand the human landscape in which the law operated. To nurture that perspective, he added compulsory courses in economics, history, psychology, and the social sciences. He also set up the Institute of Human Relations on campus as a center where law professors could "work with economists and sociologists and psychologists to make those connections between the law and the social scientists that were essential to a full understanding of the law's role in modern society." As Hutchins saw it, "The object of a law school education was to produce educated lawyers and not merely lawyers who knew the rules and how to manipulate them."

Hutchins's plans for Yale seemed to electrify young Bill Douglas. After hearing the dean speak at a suburban country club dinner in May 1928, Douglas buttonholed him in the club's locker room and the two young men—they were both just twenty-nine—sipped bootleg booze and talked until well into the night. Within a few weeks, Hutchins had persuaded Douglas to move to Yale.

In private practice, Douglas had hewn fairly close to the traditions of his profession, even the less seemly ones. As a young associate at Cravath, Henderson & de Gersdorff, he had worked on a railroad bankruptcy that was a textbook example of how Wall Street insiders and their lawyers manipulated the process to shortchange ordinary creditors and investors. But by the time he met Hutchins, Douglas had been teaching law for a year at Columbia, where his mentor Underhill Moore was an early advocate for legal realism. Like Moore and Hutchins, Douglas was growing impatient with what he called the "how-to-do-it trade school" approach to legal education. As he wrote decades later: "Why spend one's life teaching bright youngsters how to do things that should not be done?"

He moved to Yale in the summer of 1928 with a brain buzzing with fresh ideas for changing how business law was studied and taught. As one biographer put it, "He wanted students to learn how corporations worked—how they were formed, financed, managed, merged, reorganized and, occasionally, dissolved."

Hutchins encouraged his faculty to do field research and was especially supportive of studies that included collaboration with other disciplines. Douglas was hungry for exactly that kind of intellectual exercise. Under the flag of the Institute of Human Relations, he teamed up with Dorothy Swaine Thomas, a gifted young sociologist and statistician, to conduct a field study of small-business bankruptcies. He persuaded U.S. District Judge William Clark in Newark to open his busy docket to the researchers, who spent months interviewing "distraught owners of small grocery stores, restaurants, and retail clothing stores" about their personal roads to ruin. He and Thomas interviewed the debtors' accountants, their local Better Business Bureaus, their employees, their creditors. Douglas wanted to learn everything he could about how the dry facts of business law shaped the real-world experiences of business people.

In the shadows of the booming 1920s, tens of thousands of businesses in America had gone broke—nearly 37,000 a year, on average, since the end of the war. Courts had handled more than 57,000 new cases in the first half of 1929. From 1925 to 1928, the courts dealt with nearly 200,000 bankruptcies—more than twice the number of ordinary civil lawsuits in the trial courts and appellate courts in that period. Railroads were chronic debtors, regularly restructuring their liabilities via court-appointed receivers. Typically, as in the case Douglas worked on as a young Cravath associate, these receivers were boardroom insiders with little concern for small creditors, modest investors, or idled workers. American farmers, who had been encouraged to boost their harvests during the war, were now facing a glut that had pulled crop prices down to ruinous levels. Their distress pushed many regional banks, farm supply companies, and retail businesses into bankruptcy. As that pitiless process ground forward, Florida's overblown real estate bubble popped in 1925, generating more business failures and bank losses. The impact of the October crash was still uncertain. So far, the collapse of the Foshay utilities conglomerate had been an isolated event, but clearly such top-heavy public utility holding companies were vulnerable to a weak stock market.

Although his first focus was on small-business failures, Bill Douglas had not ignored these larger bankruptcies. As his reputation grew, he was recruited by the U.S. Commerce Department to study corporate failures in the Philadelphia area. In both research projects, Douglas kept digging deeper into the subsoil of business life, looking for the root factors that caused businesses to fail. If those factors could be identified and addressed, he reasoned, there would be fewer failed businesses, fewer ruined lives.

BILL DOUGLAS, JUST THIRTY-ONE years old in 1929, knew more about ruined lives than most of his fellow law professors at Yale. His widowed mother had often recounted how, when he was a child in the first years of the century, she had lost her savings when her lawyer unwisely invested the money in an ill-fated irrigation project near their home in booming Yakima, Washington. The project's failure left the Douglas family with little but a roof over its head and barely a penny to spare. These tales were not quite accurate, as he later learned, but the belt-tightening was real, whatever its cause.

With big dreams, a plainspoken eloquence, and a near-photographic memory, Bill Douglas eked out an education with before-school jobs delivering papers, after-school jobs doing janitorial work, all-summer jobs picking fruit, and school-year jobs teaching and tutoring other students. A high school valedictorian, he worked his way through tiny Whitman College in Walla Walla, Washington, and then hitched train rides east with nearly empty pockets to begin working his way through Columbia Law School.

Since his graduation from Columbia in 1925, he had been as skittish as a grasshopper. He worked at the Cravath firm in Manhattan, but he missed the open vistas and empty acres of his western home and never felt at ease in the city's crowded stone canyons. He traveled back to his beloved mountains for a brief stab at private practice in Yakima, but found the work dull and unrewarding. He returned to Manhattan to teach at Columbia Law School, and in mid-1928 made his move to Yale. Less than a year later, Hutchins was lured away to head the University of Chicago. Douglas was tempted to follow his young mentor, but Yale gave him a raise to keep him and he stayed on to pursue what he saw as a worthy experiment in making the law "more relevant to life."

At Yale, Douglas was far more interested in his research than in his students, some of whom he dismissed as the "spoon-fed, coddled, pampered" sons of privilege and wealth. Thomas I. Emerson, a Douglas student who became a noted civil rights scholar, later recalled that students saw Douglas as a pampered "big-city lawyer" who had been lured from Wall Street to Yale by a fat pay package. "It never occurred to us that Douglas was a country boy who came to New York with six cents in his pocket," Emerson said. From Douglas's first months on campus, he displayed the irreverent rejection of conformity that would become his lifelong trademark—childish stunts with a few faculty friends, tipsy or flirtatious behavior that pained his staid and more conventional wife, Mildred, and a frank and unapologetic hunger for admiration or, failing that, attention.

A brusque but brilliant young man in a big hurry, Douglas had quickly taken up the study of business failures and how creditors, investors, and employees fared in the legal process that followed. From his bit part in that railroad bankruptcy to his ongoing study of big and small corporate failures, he knew the process from the inside out. His research in Newark and Philadelphia had attracted the attention of President Hoover's Commerce secretary, and had been written up both in important law journals and in tabloid newspapers. Almost overnight, he had become widely known as an articulate authority on every aspect of corporate bankruptcy law.

And that had put young Bill Douglas in exactly the right place at the right time, because the bankruptcy work of the New York court system had just plunged into a lurid, slow-moving scandal.

In January 1929, the city had learned of the attempted suicide of a minor federal court clerk and the disappearance of his cousin, a lawyer who had recently been indicted for stealing from estates he handled as a court-appointed bankruptcy receiver.

Matters had accelerated in February when a federal grand jury in New York found widespread abuses in the federal court's handling of bankruptcy cases and accused a federal judge of "serious indiscretions" in appointing bankruptcy receivers, including the fugitive lawyer. The scandal had burst onto the front page in early March, with news that the federal judge's stepson had mysteriously wound up with a luxury car that had been owned by a bankrupt chain of local candy stores. The judge was overseeing that bankruptcy case—a small, simple case whose court-appointed receiver nevertheless was paying fees to three friendly lawyers and paying nothing to the retail chain's creditors. The same month, the same federal judge had been accused in Congress of appointing favored attorneys as bankruptcy receivers in exchange for their hiring the judge's friends and relatives.

Then in April, the storm of scandal had hit hurricane force. The federal judge resigned, becoming only the second federal judge in New York City history to step down under the cloud of criminal allegations. The fugitive lawyer surfaced in a Philadelphia hotel and agreed to meet there with federal prosecutors. Moments before the meeting, as the prosecutors waited in an adjacent room, he had poisoned himself, leaving behind a long confessional letter that turbo-charged the scandal and further stained the reputation of the bankruptcy courts.

The federal inquiry had been expanded and deepened under the direction of Judge Thomas D. Thacher, a formidable figure in New York legal circles. By the fall, expert witnesses had been called before Judge Thacher to present their ideas for reform. One of them was Professor Douglas from Yale. As the hearings rolled forward through the fall, Douglas had courted reporters, consulted with the U.S. Commerce Department, attended important policy conferences, and formed friendly ties with a number of influential jurists and political figures in New York and Washington. Indeed, within a few months, Judge Thacher would leave the bench to become President Hoover's solicitor general in Washington, where he would undertake a national study of bankruptcy courts and call again on Douglas for expert advice. With his star on the rise from Wall Street to Washington, Douglas felt confident that his unconventional research methods would get a respectful hearing anywhere in the federal court system.

But on that cold December morning near the end of the wild ride of 1929, none of his newfound fame was helping Douglas sell the idea of giving IQ tests to all the business failures coming before the bankruptcy judge in Newark, New Jersey.

Judge Clark cautioned that the IQ test might provoke opposition among the debtors—indeed, they would likely "take it as an insult," he said, and he would not order them to cooperate. But later, something about the out-of-the-box idea apparently appealed to the judge, who was in some ways as unconventional as Bill Douglas. He decided that if some debtors occasionally volunteered to be tested, he would not object.

It wasn't what Douglas wanted—indeed, this haphazard testing would render the research results useless from any scientific standpoint. But still, it could produce some intriguing findings, some fresh headlines, and some additional gloss on Douglas's growing national reputation. As one biographer would later see it, this outcome was typical of how Douglas could so often turn his missteps into success. "He picked a hot topic, positioned himself in front of the issue by posing the right questions for future study, and then left that often tedious work for others."

Undaunted by the judge's limitations on his outlandish IQ testing idea, Douglas happily boarded the evening train back to New Haven.

* * *

THE DREAM OF "DEREGULATING" AMERICAN FINANCE HAS NEVER lost its appeal in America's conservative circles. Even "neoliberal" Democrats in the 1990s gave lip service, at least, to the idea that federal market regulation is a *burden,* not an *asset,* and that the ideal should be an unregulated market free to maximize profits for investors and raise capital for American business.

But no one who makes those arguments today has ever actually experienced an unregulated financial world in America. Today's Americans have lived their entire lives under financial protections first enacted ninety years ago. They have always had "a cop on Wall Street." They have never experienced the financial jungle of unregulated capitalism.

These four men had.

In October 1929, after a decade of increasingly reckless corruption, Americans watched in horror as an unregulated Wall Street collapsed, helping to drag a great nation to its knees.

Over the next ten years, a majority of Americans would come to believe that only Uncle Sam had enough power to restrain the ruthless greed that had undermined the nation's economy.

During that pivotal decade, from 1929 to 1939, the work of these four flawed but remarkable men—the deft politician Franklin Roosevelt, the polished conservative Dick Whitney, the buccaneering Joe Kennedy, and the irrepressible Bill Douglas—would help fundamentally change the way "other people's money" would be handled in America.

The decade was an argument between two sharply differing visions. One vision was for an American future that looked very much like the past, with clear lines of privilege and a firm hierarchy of

power; the other vision was for a future in which a national commitment to fair play would open the door of opportunity to the largest
number of Americans possible. The debate is as fundamental to the
nation's well-being now as it was then: How does a democracy fairly
share the benefits of its economy with its citizens?

Capitalism, without argument, can generate great wealth and opportunity for those who participate in it, and the ideal of democratic
capitalism is that anyone *can* participate. Financial markets are the
central nervous system of capitalism. How those markets operate,
then, determines how capitalism shapes society.

How those markets *should operate* was a fundamental debate in
the 1930s.

Should Wall Street be the exclusive preserve of people who were
sophisticated enough to look out for themselves? Could they generate enough wealth to sustain the larger society? Dick Whitney, who
battled to save practices he thought made markets work better,
would have answered "yes." He believed that the wise stewardship of
Wall Street's elite would keep unregulated markets healthy and let
the benefits of capitalism spread, indirectly, to the rest of the population. He was not alone in this belief—millions of affluent Americans
agreed with him, and millions more still do.

But would ordinary Americans tolerate a freewheeling capitalism that laid its heaviest burdens on the backs of the "little guys"
while steering most of its benefits into the pockets of the "big guys"?
How long would ordinary citizens wait for some fair share of the
wealth to dribble down to them? Franklin Roosevelt believed that
this "trickle-down" form of capitalism, always unfair, had become
dangerously untenable amid the brutal suffering of the Great Depression. For reasons of their own, Joe Kennedy and Bill Douglas
enlisted in FDR's campaign to spread the benefits of capitalism
more widely and more fairly. They were determined to make Wall
Street a place where ordinary Americans could pursue their own
prosperity instead of waiting for crumbs to fall from the tables of
privilege. This unprecedented effort led by Roosevelt would help
build America's postwar middle class and would make the American
marketplace the envy of the world.

In the process, the battle waged by these four men would prove that government could level the American playing field of opportunity for future generations. Wisely led, government could regulate markets without ruining them; it could rein in the ruthless without stifling the worthy. Government could undertake big, difficult, controversial things like market regulation and make them work. It could change the world—if it dared.

CHAPTER TWO

DESCENDING INTO SILENCE

DECEMBER 31, 1929–MARCH 4, 1933

AT 1:30 P.M. ON NEW YEAR'S EVE, THE LAST DAY OF TRADING in 1929, a party broke out on the floor of the New York Stock Exchange.

The snappy regimental band of the 369th Regiment, the famed "Harlem Hellcats," had marched onto the trading floor, climbed up on a temporary bandstand, and burst into loud, lively music. At one of the trading posts, laughing traders ceremonially burned a copy of an October newspaper reporting on the Black Thursday crash. Others cheered, threw confetti, blew noisemakers—and, occasionally, conducted some year-end trades. The exchange's stock ticker, fed by clerks seated around the edge of the trading floor, sent the details of these trades out on the ticker in sporadic bursts.

Then, just after the closing bell rang at 3 P.M., the tickers suddenly fell quiet for almost a full minute.

For many American investors, this might have been a moment of silence to mourn their lost fortunes. Since the panicky days of late October, the market had continued to stumble downhill until mid-November, erasing roughly half its value at its September peak. Small investors trading with borrowed money were wiped out in the first few hours of Black Thursday. Over the next few weeks, big investors watched slower waves of selling wash away the profits of a year, or perhaps a lifetime.

Finally, on November 14—a day after Treasury secretary Andrew Mellon proposed an income tax cut, and the Federal Reserve Board cut interest rates—the market rallied and kept a grip on its gains. It began to look like the bull market of the 1920s was getting back on its feet. The rally gained strength in December. By Christmas, the market had reclaimed more than half its losses.

This welcome rally had come too late for some woefully unlucky people. James J. Riordan, the banker and Democratic donor whose suicide on November 8 was front-page news, was not the only one who found the damage caused by this wild, unregulated market just too much to bear. In the weeks and months after the crash, an uncounted community of despairing investors had also given up on life. On October 29, a Kansas City insurance executive attempted suicide at his club. The next day, a New York man's body was fished from the Hudson River with his broker's cash demands in his pocket. On November 12, two ruined investors turned on the gas in their homes. One was an obscure cigar maker, aged sixty, who died in a small apartment in the Bronx; the other was a prominent utility president, aged sixty, found dead in the third-floor bathroom of his Rochester mansion. On November 16, a distraught wholesale grocer died in a leap from his Manhattan lawyer's office window. The same day, an engineer in Scranton doused himself with gasoline and lit a fatal match. On November 23, a broker in St. Louis poisoned himself rather than face selling his seat on the New York Stock Exchange. On December 11, a ruined investor jumped in front of a subway train in the Bronx. On Christmas Day, an unemployed broker, hoping to leave his insurance benefits to his family, shot himself outside a police station in Jersey City, New Jersey. Two days later, a prominent Baltimore broker, a few days away from hosting his daughter's debutante party, shot himself in a parking garage near his home.

Little is known about the life of Wellington Lytle, age twenty-two, who shot himself in a Milwaukee hotel room on December 7, except that he possessed a rare sense of humor: he left behind four pennies and a suicide note in the form of a will, leaving his body to science, his sympathy to his creditors, and his soul to Treasury secretary Andrew Mellon.

Common wisdom today is that the wave of postcrash suicides is mere folklore, fed by a few lurid examples like Jimmy Riordan. But these specific suicides certainly happened; they and many others were reported in dozens of local papers. It is equally certain that many other deaths of despair occurred as a result of the market crash but were covered up as "accidents" to soothe distraught relatives, or were reported in small newspapers whose archives are lost to us now. The 1929 crash of the reckless, unregulated market of the Roaring Twenties inflicted real damage on real people, more damage than some of those people could bear.

But on New Year's Eve of that year, such ghosts had been chased from the NYSE trading floor by the peppy Harlem Hellcats—and by the confident forecasts from notables like Mellon and Hoover, who predicted the current rally would continue. The light New Year's Eve trading was going smoothly, amid the celebrations. Then, there was that curious pause in the ticker's chatter, just after the final bell, a silence long enough to attract worried attention beyond the walls of the exchange.

The reason was clear to anyone actually on the NYSE trading floor: it was patriotism, not panic. At that moment, as the closing bell stopped clanging, the Harlem Hellcats had broken into the national anthem and everyone on the floor—including the clerks tending the ticker—had spontaneously stood to attention. That final bell was rung by exchange president Harry Simmons, returned from his long October honeymoon and carrying out this ritual year-end task for the last time. When the exchange elected its president in May, Simmons expected to put his gavel into the steady hand of Dick Whitney.

As this exuberant afternoon showed, neither Wall Street nor Washington had fully grasped the damage done by the October crash. Since relatively few Americans owned stocks, most pundits expected nothing worse than reduced spending on luxury goods by wealthy shoppers like Dick Whitney, Joe Kennedy, and their wives and girlfriends. They thought "average" Americans would ignore the crash and keep shopping for clothing and cars, furniture and appliances. They were ignoring the extremely lopsided flow of wealth fostered by the policies of a plutocratic decade.

As one history of daily life in that period noted, "Even at the end of the economic surge of the 1920s, poverty was the usual situation for at least two-fifths of the American population." Farmers, miners, lumbermen, and factory workers all fell behind in the 1920s; by 1926, more than a third of the population, or about 44 million people, lived on less than $1,000 a year, half what that era's experts said was necessary for the basics of life. Middle-class families, those making about $15,000 a year by the end of the decade, had fared better—but, in the process, they had arrived at the end of each year with more debt than they had when the year began.

By contrast, the very rich in America had gotten *very much* richer in that gilded decade. By 1929, the richest 10 percent of the population was receiving fully half the national income; the richest *one-tenth of 1 percent* was getting nearly a quarter of the national income. One newspaper editorial in January 1929 cited figures from the Federal Trade Commission showing that "thirteen per cent of the people own 90 percent of the wealth." And when the market crashed and those very rich people suddenly felt very poor, their belt-tightening caused pain far beyond the fur salons and jewelry boutiques of Manhattan and Chicago.

The results were "chain-reactive," wrote Kenneth S. Davis, an award-winning presidential historian: "Domestic servants were laid off, clerks in expensive stores were laid off, employees of luxury manufacturers were laid off, construction workers employed on expensive housing projects were laid off." Those suddenly jobless workers cut their own spending, triggering more layoffs in the industries that catered to them, which in turn caused the idled or worried workers in those industries to cut back. *The Wall Street Journal* recounted a suspiciously apt anecdote: A postcrash stockbroker told his milkman that at least the crash wouldn't hurt *him*—people would always buy milk, right? The milkman set him straight. Yes, people were still ordering milk, but so many had cancelled their orders for *cream* that his business was down by $400 a month.

Not all the damage had trickled down from the market crash; some of it was built into the very architecture of the previous prosperity. In an address to party leaders in Boston in September 1928, Hoover's campaign manager, Hubert Work, had presciently described how precarious life was for middle-class consumers: "They owe money on their homes, their radios, their automobiles, their electric washing machine and many other luxuries . . . They have laid wagers on continuing prosperity." If the boom faltered, he warned, all that debt would "bury millions beneath it with hardship unprecedented in any former period of depression." Oddly, he saw this as proof that the country should reelect Hoover, who vowed to sustain the lopsided boom, not as proof that economic security still eluded even the nation's more affluent families.

At first, President Hoover seemed to be taking aggressive steps to stimulate the economy after the 1929 crash. He initiated an income tax cut. He convened White House conferences where corporate leaders promised future spending that would sustain payrolls. He vowed he would approve any railroad mergers needed to boost growth in that vital sector. He urged the nation's governors to speed up any public construction projects on the drawing board, and amped up the federal government's construction plans. Hoover's effort fell far short of what the crisis demanded, but it went further than old guard Republicans like Andrew Mellon and Dick Whitney thought it should. Like Hoover, Whitney believed in a very limited role for government. He met secretly with Hoover on October 15, 1930, "to counsel him on financial policy," according to market historian Barrie A. Wigmore. We don't know what advice Whitney privately gave the president, but he laid out his own long-held views publicly in a speech in November 1933: "Fundamentally, the government has no right [to a role] in business, and no right [to a role] in relief work . . . [a] dole from the government means the breakdown of all morale." But Hoover's activism in late 1929 and early 1930, however reluctant, impressed a host of pundits and business analysts, who confidently expected the economy would quickly recover.

Out beyond Washington, as 1930 grew older and leaner, confidence was harder to sustain. More than 3 million workers had lost their jobs in the first six months after the Wall Street crash. Banks that had speculated widely and unwisely before the crash were looking shaky; panics had closed banks in Toledo, Omaha, and Los Angeles. Farm prices were falling—wheat prices fell 45 percent from the 1929 highs—and rural banks were feeling the pain along with their borrowers. Foreign trade was shrinking under the weight of a profoundly unwise and ill-timed tariff law that Hoover signed in June, and that shrinkage was hurting both farmers and manufacturers.

The early 1930 market rally hadn't been enough at first to lure Joe Kennedy back east from Hollywood, where he was working on a new comedy for Gloria Swanson. But by spring, Kennedy's restless gaze had been caught by a new attraction: a faint rising star in national politics. While it is doubtful Kennedy had ever actually crossed swords with Franklin Roosevelt during the war, as he later claimed, he had gotten at least one of Roosevelt's friendly letters in support of Al Smith's presidential campaign in 1928. Kennedy hadn't responded, but he was clearly still on some list in Roosevelt's head. In the spring of 1930, Roosevelt's Hyde Park neighbor and friend Henry Morgenthau Jr. asked the film tycoon to join him for lunch with the governor in Albany. Kennedy made the trip upstate and his lunch with Roosevelt grew into a full afternoon's conversation.

Neither man preserved notes on their talk, but two topics were at the front of FDR's mind at the time.

Roosevelt was in the middle of a fight with state lawmakers over the hydroelectric potential of the St. Lawrence River and other major New York waterways, a cause he had supported since his years in the state senate nearly two decades earlier. Roosevelt wanted private power companies in the state to serve the public's interest, with publicly owned power systems set up to serve the rural areas unattractive to private utilities—and to provide a "yardstick" to keep private rates competitive. The Republicans who controlled the state legislature wanted none of that. Private utilities "must never be our masters," Roosevelt might have said, repeating comments he'd made earlier. "They must be our servants . . . well paid, as all good servants should be, but our servants still."

Roosevelt's crusade was putting him at odds with Wall Street's most ferocious forces—forces Joe Kennedy knew well. The public utility holding companies were designed by Wall Street investment bankers, underwritten by Wall Street brokerage firms, and listed on

Wall Street's stock exchanges. Like the Silicon Valley giants of the future, they controlled technologies that could radically transform society; investors were dazzled by visions of the wealth these companies could generate almost overnight. If FDR challenged the private titans of the power industry, he would have a serious fight on his hands.

Shortly before his luncheon with Kennedy, Roosevelt also had signed into law a set of weak banking reforms endorsed by the state advisory board FDR created after the back-to-back failures of City Trust Company and Clarke Brothers the previous summer. The new laws did little to protect small savers, and did nothing to require better stewardship by bank directors or to keep bankers from speculating on Wall Street with depositors' money. FDR was relying on honest bankers deterring dishonest bankers through self-regulation.

As for Kennedy, he had gone to Albany to look for a leader who could save the country from the "paralyzing disorder" he feared would occur if the Depression continued. As historian Doris Kearns Goodwin later wrote, Kennedy believed America needed a government "strong enough to demonstrate to both the radicals and the ultraconservatives that capitalism could be saved so long as it was transformed." Kennedy also felt that the levers of power were shifting. "In the next generation," he told a friend, "the people who run the government will be the biggest people in America." He intended to be among them, and his trip to Albany was a step in that direction.

Whatever the governor and the film tycoon discussed during that long afternoon visit, Kennedy was clearly impressed—and reassured. "I knew that big, drastic changes had to be made in our economic system and I felt that Roosevelt was the one who could make those changes," he said later. "I wanted him in the White House for my own security and the security of our kids."

According to his wife Rose's memories of these months, Kennedy "saw that the country was heading toward a potential explosion" and was anxious to help elect "a leader who would lead."

But for Kennedy, playing a role in national politics would mean stepping into a less forgiving spotlight than he enjoyed with Hollywood reporters and blasé Wall Street gossips. In their irreverent world, his cutthroat boardroom deals and adulterous bedroom romps made Kennedy seem masterful and suave. In the harsh glare of post-crash politics, his escapades—the indiscreet affair with Gloria Swanson, his alliances with the "pools" that manipulated stock prices in the 1920s, his rough treatment of creditors and investors in several recent Hollywood mergers—could make him look like just another predatory, unethical plutocrat. But after nearly four years in the film industry with a sideline in market speculation, Kennedy may have longed for—what? Visible power, a larger purpose? Maybe. Prestigious future opportunities for his sons? Definitely.

Whatever Kennedy's specific hunger was, as the spring of 1930 rolled toward fall and the nation rolled deeper into a bitter depression, he began to tidy up his life, refocusing on publishing, radio, and finance—realms where he could be of immense help to Roosevelt's political ambitions. At some point after this Albany visit in 1930, Kennedy spoke by phone with a friend—one of President Hoover's top fundraisers, as it happened—and told him to get ready to write down the name of the next president of the United States. "You're not hearing much about him now but you will in 1932," said Kennedy. "It's Franklin D. Roosevelt. And don't forget who told you." When he got back to his home in Bronxville, New York, after his long afternoon upstate, Kennedy sounded even more certain: Franklin Roosevelt, he told his wife, was "the man who could save the country."

IT WAS GROWING CLEARER by the late summer of 1930 that America needed saving—not just from its worsening economy but also from the alarming political discontent erupting from the extreme Left and the radical Right. As one biographer would later note, FDR was facing a world where "democracy was on the run, discredited even by subtle minds as a hopelessly cumbersome way to meet the challenges of the modern age."

Conservative lawmakers and editorial writers of the era preferred crusading against the unruly Left. And leftist political organizations were, indeed, growing stronger as hardship spread. In the spring of 1930, communist marchers had clashed with police in New York and at least a dozen other major cities. A confrontation between a truck-load of communist activists and police outside an American Federa-tion of Labor gathering in Boston produced what one police official called the worst riot in the city since 1917. In the fall of 1930, the strongly left-wing Farmer-Labor Party would overwhelmingly win the governor's race in Minnesota, and left-leaning parties strength-ened elsewhere. By then, other desperate citizens were losing pa-tience with the ballot box. According to T. H. Watkins, a historian of the Depression, "There probably had never been so many eruptions of public unrest in such a short period of time over so wide a spec-trum of geography and population" as those that would occur over the next twelve months. By mid-1931, with crop prices at their lowest point in twenty years, the nation's farmers would be on the edge of violent ferment, led by increasingly radical organizers like national farm activist Milo Reno out of Iowa and the communist organizer Ella Reeve Bloor in North Dakota. In the fall of 1931, hundreds of angry farmers would storm a local jail in New London, Iowa, to free one of their leaders, prompting the state's governor to move in two thousand troops and declare martial law. By 1932, thousands of pro-testors would have invaded the statehouses in Nebraska and Wash-ington State and barricaded roads in Iowa and Wisconsin. That summer, more than a thousand farmers would surround a jail in Council Bluffs, Iowa, demanding the release of fifty-five protestors arrested by police. Foreclosure agents would be met with nooses and guns. Grocery stores would be looted by hungry families when char-itable relief ran out. Late in the summer of 1932, Milo Reno argued in an essay published in *The New York Times* that the lack of congres-sional help showed "that farmers can no longer hope for economic justice through legislation. They have been deceived, misled and be-trayed." So-called "food riots" were erupting in the cities, as well, along with angry neighborhood protests triggered by evictions. Communist and anarchist agitators were at every public gathering—union marches, left-wing political rallies, registration drives to re-cruit Black voters, even fearful crowds of depositors outside shaky banks—trying to provoke the police into violence that would feed the workers' anger.

But there was an equally dangerous threat from the Right. Alarmed by the gathering fury on the Left, some among the anxious rich began to support a rightward surge toward anti-democratic fascism. From a stream of laudatory American journalism, they knew how Italian strongman Benito Mussolini, known as Il Duce, was using an iron fist to deal with the "Bolshevik" labor organizers in his country. Since 1922, Mussolini's increasingly harsh totalitarian regime had attracted admiration from his nation's industrialists and bankers—and from their powerful counterparts in London and New York. The Morgan managing partner Tom Lamont kept an autographed photograph of Mussolini on his office wall; asked about the regime's brutalities, he would sidestep the question and comment only on Italy's robust economy. In Germany, too, big bankers and industrialists found much to like in the angry anti-communist rhetoric of Adolf Hitler, who made no secret of his contempt for labor unions—and for democracy. As early as the mid-1920s, Hitler had attracted financial support from American industrialist Henry Ford purely on the strength of their shared hatred of Jews. Indeed, while Lamont displayed a photo of Mussolini in his office, Hitler's office featured a large photograph of Henry Ford. Hitler was still seen as a crank by many in Washington, but his party increased its vote tally by eightfold in the 1930 elections, making it the second-largest party in the German parliament. Iron-fisted fascism seemed to be on the rise and, more ominously, it seemed to be producing prosperity that ballot-box democracy had failed to deliver for Americans.

Some of America's intellectual fascists in 1930, who ranged from the fiercely anti-Semitic magazine publisher Seward Collings to the former liberal-leaning diplomat Lawrence Dennis, simply seemed to hold a "vague hope that, if necessary, some American Mussolini would appear to save the country from an American Lenin," as historian Arthur M. Schlesinger Jr. put it in one account of this period. Dennis, who would soon publish *Is Capitalism Doomed?* and his subsequent manifesto *The Coming American Fascism,* did not see any clear candidate to lead a fascist movement but he argued that Amer-

ica's long dominance by big business "made fascism logical" for the
country because Americans were "the most organized, standardized,
regimented and docile people in the world." Because the radical
Right wrongly defined communism as a Jewish-bred threat, anti-
Semitism was a common thread among the homegrown fascists and
anti-communists, including those rallying around the influential
radio rabble-rouser Father Charles Coughlin of Detroit. Mob violence never seemed far away from Jewish neighborhoods in some
American cities.

In contrast to the radical fascist and communist disciples, main-
stream Americans in the early 1930s seemed to Schlesinger to be "a
people who had lost faith, not just in government's ability to meet
the economic crisis but almost in the ability of anyone to do anything." It was a time, Joe Kennedy later said, when he felt he "would
be willing to part with half of what I had if I could be sure of keeping, under law and order, the other half."

President Hoover was not opposed to some forms of government aid for frantic bankers and struggling corporations. But his
advice to suffering citizens was to use their ingenuity "to fight their
own battles" and "be masters of their own destiny." This was "not
the easy way," he said, "but it is the American way." Hoover seemed
genuinely ignorant of how many Americans were suffering, and
how much. Despite mounting evidence, he was certain no one was
starving; he felt sure everyone was fairly healthy, and believed there
was work for those who really looked for it. (He once claimed that
the iconic sidewalk apple sellers of the Depression were men who
had left other jobs because selling apples was more profitable.) He
sincerely thought public works relief programs for the jobless—like
those FDR had on the drawing board in New York State—would
"crack the timbers of our Constitution."

What Governor Roosevelt feared would "crack the timbers" of
the republic was the iron-hard despair and stony hardships falling
on its people, who could see no hope for themselves or their families.
By October 1930, with fully 20 percent of New York's labor force out
of work, Roosevelt knew that local charity—the only source of help
that Hoover would endorse—would be disastrously unequal to the

suffering in the land. Community-based charities were set up to deal
with hardships that came single file, case by case. How could they
cope when one out of every four or five families in town was in desperate need at the same time? Roosevelt feared America would become a tinderbox for violent extremism from the Left and the Right
if its political institutions could not meet the most basic needs of its
people.

AMID THE NATIONAL HARDSHIPS of 1930, Dick Whitney had
enjoyed a remarkable year.

In May, he had become the youngest man ever elected president
of the New York Stock Exchange, and he made himself utterly at
home in his new realm. He left his old offices at 15 Broad Street for
a new wood-paneled office suite with its own private dining room.
His enormous sixth-floor boardroom was even more magnificent.
Under a translucent skylight, walls of apple green were embellished
with gilded arches and pilasters. Wide caramel leather armchairs
were arranged on three semicircular platforms that stepped down to
the well, an open area in front of the raised presidential podium.
Above the podium was a large, elaborately carved wooden wall clock.
In a place of honor was a huge red malachite urn on a green malachite column; taller than any man in the room, this Fabergé creation
had been a gift from the Russian czar in 1904, after the exchange had
successfully listed its first issue of imperial bonds. The room looked
like a place where big things happened—and no one looked more at
ease in it than Dick Whitney.

His speeches were covered in the press. He was invited to important events, such as the Bond Club's luncheon in May for Ivar
Kreuger, the famous Swedish match monopolist. Whitney had
drop-in privileges at Hoover's White House, and was treated with
great deference by most of the powerful Republicans in Congress.

There were, however, two sore spots between Whitney and Washington that would grow more inflamed after April 1930, when the
stock market reversed course again and began an epic decline.

The more visible issue was short selling, a professional strategy used by speculators to profit in a declining stock market. To sell short, a speculator would first identify a company whose stock seemed overvalued. He would then arrange to borrow a block of its shares from a broker, who had custody of the shares owned by other clients. Having borrowed the shares, the speculator promptly sold them—"selling them short." If the speculator was right and the share price tumbled, he could replace the expensive borrowed shares with cheaper shares purchased in the market—a step known on the Street as "covering" his position—and claim his profits on the original short sale. But if he was wrong and the stock continued to climb, he still had to replace the borrowed shares—even if it took his entire fortune to do so.

Hoover hated short selling, mistrusted those who did it, and wanted it stamped out. Whitney acknowledged the practice could be abused but believed it nevertheless was essential to maintaining a healthy balance between pessimism and optimism in the marketplace.

They were both a little right, and a little wrong. President Hoover was right that short sellers could "demoralize" the market by deliberately spreading false rumors to drive down a stock's price, and the NYSE's vague rules against such deceptive trading were weakly enforced. But Whitney was also right: short selling, conducted without false rumor-mongering, would tether market prices to some rough approximation of reality. When blind enthusiasm ran wild, short sellers represented the contrary viewpoint, the ballast that could steady the ship. And when markets tumbled and other investors suddenly wanted to sell everything, short sellers covering their positions could be counted on eventually to step in and buy, since they had to purchase shares to replace the ones they had borrowed before they could pocket their profits. In the next few years, Whitney would educate a host of politicians and journalists about the importance of short selling and help devise rules that would allow the practice to survive in the American market—a signal accomplishment that would help those markets work better.

The second point of stubborn dispute between Hoover and Whitney was the practice of "trading on margin," which simply means buying shares with borrowed money. In the years before the crash, brokers would routinely lend investors up to 90 percent of the purchase price of the shares, with no objections from Whitney's stock exchange. Smaller, younger brokerage houses actually used more generous margin loans as bait to lure customers away from larger, older firms.

When the market was soaring, margin trading seemed to make everyone happy except President Hoover. Investors loved being able to borrow money from their broker to buy up to ten shares of stock when they only had enough cash to buy one share. If the stock price doubled—as it *surely* would—their lives would be transformed. Corporations loved the money they made by lending their spare cash to Wall Street to finance these loans. Banks had their depositors' cash to lend but they also could borrow from the Federal Reserve and lend out that money to Wall Street at a profit. Of course, Wall Street and the NYSE loved the commissions generated by margin trading.

All this sweet calculus would turn sour when markets fell. But, as Wall Street knew, only the investors would really suffer from falling stock prices. If the value of their portfolios dropped close to the sums they owed their brokers, they would be asked to produce more cash as collateral. If they could not do so, the brokers would sell their stock to cover their debts. The brokers would get repaid and the customers would get nothing.

Hoover hated margin trading. As early as 1925, he chastised corporations for using their cash to finance Wall Street's drunken party instead of investing it in their own businesses. From the moment Hoover took office, he had tried to discourage loose credit policies. But without adequate regulation, Whitney and the nation's bankers and corporate treasurers could ignore Hoover, and did. In this dispute, the balance of historical evidence is on Hoover's side.

Whitney had crafted masterful defenses for speculative short selling and margin trading. In his speeches, he deftly defined "investment" and "speculation" in ways that defied Hoover's contention that the former was good and the latter was evil. Speculators were those who bought and sold to make a short-term profit, Whitney explained. Investors were those who bought to enjoy long-term div-

idend or interest payments, and sold when their needs or expectations changed. Markets could not function without both kinds of
transactions, he rightly argued—and his argument remains a valid
one to make to lawmakers who are quick to condemn "speculation"
in any market downturn. Speculators lubricated the market for investors, making short-term purchases when long-term investors
wanted to sell, and selling for a quick profit when long-term investors wanted to buy. As for margin trading, Whitney was just as firm,
but nowhere near as farsighted. "One can buy almost anything
through installment payments," he would say. Margin trading was
simply "installment buying of securities," perfectly respectable if not
carried to "spendthrift" extremes. He was wrong. History would
prove that trading with borrowed money, whether through old-
fashioned margin loans or modern financial derivatives, would always be carried to "spendthrift" extremes if Wall Street had its way.

Glowing coverage of Whitney's speeches was almost the only
good news Whitney got as he stepped into October 1930, a month
almost as trying for Wall Street as 1929's bleak October. The market
dropped relentlessly. Even large firms were under pressure; small
ones were merging in hurried shotgun weddings. Few corporations
dared to sell new shares of stock, so underwriting fees were scarce.
And there was a mounting docket of evidence that Whitney's world
did not subscribe to the lofty ethical principles he'd claimed.

Tuesday, September 30, opened this dismal month. At 1:30 P.M.,
Whitney climbed the familiar podium steps to report the failure of
J.A. Sisto & Company, a small firm that had handled Italian bond
issues for Mussolini. This was only the fourth NYSE firm to become
insolvent since the crash, but it was by far the largest and best known.
When Whitney stepped down from the podium, trading resumed
and the market plummeted, pushing prices to their lowest levels of
the year before a weak last-hour rally.

Three days later, on Friday, October 3, 1930, a long-simmering
mess boiled over. Manhattan Electrical Supply Company, whose
ticker symbol on the NYSE was MSY, had been a bad-boy stock for
more than three years. It soared, it plunged, it doubled in a day and
fell by half the next day, it had once ceased trading entirely for five

days without explanation. Press reports claimed these gyrations were the result of "pool" manipulations that had cost MSY investors at least $6 million; one brokerage firm had been ruined during one of these episodes. Too many times to be credible, the NYSE had opened an inquiry; each was reported with great fanfare and closed without serious consequences for anyone involved.

But on this Friday, Wall Street learned a federal grand jury in Manhattan had actually indicted six people for manipulating MYS shares on the NYSE in May 1930. The defendants included a notable trader and several employees of a prominent member firm, Prince & Whitely, although the brokerage firm itself supposedly did not know about the conspiracy. Federal prosecutors said this was the first time they had ever prosecuted anyone for operating a manipulative pool, although the practice had been an open secret for at least a decade. For Wall Street and the journalists who covered it, price manipulation was a fact of life.

No, the grand jury said: price manipulation was a crime.

The next week brought more bad news. On Thursday, October 9, the market learned that Prince & Whitely, the supposedly innocent employer in the MYS case, was broke. With seven hundred employees and nearly ten thousand clients across the country, Prince & Whitely had been a respected name on Wall Street for nearly fifty years. The market reaction was swift and severe: prices fell to levels not seen since mid-November 1929, at the nadir of the great crash. No stocks were spared, but those promoted by Prince & Whitely were closest to the line of fire. These included Prince & Whitely Trading, a mutual fund underwritten by the failed firm. Prince & Whitely's collapse was front-page news everywhere the firm did business, with most market veterans figuring the firm was a belated casualty of 1929.

In reality, the firm was a casualty of its own dishonest greed. Its practices offered a primer on how unethical brokers of that unregulated era cheated the system, deceived the stock exchange, and defrauded their clients.

The firm had supported the prices of the stocks it promoted by manipulating the market—small surprise given the prior week's indictments. It had also milked the ostensibly independent mutual fund it sold to the public; it could do this because the mutual fund's directors and the brokerage firm's officers were the same people. A few months earlier, the firm "borrowed" $1.5 million worth of securities from the captive fund and doctored their books to hide the "loan." The cooked books also showed the firm owned millions of dollars of other securities that in truth belonged to its clients. Finally, there was the firm's corrupt deal with the president of a trucking company listed on the NYSE; the executive used Prince & Whitely in a plot to drive up his company's stock price so he could profitably exercise some options. Unfortunately, Prince & Whitely didn't get paid in advance and the executive stiffed the brokerage firm for $300,000. That, the senior partner later testified, was "the straw that broke the camel's back."

Despite this sordid October, Dick Whitney was still firm in his belief that the New York Stock Exchange was fully capable of policing its own members and enforcing its own rules without any interference or oversight from Washington.

AS ELECTION DAY—TUESDAY, NOVEMBER 4, 1930—rolled closer, Roosevelt faced his own platter of scandals served up by Tammany Hall, the corrupt Democratic machine in Manhattan. Samuel Seabury, a civic reformer of unquestioned rectitude, had presided over a series of hearings and investigations that exposed appalling corruption. One of his reports, for the state's appellate court, showed that judges had paid bribes to get onto the bench and corrupt vice squads on the police force had framed innocent women for prostitution and demanded bribes to drop the charges. In a separate study of the administration of Mayor Jimmy Walker, Seabury found evidence that zoning variances and valuable leases had been awarded to bidders who paid the biggest bribes. And in a third sweeping study, done directly for Governor Roosevelt, Seabury examined whether Tammany's handpicked district attorney was so incompetent that financial frauds could be committed with impunity in New York City, the nation's financial capital. Seabury cited the Prince & Whitely matter as one of eighteen financial fraud investigations in 1930 alone that were neglected or mishandled by the district attorney. The other cases dealt with looted mutual funds, securities stolen from customers, manipulated stock prices, and fraudulent investments.

Neglect and incompetence were not the only obstacles to prosecuting fraud; jurisdictional disputes were a chronic problem. Wall Street frauds could be pursued by the state attorney general's securities bureau, by the bigger but busier federal prosecutor's office, or by the ineffective Manhattan district attorney's office. With a *simple* high-profile case, the three agencies would stumble over each other to grab the case and dominate the headlines. With a *complicated* low-profile case, each would defer endlessly to the others and nothing would get done. Even the landmark MSY pool manipulation case promptly fell into a crack between federal and state jurisdiction and languished; the Prince & Whitely fraud case would drag on until the senior partner's death in April 1933 made it moot.

Understandably, the Republican candidate for governor in 1930, a former federal prosecutor named Charles H. Tuttle, ignored FDR's attacks on utility companies and tried instead to hang every Tammany scandal around Roosevelt's neck as he campaigned for reelection. But when the ballots were counted on November 4, 1930, New York's voters showed that cheaper utility bills were more important to them than Tammany scandals. Roosevelt was returned to Albany in the biggest landslide in the state's history, trouncing his opponent by more than 725,000 votes—a larger margin of victory than Al Smith ever got. FDR carried many upstate precincts that had not voted Democratic in decades.

It was a victory that attracted attention across the country, putting FDR on the radar for party leaders looking ahead to 1932. One of his ardent allies, State Democratic Chairman James J. Farley, soon said out loud the thought that had struck Joe Kennedy during his springtime visit to Albany. "I do not see how Mr. Roosevelt can escape becoming the next presidential candidate of his party, even if no one should raise a finger to bring this about," Farley said. Joe Kennedy was ready to raise not just a finger but a big pile of cash to help Roosevelt win the presidency in 1932. FDR himself was still quietly coy about his plans, but Farley and Kennedy were ready to roll and the governor did nothing to discourage them.

The national Democratic party was celebrating its own overwhelming victory in the 1930 midterm elections. It won control of the House for the first time since before the war and cut the GOP's margin in the Senate to a single vote. Party leaders grew more hopeful that Hoover could be beaten in 1932. But who was the best candidate to do that? The 1928 presidential loser, the Catholic pro-business conservative Al Smith? Or his onetime protégé, the progressive and popular but polio-stricken New York governor Franklin Delano Roosevelt?

Despite a drenching rain, state Democrats produced an exuberant homecoming when the governor returned to Albany the day after the election. But if Roosevelt had listened carefully, he'd have heard an ominous sizzle behind the cheering. It was the sound of a long fuse, stretching back more than a year, that was about to blow up one of the biggest banks in New York City. The explosion, its causes, and its aftermath would give Roosevelt a lesson in financial regulation he would not forget.

The doomed institution was the Bank of United States.

Not "the Bank of *the* United States." The bank was not an arm of the federal government. It catered to immigrant garment workers and their families, their shopkeepers, their teachers and social workers, their working-class neighbors in the tenements around the bank's first office on the Lower East Side. Few of them likely understood the significance of that missing word in the bank's name. A rival bank did, and in 1913, it petitioned the state banking superintendent to bar the deceptive name, but he ruled that the name could remain—and some years later, joined the bank's board of directors.

By 1930, the bank was the eighth largest in the country. It also was a textbook example of what had been going awry, for nearly two decades, in the poorly regulated and overlapping worlds of banking and Wall Street. Official Washington had long been divided over whether it was even legal for commercial banks, taking deposits and making loans, to also be investment banks, underwriting and selling securities. Indeed, President Taft's solicitor general and his attorney general had both concluded in 1911 that those dual roles violated federal banking laws. But banks simply ignored those opinions and forged ahead—and, in those days of government deference to business, nobody stopped them. In 1927, Congress ratified reality with the McFadden Act, which belatedly blessed national banks' securities operations. Like most other large banks, the Bank of United States had created a spuriously "separate" affiliate that traded securities.

In a common practice, the affiliate's stock certificates were printed on the reverse side of the bank's own stock certificates, so a shareholder of one was unavoidably a shareholder of the other. And like many other bankers of that era, its officers and employees had aggressively marketed Bank of United States shares to its own depositors. This ignored an inconvenient legal reality: in a crisis, bank *shareholders* could be called on to make up losses owed to bank *depositors*. Depositors who became shareholders were, in effect, guaranteeing their own nest eggs. In another common act of magical thinking, the bank loaned its executives, directors, and big clients the money they used to buy the bank's own shares, which were the sole collateral for those loans. If a crisis caused the bank's share price to fall, the collateral for these loans would be worth *least* when it was needed *most*.

In the summer of 1929, New York's state bank examiners were working under the direction of Joseph A. Broderick, Governor Roosevelt's new banking superintendent.

In his late forties, Broderick was a slim and elegantly tailored man with prematurely silver hair and sterling credentials. As an experienced bank examiner, he had been drafted in 1914 to work on a technical committee shaping the newborn Federal Reserve System and then served as the Fed's chief examiner and secretary. He moved on to a vice presidency at a major bank in Manhattan. One historian called him "a man of courage and imagination," as fit to deal with a banking crisis "as anybody in the land."

But he had inherited a demoralized, undersized staff at the state department of banking, tarnished by the bribery and cronyism scandal at City Trust Company. The slow liquidation of City Trust was a daily drain on his time and attention. And by law, he had few good options for dealing with a badly managed bank: if he closed a bank that was still solvent, shareholders would sue and depositors would panic. His duty, as he saw it, was to "exhaust every possible resource to save the situation before deciding that the doors must be closed."

By September 1929, examiners who had analyzed the Bank of United States during the summer warned Broderick that the giant institution, while solvent, was being very badly managed. Broderick met twice with the bank's executives and sternly advised them to seek a stronger partner. They actually tried; with his help, they opened negotiations with a midsize Wall Street firm. The deal died in the wake of the October crash. Thereafter, the bank's partners assured Broderick that they were putting their house in order, but secretly they merely increased their desperate reliance on shell games and deceptive accounting.

The market crash had also shaken more than 1,200 other banks under Broderick's supervision. With his staff stretched thin, Broderick didn't send examiners back to the Bank of United States until July 1930. It took the examiners more than a month to make sense of the bank's books and figure out what had happened. Their final conclusion was shocking: the bank's surplus capital had been completely wiped out by a host of bad loans and illiquid real estate investments. The examiners raised the alarm in a report to Broderick in mid-September. He quickly realized that nothing but an immediate merger with a stronger institution could save the bank. He began to search for a willing suitor.

On Monday, November 17, the freshly reelected Governor Roosevelt joined in the search, clearly realizing the scale of the crisis. In the afternoon, he cajoled a trio of powerful bankers in the living room of his townhouse on East Sixty-fifth Street in Manhattan. Later that day, he phoned two other important bankers and urged them to help. When he left a few days later for his therapeutic visit to Warm Springs, he deputized Lieutenant Governor Lehman to support Broderick's promising efforts.

The matchmaking marathon nearly worked. By December 10,

Broderick thought he had a deal with a consortium of banks. There wasn't a moment to lose: that afternoon, thousands of nervous depositors had gathered outside a few of the bank's branches, apparently reacting to a rumor spread by a merchant in the Bronx who falsely claimed his local branch's employees had refused to let him sell some of his bank shares. The bank's executives had managed to cover that sudden spate of withdrawals, but a panic was an hourly threat. The paperwork to rescue the imperiled institution was being prepared as the bankers in the consortium waited in a palatial conference room at the New York Federal Reserve Bank. But shortly before midnight, two bankers suddenly balked, concerned that the failing bank's assets could not be reliably valued, and the others refused to go forward without them.

Broderick raced to the bank but it was nearly 1 A.M. before the weary, fractious group would hear him. He begged them to save the deal—and, with it, the life savings of the bank's 450,000 working-class depositors. He told them that the bank had supplied credit to "small merchants, especially Jewish merchants," and its closing "might and probably would result in widespread bankruptcy among those it served." He candidly admitted the bank had been run by men who should "never have been in the banking business," but he said he had tried "to correct their errors and reform their methods." At last, he asked if the decision to let the bank fail was final.

It was. Still wary of taking on millions in murky liabilities, the bankers would not budge. Disgusted and exhausted after three nights without sleep, Broderick warned the men around the table that they would be making "the most colossal mistake in the banking history of New York" if they let the Bank of United States collapse. Then he rushed from the room, found a telephone and called Lieutenant Governor Lehman at his Park Avenue apartment. Lehman told Broderick to ask the bankers to remain until he could get there, and hurried out to flag a taxi. Out of respect for his office or for his Wall Street pedigree, a small group of bankers stayed. Lehman arrived at 2:45 A.M. and made his own appeal, just as heartfelt as Broderick's—and just as futile. When the meeting broke up at 4 A.M., the bank's fate was certain. At 9 A.M. on Thursday, December 11, the closure notices went up on the doors of its branch offices across the city.

THE COLLAPSE—AT THE TIME the largest bank failure in United States history—exploded onto the front pages of newspapers across the country and even hit the financial pages of newspapers abroad.

It wasn't the first bank failure that year. "More banks failed in this country in 1930 than in any previous year," *The New York Times* reported in 1931. Federal Reserve records show that more than eight hundred banks failed between November 1930 and the end of January 1931, a three-month casualty list that did not include smaller bank failures outside the Fed system.

These were not just statistics. In the 1920s and early 1930s, a bank failure could mean overnight destitution for modest savers. Wealthier depositors, plugged into the same social class and business circles as their bankers, sometimes saw the red flags early and quietly retrieved their cash. When one of these "invisible runs" forced a bank to close, its modest depositors had little hope of immediately getting their own money. If they were lucky, they might recover something after a lengthy liquidation. If they were very lucky indeed, a solvent bank might take over their bank and it would reopen in a few weeks, or months. But if they were very *unlucky* and had invested in the stock of the bank that held their savings, they might be on the hook as shareholders to pay out twice the value of their investment to help repay depositors. It was a crapshoot, and on the day a bank failed, its modest customers had no idea which fate would be theirs. Little wonder that bank failures, like the market crash, triggered documented suicides among desperate depositors. A poignant editorial cartoon of the day showed a thrifty squirrel asking an impoverished man on a park bench why he hadn't saved for a rainy day while times were good; holding a newspaper headlined "Bank Failures," the man answered, "I did."

The Bank of United States saga would end with several of its senior executives in prison, but their behavior was hardly uncommon in that era. Most major cities had seen local banks fail from corrupt management, stock manipulation, and political or corporate crony-ism. Some state bank overseers had simply been bought by the bank-ers they supervised, who paid with campaign contributions and lenient loans to finance the officials' own real estate and stock mar-ket speculations.

But for Franklin Roosevelt, the collapse of the Bank of United States was an icy shock, one that forced him to reconsider the gentle treatment he had approved after the bank failures of 1929. Back then, he had ignored Robert Moses's call for tighter bank regulation and, instead, had agreed to far more limited reforms that relied heavily on bankers policing one another. FDR had believed those steps would be enough to prevent another scandal. And yet, here was another scandal—one inflicting exponentially more damage on depositors and on his own reputation.

The failure fueled Roosevelt's "widening, deepening disillusion-ment with the banking community," one biographer would later write. His exasperation was evident a few weeks later when he urged bank-coddling legislators to enact reforms proposed by Broderick. So far, he said, "there has been visible only a campaign of opposition not only to this bill but to the other remedial bills [Broderick] of-fered this year." The legislature, perhaps shaken by the giant bank's collapse, finally granted a few of Broderick's requests, expanding his staff of examiners and giving him greater discretion to deal with weak banks. From January to June 1931, Broderick tirelessly recruited more and better trained examiners under a civil service waiver backed by FDR. At congressional hearings in Washington in early 1931, Broderick presciently told lawmakers he was pushing for a state law to require state banks either to close their stock-trading affiliates or stop accepting customer deposits. The New York regulator's views clearly changed the mind of the overlord of those hearings, Senator Carter Glass of Virginia, who previously had not supported a sepa-ration between commercial and investment banks.

Broderick was still being politically attacked for not having acted sooner to close the Bank of United States, making him a political liability for FDR, whose quiet campaign for the presidential nomi-nation was becoming more visible each month. But Roosevelt stood by his bank superintendent, saying he had faith in Broderick's "complete integrity." The governor was furious in October 1931 when a special prosecutor—one with close ties to FDR's enemies in Tammany Hall—got Broderick indicted on flimsy misdemeanor charges of neglect of duty. The Albany correspondent for *The Brooklyn Daily Eagle* reported that his sources thought the indictment was "a subtle attempt on the part of Tammany" to derail FDR's presidential ambitions and clear the way for Tammany's preferred candidate, former governor Al Smith. The statehouse reporter for *The New York Times* had a different view; he noted that "friends of Governor Roosevelt" believed Tammany leaders were trying to force FDR to "bargain for consideration for his banking superintendent in return for a lenient attitude toward Tammany officials under fire" in the ongoing investigation of New York City's government. If so, Tammany's plans backfired: Roosevelt rose fiercely in defense of Broderick, giving the press "a thick file" of letters he had received supporting the superintendent, and vowing to testify in Broderick's defense. "Governor Backing Broderick to Limit," blared *The New York Times*. The *Brooklyn Eagle* reporter observed, "When the firing began, Roosevelt got into the trench with Broderick. He has been there ever since."

By the time of his indictment, Broderick already had fully justified FDR's trust in him as a regulator. He had sent an enlarged team of well-trained examiners out to look for weak or mismanaged banks across the state. Armed with the new powers FDR had wrung from the legislature, he closed shaky banks or merged them with stronger institutions. By August, fuming legislators who wanted to hold a hearing on the superintendent's alleged neglect of his duties gave up when Broderick could not attend because he was too busy closing three weak banks on the same day. The full measure of Broderick's success would become clear as the Depression deepened and the nation's financial system grew weaker. By winnowing out the worst banks and pushing mediocre ones to get stronger partners or fresh capital, Broderick helped shelter his state's banks from the growing storm that would sweep away nearly a third of the banks across the country.

That rapid deterioration in the nation's banking system had become a daily nightmare for President Hoover, who had his own dis-illusioning encounters that fall with bankers—most notably with the immensely wealthy banker who served as his Treasury secretary. Andrew Mellon's family controlled every bank in Pittsburgh except, as it happened, the Bank *of* Pittsburgh. In mid-September 1931, a sudden panic by some of that bank's seventeen thousand depositors had pushed the bank to the brink. Hoover personally negotiated a deal that would save it. But the deal required the Mellon interests to contribute to a local syndicate—and Mellon refused to chip in un-less *his family* was given majority control of the bank. The bank's directors refused, and the bank was closed. Hoover was aghast that Mellon had placed "private interests above the public weal," one Hoover biographer would note.

Hoover almost immediately had much larger worries. On Sun-day, September 20, 1931, the Depression-wracked British govern-ment announced it was going off the gold standard. A number of other struggling nations quickly followed, delivering a massive shock to the global banking system. Europeans began to pull gold out of American banks to bolster their own banks. The number of bank failures skyrocketed. Cash withdrawn during these regional panics was not being put back even after the panics passed. Affluent savers moved their cash into rented safe-deposit boxes; more modest ones relied on a coffee can in a closet or a cigar box under a bed. Ameri-cans were losing faith in the safety of the banking system.

Hoover knew restoring that faith was an urgent matter. But just as he felt charities should deal privately with the public's loss of in-come, he believed the bankers should deal privately with the public's loss of confidence. He continued to believe that the government should not take any direct role in addressing the bank crisis and in-sisted that any safety net for the banking system had to be woven by bankers themselves. At a secret meeting with bankers in Mellon's palatial apartment in Washington, he urged them to form a volun-tary fund, to be called the National Credit Corporation, that trou-bled bankers could tap to pay depositors quickly while the banks did the slower work of liquidating their frozen assets. The bankers, who included Tom Lamont and George Whitney from J.P. Morgan,

weren't enthusiastic; they agreed to the fund solely as a stopgap measure, but insisted a government-backed reserve was required. Lawmakers, also called to a private meeting with Hoover, questioned the
logic of a voluntary fund backed only by the beleaguered banks it
was set up to rescue. Eventually, Hoover accepted reality; in late
January 1932, he signed the law creating the Reconstruction Finance
Corporation. Despite his initial opposition, he later cited it as a
signal achievement of his presidency.

The gold crisis besetting Hoover would also become an emergency for Dick Whitney at the New York Stock Exchange.

By September 1931, Wall Street had taken a brutal beating.
Venerable firms had failed and a "pervasive air of pessimism and
resignation" was infecting the market, one market historian would
note. Although Whitney still disagreed with Hoover about short
selling, he yielded enough in early 1931 to require floor traders to
maintain daily records of their short sales—a deft move that proved
short sales were much less influential in setting the market's direction than Hoover imagined. But Whitney refused to acknowledge
the fundamental weaknesses besetting the exchange. With the rise
of more complex securities and more byzantine holding companies
during the late 1920s, the exchange was incapable even of understanding the securities listed there, much less evaluating them. As
historian Michael Parrish observed in his study of New Deal securities regulation, the eight NYSE members who served on the exchange's volunteer "stock-list" committee conducted little more than
a cursory examination of most applications. Some companies, including several controlled by the famously secretive "Match King"
Ivar Kreuger of Sweden, simply refused to give the panel any information at all—and were still listed. Market manipulations continued unpunished. The financial integrity of member firms was largely
taken on faith, with little verification. To claim, as Dick Whitney
repeatedly did in speeches and congressional testimony, that the
NYSE was competently policing itself was absurd.

Britain's move away from the gold standard in September 1931,
therefore, put intense pressure on an exchange already under stress.
The news from London, which had been announced during the

night, would plunge the NYSE trading floor into what *The New York Times* called "one of the most exciting days in Wall Street since the market collapse in the autumn of 1929." And as in the autumn of 1929, Dick Whitney personally took charge and pulled his ship safely into port. Whitney proved again the wisdom of doing everything possible to keep markets open in turbulent times, a lesson that would guide future market leaders through future crises. What was remarkable, though, was *how* Whitney managed to keep the exchange open in the fall of 1931. For the first time in its recorded history, it temporarily banned short selling.

At 9:15 A.M. on Monday, September 21, Whitney had summoned the governors to their sixth-floor boardroom. The mood was jittery. As New Yorkers had slept, trading in Paris had been wildly erratic. Other major European exchanges either didn't open at all or opened and quickly closed in disarray. The NYSE was now the only major marketplace where investors could react to the news from London. Whitney thought of the crisis sparked by the outbreak of the European war in July 1914, at the dawn of his NYSE career. Then, too, every major European stock market suddenly closed down and, at the request of the U.S. Treasury, the NYSE closed, too. It did not open again for nearly five months. Whitney had no intention of closing today, but he couldn't let the trading floor face the day totally undefended. He got the board's approval for a resolution that "short-selling during the present emergency would tend to bring about a condition of demoralization in which prices would not fairly reflect market values." Therefore, it would be temporarily banned. Other stock exchanges across the country quickly followed suit.

In New York and elsewhere, there was a sharp, violent sell-off at the opening bell. Foreign bond prices plummeted; stock prices followed. "Other exchanges were completely disrupted," *The New York Times* reported, "and for some time no quotations at all or purely nominal ones were available." But by the afternoon, trading had steadied and many prices recovered, at least partly because Whitney's decree had forced short sellers to buy the shares they needed to close out their positions and take their profits. The emergency short-sale ban was lifted two days later, but on October 6, the exchange quietly imposed a new rule that permanently barred short sales in stocks that were already falling in price. Under this new rule, a stock could not be sold short unless its previous sale had reflected a level or rising price. Coupled with the new short-sale reporting require-ment enacted in May, this new rule marked a significant effort to preserve an essential trading strategy while still placating President Hoover.

Hoover was not placated. As he saw it, if short selling was a threat during this crisis, it was a threat in any declining market. But he still flatly opposed any governmental interference in market affairs. In January and February 1932, he twice summoned Whitney to the White House to argue that the exchange itself should ban short sales. Whitney never spoke publicly about these trips to the wood-shed, but according to Hoover, "Whitney made profuse promises, but did nothing." At the second meeting, on February 16, Hoover threatened that if Whitney didn't act, he would push Congress to investigate the exchange "with a view to Federal control legislation."

Without abandoning his "hands-off" approach to business regu-lation, the furious president kept his vow—his goal was to force Whitney to act, not to insert the federal government into the mar-ket. On March 4, 1932, with his support, the Senate opened an inves-tigation into the NYSE and all its practices—an inquiry that would extend years into the future with results neither Hoover nor Wall Street could have anticipated. Whitney would testify before the panel repeatedly in 1932, easily frustrating a series of weak investiga-tors. He went public, defending short selling and margin trading in a movie newsreel, in speeches, and in articles for national publica-tions. Every argument boiled down to the same fundamental truth: if the only road open to market pessimists was to sell whatever stock they owned and walk away, the result would be a less liquid, more volatile market for those left behind. His campaign earned public praise from columnist Walter Lippmann, perhaps the nation's most influential media voice, and private applause from corporate board-rooms. More and more, Whitney was sounding like the voice of reason on Wall Street.

But by every measure except his public influence, Whitney's

world was shrinking. As 1931 ended, stock-trading volume was down to levels not seen since 1926; bond trading had dropped to levels not seen since 1924. The value of a seat on the NYSE had melted away, reducing the wealth of every member on the exchange, including its president. Corporate dividends dwindled, municipal bonds defaulted, and foreign bond prices bottomed out. Whitney's own bond-trading firm was steadied by loans from his brother, the Morgan partner.

When Whitney had closed the New Year's Eve session in December 1930, the Dow had stood at 164.58 points, well below its bubbly pre-crash peak of 381.17 points on September 3, 1929. With little to celebrate, the traditional afternoon of band music had been canceled. Now, as the 1931 trading year came to a silent and joyless close, the Dow stood at 77.90 points, less than half its 1930 closing price and fathoms below its 1929 level. The first week of January 1932 saw an erratic decline that would persist until early July 1932, when the index would hit 41.22 points. In a little less than three years, the Dow would fall nearly 90 percent below its 1929 crest.

In Albany, Governor Roosevelt was doing all he could to expand his administration's response to individual hardships and his effort surely helped millions of New Yorkers survive that bleak winter. But after Roosevelt announced his candidacy for the Democratic presidential nomination on January 22, 1932, he broadened his focus. If he won the nomination, he would have to lay out plans for reviving an entire nation sinking into desperation. While Joe Kennedy and others were filling the war chest he would need to take his case to America, Roosevelt gathered a small team of advisors to help him define what his case should be. FDR initially referred to the group as his "privy council," but it soon became known as his "brain trust."

The idea for the brain trust took solid form on a March evening in Albany. FDR was in his study, smoking and talking with Samuel I. Rosenman, a lawyer in his midthirties who had drafted bills and written speeches for Al Smith before joining FDR's team in late 1928. On this chilly evening, Rosenman worried out loud about the coming campaign. "If you were to be nominated tomorrow and had to start a campaign trip within ten days," he told the governor, "we'd be in an awful fix . . . It would be pretty hard to get up intelligent speeches overnight on the many subjects you would have to discuss."

He suggested bringing together some experts who could discuss these national issues with FDR.

"Do you have anyone in mind?"

Roseman said he knew who should *not* be consulted: the business titans, financiers, and national political leaders typically recruited for this role. Their ideas had been discredited by events.

"My idea is this: Why not go to the universities of the country?" He argued that university professors would be likely to "get away from all the old fuzzy thinking" and could give Roosevelt fresh ideas on "such things as the relief of agriculture, tariffs, railroads, government debts, private credit, money, [the] gold standard—all the things that enter into the present crisis."

Roosevelt thought about it, smoking and staring at the ceiling. "Okay," he said. "Go ahead." A few minutes later, as FDR got into bed, he briefly worried that his consultations would leak too soon, but he wasn't deterred. "We'll just have to take our chances on that," he told Rosenman.

Rosenman promptly recruited Raymond Moley at Columbia University, a widely respected expert on criminal justice administration who had already earned the trust of Louis Howe, FDR's crusty political guru. Ray Moley was, quite simply, the perfect choice for the job. Well organized, shrewd, pragmatic, and widely knowledgeable, he had what one FDR historian would call "a veritable genius for 'boiling down' a huge seething cauldron of fact and idea into succinct, forceful, clearly logical expository prose." Moley sat down in March with Rosenman and Basil "Doc" O'Connor, FDR's former law partner and current campaign advisor, and drew up a list of experts whose views would fit with Roosevelt's political philosophy— which Moley described later as "a profound feeling for the underdog, a real sense of the crucial imbalance of economic life, [and] a very keen awareness that political democracy could not exist side by side with economic plutocracy."

The list started with his Columbia colleague Rexford G. Tugwell, a creative agricultural economist whom Moley compared to "a cocktail—his conversation picked you up and made your brain race along." Then Moley added Adolf A. Berle Jr., a prickly but brilliant Columbia law professor. Berle had entered Harvard as a fourteen-year-old in 1909; in 1916, at age twenty-one, he graduated from Harvard with a bachelor's and a master's degree in history and a law degree. Within months of joining the brain trust, he would be celebrated as the co-author of *The Modern Corporation and Private Property,* an enormously influential study of corporate power in America. A few other experts would be consulted on specific issues. But Moley, Tugwell, Berle, Rosenman, and O'Connor were the core of the brain trust through the long campaign. They would develop speeches on everything from falling wheat prices to foreign war debts. Sparring with one another over office desks and dinner tables in New York and at FDR's fireside in Albany, they helped Roosevelt polish the themes that would drive his campaign.

As they worked, a parade of businessmen behaving badly marched into the headlines, reinforcing Roosevelt's increasingly dim view of business morality.

On Sunday, March 13, 1932, Wall Street woke up to the chilling front-page news that the Swedish match monopolist Ivar Kreuger had killed himself in his Paris apartment the previous morning. For years, he had been feted by kings and prime ministers—he'd met privately with President Hoover just two months earlier. Kreuger's vast empire, built on the world's universal demand for the simple wooden match, was supposedly worth more than $1 billion. But for months, he had secretly and frantically been searching for loans to cover some urgent debts. When American banks failed him, he sailed to France for meetings with his bankers and business aides. They were waiting for him at a nearby hotel when his body was found.

News of his death supposedly was withheld until stock exchanges in America closed their Saturday morning sessions. But someone in the know was dumping Kreuger-linked securities on the NYSE that day, and eager but ignorant American investors were scooping them up, thinking they were bargain-priced blue chips. By Monday morning, the Swedish stock exchange had closed down completely so its government could sort out the facts about the Kreuger empire. But Dick Whitney allowed Kreuger securities to continue trading on the NYSE, although no one could possibly assess their current value.

Within two weeks, auditors at Price Waterhouse reported that the Match King's companies were insolvent. The verdict was premature: some valuable assets were later found in the wreckage, although not enough to fully compensate investors. As one Kreuger biographer would note, "Given the rules of the game at the time, it is difficult to say that much of what Ivar did was illegal." But legal or not, Kreuger had built his reputation on a foundation of secrets, lies, accounting gimmicks, tax dodges, overpledged collateral, and forged assets—and Wall Street had fallen for it, leaving investors exposed to significant losses. His collapse soon brought down the firm of Lee, Higginson & Co., the Wall Street firm that brought his securities to market.

In April 1932, with the Kreuger aftershocks still in the headlines, investors watched in disbelief as the utility empire built by Samuel Insull began to collapse in Chicago. Its complexity would befuddle auditors for years but its inability to pay its immediate debts was clear. As many as 600,000 investors were hurt by the collapse, with losses that exceeded $1 billion in modern terms. Again, public investors were allowed to trade Insull shares in the dark on the NYSE and other exchanges while bankers and other insiders were privy to financial details that Insull had shared exclusively with them.

The elderly Sam Insull, a widely admired folk hero who started out as an aide to the genius inventor Thomas A. Edison, would later be acquitted of charges that he deliberately defrauded investors. As in Kreuger's case, much of the harm was done not by what was illegal but by what was *legal:* he simply piled so many complex securities, bank loans, self-dealing service contracts, and unearned dividends on a base of local power companies that no one could tell what the resulting pyramid was worth. Insull's use of opaque interlocking holding companies was only slightly more elaborate than the industry standard. In 1932, just eight vast holding companies controlled three-quarters of the shareholder-owned utilities in the country. That control was routinely exercised far out of view of the investors who owned the companies' shares. Challenged years later in a Chicago court about one of his misleading prospectuses, Insull said, "Show me any [prospectus] where it is done any other way!"

Roosevelt immediately found an occasion to respond to the news from Chicago—one guaranteed to attract national attention. On April 18, he arrived in St. Paul, Minnesota, to give the keynote address at that evening's annual Jefferson Day dinner. This address to the party faithful from across Minnesota and from five neighboring states would be his first speech outside his home state, and it was widely seen as the launch of his national campaign for the presidency. Roosevelt's train had arrived at the elegant Union Depot in St. Paul a few minutes after 7 A.M. that rainy Monday morning, but FDR and Eleanor stayed on board for two hours, greeting local party leaders and talking with members of the press who squeezed into the narrow parlor in the Pullman car. "I didn't think there would be so many of you!" Roosevelt called out as the reporters trooped aboard.

A little after 9 A.M., the Roosevelts left their train and got into limousines for the motorcade that carried them past cheering crowds to their hotel. For much of the day, FDR and his wife went their separate ways to receptions and meetings with local and state officials—Eleanor was universally described in the press as "charming." That evening, they met up again at the vast new St. Paul Auditorium Arena, where they sat at a 200-foot speakers' table and looked out over an enormous crowd. More than 2,500 diners filled the arena floor; another 6,000 peered down from the surrounding gallery. The ovation for Roosevelt was deafening.

A handful of other speakers, including Eleanor, gave short remarks. Then Roosevelt rose and managed to shift himself behind his heavy floral brocade dining chair. Resting his elbows against its back, he stood with a sheaf of papers in one hand and gave a speech that made news across the country. Most of the speech had been written several days earlier, and part of it was aimed at rebutting a claim Al Smith had recently made that Roosevelt's calls for policies to help "the forgotten man" were a call for class warfare. In reply, FDR said early in the speech that he was calling for "a true concert of interests" in which all Americans could prosper together.

But after the Insull failure, FDR had personally inserted a lengthy passage into his text citing the need for better regulation of power utilities, one of his first shots in what would be a very long war. "Those who have read the papers these past few days have seen an example of the vast national scope of the public utility structure," he said. Such entities were so complex, he continued, that he suspected even "those far in the upper reaches of such a structure" would concede the need for reform and regulation. Electricity was rapidly becoming the lifeblood of the country's economy. The problem of generating and distributing it was therefore "national in its scope and can be solved only by the firm establishment of national control," he said.

Meanwhile, Kreuger's collapse had opened Dick Whitney to ridicule in Washington. Fiorello La Guardia, New York City's irrepressible Republican congressman, blasted Whitney for the exchange's failure to scrutinize $250 million worth of Kreuger bonds underwritten by Lee Higginson and listed on the NYSE. "Let us suppose Mr. Whitney was head of a grocery association and Mr. Lee Higginson, who sold the Kreuger bonds, was selling baked beans," La Guardia argued. "Under the same circumstances, had beans been the commodity, both of them would be under indictment today."

The following month, the Senate's ongoing Hoover-inspired investigation of the NYSE produced another black eye for Whitney. Wall Street insiders had long known the details of the pools that manipulated prices on the exchange. Now the public learned some of them, too.

One of the most complex deals examined by the senators involved a broker at an NYSE member firm who organized a pool to rig the stock of General Asphalt, a company on whose board he served. That board then approved steps almost certain to drive up the stock's price. His pool profited handsomely from his inside knowledge, but he brazenly claimed the timing of all these helpful corporate actions had been merely a coincidence.

But the biggest headlines of these hearings focused on the disclosure that the NYSE's designated "specialist" for trading in the widely followed RCA stock, a prominent swashbuckling Wall Street figure named Michael J. Meehan, had actually been part of the pool that had rigged RCA's stock in March 1929. Dick Whitney had insisted in prior testimony that there were rules against such behavior by specialists, the exchange members who had a duty to maintain a continuous market for specific stocks. A young broker who worked with Meehan on the floor told the senators he didn't think the prohibition applied during very active markets. Meehan had arranged for his profits from the RCA pool to be paid to his wife, since exchange rules did seem to bar him from pocketing the money himself.

AS THE AMERICAN ECONOMY continued its merciless decline, Joe Kennedy's support for FDR grew stronger. "I was really worried," he said later. "I knew that big, drastic changes had to be made in our economic system and I felt that Roosevelt was the one who could make those changes . . . I was ready to do anything to help elect him." In limousines and private planes, he crisscrossed New England, raising money for FDR—some of it secretly contributed by Republicans who had lost patience with Hoover. By one account, Kennedy gave the campaign $25,000, loaned it $50,000, and raised another $100,000 from his circle of acquaintances—substantial amounts in those days. In May, Kennedy was FDR's quiet envoy to the California court of William Randolph Hearst, the media king whose newspaper editorials and public pronouncements influenced millions of voters, in the first of many efforts he would make to entice Hearst to support Roosevelt.

Roosevelt had arranged his campaign travel so he could be in a New York City courtroom on April 29, 1932, to testify at the criminal trial of his banking superintendent, Joseph Broderick, accused of neglecting his official duties. For about a half hour, he defended Broderick's integrity and claimed equal responsibility for the decisions that had been made during the Bank of United States crisis.

On May 28, an hour or so before dawn, a weary jury vindicated FDR and acquitted Broderick, a verdict cheered by more than three dozen friends who had sat with him during the long vigil.

By that time, Roosevelt was back on the campaign trail, where conservative Democrats led by Al Smith and conservative Republicans backing Hoover continued to attack FDR's comments about helping the "little fellow" as a call for "class warfare." They never applied that label to Hoover's Reconstruction Finance Corporation, the emergency lending program set up in January 1932 to help the "big fellows" in banking and business.

Roosevelt wasn't bashful about calling out these blind spots. In one speech, he rejected the idea that "if we make the rich richer, somehow they will let a part of their prosperity trickle down through to the rest of us." His notion, he said, was that "if we make the average of mankind comfortable and secure in their prosperity, it will rise upward just as yeast rises upward." He frequently warned that if big business used its power in ways "contrary to the public welfare," the government must intervene.

In later decades, some would claim Roosevelt was deliberately vague about the New Deal and won in 1932 simply because he wasn't Herbert Hoover. "Vague" might apply to FDR's views on the gold standard and future budget deficits, but it absolutely did not apply to his views on regulating business and Wall Street. The media coverage of his campaign proves that. It began as early as April 1932, with the local coverage of FDR's post-Insull speech in St. Paul. Like many other major newspapers, the *Minneapolis Star* and *Minneapolis Journal* described the speech as a deft rebuttal to Al Smith's charge that FDR was fomenting "class warfare." But while that was the primary focus of Washington pundits, the Minneapolis newspapers also saw the speech as proof that "Governor Roosevelt plans to make the power question an outstanding issue in his campaign," as the *Minneapolis Star* put it. And that mattered, the newspaper explained at some length, because Minnesota Power & Light was among the utilities pushing to inflate the value of their capital investments to justify higher rates for local consumers. Utility regulation was a pocketbook issue in homes all across the country and Roosevelt knew that, even if the pundits didn't.

In a radio address on July 30, he called for "regulation to the full extent of federal power" of *all* utility holding companies selling securities or power in interstate commerce, including rules governing the rates they charged consumers. On September 22, *The New York Times* carried a front-page list titled "Roosevelt's Utilities Program." It could hardly have been more specific: it called for public utilities to disclose their capital structures, balance sheets, and profits; the ownership of their stocks and bonds, including those owned by officers and directors; and all intercompany contracts that enriched insiders. Beyond the utilities industry, Roosevelt promised he would require *all* companies to publicly disclose the full truth about their finances before they sold securities to the public. He vowed to support a law separating investment banks and commercial banks, as his friend Joe Broderick had proposed two years earlier in New York. He said he would create "quicker methods" to get money back to depositors after bank failures, and would impose "more rigid supervision" on national banks. In August, in a speech in Columbus, Ohio, he repeated much of this regulatory platform, including "the use of federal authority" to regulate "the many exchanges in the business of buying and selling securities and commodities."

Roosevelt made it crystal clear during his campaign that he intended to radically change the way Washington dealt with Wall Street and the way Wall Street dealt with the public. As New Deal historian Eric Rauchway has shown in his research, a vote for FDR in 1932 was a vote for an unprecedented degree of federal financial regulation—Hoover knew it, Wall Street knew it, and the voters knew it.

As Roosevelt barnstormed the country, Joe Kennedy was among the regular travelers on the campaign train. Gradually, "in the friendly intimacy of the campaign train the man from Boston became one of the inner circle," one aide reported. Before Kennedy headed west to the Democratic National Convention in Chicago, he promised Roosevelt he would "keep my contact with WR [Hearst] on a night-and-day basis." Roosevelt stayed in Albany, sitting by an open telephone line from Chicago, as his team waged a fierce battle against Al Smith's forces.

Roosevelt's battle to win the nomination at the 1932 Democratic convention was a master class in backroom bargaining and subtle arm-twisting.

As the voting began in Chicago on June 30, FDR was fewer than 100 votes short of having the two-thirds majority needed to claim the nomination. But his Tammany-backed rival, former governor Al Smith, held 190.5 votes and would never release them to Roosevelt. The votes to put Roosevelt over the top would have to come from elsewhere—and Jim Farley, FDR's astute navigator at the convention, managed to find them. Through a long night and three ballots, Smith's backers in the gallery booed at every mention of Roosevelt's name. Still, Jim Farley's team kept every FDR delegate on board and pried away a few additional votes.

Then, through intense backstage negotiations, ninety delegates from California and Texas were wrangled into Roosevelt's corner. Joe Kennedy aided the cause by helping to persuade publisher William Randolph Hearst that his preferred candidate, the conservative House Speaker John Nance Garner of Texas, could not win the nomination. At Hearst's word, Garner released his delegates to Roosevelt after Farley vowed to support Garner as FDR's running mate. The California turnabout was led by progressive William Gibbs McAdoo, President Wilson's son-in-law, who blamed Al Smith for the 1924 deadlocked convention that cost McAdoo that year's presidential nomination. The deal assured FDR would win the nomination.

In the governor's mansion in Albany, Roosevelt and members of his family and staff were following the convention news on the big wooden console radio in the parlor. At one point, Roosevelt picked up the phone with an open line to the Chicago hotel suite where Louis Howe and Jim Farley were stationed. His Albany guests saw Roosevelt beam and say a few words—"Good! Fine! Excellent!"— but he did not share any news as the balloting resumed. Once California's vote was announced, the remaining votes he needed were quickly gathered as delegates who had been pledged to various "favorite sons" moved into Roosevelt's camp. Garner was unanimously chosen as FDR's running mate. Al Smith, whose delegates stayed loyal to the end, stalked out of the convention without comment and caught a train for home. Roosevelt won by 945 votes to Smith's 190.5 votes but, as *The Evening Star* in Washington observed, "No effort was made to make the election unanimous."

In Albany, cheering supporters filled the governor's mansion as soon as McAdoo had spoken in Chicago. An exultant Roosevelt promptly sent off appreciative telegrams to Garner and McAdoo. Then FDR gathered Eleanor, sons John and Elliott, and a few close aides and boarded an airplane bound for Chicago. For the first time, a candidate would accept his nomination in person at his party's convention. The flight was slowed by turbulent headwinds, but huge, patient crowds greeted Roosevelt at the Chicago airport and outside the convention hall. His speech galvanized the exhausted delegates and, in its final paragraphs, gave his future administration the label it bears to this day. "Never before in modern history have the essential differences between the two major American parties stood out in such striking contrast as they do today," he said. Republican leaders "have held out no hope, they have pointed out no path" for recovery. Millions looked to the Democrats to provide "more equitable opportunity to share in the distribution of national wealth . . . Those millions cannot and shall not hope in vain," he said. "I pledge you— I pledge myself to a *new deal* for the American people . . . a new order of competence and of courage."

Back in New York a few days later—the Roosevelts took a train home—FDR and three of his four sons boarded a graceful 40-foot sailboat for a relaxing postconvention cruise north along the New England coast to Maine. Joe Kennedy, Jim Farley, and other close campaign aides followed along in a 95-foot yacht, where they convened nightly planning sessions. Ever restless, Kennedy soon returned to shore but he seemed to be waiting for the FDR craft at every port.

Defeating Al Smith and the conservative forces in his own party at the convention was arguably more difficult for Roosevelt than defeating Hoover in the election. Ultimately, the race seemed to turn on contrasts in their core beliefs. Hoover had lifted himself out of harsh, unloving poverty and believed everyone could do the same, even in the hardest times, if they just worked hard enough. Roosevelt, coddled as a child and untouched by poverty, had been taught by polio that fate could smash into anyone's life at any moment. Despite the grinding Depression, Hoover still thought Americans could perform the impossible task of pulling themselves up off the ground by tugging on their own bootstraps. Roosevelt, whose "boots" were strapped onto heavy leg braces each morning, knew that any American, on any given day, might suddenly need a helping hand just to rise up and walk. To Hoover, government's job was to encourage big business to lead the march to prosperity and then get out of the way. To Roosevelt, government's job was to make sure the march of big business didn't trample over "the little fellow" and damage the roadway.

FDR's case that the federal government had a duty to relieve the nation's suffering was denounced by Hoover and his supporters as un-American and socialistic, a dangerous repudiation of the "rugged individualism" that Hoover saw as the soul of American culture. To counter those attacks, Roosevelt often framed his New Deal as merely a fresh expression of traditional progressive ideas that dated back decades to William Jennings Bryan, Teddy Roosevelt, and Woodrow Wilson—ideas that had been smothered by the selfishness of the 1920s.

But with the New Deal, Roosevelt was challenging both the sharp-edged creed that worshipped private capital *and* the sepia-tinted progressive ideas that romanticized Puritan values and small-scale commerce. Roosevelt's New Deal was neither an emergency response to a temporary economic crisis nor the nostalgic pursuit of a simpler past. It was a clear-eyed vision for a new century, a blueprint for a liberal government that could be as powerful in protecting Americans as unregulated capitalism had been in exploiting them. For him, more than for any president before him, the presidency was a vehicle for actively shaping and nurturing a modern industrial economy that could give real hope and opportunity to

Americans on every step of the social staircase. A racially segregated society would distort his vision and delay his dream for millions of people; even so, FDR did not doubt that each step toward a fairer economy was a step toward a healthier democracy.

ON ELECTION DAY, NOVEMBER 8, 1932, Roosevelt carried all but six states in a landslide that expanded the Democrats' power in the House and Senate and swept FDR's lieutenant governor, Herbert H. Lehman, into the governor's chair in Albany. But the Constitution—in language already repealed for future elections—required Roosevelt to wait until Saturday, March 4, 1933, to be sworn in.

As he waited, the nation descended into the worst winter of the Depression. Parts of the farm belt were drying up and starting to blow away. Untold hosts of people were homeless or living in shacks made of tin scraps or old boxes; photographs from the era show families scouring landfills for salvageable food or saleable goods. Others were painfully choosing whether to spend their scant funds on heat or groceries. Private charities were exhausted; churches, museums, colleges, men's lodges, women's clubs, and scout troops were all struggling as donations dried up. A record number of businesses had failed that year; those that survived had done so by cutting millions of workers off their payrolls. At least 25 percent of American workers—nearly 13 million people, at a minimum—were unemployed; it is likely the national tally was much higher and it is certain the toll in some cities was higher still. Democracy itself was being tested. In November, the nation had overwhelmingly elected a man who promised to help, but his hands were tied for months.

It seemed the social order had finally slipped off its axis on February 15, 1933. During a Miami evening rally, an assassin fired five shots at Roosevelt, who was spared when an alert woman bravely jostled the gunman's arm. As the assassin was wrestled to the ground, the president-elect hauled one nearby victim, the fatally wounded mayor of Chicago, into his limousine and held him in his arms as they sped to the hospital. Afterward, FDR seemed utterly himself; his only visible reaction was his concern for the mayor and the others who had been shot. One close aide recalled, "I have never in my life seen anything more magnificent than Roosevelt's calm that night."

There was worse, still, for the nation to endure before the inauguration. Days before FDR's miraculous escape, a major bank in Detroit, the hub of the nation's supposedly impregnable auto industry, had been hit with a run and was in danger of failing. A desperate Treasury official sought help from auto titan Henry Ford, warning him that the Detroit failure could be disastrous for the whole country. Ford refused. "Let the crash come," he said, and it did. A desperate Michigan governor and, soon, governors in nearly every other state closed their banks or severely restricted withdrawals.

By the time Roosevelt boarded his train to Washington on Thursday, March 2, consumer spending had virtually stopped. By late Friday evening, March 3, when he went to bed in a suite on the seventh floor of the Mayflower Hotel in Washington, only New York's mighty banks were still open. When he woke up on Saturday, they, too, were closed. Before dawn that morning, Governor Lehman had declared a two-day "holiday" at the pleading of the New York Federal Reserve Bank; the moratorium would last days longer.

Stocks can't be paid for if banks aren't open. Dick Whitney had no choice but to close the New York Stock Exchange. Before the opening bell on Saturday morning, March 4, he climbed up to the podium over the trading floor and announced a two-day closure, only the third in the exchange's history. Two days would come and go but, as long as the banks were closed, the exchange would also remain shuttered.

It must have been a bitter pill for the man who, almost single-handedly, had kept the exchange open through the 1929 crash and the 1931 gold crisis. The trading floor was hushed by his words. The tickers sent the news out across the country, and fell silent.

Like the great suffering nation, the world of Wall Street grew ominously quiet, waiting for Roosevelt.

CHAPTER THREE

CONFIDENCE, COOPERATION, AND CREATION

MARCH 4, 1933–JUNE 30, 1934

THE SLEEK PIERCE-ARROW TOURING CAR GLIDED UP TO THE portico of the White House. In the jump seats behind the chauffeur were two top-hatted congressional leaders. Behind them, bundled up against a raw morning, were Franklin and Eleanor Roosevelt.

It was 11 A.M. on Saturday, March 4, 1933—Inauguration Day. Not since Lincoln took the oath of office in 1861 had this American ceremony been conducted under more desperate circumstances. Millions were homeless, jobless, hopeless, and hungry. The rusting wheels of industry were barely turning. Before sunrise that morning, the engines of finance had stopped. Almost every bank in the nation was closed; without those banks, the nation's markets were paralyzed. Radicals on the Right and Left were disgusted with democracy's failure to address this calamity and some longed for a strongman to take charge. Democrat Al Smith, just weeks earlier, told a business conference that the Depression, like a war, required that the government "lay aside the red tape and regulatory statutes" and become "a tyrant, a despot, a real monarch." Columnist Walter Lippmann told FDR privately in February that he might have "no alternative but to assume dictatorial powers." But perhaps the best evidence of this hunger was that publisher William Randolph Hearst was helping to write and produce an MGM film, *Gabriel Over the White House,* in which a weak Harding-like president is transformed by some divine encounter into a heroic dictator who shuts down Congress and rules alone. Hearst believed the film would be widely popular.

Roosevelt had left the Mayflower Hotel that morning for his last journey as a civilian; when he next got into this car, he would be president of the United States. But for the next hour or so, that office was held by the sour-faced man crossing the White House portico to join him for the ride to the Capitol. Herbert Hoover extended a hand to Eleanor, who had jumped from her seat to join First Lady Lou Hoover in a separate car. As Hoover stepped into the car, FDR smiled broadly and extended his hand. Hoover briefly grasped it, mumbled a few words, and sat down, his top hat on his lap. Aides tucked a blanket over the two men's knees.

Despite a few attempts by Roosevelt—"Lovely steel," he chirped as they passed a government construction site—it was a sullen drive. Hoover had deep, irreconcilable issues with FDR, differences that he would help embed in the genetic code of his party. His contempt for the crippled New York politician beside him seared away any social graces he might have mustered. He had refused to permit formal photographs: "I will never be photographed with that man. I have too much respect for myself." He had offered the Roosevelts only teatime at the White House rather than the customary dinner party, and had used even that scant hospitality to flog his policy disputes. Hoover was furious because Roosevelt had refused to repudiate his "so-called new deal" after the election and adopt Hoover's own pro-business, anti-regulatory policies—the only hope Hoover had seen for restoring public confidence in the banks. More immediately, Hoover had refused to address the spiraling bank crisis without Roosevelt's public support.

Roosevelt had been bemused by Hoover's naïve demand that he repudiate the New Deal; only a child would expect him to betray the voters who had overwhelmingly picked his platform over Hoover's. But FDR was shocked at Hoover's refusal to use his own presidential power to do what his own advisors were begging him to do: declare a national bank moratorium to give regulators time to deal with a crisis that threatened the savings of millions of people and the flow of credit to agricultural and industrial America. We only have one president at a time, FDR kept saying to Hoover, no doubt silently adding ". . . and for now, it's *you.*"

Roosevelt firmly believed Hoover, as president, had the power to close the banks in a national emergency, thanks to a wartime law adopted in 1917, amended in 1918, and never repealed. A long-serving member of the Federal Reserve Board had visited Roosevelt's home in Hyde Park during a bitter December snowstorm to brief him about this option, which had already been explained to Hoover to no effect. FDR had one of his aides research the law; the aide reached the same conclusion the Fed member had.

But Hoover had disagreed and, throughout the day before the inaugural, he continued to resist all the arguments in favor of a moratorium. After Roosevelt, during a phone call to the White House late the previous evening, had repeated his mantra about "one president at a time," Hoover had abruptly hung up and gone to bed. The Hoover Institute at Stanford later noted that Hoover "never forgave Roosevelt and spent the rest of his life holding FDR in bitter enmity."

Thus, Roosevelt—waving his hat a few times to acknowledge cheers from the crowd—was making this strained and nearly silent journey into his presidency.

Under threatening skies, the Capitol grounds were crowded. Umbrellas popped up like dark mushrooms during brief lashes of rain. All the cutting-edge technology of a new communications age was on display. Newsreel cameramen perched on platforms high above the spectators, ready to rush big wheels of film into urban movie theaters before nightfall. Radio microphones would beam Roosevelt's words across the country and far beyond; fascists, communists, democrats, and aristocrats around the world would take the measure of this new American leader. Roosevelt stood solemn and hatless as the oath was administered, his hand on a thick Dutch family Bible that was a century older than the Constitution he swore to "preserve, protect, and defend." His customary grin was gone; one reporter declared FDR's closest friends would scarcely recognize this somber figure.

Then Roosevelt began to speak in his patrician tones, with an opening that was nearly a prayer and a speech that was almost a sermon.

"President Hoover, Mr. Chief Justice"—a heartbeat pause—"my *friends*. This is a day of national consecration."

Americans expected candor from him, he said, and they would get it. Despite its current troubles, "this great nation will endure as it has endured, will revive and will prosper," he told them. "So first of all, let me assert my firm belief that the only thing we have to fear is fear itself—nameless, unreasoning, unjustified terror which paralyzes needed efforts to convert retreat into advance."

The nation's problems "concern, thank God, only material things," he said. But his recital of them was grim enough: "The means of exchange are frozen in the currents of trade; the withered leaves of industrial enterprise lie on every side; farmers find no markets for their produce; the savings of many years in thousands of families are gone. More important, a host of unemployed citizens face the grim problem of existence, and an equally great number toil with little return. Only a foolish optimist can deny the dark realities of the moment."

But this distress "comes from no failure of substance," he said. "Nature still offers her bounty and human efforts have multiplied it. Plenty is at our doorstep, but a generous use of it languishes in the very sight of the supply."

This, he continued, was because those who ruled "the exchange of mankind's goods" had failed "through their own stubbornness and their own incompetence." Their values were those "of a generation of self-seekers." It was time to "apply social values more noble than mere monetary profit." The current hardships "will be worth all they cost us if they teach us that our true destiny is not to be ministered unto but to minister, to ourselves and to our fellow men."

To the business powers that had ruled the prior decade, Roosevelt said: "There must be an end to a conduct in banking and in business which too often has given to a sacred trust the likeness of callous and selfish wrongdoing." Confidence "thrives only on honesty, on honor, on the sacredness of obligations, on faithful protection, on unselfish performance; without them it cannot live."

Words were not enough, he said. "This nation asks for action, and action now." The applause burst out more frequently as he laid out the actions he planned to take—foremost, "to put people to work," but also to impose "a strict supervision of all banking and credit and investment" and to end "speculation with other people's money."

He was confident that the Constitution was "so simple and practical" that this crisis could be met within its framework. He would work with Congress to enact "the measures that a stricken nation in a stricken world may require." But if Congress did not act, he warned, he would "ask the Congress for the one remaining instrument to meet the crisis—broad executive power to wage a war against the emergency as great as the power that would be given to me if we were in fact invaded by a foreign foe."

Was this the vow of the strongman too many people longed for? The roar of approval was the loudest of the day. In the ranks behind Roosevelt, his wife, Eleanor, cringed at the crowd's readiness to cheer this extreme contingency, knowing her husband had no appetite for dictatorship.

Roosevelt insisted "the people of the United States have not failed" in the work of governing themselves. Instead, they were relying on democracy to produce "direct, vigorous action" from their elected leaders. They "have made me the present instrument of their wishes," he said as he concluded. "In the spirit of the gift, I take it."

One of Eleanor's biographers captured the impression her husband made on the crowd, and on the nation: "Franklin Roosevelt flooded the dark day as if he were made of light, a big bold electrified sign on a hillside heralding the American notion that *Things Can Be Fixed*. He himself could not be made afraid."

By midafternoon on Inauguration Day, he had submitted the list of his cabinet nominees to the Senate and, in less than an hour, they had been unanimously confirmed. At 6 P.M. the same day, he gathered them to the White House to be sworn in as a group and told them to take charge of their departments immediately. He invited congressional leaders to meet with him the next day, and got his staff working on an executive order and an accompanying bill to deal with the banking crisis.

Eleanor, who had attended her uncle Theodore Roosevelt's inauguration when she was a child, presided over a luncheon buffet in the East Room; allocated bedrooms—FDR's bed and her own were too short, so she ordered longer ones; and greeted visitors, including the intrepid woman who had deflected the assassin's aim on that fateful February evening in Miami. Wooden ramps, built in the last days of Hoover's term and stowed in the shrubbery, were put in place to ease Roosevelt's way around his new home. His longtime personal secretary, Marguerite "Missy" LeHand, and his gnome-like political mentor, Louis McHenry Howe, were installed as full-time residents, with bedrooms on the third floor. Members of his Albany secretarial staff and several of his "brain trust" advisors had come with him to Washington. The grown Roosevelt children and their young families were boisterously present. The liveliness dispelled the bitter gloom of Hoover's last months in office.

On his first morning as president, Roosevelt had breakfast in bed amid stacks of letters, memos, and newspapers—a habit since his days in Albany. It was Sunday so he attended church with Eleanor, another habit for this longtime Episcopal vestryman.

Then, he went back to work.

"The hours between Mr. Roosevelt's inauguration and the night of March 9 were among the maddest Washington has ever experienced," one observer recalled. "Conferences ran practically without interruption for four days and nights."

At his first cabinet meeting on March 6, FDR confronted his attorney general. When would his formal opinion on the 1918 law be ready? It *was* ready, and it matched those Roosevelt had already gotten: in this national emergency, FDR had the power to close the banks. A proclamation was drawn up calling for a four-day bank moratorium and an embargo on the hoarding of gold and silver, with severe fines and jail terms for anyone who defied the rules. Congress would reconvene on Thursday, March 9, and FDR intended to hand them a bill to formalize these emergency measures.

Meanwhile, the country had to keep running. Waivers were granted to finance food shipments, payrolls, and medicines. A new form of currency, Federal Reserve Notes backed by bank assets rather than gold, was printed for emergency use when banks reopened. Banks were ordered to give customers access to their safe-deposit boxes to retrieve hoarded currency and gold. Dozens of other smaller problems had to be anticipated, and solved.

"Action, and action now," the new president had promised. On Thursday morning, the cautious editorial page at *The New York Times* concluded that he had kept his vow. The banking moratorium, which might have alarmed the country, instead "seemed to cheer it up." The editors concluded, "In the midst of our bad luck it is strengthening to the public morale to feel that it is good luck to have such a president just now."

That same day, March 9, the emergency banking bill—taken largely on faith by lawmakers—passed the House of Representatives shortly after Congress came back into session. The Senate approved it a few hours later and FDR signed it into law that night, his sixth evening in the White House. The new law laid out a process for closed banks to be examined, shored up where necessary, and reopened. The Reconstruction Finance Corporation was authorized to provide the fresh capital necessary to turn shaky banks into sound ones. State banking regulators would work in parallel to examine and reopen the banks under their jurisdiction. Roosevelt's plan to address the banking crisis was in place—a plan Hoover could have implemented months earlier.

Indeed, shortly after FDR had been sworn in, an outline for a bank moratorium law had been handed to Roosevelt's team by Hoover's lame-duck Treasury secretary Ogden L. Mills, who was FDR's Hudson valley neighbor and Harvard classmate. The Mills memo was based on executive orders and draft legislation that Mills and his staff had futilely urged Hoover to implement. As the crisis worsened on Friday afternoon, March 3, Mills had invited William H. Woodin, Roosevelt's choice as Treasury secretary, to join in the marathon staff meetings at the Treasury building. Will Woodin, a sweet-tempered industrialist, was joined at various times by brain-trust members Ray Moley and Adolf Berle. At some point during that long Friday night, Moley had awakened from a short nap on an office sofa and seen "an unforgettable picture. Mills sat behind the desk of the Secretary of the Treasury, Woodin on the other side. The long days and nights after, Woodin was to sit behind the desk and

Mills in front. Otherwise nothing was to change in that room." These people, Moley wrote in a later memoir, "had forgotten to be Republicans and Democrats. We were just a bunch of men trying to save the banking system."

After breakfast on Inauguration Day, Ogden Mills had spent his last hours in office drafting what he vaguely called "a tentative outline of a possible line of approach to the solution of our banking problem." Even after his term ended at midday, Mills and his key aides had stayed on to help. After round-the-clock sessions—to revise and refine the plan, to consult key senators, to wrangle regional Fed officials into line—Woodin and his exhausted bipartisan team finished the emergency bill at 2:30 A.M. on Tuesday, March 7. One of the Hoover holdovers recalled trooping next door to the White House on the morning of Thursday, March 9, with a huge map, borrowed from the Fed, that was studded with colored pins marking the location and financial condition of all the national banks subject to the new law. "The president thought it was great," the official recalled.

But while Roosevelt may have loved the map, he had left the plan's gritty details to the men huddled in the Treasury building. His own policy goal was clear and simple. While Hoover still claimed people were fleeing banks because they didn't trust the New Deal, Roosevelt understood that people were fleeing the banks because they *didn't trust the banks*. Thousands of banks had failed; billions in savings had been lost or frozen. For bank customers, as for the country, the worst fear was fear itself. FDR needed a plan concrete and practical enough to assure people that any bank that reopened after the "bank holiday" could be trusted. Beyond all odds, and beyond all the intricate legislative language, that was what his team delivered.

JUST HOURS AFTER CONGRESS passed the banking bill, Roosevelt called its weary leaders back to the White House to brief them on an emergency belt-tightening bill that would reduce federal salaries and revise veterans benefits to save $400 million. The bill terrified Congress, which feared a backlash from civil servants and veterans. It also worried a few farsighted economists who believed that more federal spending was needed to prop up the economy until the New Deal relief programs kicked in.

But Roosevelt was thinking like a salesman, not an economist or a lawmaker. To those in the world of finance and business, the federal deficit was not just a number written in red ink; it was concrete evidence of how unqualified the federal government was to run anything. To establish his credibility in those precincts, Roosevelt had to address the deficit right away, even if he had to deepen it later. When the bill passed the House on Saturday, March 11, Democrats cast 92 votes against the bill but enough "fiscally conservative" Republicans supported it to cover the defections. The bill would face days of debate in the Senate, but it would pass—along with a bill from Roosevelt to legalize beer, a wildly popular step away from Prohibition and a deft media distraction.

On March 12, FDR's second Sunday night in the White House, he gave the first of what he later called his "fireside chats," an informal radio broadcast in which he spoke directly to the American people. His topic, of course, was banking—but banking as understood by citizens whose financial lives were limited to home mortgages and savings accounts. He gave a quick tutorial in how banks worked, explaining that they used most of the money deposited with them to make loans to farmers and businesses, keeping just enough to "cover the cash needs of the average citizen." Then he walked them through the anatomy of the banking panic: the blind fear, the sudden extraordinary demands for cash, the impossibility of selling "perfectly sound assets" at a moment's notice except "at panic prices far below their real value." Finally, he promised that sound banks would be reopened "as fast as the mechanics of the situation will allow." He was confident, he said, that when people found "that they can get their money—that they can get it when they want it, for all legitimate purposes," their fears would evaporate.

He concluded, "We have provided the machinery to restore our financial system, and it is up to you to support and make it work. It is your problem, my friends, your problem no less than it is mine. Together we cannot fail."

And together, they did not fail. With heroic efforts by bankers and regulators, banks began to reopen on March 13. In major cities, then in smaller cities and towns, people lined up to make deposits, not withdrawals. In barely a week, the country's banking system had been rescued from the consequences of a decade of greed and folly— *without* the repudiation of the New Deal that Hoover had stubbornly demanded. When the stock market reopened on March 15, ten days after its abrupt closure, prices rose 15 percent above their closing value on March 3. Even the princes of Wall Street were impressed. The House of Morgan cabled its London affiliate that "the whole country is filled with admiration for President Roosevelt. The record of his accomplishment in just one week seems incredible because we have never experienced anything like it before."

In the fireside chat that helped turn the tide, Roosevelt said most banks had been soundly managed. But he added that "some of our bankers had shown themselves either incompetent or dishonest." He could scarcely have pretended otherwise, given the evidence from the Senate Banking Committee hearings that had begun back in February 1932.

The Wall Street investigation, originally sparked by Hoover's misguided hatred of short sellers, had an unpromising start. Dick Whitney, called often as a witness during the spring of 1932, had no trouble outwitting his ill-prepared inquisitors.

Neither Hoover nor the Senate committee had ever mustered any evidence that short sellers had engineered the long bear market. But on Friday, April 8, 1932, the Senate cloakroom had been swept with unconfirmed rumors that a massive "bear raid" of short selling would be conducted the next day. The committee had immediately summoned Dick Whitney to come before the committee on the following Monday with the names of all the short sellers on the NYSE and all the stocks affected by short selling in excess of ten thousand shares.

Whitney had appeared without the information demanded, explaining that 175 exchange staffers were still working diligently to assemble the data from the files of 25,000 brokerage offices. The rumored raid had not happened; the committee's chief counsel had known little about how the stock exchange worked. The hearing, instead, had become a forum for Whitney to present his own data showing that short selling had not been a factor in recent market routs. Indeed, he had testified that short selling had accounted for less than 5 percent of all NYSE transactions since the Depression began.

Coverage of his testimony shows he had commanded the stage. *The New York Times* had led the next day's paper with a lengthy account of his performance, noting that he had "ranged from financial dissertations to pointed political observations." The audience of nearly five hundred spectators who had squeezed into the hearing room had laughed at his jokes and listened raptly to his explanations. "The testimony was sufficiently interesting to hold the audience throughout the day."

The committee, with little staff expertise, had not been able to make much of the short-sale information the NYSE supplied, so Whitney's next three appearances as a witness had been little different from his first. No, he had testified, he had no knowledge of any manipulative trading on the NYSE. He did not see any need for changing the way the exchange operated. If such a need arose, he and the exchange's other governors would take care of that themselves.

The hearings had petered out by the end of June 1932. By the end of the year, the committee's progressive Republican chairman, Senator Peter Norbeck of South Dakota, had hired and fired three chief counsels, the third after less than a week. Without a chief counsel, the investigation had become rudderless—there was no one even to compile a final report for the Senate.

By January 1933, there had seemed little chance that this once-ballyhooed investigation of Wall Street would produce anything beyond some flattering front-page articles for Dick Whitney's scrapbook. Then on January 22, 1933, with the investigation due to expire when Congress adjourned for the inauguration on March 4, Senator Norbeck had made a Sunday afternoon telephone call to the Manhattan apartment of lawyer Ferdinand Pecora.

"Ferd" Pecora was a Sicilian-born success story, a short athletic man with a square pugnacious jaw and a distinctive curly black pom-

padour. In a society where the legal elite quietly sneered at the lazi-
ness of "swarthy" southern European immigrants, Pecora worked his
way through New York Law School and then became a tireless prosecutor in New York City. As chief assistant district attorney, he had
won the bribery conviction of New York's crooked Tammany-backed
banking superintendent in 1929. When his boss resigned shortly
thereafter, the incorruptible Pecora found his own path to promo-
tion blocked by a resentful Tammany boss. He quit and went into
private practice, making money with routine business litigation and
corporate legal chores. Then, his home telephone had rung, with a
U.S. senator on the line.

Norbeck had offered Pecora the job of chief counsel for the Wall
Street investigation. The position seemed to have few attractions—
indeed, Norbeck had already been turned down by several other lawyers. The pay was low, the media had lost interest, and the inquiry
would shut down in less than two months. Would Pecora take the
job?

He would. Pecora had been bored in his law practice, and he
loved investigative work. He had asked his partners to cover for him
for a few weeks, taken a night train to Washington, and walked into
Senator Norbeck's office the next morning. He had explained that,
rather than just drafting a final report, he wanted to use the next few
weeks to hold additional hearings. Norbeck had agreed.

There hadn't been a moment to waste. The new chief counsel had
returned to New York that afternoon and rented a suite of cheaply
furnished offices in the same midtown building that housed his law
office. The location was a subway trip away from the downtown
banks and brokerage firms whose records he would examine. He had
hired a handful of lawyers, an accountant, and a statistician, and inherited an economist and a few other staffers from his predecessors.

After a week on the job, Pecora had quietly sent subpoenas downtown to the chairman of one of the largest banks in the country:
Charles E. Mitchell of National City Bank, one of the bankers who
had financed Dick Whitney's historic buying spree on Black Thursday, 1929. After becoming the bank's president in 1921, Mitchell had
plunged into the securities markets through the bank's alter ego,

National City Company. By 1929, National City Company had become one of the largest securities retailers in the world. Mitchell and a few of his lieutenants had been summoned to appear before the committee on February 21.

Pecora had underplayed the epic nature of these subpoenas. He was just "fact-finding," he told reporters. In reality, he was planning to question Mitchell about his bank's entire track record of selling securities to the public, an explosive new line of inquiry for the committee. Reporters knew that Mitchell already had been quizzed by the committee in June 1932 about a copper stock manipulation and he had emerged unscathed. They had expected little from this return visit.

Pecora wanted to get right to work on the Mitchell investigation, but Senator Norbeck had announced in November that the committee would soon produce "sensational" hearings into the collapse of the Insull utility empire, so Pecora had to begin his digging on that thoroughly trodden ground. He had managed to wring some front-page news from a prominent bank chairman in Chicago, whose institution had been an almost bottomless source of credit for Sam Insull. The banker had admitted the bank "violated the spirit" of an Illinois law that limited how much a bank could lend to a single company. While on paper, the loans went to different fiefdoms, they all added up to Insull. They also added up to more than three times the state cap.

General Electric was one of Insull's biggest creditors and its chairman, Owen D. Young, was one of the most capable businessmen in the country. But under questioning from Pecora, the executive had conceded that Insull's holding companies were so complex that it was "impossible for any man, however able, really to grasp the situation." Young had added, "I believe Mr. Samuel Insull was very largely the victim of that complicated structure, which got even beyond his power, competent as he was, to understand it."

This new evidence from Pecora would arm FDR in future battles over regulating utility holding companies. But the Insull hearings had also exposed Pecora's weak grasp of investment banking, and the press corps had grown even less interested in his upcoming date with the chairman of the formidable National City Bank, a forerunner of today's giant Citibank. What the reporters had not known was that Pecora's staff had been conducting a penetrating inspection of the bank's records since February 9. Nor had they seen Pecora himself poring over the bank's board minutes in every free moment, storing reams of data in his phenomenal memory.

What had happened when Pecora finally put Charles Mitchell under oath had been astounding. On Tuesday morning, February 21, 1933, Mitchell had taken the stand with "the manner of a powerful man irked at wasting his time." Five days later, on Sunday night, he had resigned all his positions at the bank.

Under questioning by Pecora, Mitchell had acknowledged a remarkable array of sins. The bank had used its securities arm—and its shareholders' money—to bail itself out of unwise loans to Cuban sugar producers. His bonus system had encouraged his executives to use heavy-handed sales pressure, to underwrite unworthy new issues, and to give tainted investment advice to depositors. The bank's securities arm had manipulated the prices of certain stocks, including the bank's own shares. The bank had made interest-free loans to about a hundred senior employees during the 1929 crash so they could hang on to bank shares they bought on margin, even as its securities affiliate was selling out the margin accounts of its customers. Fully 95 percent of these supposedly secure insider loans still had not been repaid; some of them had been sold to the bank's securities arm to get them off the bank's books. The bank's securities arm also had sold investors more than $116 million worth of now-worthless Peruvian and Brazilian bonds without disclosing the bank's own dire assessments of those borrowers. One confidential memo described "the complete ignorance, carelessness and negligence" of certain state officials in Brazil; the prospectus for that state's bonds praised the "prudent and careful management of the state's finances."

It had been a comprehensive catalogue of shockingly routine abuses committed by dozens of executives at one of the nation's most powerful and respected banks. What one magazine called "The Damnation of Mitchell" actually had been the damnation of a generation of big-city bankers who had admired and copied National City's unethical conduct.

When National City Bank's directors had gotten Mitchell's sudden letter of resignation on February 26, they had felt they should consult Washington leaders before accepting it, given the accelerating number of bank failures and closures that month. President Hoover had told them he thought Mitchell's departure would actually help the bank's reputation, not hurt it. President-elect Roosevelt had been astonished that the directors had even asked. "These New York bankers haven't any more notion of public psychology than a chicken," he had said as he hung up the phone.

Mitchell's resignation had not ended Pecora's inquisition, as some bankers had hoped. Indeed, the Senate had promptly extended the committee's lease on life into the new administration. One of the last witnesses before the inauguration recess had been Dick Whitney, who had "fenced for four hours" with Pecora over whether federal regulation of the stock exchange was necessary. A few weeks later, Whitney would make the same futile arguments directly to Roosevelt, whom his brother, George, had known—and disliked—since their days at Groton and Harvard.

On March 22, 1933, as the senators turned their attention to FDR's urgent legislative agenda, Pecora quietly invited Tom Lamont, Morgan's managing partner, and John W. Davis, the firm's foremost lawyer, to his drab midtown offices in New York. He told them his staff needed to see the firm's records for the next phase of his inquiry. Lamont and Davis pulled every string they could reach to block this demand and, if possible, remove Pecora—including an appeal directly to Roosevelt during a long White House visit the next day. But Roosevelt stood firm and Pecora won. He and his men trooped into the Morgan bastion at 23 Wall Street in April, armed with a subpoena for specific partnership records going back many years; for more than a month, they examined the files and took notes.

One day in the first week of April, Pecora took a lunch break from the Morgan records in Manhattan to meet William O. Douglas, the young firecracker on the Yale law faculty.

"He wants me to make a study for him which will be used in his investigation of the stock exchange," Douglas wrote a friend. "As you know, he hopes to be able to present at the close of his investigation a regulatory bill covering stock exchange operations."

It's not clear what drew Pecora's attention to Douglas. An avid reader, he may have come across two provocative papers in *The Yale Law Journal* that Douglas had co-authored over the previous year. Both dissected the ethical conflicts embedded in the machinery of the securities industry—and both displayed a granular understanding of Wall Street that Pecora lacked. In any case, Pecora told Douglas during lunch that he was looking for real-life examples of dubious practices by the big brokerage houses. He knew these anecdotes were catnip to the press and bolstered the case for reform in Congress. And Bill Douglas had a gift for finding such stories, as he'd shown in his celebrated examination of why businessmen went bankrupt.

Shining through that scientifically flawed study, whose sample size had been curtailed by the bankruptcy judge overseeing the cases, was Douglas's bottomless curiosity about the lives and problems of ordinary people. Like Pecora, he loved a good story. He'd polish and practice each one in the living room of his New Haven home until he found the most effective "off the cuff" way to tell it. And he had found a mother lode of stories in his bankruptcy "clinics." His research seemed to have softened the harsh viewpoint that once led him to dismiss failed businessmen as "almost morons." He came to see the tragedy of the events that had blown these men onto the rocks. "Some cases were pathetic and sad—a life time of frugality and hard work" undone by ill-considered speculation, he noted in his report on the study. A laundress who made $33 a week scraped together a $5,000 nest egg over many years and used it, in the fall of 1928, to buy two prominent stocks on margin; she was wiped out in the October crash. A couple, a laborer and a stenographer who together made about $200 a month, were enticed by a market tipster and lost about $5,000 in the crash. Businessmen were busted by investments in Russian and German bonds, volatile Chicago commodities, and Florida real estate, pitched at them both by respected bankers and by deceitful hucksters.

Douglas's groundbreaking work had gotten national attention, and Yale had awarded him an endowed chair the previous summer. He was working hard and having a ridiculous amount of fun. He and a faculty sidekick invented a wry game called "the get-ahead system." One got points by getting publicity, Douglas later explained. "Favorable publicity preferably, but any publicity was better than none at all."

And perhaps that was why Douglas was cool to Pecora's offer: whatever work he did would be publicized only through Pecora's committee. Douglas turned Pecora down, telling him that "everyone knew what the dire effects of unlimited speculation were" and it would not be helpful for him "to count the number of people who had jumped off buildings, fired their maids, sold their Lincolns, or stolen their employer's money."

It was a missed opportunity for Douglas. In May 1933, Pecora's examination of J. P. "Jack" Morgan Jr. and his imperious partners, Tom Lamont and George Whitney, was front-page news everywhere in the country.

The House of Morgan was a far cry from the hurly-burly of National City's sales operation but the "Insiders Only" sign still hung over the door. Pecora forced Jack Morgan and George Whitney to explain why the firm secretly invited certain well-placed people—corporate titans, elite bankers and lawyers, and powerful political leaders in both parties—to purchase new securities at prices well below the market's advance bids. The answer could only be that the partners were buying tolerance and influence. Pecora produced a letter from one influential Democratic Party official thanking George Whitney for one such gift, saying he hoped "the future holds opportunities for me to reciprocate." Even more conclusively, Tom Lamont had arranged one of these windfalls specifically to reward someone who had given congressional testimony helpful to the firm.

This so-called "preferred list" maintained by the Morgan partners—sometimes called "the gravy train"—was hardly as malignant as the deliberate falsehoods Charles Mitchell's National City team used to sell Latin American bonds to unsophisticated public investors. The wealthy passengers on the Morgan "gravy train" actually faced almost no risk of loss, unlike the hapless foreign bond buyers. But the largess was a national sensation and it wounded the firm, badly. "The brightest angel on Wall Street had fallen," as one Morgan biographer would later put it. "In every instance, Morgan & Company could claim the technical legality of their policies," a Senate historian wrote, "while Pecora could demonstrate how far they had gone to stretch their legal and ethical standards." Columnist Walter Lippmann felt personally betrayed; like many senior journalists, he had been charmed by several Morgan partners and trusted the firm's integrity. *The New York Times,* in an editorial titled "Why It Hurts," expressed the "surprise and regret" that Morgan's "warmest friends" felt on learning that the firm had "failed under a test of its pride and prestige" and stooped to employ "the small arts of petty traders." That mistake over time had "swollen into a grievous fault" and the firm had thereby "sacrificed something intangible, imponderable, that has to do with the very highest repute." Other journalists began to refer to the financial executives trooping past Pecora as "banksters," the close cousins of the gangsters of Prohibition's lawless culture.

BEFORE THE MORGAN CIRCUS began, Roosevelt had sent Congress a hasty version of a "truth-in-securities" bill that gave the Federal Trade Commission an almost free hand in determining which securities could be sold to American investors. The FTC would be empowered to reject any new securities issue it deemed unwise. Congressman Sam Rayburn of Texas, the man who would have to get this bill and several other FDR proposals through the House of Representatives, hated the draft. "We have passed a lot of laws since we met here on the fifth of March," Rayburn told his committee members, "but I do not think we have given anybody that much power yet."

Rayburn turned to Ray Moley, FDR's confidential advisor since the dawn of his presidential campaign in Albany. "I need help on this thing," Rayburn said. "I need somebody who knows something." Moley reached out to Felix Frankfurter, an expert in utility regulation at Harvard who had known Roosevelt since their days in the Wilson administration. In a move that shaped history, Frankfurter dispatched three of his young protégés to help. One was James M. Landis, a Harvard law professor deeply schooled in state-level securities regulation. The second was Benjamin V. Cohen, a Harvard-trained New York lawyer with a thorough grasp of the British Companies Act, a possible template for FDR's effort. The third was Thomas G. Corcoran, a brash but irresistible legal gadfly already working in Washington as counsel to the Reconstruction Finance Corporation, which he irreverently dubbed "the Resurrection Finance Corporation." Under Rayburn's loose supervision, the three young men quickly produced a groundbreaking new bill the Texan could support.

The bill won Roosevelt's support, as well. In a message to Congress on March 29, 1933, the president said the federal government had a duty "to insist that every issue of new securities to be sold in interstate commerce shall be accompanied by full publicity and information, and that no essentially important element attending the issue shall be concealed from the buying public."

The bill still charged the FTC with administering the new law. But as FDR preferred, it relied on sunshine—honest public disclosure of all the information people needed to make their own investment decisions—instead of the subjective veto of a few FTC commissioners reviewing the merits of each new business venture. It also imposed serious penalties on anyone who violated the law, from lofty corporate directors down to the lawyers, accountants, and other hired hands. This shift from "merit review" to "full disclosure" ranks as a revolution in regulatory practice. How could Wall Street—which had hidden the risks of those Peruvian and Brazilian bonds—possibly deny that the public had the right to demand the truth, and the whole truth, before they invested? Had not Dick Whitney himself already urged companies listed on his exchange to give investors more information about their finances?

As the legislation's co-author Jim Landis later put it: "My fundamental belief is that if the truth is told about these things then it is up to the parties to decide whether they want to buy them or not."

Landis later recalled that Rayburn "didn't know anything about securities" but "he knew when a man was an expert on his subject, when he was telling the truth." Rayburn steered the new full-disclosure bill through Congress and on May 27, 1933, Roosevelt signed it into law, handing the pen he used to Rayburn.

"Events have made it abundantly clear that the merchandising of securities is really traffic in the economic and social welfare of our people," Roosevelt said as he signed the bill. "Such traffic demands the utmost good faith and fair dealing on the part of those engaged in it." Any hope Wall Street had for lax enforcement faded when Landis was hired as an FTC consultant. Five months later, FDR appointed him to a vacancy on the commission, and his career as a significant New Dealer was launched.

Pecora's exposure of the conflicts and mischief caused by the securities operations of major banks gave Senator Carter Glass, a conservative Democrat from Virginia, evidence to support his own emerging view that banks should be forced to shed their securities affiliates, a view borrowed from New York state banking superintendent Joseph Broderick and supported by President Roosevelt. As Pecora had shown, banks had used depositors' money to make loans to finance their securities units' underwriting activities and stock market speculations, exposing the banks to ruinous losses. They had also loaned their depositors' money to customers of their securities units, and had even dumped their banks' bad loans and unsold securities into their customers' portfolios.

Senator Glass, however, opposed setting up any sort of federal insurance program to protect depositors at failed banks—a view also shared by FDR, who saw deposit insurance as a temptation to reckless bankers. But with so many nest eggs lost in recent years, American savers were desperate for deposit insurance. One of their most vociferous champions was Congressman Henry B. Steagall, an Alabama Democrat who cautioned before the 1932 election that "this fellow Hoover is going to wake up one day and come in here with a message recommending guarantee of bank deposits, and as sure as he does, he'll be re-elected." Steagall's view had strong congressional support. Betting correctly that FDR would compromise rather than veto his prized bank reform effort, Steagall joined with Glass to win passage of a banking bill that gave them both what they wanted most.

The Glass-Steagall Act—officially, the Banking Act of 1933—was signed by FDR on June 16, 1933. It was a complex law, limiting the use of bank loans for stock speculation and barring the payment of interest on checking accounts. But notably, it created a temporary program that would ultimately become the Federal Deposit Insurance Corporation, which finally made banks a safe haven for the savings of ordinary American workers trying to improve their lives. And it gave giant Wall Street banks a year to decide whether to accept deposits or underwrite securities—it barred them from doing both. The National City Bank did not need a year to decide; right after Charles Mitchell resigned, it announced it was disbanding the securities-selling army he built.

THE EARLY PECORA HEARINGS did not just build a bulletproof case in Congress for Wall Street regulation. They also helped build a bulletproof case in the Oval Office for ignoring the ambitions of Joseph P. Kennedy.

As a major donor and fundraiser for FDR, Joe Kennedy wanted to be named secretary of the Treasury. After election night, Kennedy stayed on in New York, waiting for a call that didn't come. On December 10, 1932, he attended the Gridiron Club dinner in Washington, the capital reporters' annual spoof of officialdom, but could not wrangle a private moment with FDR. Later that month, after a weekend visit to William Randolph Hearst's magical estate on the California coast, he forwarded some memos from Hearst to Roosevelt along with a note saying, "If you want me to come to Albany right away, I will be very happy to do so, or call me on the telephone." There was no response.

In reality, Kennedy's chances of becoming Treasury secretary were never good. Roosevelt, determined to frame his own policies, clearly wanted an amenable fellow in that post, not a scrappy deal-maker with a mind of his own. And FDR's trusted mentor, Louis

Howe, didn't like or trust Kennedy. But Pecora's work was surely the final blow; for now, at least, Roosevelt simply could not put a "bankster" into the cabinet.

Kennedy sulked in humiliated rage at his rented mansion in Palm Beach, where presidential advisor Ray Moley visited him for a few warm days of rest in February 1933. "I heard plenty of Kennedy's excoriation of Roosevelt," Moley later reported. Kennedy shared his angry criticism widely within his circle. As the silence from the Oval Office continued, Kennedy "let everyone he came into contact with know what he felt, and in the bluest language," Moley said. Washington got a whiff of the brimstone when Kennedy shocked a friendly senator by saying he might sue the Democratic National Committee for repayment of his campaign loan. The tantrum became gossip fodder on Wall Street when Moley tried to placate his friend by making him a delegate to a London monetary conference. The leader of the American delegation, a prominent Wall Street figure, threatened to resign rather than accept Kennedy, whom he called "a completely irresponsible speculator who has been spreading malicious stories about the president."

The critic was well-informed. Besides spreading malicious stories about the president, Kennedy also had plunged back into his pre-campaign life as a Wall Street speculator, engaging in exactly the kind of unsavory pool operations that Pecora was determined to expose and Roosevelt was determined to stop. Although Kennedy denied doing any bearish trading, one historian found evidence that he was "dealing in hundreds of thousands of dollars and that most of his profits came from driving various company stocks down by selling short."

One adventure did later come into clear focus, thanks to Pecora. In the summer of 1933, investors were speculating on which stocks would benefit from the anticipated repeal of Prohibition. That gave rise to an audacious idea: instead of chasing stocks that really would benefit from repeal, as one Kennedy biographer put it, "why not boost a stock that only *appeared* to be caught up in the coming 'booze boom'?" That idea was born in the resourceful mind of Henry Mason Day, a senior partner in the firm of Redmond & Co. Those who chipped in to exploit Day's ingenious idea included Kuhn, Loeb & Co., Lehman Brothers, two smaller brokerage firms, and two individuals: Walter P. Chrysler and Joseph P. Kennedy. The stock they settled on was Libbey-Owens-Ford Glass Company (LOF), a plate glass manufacturer that unsophisticated investors might (and did) confuse with Owens-Illinois Glass Company, a major producer of glass bottles. After Day's lieutenant on the NYSE trading floor had churned up a storm of illusory trading, the LOF stock had risen by more than $10 a share and Joe Kennedy had made at least $60,805, his share of the nearly $400,000 total profit reaped in just a few months. He invested some of his profits in real "repeal stocks" like Owens-Illinois and National Distillers, tripling his money on the latter by the end of the year.

By the time the LOF pool was quietly up and rolling, Kennedy had papered over his feud with Roosevelt. With friends counseling patience and his anger cooling, he sent FDR a telegram in March 1933 praising the work of the new administration. In mid-May, Roosevelt had sent a personal reply: "I have been meaning for some time to write to you and tell you of my real appreciation of all that you did during the campaign. I need not tell you how helpful you were, to say nothing of the joy you added when things were most difficult." He invited Kennedy to visit the Oval Office on his next trip to Washington, and Kennedy did so.

"Hello, Joe," Roosevelt boomed. "Where have you been all these months? I thought you got lost."

The conversation was cordial but subdued. There still was no room in the Roosevelt administration for the Wall Street speculator.

There was, however, room for Joe Kennedy in the hearts of some important people around Roosevelt. In the spring of 1933, Kennedy deepened his relationship with Ray Moley, even offering to help raise private funds to defray Moley's living expenses while he served in Washington. Moley declined the offer, but did not condemn Kennedy's ethics for making it. Kennedy also courted Missy LeHand, the presidential secretary he had charmed on the campaign trail with special side trips and seats for a World Series game when FDR's train paused in Chicago. And he utterly dazzled young James Roo-

sevelt, the president's twenty-six-year-old son. Jimmy Roosevelt had
political ambitions and a thirst for financial success, but was "naïve
and inexperienced," as the astute Roosevelt aide Tommy Corcoran
put it. Kennedy quietly steered business to Jimmy Roosevelt's insurance agency in Boston and hinted at financial support for future
campaigns. In February 1933, as the stony silence from FDR continued, Rose and Joe entertained young Roosevelt's wife and sister-in-
law in Palm Beach—James was invited but couldn't make it. In the
summer of 1933, Kennedy invited the couple to the family's sprawling seaport home in Hyannis Port, Massachusetts.

In September 1933, it was front-page news when the young Roosevelts set off from New York for a European trip on the luxury liner
Europa. Before boarding, they gathered at the Roosevelt townhouse
on East Sixty-fifth Street for a "bon voyage" family dinner. Also
traveling that night on the *Europa* were Joe and Rose Kennedy, and
their oldest son, Joe Jr. Press accounts noted that the Kennedys were
"the only outsiders invited to the family reunion and dinner" at the
Roosevelt home.

Kennedy had his own agenda for his London visit: tying down a
valuable liquor distribution contract for his new business venture,
Somerset Importers. He hoped the Distillers Company Ltd. would
tap him as the exclusive importer of its Haig & Haig Scotch, Gordon's Dry Gin, and Dewar's White Label Scotch. When the Kennedys and Roosevelts arrived in London, Joe took Jimmy along for
lunch with one of the Distillers executives—but it's likely the meeting impressed the young Roosevelt more than he impressed his
British host. Joe Kennedy already had a formidable reputation in
London as a movie industry dealmaker; he was an ideal partner for
any distiller eager to reenter the vast American market after Prohibition. Besides having ties to FDR that predated his presidency,
Kennedy "was fabulously wealthy with abundant cash to spend. He
was a brilliant businessman and a consummate salesman and pro-
moter who could be counted on to get the whiskey into the right
hands—for the right price," one biographer would note. After he
secured the deal, Kennedy steered the business of insuring the liquor
shipments to his young friend, a continuation of his prior patronage.

Their unequal friendship would later give rise to reports that James Roosevelt had been the key to Kennedy's liquor industry success, but that is simply not credible. Kennedy did not need the president's son by his side to advertise his New Deal ties. He got his federal import licenses, expanded into domestic rum production, and made another enormous fortune on his own, as he had done on Wall Street and in Hollywood before he had met any of the Roosevelts.

The new liquor business, begun during Kennedy's long pout over his exclusion from FDR's administration, would be just as successful as his earlier ventures. "Until 1946, when Kennedy sold the company, Somerset would function as the family cash cow," wrote one biographer.

BY THE END OF 1933, those working on Roosevelt's financial reforms were facing a changed political landscape. As one legal historian noted, the first hundred days of FDR's presidency were "that rare time when money talked and nobody listened." But after failing to block the 1933 act, the old guard warriors on Wall Street had rallied to Dick Whitney's flag to battle any further regulation—although the Pecora hearings showed the work of reform was far from done.

At Yale, Bill Douglas watched with envy as several associates found jobs with the New Deal. He decided to make himself an expert on the new securities act. He initially defended the law, noting in a lengthy letter to the editor of *The New York Times* that "the bankers and the issuing corporations can take care of themselves. But the investors cannot." But by the end of 1933, he had joined the chorus of those who argued that the law didn't go far enough to protect investors from Wall Street's predatory culture. He favored a regulatory effort to change that culture, which he said showed an "amazing absence of social consciousness on the part of directors and business executives."

Douglas's attacks on the law from the sidelines infuriated its co-author Jim Landis, who complained bitterly to Frankfurter. His mentor replied that Douglas was trying to appeal to "the people in the big offices and the business schools, among whom he likes to appear a sound and knowing fellow." In reality, Douglas was trying to appear "a sound and knowing fellow" to the New Dealers working for Roosevelt, but the thin-skinned Landis nursed a long grudge.

In their small New York offices, Ferdinand Pecora and his staff worked through the Senate's summer recess in 1933; there seemed to be no end to the evidence of "bankers behaving badly." But the abuses Pecora examined in the fall were arguably more significant to future American investors than anything exposed in the flamboyant Morgan hearings in the spring.

On October 2, 1933, Clarence Dillon, the founder of Dillon, Read & Co., was called to testify. Pecora covered some familiar ground: Dillon's firm had run sixty-five manipulative stock pools between 1927 and 1931, and had kept bondholders in the dark about an electrified railroad in Brazil that was financed but never built.

But some of the most illuminating testimony focused on how Dillon's firm had used, and abused, the investment trusts it created and controlled.

In the 1920s, mutual funds came in two varieties. Open-ended funds constantly issued and redeemed their own shares, just as modern mutual funds do. Closed-end funds, called "investment trusts," issued a fixed number of shares that traded on the stock exchange, a forerunner of the modern exchange-traded funds (ETFs). Of course, both types of funds used their investors' money to buy a diverse portfolio of securities. But investors in an open-ended fund could sell their shares directly to the fund at a price determined by the daily closing prices of the securities in the portfolio. Investors in the closed-end investment trusts had to sell their shares in the open market for whatever they would fetch—which might be a fraction of their portfolio value in a market panic. These closed-end trusts had boomed during the great bull market but had been a disaster for investors since the 1929 crash.

For years, an unregulated Wall Street had played greedy games with the money Americans put into these investment trusts. Dick Whitney himself had seen how partners at Prince & Whitely, the NYSE firm that sank into scandal in 1930, had used their control over an affiliated investment trust to arrange a "loan" of trust assets to their failing and corrupt brokerage firm. In the spring of 1931, Whitney had publicly urged investment trusts to be more forthcoming with investors, saying "publicity and publicity alone can prevent evil practices." But in the fall of 1933, Pecora demonstrated just how common and damaging such "evil practices" were.

By holding all the voting shares and selling nonvoting shares to the public, Dillon's firm could control its investment trusts without chipping in more than a small fraction of their own capital. That let the firm use the trusts as piggy banks to finance its own deals, purchase shares its partners wished to unload, or gain leverage over other corporations. In one case exposed by Pecora, Dillon used $10 million earned by one trust—which could have gone out as dividends to its shareholders—to buy a controlling stake in a second investment trust, created and sold to the first trust by Dillon's firm for reasons Dillon could not adequately explain. One financially savvy senator was stunned. Using one trust's assets to buy control of another trust for the sole benefit of Dillon's firm was "rotten ethics" and "reprehensible," he told Dillon, who casually replied that he saw no reason, even in hindsight, to have done anything differently.

In another dubious transaction, the firm sold two blocks of nearly busted railroad shares to the trust during the worst weeks of the 1929 crash, leaving a trustee trying to explain later to Pecora why he thought it was a good idea for the trust to *buy* those specific shares at the same moment that his brilliant investment advisors at Dillon's firm thought it was a good idea to *sell* them.

"I know they believed in railroad shares at that time," the trustee said vaguely.

Pecora asked, "If they believed in railroad shares at that time, will you explain why they parted with their railroad shares at the time to your investment trust?"

"That I don't know," the trustee admitted.

Dillon was not unique. Cyrus Eaton, a famous Chicago investor, forced an investment trust he controlled to take out a loan to buy some securities that Eaton's brokerage firm had to unload. Samuel Insull, Eaton's rival tycoon in Chicago, used two captive investment trusts as tools to secure his own control of his public utility empire, as his son admitted under questioning from Pecora. The House of Morgan turned its United Corporation, an investment trust that promised shareholders a diverse portfolio, into a vast undiversified utility holding company. Between 1929 and 1933, more than three dozen NYSE member firms promoted their own investment trusts for listing on the exchange, a conflicted arrangement that Dick Whitney had tried to curb, without much success.

Indeed, Otto H. Kahn, the head of the Kuhn, Loeb investment house, belatedly conceded to Pecora from the witness chair that there should be "a general rule" that "investment trusts must deal at arm's length with every comer, including those who created it."

Despite the damage these investment trust abuses inflicted on modestly affluent investors, Washington reporters apparently weren't interested. By the early fall of 1933, the Pecora hearings had slipped from the front pages to the financial pages.

Then, in October, Pecora squared off against another Wall Street statesman and his investigation was back on the front page. Albert H. Wiggin, another of the banking lords who had financed Dick Whitney's exploits on Black Thursday, was known as "the most popular banker in Wall Street." He was certainly one of the best paid. He had retired as Chase National Bank's chairman in December 1932, but he still held paid positions on nearly five dozen corporate boards and served on the executive committee of the Federal Reserve Bank of New York while collecting lavish retirement income from Chase.

Based on earlier hearings, reporters may have expected to learn that Wiggin had dodged his taxes. But, in fact, he had written remarkably large checks to the IRS. Digging deeper to find the source of that income, Pecora found Wiggin had used private shell companies not just to profit personally from pool manipulations but also to profit from the decline of his own bank's shares by selling those shares short. This was a stunning act of malpractice, since a bank chairman's only priority should have been to see his bank prosper, not to see its share price decline so he could collect more than $10 million in short-sale profits.

Wiggin explained his unscrupulous actions as a product of "the times," as if the roaring bull market of the 1920s had trampled on Wall Street's ethical judgment without anyone realizing it. Kuhn, Loeb's Otto Kahn similarly acknowledged that Wall Street's past was nothing to be proud of—but also was nothing that required immediate federal regulation. "We were all sinners," he told Pecora. "If we indulge again in practices that are socially, economically, and—from the point of view of the country—undesirable, I think the policeman ought to be ready to step in."

These revelations in late 1933 seemed to cause lawmakers on Capitol Hill more dismay than outrage. Perhaps lawmakers were beginning to doubt whether any banker's behavior over the past decade could withstand public scrutiny. The uneasy senators wanted Pecora to get back to the original mission, a study of the methods and machinery of the New York Stock Exchange.

And Pecora was ready. His staff had been gathering evidence for months. They had prepared a questionnaire for the exchange's member firms, but Dick Whitney had refused to distribute it. Flushed with rage, he had told two Pecora staffers who came to his office: "You gentlemen are making a great mistake. The exchange is a perfect institution." Pecora had sent the questionnaire out on his own, and his staff spent months analyzing the financial data it produced, adding up commissions and profits, documenting conflicts and careless oversight, and tracking the manipulative trading that persisted to that very moment.

Besides placating his Senate bosses, Pecora was making a strategic choice by turning his spotlight to the stock exchange. His entire mission had been to build an ironclad case for regulating Wall Street—and the regulation of stock exchanges was moving to the forefront of the Roosevelt agenda.

ROOSEVELT HAD SET HIS advisors to work on a stock exchange bill soon after the 1932 election, seeing it as a necessary companion to his "truth in securities" proposal. That effort had slowed during the summer of 1933. By the fall of that year, Roosevelt was determined to get a workable exchange regulatory bill he could send to Congress early in 1934. But as he often did, FDR had put several teams to work on drafting legislation, letting them fight over the details before he finally stepped in with his own preferences. And the fights that fall and winter were long, complex, divisive, and deeply frustrating for dedicated reformers like Jim Landis and Ferdinand Pecora. Roosevelt's Commerce Department set up an advisory committee strongly tilted toward Wall Street and produced a timid proposal that Whitney himself could have drafted. A more credible effort was drafted by a former FTC chairman, but it was deemed unworkable by Sam Rayburn in the House. Finally, an ad hoc team came together: some senior Pecora staffers, some young FTC aides, the new FTC commissioner Jim Landis, and his two colleagues from the 1933 battle, Ben Cohen and Tommy Corcoran.

After more than a dozen revisions and countless sleepless nights and weekends, the team came up with a regulatory plan they considered very tough but still practical. The bill would have required all exchanges to register with the FTC, which would have sweeping powers over their rules; it also would have regulated margin trading, set debt limits for member firms, banned pools and other manipulative practices, and barred exchange members from trading both for themselves and for public customers. Reflecting FDR's reliance on sunshine, the bill required corporate insiders to disclose their trades in company stock and listed precisely what financial information corporations had to disclose. The draft, called the Fletcher-Rayburn Bill, was introduced in the House and the Senate in mid-February 1934—and Wall Street exploded, loudly condemning the bill as drastic, draconian, deadly for capital markets, and ruinous to corporate America.

As on Black Thursday in 1929, Dick Whitney became the face and voice of Wall Street, expressing its implacable opposition to this New Deal regulatory effort. He rented a Washington mansion, instantly dubbed "the Wall Street Embassy," where his senior staff and a team of lawyers and lobbyists pressed their case in potentially sympathetic corners of the capital. He met personally with the Commerce Department panel, persuading its more conservative members that "self-regulation" was a better approach than the pending bill; the group ultimately proposed "a weak and friendly" industry-dominated oversight board and left the exchanges largely free to police themselves. Whitney expanded his attack to include not only the proposed stock exchange bill but also the "truth in securities" law passed the previous year, claiming that it was responsible for sluggish activity on Wall Street. Unless there was an immediate U-turn toward deregulation, he claimed, the Depression would persist and Wall Street would become "a deserted village." He wrote the CEO of every corporation listed on the NYSE, urging them to register their opposition with Congress and they had forcefully done so. The pressure reached down to low-level corporate employees, who dutifully followed orders and sent their own protests to Washington.

At every opportunity, Whitney insisted that stock exchanges could police themselves without any interference from government bureaucrats. Indeed, he staged a bit of "self-regulatory" theater in February 1934 by having the NYSE board of governors approve new rules he claimed were more stringent than anything the New Deal was proposing. The rules explicitly barred members from profiting from manipulative pools and curbed how specialists could use the inside information they had about the flow of market orders. A compliant press corps did not ask Whitney why these rules had not been imposed years earlier or whether they would be enforced with more vigor than the rules that were supposed to have deterred specialist Michael Meehan from helping to run the RCA pool in March 1929.

To drive home the point that the NYSE was derelict at self-regulation, Pecora produced evidence that, as recently as the previous summer, exchange members were running successful pools to puff up certain liquor-industry stocks—and the exchange had done nothing about it. The pool that enriched Joe Kennedy was just one example trotted out in these hearings.

But Whitney was gaining ground. He met with representatives of thirty brokerage firms to encourage them to enlist in the battle. He organized nearly fifty thousand employees of brokerage firms in New York City to add their protests. At his urging, New York brokerage firms reached out to their regional offices to solicit further opposition. "Congressmen reported receiving vast numbers of letters, telephone calls, and telegrams," decrying the bill's "wholesale 'goose-step' regimentation" of American business, one historian noted. Even some who favored stock exchange regulation began to express doubts about whether this bill was the best way to proceed. Public and congressional support for the legislation began to melt away. By March 5, the first version of FDR's stock exchange bill was dead.

Franklin Roosevelt's credibility and the momentum of his financial reform agenda were both in peril. FDR firmly believed federal regulation was the only way a tone-deaf Wall Street could ever regain the public's trust and prosper again. The end was not in doubt, merely the means. Recalling advice he'd gotten from President Wilson, Roosevelt shrugged off the Democratic infighting over the bill, saying that "Republicans never want to do anything, so they're always united. But we Democrats want to do things" and get "disunited" over *how* to do them.

Rather than give up on his reform promises, he "assumed personal direction of the effort to rewrite the bill." With Landis at his side to provide the legislative language, FDR quickly negotiated practical compromises with the Federal Reserve Board, his own Treasury Department, leading investment and commercial bankers, and even with a few reform-minded members of the NYSE itself. He bent far enough to accept some amendments to the Securities Act of 1933. But he refused to drop the stock exchange bill or fatally weaken it, and he put Landis in charge of vetting any changes to the 1933 law to ensure they did not impair its mission.

On March 19, 1934, a new version of the Fletcher-Rayburn Bill was introduced in the House, with Roosevelt's considerable political muscle behind it. "The country as a whole will not be satisfied with legislation unless such legislation has teeth in it," and this bill did, he told its congressional sponsors in a letter on March 26. He added a warning: "I do not see how any of us could afford to have it weakened in any shape, manner, or form."

The revised bill was a web of compromises. Like the original, it required all stock exchanges to register with the government and get approval for their rule books; it also prohibited specific manipulative trading practices. To win support from New Dealers, it left the securities laws under the administration of the Federal Trade Commission, rather than under the weak oversight board Whitney favored. It gave the Federal Reserve the power to set margin loans within statutory limits, but to reassure Wall Street, the effective date of that rule was postponed to give margin traders time to adapt. It allowed exchange members to trade both for their own account and for customers, but ordered a study of how to address that inherent conflict in the future. But as Roosevelt warned, there would be no compromise on the fundamental goal: if the bill became law, the nation's stock exchanges were going to be regulated by a law "with some teeth in it."

The new bill was quietly accepted as workable and, indeed, inevitable by some on Wall Street. But three days after its introduction, Dick Whitney told Sam Rayburn the amended bill was no better than the original, and renewed his attack. He proposed a long list of changes but would not commit to supporting the bill if those changes were made. Further hearings were held, but Whitney never faltered in his opposition. Weary from the relentless attacks, Rayburn warned the Wall Street lobbyists: "There is going to be a bill of some kind, and we might as well make up our minds to that." But Whitney would not concede the point. In a personal letter to Roosevelt on April 12, Whitney repeated his claim that the new bill retained "many of the dangerous and deflationary features of the original bill and I am confident that its enactment would be a disaster." He appealed for another meeting with FDR.

This time, Roosevelt fobbed Whitney off on Jim Landis—who turned the meeting into a bit of New Deal theater by treating Whitney to a 45-cent lunch brought up to his office from the FTC canteen. Whitney was not disarmed: he repeated his exaggerated claims about the vast damage the exchange regulation bill would do to Wall Street. Encouraged by his opposition, a few conservative lawmakers warned that the bill would push the country "along the road from Democracy to Communism."

Speaking for the bill when it finally reached the House floor on April 30, Rayburn said that it had been drafted "under the pressure of the most vicious and persistent lobby that any of us have ever known in Washington." Whitney and his Wall Street forces "would, I am convinced, protest against it in any form so long as there was a tooth left in it."

Roosevelt and Rayburn had read the country far more accurately than Whitney had. As a Rayburn biographer would note, "The public was demanding that the stock markets be brought under government supervision, and only a handful of House members were willing to risk their own political future by taking Wall Street's side." The bill passed the House with only 84 votes against it. A slightly different Senate version passed easily, 62 to 13, on May 12. Despite Whitney's dire harangues against the bill, it left the economic architecture of the NYSE trading floor essentially intact. Specialists would remain at their posts and traders would remain temporarily free to pursue their own profits while handling customer orders, albeit with greater federal oversight.

The new law, which would go into effect on July 1, was "a marvel of irresolution," as one historian described it. Instead of laying out a list of "do's and don'ts," Congress gave those who would administer the law the task of writing new market rules as needed and called for studies of the corporate bankruptcy process and the amorphous over-the-counter stock market. But fundamentally, the law gave its administering agency "vague powers to use its discretion" in deciding how to regulate Wall Street.

The identity of that administering agency became the final bout in this wrestling match. Roosevelt told reporters he favored putting the FTC in charge, as Rayburn's House version proposed. But Senator Glass, who favored fragmented government as a defense against despotic government, got Senate support for the creation of a bipartisan five-member commission to administer the law—an idea already endorsed by Whitney and his allies, who felt sure they could capture any young agency trying to regulate them. Rayburn ultimately accepted the senator's idea, after being assured by Roosevelt that Wall Street would not dictate his appointments to the new body.

A defeated Dick Whitney tried to sound gracious, saying the

new act would be "a constructive measure" if it could be "ably, wisely and judiciously administered." He had just been elected to his fifth term as NYSE president. The floor traders and specialists who supported him made up roughly two-thirds of the governing board's membership. But there were a few exchange members—notably those whose firms dealt with members of the public—who were growing weary of his hostility toward the New Deal. They felt regulation was the price Wall Street must pay to regain the public's trust, and they began to talk privately about how to end Whitney's war with Washington.

On June 6, 1934, Roosevelt signed the Securities and Exchange Act, using several pens to do so. Jim Landis, so important to the survival of the bill, was out of town but FDR handed pens to three of his allies: Ferdinand Pecora, the driven Sicilian immigrant who had exposed Wall Street's sins; Ben Cohen, the brilliant Jewish lawyer with a gift for writing sound statutes; and Tommy Corcoran, the charming networker from "lace-curtain Irish" roots in Rhode Island. All three men had been summoned to Washington from the diverse edges of the legal profession to help challenge and change Dick Whitney's patrician and powerful Wall Street.

As Roosevelt handed the final pen to Pecora, he impishly asked, "Ferd, now that I have signed this bill and it has become law, what kind of a law will it be?"

Pecora replied, "It will be a good or bad bill, Mr. President, depending upon the men who administer it."

Who *would* administer it?

By law, FDR had to pick two Republicans. He chose FTC commissioner George C. Mathews and Judge Robert E. Healy, the FTC's general counsel. "Bud" Mathews, a forty-eight-year-old progressive in the midwestern mold, was a seasoned state railroad and utilities regulator with a strong background in accounting and a strong distaste for the reckless brand of capitalism exposed during the Roaring Twenties. At age fifty-one, Judge Healy—the tall, lean Vermonter pronounced it "Haley"—was an old-fashioned self-taught corporate lawyer who had served briefly on his state's supreme court. His national career was launched in 1928 when President Coolidge, looking for someone to whitewash a mandated investigation of the public utilities industry, made the mistake of thinking Bob Healy was the man to do that. For the next four years, Healy doggedly led FTC hearings that filled dozens of volumes with evidence of utility industry misdeeds. Roosevelt could hardly have found two Republicans more supportive of his reforms.

The other three members of the new stock exchange commission would be Democrats and one of those would be chairman. Most in the media expected the gavel to go to Jim Landis, the workaholic legal whiz, but he was a lightning rod for Republican anger toward the New Deal—Hoover's former secretary of state called him "the most dangerous man in the United States." In Congress, Pecora was seen as the logical chairman—and, according to his biographer, he himself thought he had the strongest claim to the job. On Wall Street, however, Pecora was perhaps the only candidate for chairman who could make Landis look acceptable. His exposure of Wall Street's sins had left deep scars.

Ray Moley, FDR's advisor, felt the first SEC chairman should be someone who at least had a chance of defusing Wall Street's resentment and resistance. Neither Landis nor Pecora could do that—but Moley thought he knew who could, if he would take the job.

The diplomacy began on April 12, 1934, before work on the law was completed. Returning to Washington from Miami, FDR paused his train trip in West Palm Beach for a quick, quiet parlor-car visit with Joe Kennedy. He invited Joe and Rose Kennedy to stay at the White House a few days later, and the two men talked deep into the night after the Gridiron Club dinner. Some weeks later, James Roosevelt made a telephone call to Hyannis Port, and at 5 P.M. on June 28, Kennedy was back at the White House. With Ray Moley looking on, the president indulged in hours of cat-and-mouse conversation before finally popping the question: Would Kennedy take on the chairmanship of Wall Street's new watchdog?

Kennedy cautioned that, during his long business career, he probably had "done plenty of things that people could find fault with."

Moley stepped in: "If anything in your career in business could injure the president this is the time to spill it."

Moley recalled that Kennedy responded with "a blue mist of pro-fanity," defied anyone to find a single "shady act" in his background, and then vowed to lead the SEC in a way "that would be a credit to the country, the President, himself and his family—clear down to the ninth child."

To many ardent and outraged New Dealers, Kennedy was a fox put in charge of the henhouse. But to Roosevelt, the very traits that disqualified Kennedy as Treasury secretary—his independence, his strong opinions, his take-charge personality, his demanding hands-on management style—made him the ideal choice for bring-ing the new watchdog agency to life. Kennedy also knew "all the tricks of the trade" that he would be regulating—"set a thief to catch a thief," FDR quipped. Kennedy was rich enough to be immune to the job's inevitable temptations. Best of all, he was a choice that would instantly disarm and confound Wall Street.

To FDR's New Dealers and much of the general public, Kennedy was one of Wall Street's own—but to Wall Street, Kennedy was what he had always been: an outsider who kept his secrets and played a solitary game.

Roosevelt announced his decision on June 30, naming Landis, Mathews, Healy, Pecora, and Kennedy to the new Securities and Exchange Commission. At Moley's request, he wrote a short note expressing his wish that Kennedy should serve as SEC chairman. But by law, the commissioners picked their own chairman—and at least two of them thought they had a better claim to the job than Kennedy did.

Kennedy had FDR's note in his pocket when he arrived at the FTC building two days later for the agency's first meeting. He would use it if he had to—but not even Roosevelt could guarantee that it would work.

CHAPTER FOUR

POWER TO THE PEOPLE

T
JULY 2, 1934–JANUARY 23, 1936

HE FEDERAL TRADE COMMISSION WAS HOUSED IN A SHABBY
temporary building on Constitution Avenue that had been built for
a war that ended in 1918. Exposed pipes crisscrossed the stained ceil-
ings; the smell of disinfectant hung in the hallways. The wiring was
dangerously old—an electrical fire in 1930 at a similar building
nearby had destroyed irreplaceable FTC records. But plug-in fans
and open windows were the only tools for coping with the heat that
baked the capital in early July 1934, driving temperatures in some
offices well over 100 degrees.

On Monday, July 2, reporters and photographers waited in an
airless hallway for the debut meeting of the still homeless Securities
and Exchange Commission. In theory, the five commissioners would
be quickly sworn in and would then elect their chairman. In reality,
the afternoon would be a tense face-off between New Deal purists
and White House realists.

A little before 3 P.M., Joe Kennedy limped in. Some weeks earlier,
he had fallen from a horse and broken his leg, but he was still jaunty
in a tan summer suit. He laughed off questions, headed into Bud
Mathews's office, closed the door to the press, and settled down to
get acquainted with Mathews and Judge Healy, the FTC's general
counsel.

Then, Ferdinand Pecora arrived from New York by way of Union
Station—sweaty, a little late, and grimly silent. At age fifty-two, he
didn't want to serve on the commission for very long; after two years

as a low-paid Senate counsel, he needed to revive his law practice and replenish his savings. But he was furious that he would not be chairman during his short SEC tenure. Without a word to reporters, Pecora followed Jim Landis into his office. Behind that closed door, Landis began the long, quiet process of persuading the legendary "hellhound of Wall Street" to change his mind about fighting publicly for the chairmanship.

The reporters in the stifling hallway grew more curious as the minutes wilted away. Perhaps the rumors of the past week were true; perhaps Pecora was defying FDR and refusing to defer to a stock market manipulator.

A few days earlier, Roosevelt had summoned Landis, Mathews, and Healy to his oval study upstairs at the White House and urged them "to take a good look at Kennedy" and keep an open mind. Roosevelt could go no further.

Joe Kennedy could, and had. He had made a quick morning call at the White House to get FDR's note endorsing his chairmanship, and then gone to the FTC to lobby Jim Landis.

Landis was just thirty-five, but seemed a decade older, with thinning hair, a stern profile, and an unseasonably dark suit on his lanky frame. But his mature manner hid his inner doubts. "Healy and Mathews would have voted for me," he later said. "They had confidence in me, more confidence than I had in myself." Could he win the trust of Wall Street? That "was a big question in my mind."

Kennedy, a decade older than Landis, had seemed boyish by comparison as he hobbled to the wooden chair Landis offered. Clearly unafraid of the Wall Street forces the agency sought to tame, Kennedy was full of energy for the task ahead. He had treated the moody Landis as a full partner in the adventure. They had talked for most of the morning. In his blunt, breezy way, Kennedy asked Landis to vote for him as chairman. "I was very impressed with him . . . [he] was the best man" for the job, Landis later recalled. Landis had shared his views with Mathews and Healy, who accepted his judgment. Thus, by midday, Kennedy had the votes he needed.

But to be elected chairman without the support of Pecora, the crusading knight of the New Deal hard-liners, would be a terrible way to begin. The SEC had to be credible to both the suspicious Wall Street leaders who hated Roosevelt and the angry Roosevelt voters who hated Wall Street. To do that, Kennedy needed more than a four-vote majority; he needed Pecora.

In that second New Deal summer, America's markets were becalmed and befuddled. The months after the inauguration had seen a rebound that "was almost inconceivable to those battered by over three years of downdrift," one market historian wrote. Some measures of economic activity doubled and tripled before the end of 1933. The stock market rallied, with daily trading volume approaching 1929 levels and bond prices seeing an "explosive rise." The Dow index at the end of June 1934 was almost twice its pre-inauguration level.

But by the time the SEC opened for business in July 1934, Main Street and Wall Street had parted ways. The improving lives of average citizens made them more supportive of FDR. But the improving lives of America's capitalists made them less supportive of FDR—fiercely hostile, in fact. Wall Street, which had quietly prayed Roosevelt could save the financial system in March 1933, was now complaining bitterly about how he was going about it.

FDR had addressed corporate America's discontent in a speech in Green Bay, Wisconsin, in August 1934. He told the crowd he'd gotten a letter from a businessman urging that the only way to restore "confidence" was for him to abolish any form of government supervision over business—restoring "the unregulated wildcat banking of a century ago," the sale of "fraudulent securities and watered stock," and "stock manipulation which caused panics and enriched insiders." He added, "If we were to listen to him, the old law of the tooth and claw would reign once more. My friends, the people of the United States will not restore that ancient order."

In the absence of that restoration, however, Wall Street had simply refused to function, claiming the Securities Act of 1933 made it impossible for new securities to be issued. As an olive branch to the Street, FDR had accepted some amendments to the act, mostly to clarify how to establish liability for false statements made to investors. But perceived flaws in the 1933 law scarcely explained the market's paralysis. When four major railroad and municipal bond issues did not attract a single underwriter in late 1933, Wall Street predictably blamed that year's new securities law—although all four of those issues were *exempt* from the law. One trusted advisor told FDR, "I am personally convinced the bankers agreed amongst themselves not to bid on these bonds." Adolf A. Berle Jr., the FDR advisor with perhaps the strongest Wall Street ties, similarly believed "there has been a tacit understanding among security houses that no issues would be floated for the time being, pending revision of the Securities Act." So Roosevelt had signed the 1933 act amendments and for good measure tapped the market-savvy Joe Kennedy as SEC chairman, gestures of peace that he hoped would get the financial engines humming again.

But Wall Street had not met its side of the bargain. There was no uptick in new issues after the Securities Act amendments, just demands for more deregulation. If Kennedy couldn't cajole these pouting capitalists back into the market, congressional support for the New Deal's financial reforms could melt away.

Thus, Roosevelt knew how much was hanging on a unanimous vote for the chairmanship. It would give Kennedy the credibility he needed to be effective. Wall Street would see he had enough moderate support to temper any "radical" impulses from New Dealers; New Dealers would see Pecora's support as proof that Kennedy would be the tough watchdog Roosevelt promised.

But could Kennedy get Pecora's support? That was presently in the hands of Jim Landis.

Around 4 P.M. on July 2, Landis put his head into Mathews's office and asked Kennedy to follow him to his own office, four doors away. There, he let Pecora make one last attempt to wheedle away the gavel, at least for the next few months.

Kennedy calmly explained his refusal was not personal, but also was not negotiable. "Roosevelt has decided that I am to be chairman," he kept insisting, "so I have no authority to make the trade." Pecora tried other arguments, other trade-offs; none would move his rival from that position. The FTC building grew silent as its staff headed home.

Finally, Landis and his two colleagues emerged. Kennedy and

Pecora led the way down the hall to Mathews's office "as chipper as two long-parted and suddenly reunited brothers," as one reporter put it. Ultimately, Pecora was a loyal Democrat; he had bowed, at last, to FDR's expressed wishes. An FTC notary swore them in, a quick executive session was held, and the stock market speculator was unanimously, if improbably, put in charge of Uncle Sam's first effort to be "the cop on Wall Street."

When the reporters came back in, Pecora smilingly shook off questions about the closed-door delay. "I will try and do my part to put the child on its feet," he said. He would later say of Kennedy, "I like him immensely . . . he knows how to do things."

Kennedy was equally gracious toward Landis and Pecora. At his first desk-side press conference, his shirtsleeves pushed above his elbows, he told reporters, "I'm no sucker." His two colleagues "know more about this law than I ever hope to know. They put their blood into it."

FROM HIS FIRST DAY as SEC chairman, Kennedy did what FDR needed him to do. He treated Wall Street with reason and respect but he did not abandon New Deal reforms. "We are not going ahead under the presumption that everybody connected with finance is a criminal," he told the press. "No honest man need fear that our commission will do anything that will harm him." But he also warned that the SEC would not tolerate dishonest dealings. He was unsparing—indeed, brazen—in condemning the Street's past sins, some of which he had committed. "The days of stock manipulation are over," he said. "Our ideas have changed. Things that seemed all right a few years ago find no place in our present-day philosophy."

As for the doubts of the New Dealers, Kennedy gave his personal pledge that the SEC would do the job as FDR intended. "Boys," he told reporters, "I've got nine kids. The only thing I can leave them that will mean anything is my good name and reputation. I intend to do that, and when you think I'm not doing so, you sound off."

Surprising his critics, Kennedy set a high bar for the agency's ethics. As soon as he accepted FDR's appointment, Kennedy put his own investments in trust "under the explicit provision that no change whatever was to be made" in the portfolio for so long as he served on the SEC. His care may have helped mute the criticism when, on July 16, his role in the previous summer's Libbey-Owens-Ford pool was cited in the Pecora committee's final report to the Senate. It surely helped that Pecora, no doubt determined to spare the infant agency any scandal, quietly stood by him after the report came out. On July 6, the SEC adopted an ethics code requiring employees to report all their trades within forty-eight hours, barring them from buying stocks on margin, and banning any trades based on information they got on the job—a rule that would later be tightened to forbid them from buying any security registered with the SEC.

Kennedy was seen as "capable of getting a tough job done without continual plucking at the presidential coat sleeve," as one historian put it. He reassured hard-liners by hiring several of Pecora's Senate investigators and the entire FTC securities division Landis had assembled. He further soothed Landis and Pecora by giving each man the SEC portfolio he most desired. Landis, the consummate draftsman and legal scholar, would oversee rule making and in-depth studies; Pecora, the tireless bloodhound, would supervise investigations of manipulation and misbehavior on the nation's stock exchanges.

Kennedy also tried to placate the less visible forces opposing him, including Tommy Corcoran and Ben Cohen, who helped draft FDR's market reforms. Over lunch in the tree-shaded garden of the popular Tally Ho Restaurant at Seventeenth and H Streets, Kennedy disarmingly asked: "Why do you fellows hate me?" He assured them "he was not predisposed to Wall Street, that he knew there were others with more knowledge of the law than he had, and that he would build a first-rate staff." It broke the ice, a bit. Kennedy also consulted their mentor Felix Frankfurter on personnel decisions— the role the professor most loved to play—and on drafting key speeches.

Frankfurter stood on one side of an ideological fault line running through the administration's vision of American business. He and his allies stood with aging Supreme Court justice Louis Brandeis, who believed "bigness," not badness, was the root of the evils that produced the 1929 crash and the Great Depression. The Brandeis circle, to simplify greatly, wanted the New Deal to use antitrust laws and tax policy to break Big Business into smaller businesses and then leave them more or less alone. On the other side of the divide, advisors like Adolf Berle and Ray Moley believed bigness was inevitable as America grew into a global economic power, and the New Deal's job was to prevent Big Business from becoming "bad business."

Joe Kennedy and Franklin Roosevelt were not locked into either camp. Although Roosevelt admired and cherished both Brandeis and Frankfurter, he needed workable ideas for building a healthier, fairer economy and he didn't much care which side produced them. As for the supremely practical Kennedy, he was ready to regulate the business world as he found it, in the belief that *bad* business, big or small, could be cured only with strong federal oversight.

Kennedy's effort to build an agency to provide that oversight was a masterpiece of public service.

He found the agency a home of its own in a building at Eighteenth Street and Pennsylvania Avenue, a short walk from the White House. He waged skillful bureaucratic warfare with the FTC to claw back money it had gotten to handle the 1933 act, work the SEC was now doing. He wrangled with Roosevelt's conservative budget bureau to get a hefty increase in the agency's second-year funding. He courted financial editors, soothed angry lawmakers, and defended his staff from unfair attacks, whether from witless ill-informed critics or from senior members of Congress—who, occasionally, were the same people.

As a haven from his workaholic habits, Kennedy leased Marwood, a vast chateau along the Potomac River built on the scale of a boutique hotel. It had fourteen bedrooms and baths, a lobby-sized living room, a game room in the cool basement, a hundred-seat movie theater in the even cooler subbasement—and a new elevator, put in at Kennedy's expense, to ease FDR's visits.

As he promised, Kennedy assembled a first-rate staff of young securities lawyers and corporate accounting experts, maneuvering deftly through civil service rules that had no job classification for "experts who could read the ticker tape," Landis recalled. For the critical post of general counsel, he drafted Judge John J. "Johnny" Burns of Boston, a bright Harvard Law School graduate who, at age thirty-three, had been the youngest jurist ever named to the Massachusetts Superior Court. Kennedy knew Burns was close to Frankfurter and would therefore have his pick of Harvard's brightest law graduates.

As usual, the office next to his own was occupied (again, at Kennedy's expense) by his longtime confidant Edward E. Moore, an immensely likeable Irish Democratic workhorse in Boston's municipal government whom Kennedy had hired away from his father-in-law in 1920. Kennedy had come to value this quietly efficient aide so highly that he named his youngest son, born in February 1932, in Moore's honor. Kennedy also hired three other capable friends—all hardworking Irish Catholics from Boston. After they were on board, he jokingly decreed "No more Irish! This place is beginning to look like the Irish Free State Embassy."

Finally, at the suggestion of Landis, he hired Yale law professor Bill Douglas to lead the agency's congressionally mandated study of corporate bankruptcies. By law, the SEC had to come up with a plan for reforming the so-called "protective committees" that were key to the bankruptcy process. These committees were supposed to protect shareholders and creditors but Douglas knew they were often manipulated by corporate insiders, their bankers, and their lawyers.

It is a testament to Landis's loyalty to the new agency that he put Douglas forward for the job. The two young men almost magnetically repelled each other. To the serious, scholarly Landis, Douglas seemed flippant and crude; to the brash, ribald Douglas, Landis seemed prissy and humorless. But by 1934, Douglas was the most authoritative expert on corporate reorganizations in the country— and Joe Kennedy insisted that the SEC hire only the best.

For Douglas, the job offer was a consolation prize. He'd hoped to be an SEC commissioner, a better paid position, but he was never even considered by those advising FDR. He was in debt, as usual, so he could not trade his Yale salary for a low-paid staff job, even though it might give him a better shot at the next commission appointment. Douglas daringly told Landis he could only accept the SEC post if he could work part-time and keep his Yale job—and his reputation was such that Landis agreed.

Douglas later recalled going to the SEC chairman's temporary office in the FTC building for the first time. He found the shirt-sleeved Kennedy at work at his desk.

"What instructions do you have for me?" Douglas asked.

Kennedy barked: "Instructions? If I knew what to do, why in hell would I get you down here?"

With the audacity of a man with tenure at Yale, Douglas said he was shocked at his tiny budget and asked for more money. Kennedy turned silently back to the work on his desk. After a few moments, he looked up. "Well, what in hell are you waiting for? Get going."

Douglas got going.

As a part-timer, he needed a strong chief of staff in Washington. He tapped his former law student Abe Fortas, who had entered law school as a precocious twenty-year-old. Soon after graduation, Fortas went to work at the Agricultural Adjustment Administration under Jerome Frank, a spirited polymath who was for Yale's law graduates what Frankfurter was for Harvard's—a one-man clearing-house for New Deal jobs. A year later, Douglas lured him away to help run the protective committee study, which Fortas did by working more hours than seemed humanly possible.

The work ethic throughout the infant agency was prodigious. Kennedy himself set the pace, undistracted by family duties since Rose had no plans to move the children or herself to Washington. At Marwood, Kennedy rose early each working day, swam naked in his pool or took a vigorous horseback ride, and arrived at his office by 8:30 A.M., with Eddie Moore toting his laden briefcase. He expected his staffers to be at their desks from 9 A.M. until 5:30 P.M., but he and most of them put in far longer hours, energized by the monumental scale of work to be done. "We were remaking the world," one of them later recalled.

The tireless Landis kept up with Kennedy. In September 1935, as the deadline neared for corporations listed on the NYSE to register with the new agency, he had cots brought in so staffers could work around the clock to process the submissions. He once kept the offices open into the weekend so a West Coast company could file a new issue, one of Kennedy's top priorities. Old FTC forms were reviewed with Wall Street lawyers and accountants, and were simplified. Temporary trading rules were worked out with stock exchange professionals. The final rules were debated by the commissioners at the big table in Kennedy's office and adopted, usually with little dissent. When final registration rules were adopted for NYSE-listed securities, Adolf Berle praised them as a "nice accommodation of the balance between public interest as evidenced by the act and the private difficulties of business men."

The key message Kennedy wanted to deliver was that *regulation could work*—it could restore the public's faith in the marketplace and level the playing field for honest professionals, without stifling the necessary work of capitalism. Taking a cue from FDR's fireside chats, Kennedy arranged to make his case in a luncheon address on July 25 at the National Press Club in Washington, with a radio hookup to a much wider audience. According to *The New York Times*, Wall Street was so eager to hear Kennedy that some traders jokingly urged the NYSE to suspend trading during the speech.

Kennedy turned to two friends from the campaign trail, Ray Moley and prominent journalist Herbert Bayard Swope, to help him draft his debut address. Swope told him "to strike a note that is definitely your own—one that is marked by courage, by independence and by understanding of the job you have before you; also by a deep sense of fairness."

The speech was a solid success. "It is my belief that the investing public will find the markets to be firmer in their foundations because of the [SEC's] safeguards," he predicted. No one at the SEC believed that Wall Street businesses "must be harassed and annoyed and pushed around," he said, but there could be no repetition of the chicanery of the past.

The New York Times applauded the speech. Swope, too, must have expressed his approval because Kennedy sent him a jokey telegram that evening: "Whadya mean I done noble. You done noble. Everybody seems to have liked it. Give me a ring tonight."

Even Dick Whitney was complimentary: "I think Mr. Kennedy has shown that he is approaching his job carefully and from a sane and sound point of view." Indeed, Whitney publicly appeared to be accepting his new watchdog. His staff helped the listed firms register with the SEC and, as the deadline neared, he personally delivered a large suitcase full of completed forms to Washington. The NYSE also created a panel of nonvoting experts to advise its board and asked Adolf Berle to join. The press was quick to see the invitation to FDR's confidant as an olive branch, of sorts, toward the administration.

Berle himself must have worried that his acceptance would be interpreted as more presidential approval of the NYSE than FDR wanted to convey. He wrote Roosevelt to be sure he was comfortable with the step.

"I think it is absolutely all right to go on that Stock Exchange Board," Roosevelt wrote back. "As you and I know, the fundamental trouble with this whole Stock Exchange crowd is their complete lack of elementary education. I do not mean lack of college diplomas, etc., but just inability to understand the country or the public or their obligation to their fellow men." FDR added: "Perhaps you can help them to acquire a kindergarten knowledge of those subjects. More power to you!"

Whitney was a gracious host when Kennedy and his fellow commissioners made an official tour of the exchange on September 18, 1934. Well before the opening bell, the commissioners and a few senior aides arrived at Whitney's spacious paneled office. After some cordial conversation, Whitney led them down to the trading floor, where the day's business was under way. After about an hour of observation, Whitney escorted them to the exchange's peach-toned dining room for lunch.

But behind this apparent courtesy was a darker reality. By one account, Whitney had put security guards around the trading floor that day to protect the visitors from verbal abuse or physical attack by his own allies, whom he regularly inflamed with complaints about Roosevelt's rules.

Within a few months, it was clear that the nation's voters were squarely behind Roosevelt, however much Wall Street hated him. Democrats overwhelmingly won the 1934 midterm elections, a rousing cheer for how the New Deal was unfolding. The SEC's vigorous headline-making work surely helped Roosevelt's cause.

Voters expected FDR to keep his vow to reform Wall Street. For now, Kennedy was willing to let Whitney implement reform in his own way and at his own pace—so long as the reforms were made. In public, Whitney seemed agreeable; but in private, he was stalling, still insisting the stock exchange was "a perfect institution" just as it was.

This was not a debate that could be infinitely postponed. The SEC was required to report to Congress on how the nation's securities exchanges worked. The report Kennedy delivered on January 25, 1935, focused primarily on the NYSE because the nation's other thirty-three exchanges largely followed its lead. With mild language and no threats of coercion, it laid out eleven "suggestions" for reform.

The three most significant ones called on the NYSE to expand the voting power of members whose firms dealt directly with the public, to overhaul how it selected its board members and officers, and to improve how it dealt with members' misconduct.

Retail brokerage firms, those serving public customers, owned more than half the seats on the exchange, but their representatives held only about a third of the seats on its governing board. The rest were held by floor traders, specialists, and other "insiders." The SEC wanted that to change. It also wanted the exchange to make it easier for board candidates to be nominated from the floor. The current method—with Whitney's allies on the nominating committee picking other Whitney allies as board candidates—had resulted in "the self-perpetuation of the 'in' group," the SEC noted.

Finally, the report found fault with how the exchange disciplined its members. The exchange's arbitration committee handled complaints from the public, but it had no public members and its rule book violated "many canons of accepted judicial procedure." An aggrieved customer could not even get a copy of a member's answer to a complaint and thus couldn't challenge errors or lies. On the rare occasions when customers were invited to appear before the panel, they could not have a lawyer present without its permission, and an adverse ruling could not be appealed. Moreover, the exchange's powerful business conduct committee, which policed its members' financial integrity and daily behavior, had vast discretion over whether to punish a trader's sins. That power had been used in the past to "discourage protests or appeals" of its decisions, however arbitrary. All that should change, said the SEC.

These reforms were a direct threat to Dick Whitney's power. Some members at retail firms were already exasperated with his war on the New Deal; giving them more power on his board was the last thing he wanted to do. As for the nominating process, it was precisely how Whitney made sure his critics held only a small number of board seats. His control of the business conduct committee gave him a highly effective tool to reward allies and keep disgruntled members in line.

Whitney had assured his colleagues at the exchange that the SEC study "would find little fault with their organization," according to one report. Members were shocked to read instead that the SEC wanted it to take steps "looked upon as possibly shattering the present methods of administration." Furious, Whitney left for Washington to "confer with members of the commission."

When the report was first released, Kennedy had privately warned the NYSE reformers he expected them to stand with him. They claimed to support reform, he told them. "Now I want you to endorse the program and let Whitney and his (profane expletive) crowd go fry." Whitney's appeal was noted by the SEC, and politely ignored; he vaguely threatened to sue to block the reforms, if necessary.

In February 1935, Whitney and his friend, the exchange's outside counsel Roland L. Redmond, had renewed their lease on the Washington mansion for the coming congressional session. The "Wall Street Embassy" was back in service. Whitney also set up three nationwide radio addresses, part of an expanded public relations campaign to defend the status quo in the American market. Despite some minor reforms and conciliatory words, the old guard's battle with the New Deal was far from over.

IN FACT, IT WAS about to explode into one of the fiercest fights Roosevelt had yet faced, the battle to reform America's private power companies at the dawn of the Electric Century.

For Roosevelt, transforming the utility industry was the key to transforming the nation. Power plants were expensive to build and maintain. On top of that, the elaborate holding companies that owned those power plants needed huge amounts of cash to pay interest and dividends to investors—and high salaries and service fees to utility insiders. It had therefore become an article of faith in the industry and on Wall Street that it was better to sell luxury-priced power in monopoly markets than to sell cheap power in competitive markets. That formula, which had left 90 percent of the nation's farms without electricity even as the total output of electricity soared, was the crux of Roosevelt's concern. He knew electric power would be the lifeblood of the future economy. Where it flowed widely, abundantly, and affordably, states could prosper and their lowliest citizens could enjoy brighter, healthier, safer lives. Where electricity remained expensive, the affluent could enjoy and profit from its gifts but the rest of the country—rural farmers, small manufacturers, working families—could not.

Roosevelt knew in his soul that an economy that served only its richest citizens was unfair and, ultimately, incompatible with a healthy democracy. Those capitalists who controlled the nation's power supply would control the nation's future—indeed, nearly half the electricity generated in the country was already supplied by just three vast holding companies. Senator George W. Norris, a progressive Nebraska Republican, could have been speaking for Roosevelt with this prophecy: "When electricity becomes common in every home, as it will, and as necessary as water, if we are subjected to the will and wish of a giant monopoly that reaches from the Canadian boundary to the Gulf of Mexico and from ocean to ocean, we will in reality, to a great degree, be slaves."

But regulating private utilities would hit Wall Street right in its wallet because they were a mainstay of the financial markets. The largest of them dictated loan terms to their bankers and designed new securities for brokers to sell. Their stocks and bonds were tucked into countless trusts and portfolios. The mergers that created huge monopolies created a river of fees for investment bankers and their lawyers. Any federal action against these utility behemoths would be felt on every corner of Wall Street.

For years, the political power of utility holding companies had been sufficient to deflect any effort at reform. The smallest utility holding companies could influence the town halls and county seats where they did business; the largest ones had an iron grip on both state lawmakers and members of Congress. Laws they opposed died in committee. Their preferred candidates for state regulatory boards were appointed and confirmed. The campaign donations they made were decisive on Election Day. The boardroom seats, legal fees, and investment banking business they doled out were coveted. As the economy began to recover in 1933, the power trust's grip on public policy got stronger every day.

Before FDR, both political parties had been the utilities' willing allies, creating what Roosevelt saw as a "political standing army" for the industry. After a state GOP chairman in Albany became a utility executive and immediately began to lobby lawmakers, his successor in 1933 had famously warned: "The trouble is not that [the former party chairman] believes in the private ownership of public utilities, but that he apparently believes in the private ownership of the state government." Indeed, in FDR's first year as governor, the powerful chairman of the New York Senate's public utilities committee se- cretly had been on the payroll of a giant utility holding company, Associated Gas and Electric (AG&E). Utilities wielded similar power in Tammany Hall and in other big-city machines, "where there was always plenty of utility money and all the more or less hid- den influence that goes with it."

The public had been largely ignorant of the utility conglomerates' grip on the levers of state and local power. That had begun to change after 1928, thanks to the extensive FTC hearings led by Judge Healy, now one of the new SEC commissioners.

On January 27, 1935, the FTC sent Congress a scathing report urging federal action to curb the utility holding companies' unsound accounting, imprudent finances, and market manipulations. "It is not easy to choose words which will adequately characterize various ethical aspects of the situation without the appearance of undue severity," the report said. "Nevertheless, the use of words such as fraud, deceit, misrepresentation, dishonesty, breach of trust and oppression are the only suitable terms to apply."

State regulation was no solution, the FTC warned, because the utility holding companies were "so vast and so complex as to pass inevitably beyond effective state control." These giants of capitalism, in reality, had never been effectively regulated by the states and, without federal help, never could be.

These complaints echoed warnings experts had been making for nearly a decade. Since 1926, an influential economist named William Z. Ripley had publicly decried the utility industry's precarious capital structure and deceptive sales practices. An Investment Bankers Association panel had found that "a considerable number" of holding company prospectuses sent to investors "do not come up to the proper standard." The abuse of utility investors had been documented by Judge Healy at the FTC. Rickety holding companies had sold securities to customers with the specious assurance, "Push the button and if the light goes on, your money is safe." In reality, holding company securities were rarely secured by the output of the subsidiary power plants—which meant the lights could go on and investors could still lose their money. (The lights had stayed on in the Midwest in 1932 while Insull's failure had wiped out tens of thousands of investors.) Holding companies had deceptively persuaded investors to trade safe, fully secured bonds of local power companies for less secure bonds of some new holding company further up the corporate pyramid. Some utilities had skimped on the reserves needed to upgrade obsolete equipment and used the cash instead to pay bigger dividends to their holding company owners. Holding companies had sold vague and overpriced management or engineering services to their own subsidiaries, paying themselves at the expense of their customers and investors.

The final insult? Having hamstrung city and state regulators from one end of the country to the other, these same companies had glibly assured investors that "the red tape of regulation which surrounds the utility" was their best insurance "against any financial juggling" that would affect their investment. Nothing could have been further from the truth.

The FTC's findings, if not surprising to experts, were specific, well-documented, and remarkably free of hyperbole. The author of a 1937 book about the investigation said of Judge Healy: "He never asserted that it was wrong or dangerous to heap up five or six corporations, native to Delaware and Maine and resident in New York or Chicago, to finance and manage the distribution of electricity to the factories and homes of Tarpon Springs, Florida or Leesville, Louisiana. He merely asked why it was done that way."

The industry's answers had only rarely been persuasive, or even coherent. Indeed, one utility financier had acknowledged in an industry magazine in 1932 that "some practices indulged in [by holding companies] during the past must be eliminated in the future."

But even the experts had seemed shocked when the FTC turned its searchlight on the hidden "propaganda" campaign by which the power industry had long controlled the public debate over power policy.

Since 1919, utility conglomerates had quietly banded together to sell the American public on the idea that private for-profit power plants were vastly superior to publicly owned municipal power plants. Evidence in industry files showed that utilities had slanted the content of high school and college textbooks on economics, civics, and business; rewarded professors who supported private power and tried to silence those who didn't; denounced public critics as charlatans, socialists, or communists; ghostwritten false or inaccurate editorials and articles for local newspapers and misleading speeches for community leaders; secretly bought controlling stakes in some newspapers to insure favorable coverage of utility issues; secretly financed supposedly independent academic research; produced films and set up radio stations that promoted private power; and ordered their employees to send bogus "grassroots" telegrams and letters to keep lawmakers in line. The industry, determined to shape public opinion "from the cradle to the grave," had even provided kindergartens with 400,000 copies of a thirty-two-page color picture book called *The Ohm Queen.*

In November 1934, the FTC had told the Senate the industry "literally employed all forms of publicity except 'sky writing,' and frequently engaged in efforts to block full expression of opposing views." The cost of all this disinformation ultimately fell on the industry's customers.

By then, Judge Healy and Ben Cohen had started work on a draft of a utility regulatory bill for Roosevelt, aiming for reasonable registration and financial disclosure rules that might win at least some support in the industry. A few months later, Tommy Corcoran had joined them. A presidential demand for an overnight rewrite forced both Cohen and Corcoran to miss Ferdinand Pecora's swearing-in as a New York state judge on January 22, 1935, the day after his resignation from the SEC took effect.

Roosevelt also arranged to meet with three industry leaders to hear their views. One was Wendell Willkie, president of the Commonwealth & Southern system, which had been largely free of the industry's worst abuses. Two other holding company executives were there, but Willkie held the floor.

An FDR aide in the room saw Willkie getting increasingly angry as Roosevelt listed the industry's abuses. "Finally, [Willkie] took his glasses out of his breast coat pocket and using them as a pointer, he leaned over . . . pointing this object at the president as he spoke." The aide was shocked at Willkie's discourtesy. The other two industry executives reacted "as if Willkie had suddenly produced a gun and started shooting," the aide said.

Willkie challenged Roosevelt: "Do I understand then that any further efforts to avoid the breaking up of utility holding companies are futile?"

"It is futile," the president answered.

Roosevelt's frustration was evident. On the Far Left, he already faced the erosion of support from socialist-leaning liberals, a growing American Communist Party, and the rise of powerful demagogues like Senator Huey Long of Louisiana, who complained that FDR wasn't doing enough to "share the wealth." On the Far Right, he faced a revival of the upper-class fascist flirtations of the early 1930s, this time with growing support from less tolerant working-class voters drawn by the fascists' racial and religious bigotry. And across the spectrum, there was this implacable resistance from most of the business community.

"To every problem, [business leaders] offered a single answer— the restoration of 'confidence' through balancing the budget, halting reform, and reducing government regulation," he complained.

Impatient progressives cited all this as proof that American business would never reconcile itself to federal regulation and that FDR should just march forward without its support. Some of them urged a government takeover of the entire utility industry.

Roosevelt, who was a "socialist" only in the eyes of enraged conservatives, refused to go that far. But he had wrestled with unrestrained utility industry power for most of his political life, and the holding company bill was where he drew the line on concessions to business. He believed utility holding companies wielded far too much power over the nation's future and should be eliminated. Attempts to change his mind, as he had told Willkie, seemed to be "futile."

With Ben Cohen and Judge Healy still working on a moderate bill for regulating holding companies, FDR put other lawyers to work drafting a bill that would abolish them, largely through a federal tax on upstream dividends. His hard-line approach was gaining support in an increasingly fractious Congress.

Ben Cohen believed abolition was simply impractical. "Although the abuses connected with the holding company have been great . . . huge amounts of capital tied up in holding companies cannot readily be untied," he wrote Judge Healy in late November 1934. His initial draft required holding companies to register with the SEC, disclose their financial architecture, get prior SEC review of new securities and acquisitions, and avoid excessive pyramid-style growth. Landis and Corcoran helped Cohen polish his bill, and by mid-January, they were ready to hand it to Roosevelt.

Advocates of abolition pushed back, knowing FDR was leaning in their direction. On February 5, 1935, Cohen and Corcoran were summoned to the White House for another tug-of-war, where they were "virtually alone in arguing for moderation." Cheerfully stubborn, Roosevelt continued to endorse abolition. Making clear and logical arguments, Cohen quietly but firmly held his ground and Roosevelt—as always, a practical crusader—finally accepted the Cohen bill as a starting point, with two presidential revisions. One was cosmetic: he wanted a tough litany of holding company abuses written into the bill. The other was fundamental: he wanted to give the SEC the power to dismantle any holding company that, by January 1, 1940, had not shown that it served a valid economic purpose in the operation of the underlying utilities.

This provision, which the utility industry deftly dubbed "the death sentence," became the front line of a long legal fight. It also caused some private skirmishing within the SEC. No fan of holding companies, Joe Kennedy nevertheless was sympathetic to the outcry from their investors and uneasy about the power the bill gave the SEC, views that Landis apparently shared. Both Cohen and Corcoran had also opposed FDR's "death sentence" clause, but they were too loyal to say so publicly. Cohen wryly wrote a friend, "Tom and I will be branded as dangerous radicals again, although we are in fact about the only real conservatives in Washington." They made Roosevelt's alterations. On February 6, 1935, Senator Burton K. Wheeler and Representative Sam Rayburn introduced the Public Utility Holding Company Act of 1935, known as the Wheeler-Rayburn Bill.

The utility holding company industry—a behemoth with at least 24 million customers, millions of investors, more than $18 billion in assets, and a national lobbying operation that was second to none—immediately denounced the bill. Striding up and down at one congressional hearing, Willkie brushed off past holding company abuses

as "foolish things" a few greedy executives had done in "a crazy period" on Wall Street—things that had never been done by responsible holding companies like his, and that would surely never be
done by *any* holding company in the future. As Whitney had claimed
about stock market regulation, Willkie warned that if this bill were
to pass, it would throw an essential industry "into a chaos of liquidation and receiverships" that would savage investors and lead to the
outright nationalization of the power business.

Rayburn must have rolled his eyes. Once again, "flagrant abuses
were freely confessed, yet the high financiers were not willing to
recommend effective reforms to prevent the repetition of such
abuses." He and every other member of Congress were sent lists of
utility investors in their districts as a warning not to vote against the
utilities' interests, and spines began to weaken.

But then Roosevelt weighed in. On March 12, 1935, he sent Congress a message saying the Wheeler-Rayburn Bill would curb a dangerous source of economic tyranny. His argument became a rallying
cry for the bill's supporters. "I am against [the] *private socialism* of
concentrated economic power as thoroughly as I am against governmental socialism," he wrote. "The one is equally as dangerous as the
other."

THAT SAME WEEK IN March, the danger of concentrated power
was also on the mind of John Wesley Hanes II, a wealthy stockbroker from North Carolina. The power that Hanes had in mind was
that wielded by Dick Whitney in the boardroom of the New York
Stock Exchange.

On paper, Hanes looked like a plantation version of Whitney's
hunt-country squire. An heir to a southern tobacco dynasty, he was
a rising partner at Charles D. Barney & Co., with a brother who was
already a powerful banker back home. Hanes was close to the House
of Morgan and had already warned Tom Lamont that the NYSE's
hard line against the New Deal was bad for business. But Dick
Whitney, apparently thinking Hanes was a reliable ally, let him join
the NYSE board and its nominating committee.

By February, reporters were starting to notice widening cracks in the foundation of Whitney's support. An advisory committee of the Association of Stock Exchange Firms, the trade group for retail firms, had openly endorsed the SEC's suggestions. The advisory panel's members included John Hanes.

Then, a month after Kennedy's list of suggested reforms was released, Hanes rose unexpectedly at an exchange board meeting to state his case, the first time he had spoken out. "His position was simple: Whitney's intransigence was alienating the public and the proposed reforms were legitimate," according to one account. "The old guard had assumed [Hanes] was safe. When he sat down, there was dead silence."

The New York Times now reported Whitney faced opposition both from John Hanes and from one of Whitney's longtime board colleagues, Charles R. Gay, a retail broker who had begun his Wall Street career as an office boy, joined the NYSE in 1911, and served quietly on the board since 1924. Whitney's allies hinted Whitney might run as an "independent" if the nominating committee didn't back him.

No one could recall a contested election for the NYSE presidency. Buoyed by his 1929 celebrity, Whitney had been unanimously elected five times before. He still was closely tied to the powerful Morgan firm. In February 1934, his stern gaze had stared out from *Time* magazine's cover. With his nationwide defense of the NYSE, he embodied Wall Street for much of the general public. That he would be tossed out of office seemed unlikely to both his critics and his allies—he simply was too powerful.

As an April 8 deadline neared for announcing an official slate, Hanes and the other nominating committee members made their choice: Charles R. Gay for president, Whitney for a seat on the board of governors. Hanes was tapped for reelection to his governor's seat, but he had taken himself out of the running for president.

There is little doubt that Richard Whitney considered a public fight to keep the presidency. But his brother, George, "would have none of it," a Whitney biographer reported. Perhaps George Whitney thought a fight would further tarnish Wall Street's image. But he also had private concerns about his brother. Dick Whitney lived an expensive, fairy-tale life. There was the Far Hills, New Jersey, estate where he raised prize-winning cattle and Thoroughbred horses. There were memberships at a host of luncheon and country clubs, and the costly hobbies he pursued as an officer of both the New York Yacht Club and the National Steeplechase and Hunt Association. He kept a large staff of servants and farmhands at his estate and a butler and household staff at his five-story townhouse on East Seventy-third Street. All this had to be supported by the small bond-trading firm that Whitney had often neglected during his presidency.

For whatever reason, Dick Whitney accepted the nominating committee's verdict. "Mr. Gay has all my good wishes and, as president, will command my warm support," he told reporters when he announced his decision. But he was vindicated by the election results: with an extraordinary turnout of nearly 90 percent of the members, he received more votes than any other nominee for any office, including his friend Charles Gay. He also put three more of his allies on the board, ousting John Hanes and two other official nominees.

Charles Gay, although he ran a prominent brokerage firm, was a nondescript figure in off-the-rack suits who lived simply in a Brooklyn townhouse. Indeed, his socially active wife was mentioned far more often in the era's newspapers than he was. Soft-spoken and conscientious, Gay hated acrimony and pursued boardroom peace at almost any price. It would be hard to imagine anyone less likely to rein in Dick Whitney.

To be sure, the exchange election had brought some mild reforms. The new governors were a bit more representative of the wider world of Wall Street. A young reform-minded retail broker from St. Louis, William McChesney Martin Jr., was elected to the board and eight senior partners of other retail firms were seated as nonvoting members to balance the views of the floor traders and specialists. The new post of "executive vice president" was created to deal with administrative details.

But at best, the election was an ambiguous victory for reformers. Dick Whitney had lost his position—but he had not lost his *power*. Not only had he easily kept his board seat, he also remained influential on the important law and business conduct committees. Moreover, Charles Gay's first act as president was to recruit former president E.H.H. "Harry" Simmons—Whitney's mentor—as his vice president. Veteran observers were quick to see the step as "a return to power of the faction recently headed by Richard Whitney," although Gay insisted the choice was simply a bid for "unity and harmony."

But Kennedy took his small victories and continued to urge business to cooperate with this new era of regulation. Finally, in mid-March 1935, he saw the first metaphorical robin of a Wall Street spring: the giant meat-packer Swift & Company of Chicago and the Pacific Gas & Electric Company of California both announced large new bond issues. A few smaller issues pushed the total bond issuance for the first two weeks of March to $120.5 million—larger than January and February combined.

Kennedy immediately capitalized on this event in a luncheon speech on March 19 at the Hotel Astor on Times Square in New York. Addressing a ballroom crowd of about a thousand "businessmen and industrialists," Kennedy gave a remarkable finger-wagging, rumor-busting, cheerleading address.

First, he chided New York City—"the barometer of the nation's business"—for its unwarranted hysteria about federal regulation. The need for the new laws was "apparent to all right-thinking people," he said. "Business must be financed. Those who do that financing—the investors—must be protected," he said. "We cannot turn back. It is idle to dream and wish for the return of a former day, with its unrestrained opportunity for unfair and dishonest practices." Investors were so mistrustful of Wall Street, he said, that "it required an agency such as our commission to help regain this lost confidence, to restore the shattered prestige of the business."

Wall Street's pessimists were wrong to blame the sluggish capital flow on federal regulation, Kennedy continued. "Happily, some able business men have agreed," he said, pointing to the executives running Swift and Pacific Gas & Electric. "Can these men, representing some of the best minds and hearts in American business, be entirely wrong, and the hesitant majority who carpingly criticize the existing law, without taking the trouble to become informed concerning it, be correct? We know better."

Unsurprisingly, given his steady success, Kennedy's welcome at the White House grew warmer every day. By one account, he made "three or four unannounced evening visits to the White House each week," where he would share cocktails and gossip with the president and perhaps a few family members or close aides.

FDR's casual visits to Marwood became more frequent, too, especially when deliveries of fresh New England seafood had arrived. The cuisine at the White House was notoriously dull, and Roosevelt relished the meals prepared by Kennedy's chef. Roosevelt swam in the pool, watched lighthearted films, played penny-ante poker, and sang along loudly to the tunes that Tommy Corcoran played on his accordion or the resident piano. These casual gatherings were a carefree respite for a president facing a crushing array of challenges.

Beyond this hospitality, there was real substance to Kennedy's relationship with Roosevelt. In the privacy of Marwood, FDR could confer secretly with business leaders unwilling to brave the press corps that stood watch at the White House. He could ask Kennedy for independent budget estimates for various programs, and consult him confidentially about monetary policy. At one point, according to historian Michael Beschloss, FDR even considered drafting Kennedy as a sort of "public works czar" to coordinate among frequently feuding cabinet members.

But by May 1935, the SEC was on its feet with a motivated and hardworking staff of outstanding lawyers and analysts. The frozen opposition of Wall Street seemed to be melting and new issues were starting to flow back into the market. Kennedy felt his job was done; he was ready to get back to his business and his family. He drafted a letter of resignation, planning to leave sometime around the agency's first birthday in early July.

Late in the warm spring afternoon of Monday, May 27, he folded the letter, put it in his jacket pocket, and left his office for the short walk to the White House. Before he reached the grounds, he saw a newsboy waving an early edition of an evening newspaper with the blaring front-page headline: "Supreme Court Wipes Out Codes." The Supreme Court had struck down the industry agreements on wages and prices negotiated under Roosevelt's National Industrial Recovery Act, a cornerstone of his economic recovery plan.

The decision revealed such a cramped view of "interstate commerce" that it cast doubt on many other reforms. The GOP leader in the House gleefully told reporters, "The whole New Deal is out the window," adding that Roosevelt should "forget all this experimenting" and "put things back on a business basis."

Joe Kennedy turned around and returned to his office. He could not resign that day—it was time for New Dealers to close ranks. He and his fellow commissioners remained grimly silent when reporters asked if the ruling was a threat to the SEC.

But Wall Street immediately rejoiced over the decision, certain that it meant the future dismantling of the SEC and the immediate abandonment of any new laws to regulate commerce or capitalism.

The next day's trading showed what new laws Wall Street had in mind. While the larger stock market slumped badly on fears that the court's ruling would lead to price and wage cuts that would tip the nation back into a depression, there was one exception to the general rout: "Utility shares played a prominent part in the early rise and in many cases resisted the later selling," one newspaper reported.

The fate of the Wheeler-Rayburn utility reform bill had been cloudy even before this legal setback. Rayburn simply could not muster the votes to include the death sentence in the House version of the bill. Wheeler was able to get his version of the death sentence passed in the Senate on June 11, but not even that strengthened Rayburn's hand. A weaker bill without the death sentence was overwhelmingly approved in the House.

Before a conference committee of lawmakers could meet to resolve their differences, scandal came to the New Deal's defense. An impromptu Senate investigation, led with brutal expediency by Senator Hugo Black, had revealed that a thousand telegrams sent to Congress to oppose the holding company act were faked by agents working for Associated Gas and Electric (AG&E). The signatures had been cribbed from phone books, payroll lists, even tombstones—and the incriminating originals had been burned on AG&E's orders, in violation of federal rules and Western Union policies. Those "grassroots" protests from "widow and orphan investors" that had terrified Congress had been bought and paid for by Howard C. Hopson, the "black sheep" president of AG&E, who admitted his company had borrowed nearly a million dollars to lobby against the bill. As one Rayburn biography noted, "From the beginning, utility leaders knew that Hopson and AG&E were the most fearsome skeleton in their closet. They were right. Once Hopson's activities were publicly aired, the battle was lost."

Senators on the conference committee crafted a slightly less draconian version of the death penalty. It spared holding companies that served a beneficial economic purpose, owned only contiguous power systems, and were not so large as to "impair the advantages of local management." (It also featured a minor provision with a major impact: it directed the SEC to make a groundbreaking study of investment trusts, since that type of mutual fund had some of the characteristics of holding companies.) The editing allowed the bill's former opponents to justify changing their votes by claiming their original objections had been addressed. Late on Saturday, August 24, the bill passed and was sent to Roosevelt.

In the same protracted session, the Senate unanimously confirmed James Delmage ("J.D.") Ross, the father of Seattle's well-run municipal power company, to the SEC seat first held by Ferdinand Pecora. His appointment to the commission assured progressives that a seasoned advocate for public power would help administer the new law. On August 26, 1935, FDR signed the holding company bill into law, effective on October 1.

The infant SEC now had to implement a law that was fiercely opposed by one of the richest, most powerful industries in the country. Was this a job that Joe Kennedy wanted to take on?

No, it was not. Kennedy opposed the death sentence provisions and thought the law gave the SEC too much power. He shared similar concerns in a public letter to Senator Wheeler, and somewhat belatedly decided it was time to resign.

After breaking the news personally to FDR at Hyde Park, he arranged for Rose and two of their children to join him on a luxury liner sailing for Europe on September 25. In his official resignation letter, effective September 23, he told Roosevelt the SEC was "strongly established as a going concern." But it would be best, he said, for someone new to see to the implementation of the new holding company law. He vowed: "I shall still deem myself a part of your administration."

That was not an idle promise. Kennedy could still get the president's ear, and he retained a proprietary interest in the SEC, working behind the scenes to protect the agency and promote the careers of his favorites. And within six months of his resignation, he had signed on to support Roosevelt's reelection bid in 1936.

Kennedy was deeply gratified by the public praise that followed his resignation, led by Roosevelt himself. Even the Wall Street scourge and former Pecora investigator John T. Flynn, who initially had been enraged by Kennedy's appointment, conceded the former speculator had become "the most useful member of the commission." Abe Fortas praised Kennedy for creating an agency where "men can live and breathe and work with a minimum of the tapes that bind." In his aw-shucks tone, Bill Douglas added, "You are such a swell administrator that all of us have felt we were working for you personally."

Roosevelt returned to the White House from Hyde Park early on Monday, September 23. Just before lunch, he met again with Kennedy to discuss the future of the commission. As he left, Kennedy told reporters on the White House steps that FDR and he both favored Jim Landis as his successor, adding that Landis was a "damn good man." Back at SEC headquarters, he told staffers at an emotional farewell meeting that Landis would give business "the fairest and squarest deal a man can get." He added, "I would deem it an honor to have him as a trustee of anything I owned." Then he joined the other commissioners in unanimously electing Landis to replace him.

In his clipped, deliberate style, Landis assured the reporters gathered in his office that there would be no revolution at the SEC. "Mr.

Kennedy's policies are the commission's policies, and there is no reason for changing them." The only new tack would be to implement the holding company act, Landis said.

Suddenly, as Landis spoke, Joe Kennedy appeared in the doorway and strode over to shake his hand. "Goodbye, Jim boy," he boomed. "Good luck to you. Knock 'em over." As Landis stood "speechless," Kennedy waved farewell to the group and quickly left the room.

Reporters "could not help notice" how different the two men were, one Landis biographer wrote. Kennedy was "tall, athletic, well-groomed, and colloquial as he wisecracked with reporters. Jim Landis was short, thin, indifferent to dress, soft-spoken, and always careful in his choice of words." An aura of command surrounded Kennedy that Landis never acquired as SEC chairman.

But despite their differences, Kennedy trusted his young successor. Indeed, he was entrusting Landis with something he clearly cherished: his reputation as the founding chairman of a highly effective regulatory agency. There would be little glory in that achievement if the SEC could not survive his departure.

KENNEDY WAS PLACING HIS trust in a very complicated man.

James McCauley Landis was born and raised in Japan, where his brilliant but rigidly exacting American father was a missionary school teacher. His German-born mother had worked as a tutor for a wealthy family before her marriage. At Princeton, Landis had only one grade below an A, a B+ in German, which he "had not bothered to study" since he learned it at his mother's knee. When his father visited him on campus, "only the B+ concerned him," his biographer reported. Landis graduated from Princeton in 1921 with a Phi Beta Kappa key, and finished Harvard Law School at the top of his class in 1924, working on the law review and supplementing his limited funds with his winnings at the bridge table. He earned "what was reputedly the highest average at the school since Louis Brandeis had graduated in 1878," although his father was no long alive to appreciate that success.

While at Harvard, Landis formed a worshipful relationship with

Felix Frankfurter, who helped engineer his clerkship with Justice Brandeis, his faculty post at Harvard Law School in 1926, and his fateful volunteer work for the New Deal in 1933.

Landis lacked the vibrant certainty that made both Roosevelt and Kennedy such successful leaders. As chairman of the commission, he seemed to be "a stern, self-confident administrator who missed no detail and mastered every situation," his biographer would observe. Socially, he was known as a prankster whose card tricks and Civil War trivia quizzes enlivened boozy evenings with other young New Dealers. But behind both the stern façade and the party pranks, Landis "suffered a lifelong crisis of self-esteem which led him to develop dependencies on strong personalities, from his own remarkable father to such surrogates as Felix Frankfurter and Joseph Kennedy." Indeed, Landis "lived perilously close to the edge of self-destruction." His marriage was an unhappy mix of long absences and stormy arguments, and his personal finances were a muddle for most of his life. Joe Kennedy could occasionally persuade him to relax at Marwood, but Landis never gave up the workaholic habits he developed as the child of an implacable perfectionist. His character may not have brought him happiness, but it helped the young agency hold its own against opposition fiercer than anything Joe Kennedy had faced.

Kennedy told shipboard reporters before he sailed to Europe that the SEC was in fine shape. In truth, Landis was taking the helm in the middle of a legal thunderstorm, with far worse weather to come.

In the summer of 1935, Roosevelt had won a series of historic legislative victories. At his insistence, Congress had enacted the Social Security Act, the Wagner Act to protect labor unions, a banking bill strengthening the authority of the Federal Reserve, and the unprecedented utility holding company act—"the most far-reaching reform measures [Congress] had ever considered," as one historian would put it. But every victory of that summer further inflamed American business leaders, who were now routinely condemning the New Deal as "an agency of totalitarian tyranny remorselessly enlarging its control over all aspects of American life." This was the "all-or-nothing" formula of Herbert Hoover: anything but totally unfettered capitalism was socialism. As the central agent of business regulation in the New Deal, the SEC was directly in the line of fire for Wall Street's verbal and legal attacks. The young agency was facing a fight for its life against some of the most powerful interests in the country.

In his first press interviews, Landis was asked repeatedly about the new holding company act. Some utility executives were meeting with the SEC the next day, and Landis told reporters he assumed the utility holding companies would cooperate with the new law. In fact, he knew they intended to fight the new law "to the last legal ditch"—that fight had already begun.

On September 16, the trustees for a bankrupt utility had asked U.S. District Judge William Coleman in Baltimore to rule that the holding company act did not apply to the utility's reorganization because the law was unconstitutional. Judge Coleman, a vocal New Deal critic, said immediately that he already "regarded the act as unconstitutional." But he preserved the façade of an adversarial case by letting some of the utility's creditors petition him for a ruling that the act *was* constitutional and thus *did* govern the current reorganization. No one could seriously argue the case was a fair and authentic test of the holding company act's constitutionality—the whole exercise bordered on courtroom stagecraft.

The SEC had been totally blindsided. All it could do was ask to appear as a "friend of the court" to make its case that the court should not take up the constitutionality issue at all. With Landis on call, Ben Cohen and Tommy Corcoran were working frantically with SEC general counsel John Burns to muster a strategically safe response before the hearing on Friday, September 27.

That hearing was the unaddressed elephant in the room on Wednesday, September 25, when nine utility executives trooped into a sparsely furnished corner conference room at the SEC's headquarters. Wendell Willkie, the tousled president of Commonwealth & Southern, and eight other top executives took their seats around the table, which held stacks of the SEC's proposed registration forms for their review.

Landis was joined by Bud Mathews and Judge Healy. A notary

swore in the commission's newest member, J. D. Ross, the public power advocate whom FDR had appointed to the commission just as the holding company act had passed Congress. The commissioners approved a few new rules and then reviewed the proposed utility registration forms. There were few complaints from the executives, who no doubt believed they would never have to fill out those forms. As a financial columnist at *The New York Times* put it the next day: "The utility industry would cooperate with the commission but with fingers crossed."

On Friday, September 27, extra chairs had to be dragged into Judge Coleman's courtroom in Baltimore to accommodate more than 150 utility executives and lawyers who had traveled from Washington and New York to watch the fireworks in the strange courtroom battle unfolding there. The attack on the holding company law would be led by the formidable John W. Davis, the legal advisor to J.P. Morgan and the man Dick Whitney wanted to hire to fight the SEC. And through a quirk in legal process, the act would be "defended" not by the SEC but by a prominent *utility industry* lawyer who was ostensibly supporting the law in this case but who was attacking the law's constitutionality in a separate case for another client. The only sincere advocate for the holding company act in the courtroom that day would be the SEC, whose "friend of the court" arguments would be anything but friendly.

The SEC's young legal team had arrived early, planning to challenge the entire case as a sham. With Ben Cohen and Tommy Corcoran seated beside him, John Burns made "a blistering 45-minute opening statement" denouncing the whole proceeding as unfair, "prearranged" and "collusive." Appearing outraged, Davis thundered that the three young SEC lawyers had made "an unworthy, an undignified, and a contemptible presentation."

The judge grudgingly agreed to hold a hearing on the SEC's complaint—but announced he would hold it then and there. Burns and Corcoran improvised, questioning the various litigants and lawyers sitting in the courtroom. The charge that the case was unfair to the SEC couldn't really be disputed. The government had only learned about the case the day it was filed. Because it wasn't an official party to the case, it had no right to appeal if the judge struck down the law. Burns had teased out "testimony from witnesses that seemed to corroborate much of his opening statement" about collusion, one legal scholar noted. But the outcome was a foregone conclusion. Judge Coleman refused to dismiss the case.

The litigation was followed closely by almost every big-city daily in the country—hardly surprising, since homes and businesses almost everywhere relied on one of the giant utility systems that fiercely opposed the new law. *The Philadelphia Inquirer* said the case had "all the earmarks of one of the most important legal battles in the history of the United States." Against the backdrop of that national interest, Jim Landis gave a national radio address on Saturday, September 28, his first as SEC chairman. He pointedly criticized the Baltimore litigation. The SEC would not obstruct any "honest effort" to challenge the act, he said, "but it must be a controversy that is real, and not a sham."

On Thursday, November 7—the day Landis opened the investment trust study that would lay the foundation for regulating the American mutual fund industry—Judge Coleman issued an opinion declaring the Public Utility Holding Company Act "void in its entirety." It was a glorious day for the law firms serving the utility industry. Utilities promptly filed fifty-eight similar legal challenges in courthouses across the country.

Judge Healy told Joe Kennedy, still in Europe, that he was missing all the fun. "You should have stayed with us," he wrote. "We get sued every five minutes."

Jim Landis was determined that the SEC would defend the holding company act on its own terms, against its preferred adversary, and in its chosen forum. But the industry was not worried. Judge Coleman's ruling seemed comfortingly emphatic: the law was "grossly arbitrary" and Congress had "flagrantly exceeded its lawful power" in passing it. The SEC's small legal team had to defend dozens of fresh lawsuits; it was surely in no position to go on the offensive.

But that was exactly what Ben Cohen and Landis decided to do. The strategy was audacious: the SEC would file its own test case, seek the dismissal of the Baltimore case and all the other regional cases on the grounds that the SEC could only be sued in its hometown, and persuade the senior court in Washington, D.C., to freeze the seven cases filed there until its test case was resolved. That would allow the SEC to put all its legal effort into its own case.

The most important goal of the SEC's lawsuit was to limit the issues that would come before the court. Unlike the utilities, which wanted the entire law overturned, the SEC wanted its test case to result in key parts of the law being upheld. Specifically, the agency planned to sue only to enforce the act's registration and disclosure requirements, Sections 4 and 5, postponing the tougher fight over the death penalty clause. Dozens of stock exchanges and thousands of companies already had registered with the SEC. Any utility holding company would have a hard time showing why it should be exempt from mere registration and disclosure.

Landis decided the defendant should be the giant Electric Bond and Share Company, known as Ebasco. "Let's pick a big one, a top one," he urged Cohen. "Take a big one and topple that one, and then the little ones would fall into line."

Cohen and Corcoran enlisted the help of Assistant Attorney General Robert H. Jackson, a brilliant presidential troubleshooter whose ties went back to the dawn of FDR's political career. The SEC's strategy would delight FDR, Jackson knew. "Roosevelt liked novel ideas, bold courses, and dramatic actions, and he liked the sort of men who could come up with such suggestions."

The SEC team quietly set up a war room in the Reconstruction Finance Corporation's offices, out of sight of anyone visiting the SEC. There, Cohen and his colleagues worked with barely a break for food, catching naps on the floor when exhaustion couldn't be fought off.

The SEC team sifted through news articles and Judge Healy's massive FTC files to document why Ebasco was the most appropriate defendant. Electric Bond and Share, created by General Electric and J.P. Morgan, was the largest utility holding company in the country, effectively controlling eight enormous foreign and domestic power systems including Wendell Willkie's. It had more than a dozen holding companies that owned more than five dozen local power companies in nearly three dozen states. Its transmission lines supplied at least 10 percent of the entire nation's electric power. Its engineering, construction, and financial units had contracts with subsidiaries all across the country. Thus, it was engaged in "interstate commerce" on a vast and indisputable scale. Moreover, it clearly was committing many of the abuses the holding company act was designed to outlaw. Best of all, it was based in New York and thus could be sued in federal court in Manhattan—where Judge Julian W. Mack, Ben Cohen's "liberal-minded" mentor, sat on the bench. If the utilities could maneuver their case before a sympathetic judge, Landis could do the same.

Two Ebasco executives were scheduled to meet with Landis on Tuesday, November 26, 1935. At about 3:30 A.M. that morning, the young men in the RFC war room put the final touches on the SEC lawsuit. An aide sped to the airport to get it onto the 4 A.M. flight to New York. The papers were in the hands of an SEC lawyer in Manhattan when the utility executives greeted Landis and settled into chairs in his office. Once again, they confirmed they would not register with the SEC as the act required. Landis thanked them for the update and saw them out. As they rode the elevator down from the tenth floor, Landis returned to his desk, picked up the phone, and told the SEC lawyer in New York to file the test case immediately with Judge Mack. The staffer was likely on his way to the courthouse before the utility executives had reached their limousine at the curb.

Ebasco and the entire utility industry were stunned. The SEC had shown it had enough guile and brilliance to make up for its lack of resources, but Landis knew it would be a long war.

He had other wars to fight, too—notably the battle against Wall Street's continued misbehavior. Many of his staff's successful cases involved small-time fraud outfits or regional brokers, cases significant mostly to the victims, but there was no bigger target than Michael J. Meehan, the legendary RCA stock market operator. Meehan had been a Kennedy ally on the Street and a donor to both Al Smith's and FDR's campaigns. Nevertheless, when the SEC found Meehan rigging the price of Bellanca Aircraft shares in mid-1935, it pounced and Landis ultimately succeeded in barring Meehan from the nation's stock exchanges.

ALTHOUGH KENNEDY'S LAST OFFICIAL act at the SEC was to vote for Landis as the next chairman, his last *unofficial* act was to urge Roosevelt to choose Bill Douglas to fill his own seat.

Roosevelt clearly had noticed the young cowboy from Yale, most likely during casual Marwood evenings. Douglas had the sassy swagger that FDR liked to see in the men around him. On December 20, 1935, Landis told Roosevelt he agreed with Kennedy's choice. FDR immediately called Douglas to offer him the seat, and Douglas immediately accepted.

On January 23, 1936, William O. Douglas was sworn in as the seventh SEC commissioner. Neither the agency nor Wall Street would ever be the same.

CHAPTER FIVE

AN OCEAN OF
UNFINISHED BUSINESS

JANUARY 1936–SEPTEMBER 1937

WHEN JOE KENNEDY HAD HIRED BILL DOUGLAS IN JULY 1934, all he knew about the Yale professor was that he was the top expert on corporate bankruptcy in the country. At their first meeting, the chairman had just one directive: "Get going."

Douglas and his lieutenant Abe Fortas had moved into a warren of offices on the fourth floor of the SEC's headquarters, down the hall from the agency's law library. From there, the small team of men and a few trailblazing women had conducted a remarkably broad study of how the bankruptcy process had long abused small creditors and ordinary investors.

The bankruptcy landscape was so vast and swampy that Congress itself had largely given up on studying it. For decades, there had been local scandals like the one in New York's federal court in 1929, when favored lawyers got paid so much there was nothing left for creditors. But at the national level, the bankruptcy abuses were rooted in Wall Street, where financial insiders—executives, directors, bankers, lawyers, and the best-connected bondholders—controlled the outcome of big bankruptcies with little regard for anyone's interests but their own.

By 1934, Wall Street was littered with defaulted bonds that had been sold before the 1929 crash. Through Pecora's work, Congress had learned about the deceptive ways Wall Street sold those securities to unsophisticated investors. Now, through the work of Bill Douglas, Congress would learn about the deceptive ways Wall

Street had shortchanged investors after those securities had gone bust.

The Douglas study was focused on so-called "protective committees," which were supposed to represent and protect investors during the reorganization process. The SEC team sent queries to more than 1,600 committees, the first of more than 200,000 it would eventually examine. The team soon found that "the corrupt practices of these groups were so commonplace that many of the respondents openly admitted their unethical and illegal practices."

Through public hearings, Bill Douglas and Abe Fortas documented these practices. Still juggling his teaching duties at Yale, Douglas would work on the evening train from New Haven to Washington, absorbing staff reports and witness transcripts. Then he would rise the next day to pose questions that would immediately "go to the jugular of the issue," Fortas recalled.

Douglas had only one response when his staffers fretted about the titans they were confronting: "Piss on 'em." He wanted no kid-glove handling of these powerful figures; in his eyes, they were no better than the fourth-rate lawyers who fleeced small-time creditors in New York in the 1920s.

At the first hearing, Douglas showed that two executives who bankrupted the huge Celotex Corporation had used shell companies to secretly take control of the new firm that emerged from the rubble. Journalists, seeing the solid evidence and nimble questioning, started to pay more attention to the hearings, and they weren't disappointed.

Douglas documented a secret fee-splitting deal between two eminent lawyers who represented competing groups in one of Ivar Kreuger's American bankruptcies. The lawyer for the Kreuger underwriter was Republican power broker John Foster Dulles. The lawyer for some irate Kreuger bondholders was the Democratic workhorse Samuel Untermyer, a New Deal advocate. These two supposed adversaries had quietly declared a truce and refrained from challenging each other's claims, without the knowledge of their clients. Questioned by Douglas, Dulles insisted that "there was nothing done here that reasonable and honorable people would not do."

Even when the probe touched on Joe Kennedy's own post–SEC business interests, Douglas did not falter. He pressed the partners at the Kuhn, Loeb firm to defend their role in the bankruptcy deal that created Paramount Pictures, one of Kennedy's new consulting clients. Kuhn, Loeb had picked all the members of the committee that was supposed to protect bondholders—but none of them actually *were* bondholders. Indeed, Kuhn, Loeb itself did not own any Paramount securities until after the committee was formed, when committee members started to trade heavily, secretly aware that Kuhn, Loeb was manipulating prices to protect their profits. The backroom dealings of the investment bankers, revealed by Douglas, prompted one angry Paramount director to decide that he had been "double-crossed" by an opposing lawyer during the long reorganization; the two men nearly came to blows in the hallway outside the SEC's hearing room.

Conflicts of interest stretched from the top of the food chain to the bottom. A Cuban sugar company's Wall Street bankers controlled all its protective committees and, coincidentally, made sure their loans would be repaid ahead of other creditors. One banker conceded to Douglas that it "might have been better" if these conflicts had not existed. Similarly, Douglas examined billions of dollars' worth of mortgage bonds sold to average investors in the late 1920s. By 1931, nearly two-thirds of these bonds were in default. The firms that sold the bonds—and speculated ruinously with the proceeds— also controlled the protective committees and "spent much of their time protecting themselves from claims of fraud."

The Douglas study went further and deeper into the bankruptcy swamp than most journalists or their readers wished to travel. Its eight-volume report to Congress—the final volume was released in 1938—was so large and so tardy that Douglas himself doubted anyone would read it.

But the hearings themselves were tough and uncompromising. They showed the SEC doing its work carefully and fairly, undeterred by personal interests or partisan rivalries. They also produced an unassailable record of the long-standing bankruptcy abuses that had hurt countless small investors and creditors for decades. Many of the reforms Douglas recommended would ultimately become federal law.

Douglas was admired within the agency even by those who chafed under his brusque behavior. Adolf Berle, the FDR advisor, had known Douglas as a faculty colleague at Columbia and found him "a moody man" who was "a bit intolerant of other people's different views." He was not easy to work with, or to work for, although he drove himself as hard as he drove others. Fortas protected the staff when he could. "I don't mean he wasn't firm," one aide said of Fortas. "But he could tell you that you were dead wrong in a nice way probably, and Douglas would just say you were crazy."

The 1935 hearings made Bill Douglas, at age thirty-seven, a media favorite. With a nudge from Tommy Corcoran, journalist Robert Kintner of the *New York Herald Tribune* had taken a shine to the young professor and featured him frequently in his columns. Other Washington journalists followed suit. Kennedy himself, in a June 1935 letter, called the bankruptcy study "one of the most outstanding and significant pieces of work which the commission has undertaken and one of the most thorough-going investigations which I have ever seen." He repeated that compliment in a *Saturday Evening Post* essay published days before Douglas joined the commission in January 1936.

Kennedy's support for Douglas initially calmed Wall Street's jitters about him. One pundit breezily noted: "Word is that Douglas will string with Landis and give the 'reasonable' element in the commission a majority. It has been evenly divided between 'reasonables' and 'radicals' ever since Kennedy quit."

But within months, columnists Drew Pearson and Robert S. Allen observed that Douglas "is expected to put backbone" back into the SEC, where the once-feared Landis had been "eating caviar a little too frequently with the boys whom once he frightened." Another pundit praised Douglas for being "illusionless about Wall Street" and claimed he, unlike Landis, wasn't "dazzled" by "luncheon invitations from George Whitney" at the Morgan firm.

These unfair insinuations must have hurt Landis, proud of his tenure at the SEC, but it isn't clear that he blamed Douglas for them. It *is* clear that Douglas and Healy frequently voted for steps they thought would toughen SEC oversight—only to be outvoted by Landis, Ross, and Mathews.

Behind his stoic manner, Landis was struggling with the pile of unfinished business that Kennedy had left on his desk.

The SEC was essentially paralyzed as a utility regulator. Some small utilities had registered but most major utility holding companies had decided simply to disobey the law until they could get it thrown out. This deliberate disobedience shocked some conservative investors, including Roger W. Babson, one of the most influential economists and investment advisors on Wall Street. He wrote FDR in late 1935 that the industry's refusal to register was "worthy of the lawlessness of the gangster" and "impresses me as one of the most deplorable mistakes which I have witnessed in more than thirty years of industrial and financial experience." Jim Landis agreed, but he had to accept this lawlessness until the agency's lawsuit against the Ebasco holding company made its way to the Supreme Court. This, he would later say, was "the bitterest fight of all."

He had opened the congressionally mandated study of investment trusts, the mutual funds of that era, but that work also was moving slowly because the SEC staffers had found so many questionable activities that they wanted to expose at public hearings. It was clear a new rule book was needed for this increasingly powerful Wall Street force—at the early hearings, Bill Douglas was already pushing for a very tough code of regulations—but Landis was nowhere close to drafting it.

The year 1936 brought other consequential but less publicized frustrations. One focused on the long-standing issue of whether members of the NYSE and other exchanges should be allowed to trade simultaneously for public customers and for their own pocketbooks. Many reformers wanted to end this conflicted practice, but Landis feared doing so would bankrupt many small firms. With both Douglas and Healy favoring a crackdown—and the NYSE protesting even the mildest reforms—the dispute "embittered all concerned." About all Landis could do in 1936 was to require exchanges to publicize the daily volume of personal trades by their members.

Another piece of unfinished business was the issue of "unlisted" trading. Wall Street had a long tradition of allowing the stock of companies not listed on an exchange to trade there at the request of any of that exchange's members. In practice, this meant a trader could give an unlisted company the benefits of a public market—which included the reassurance that exchange trading gave investors—even if that company had not met the exchange's own listing requirements. The practice was fraught with risk, but unlisted trading commissions kept the lights on at most of the nation's smaller exchanges and, again, Landis was cautious about the economic cost of reform. Congress had ordered the SEC to regulate this practice or shut it down by June 1, 1936, but Landis was nowhere close to doing either and had to ask Congress for more time.

Landis said later that eliminating unlisted trading and conflicted floor trades was "just too revolutionary. Personally, I was glad to get what I got, without trying to get into an impossible position the consequences of which I really couldn't foresee." But for many New Dealers, his caution was provoking and disappointing.

Judge Healy also grew frustrated that Landis, like Kennedy before him, did not push the agency to set clearer standards for the accountants who examined the books of registered companies. The accounting profession's old guard—the big eastern firms with their roots in Britain—praised the SEC's deference to their traditions. But some accountants yearned for a day when firms could not lure clients away with hints of a more "flexible" approach to audits.

The biggest piece of unfinished business for Landis was a congressional mandate to tame the vast unregulated over-the-counter market. This was a project that would shape the modern marketplace for a century to come, but at this point, Landis deemed it simply too daunting for the small staff of the SEC.

The scale of the over-the-counter (OTC) market had been poorly appreciated by Congress when it blithely told the SEC to set up some system for regulating it. Somewhere between 60,000 and

90,000 issues traded over the counter, compared to fewer than 6,300 issues listed on all the exchanges in the country. The OTC trading occurred with no outside supervision; even the OTC price quotes in newspapers were guesses. Only the dealers themselves knew the prices at which they had bought and sold, and the spread between those two prices could reach piracy levels.

For regulators, this marketplace was like the dark side of the moon. The national exchanges kept lists of their roughly 1,800 members; there were thousands of OTC dealers and the only place they were listed was in local telephone books. Exchanges voted on whether to accept someone for membership; anybody could hang out a shingle in the OTC market. Exchange trading left a paper trail; the OTC market consisted of invisible messages zipping through telegraph and telephone wires.

Lawmakers had also failed to grasp how diverse and consequential this unregulated market was. It was an enormous national bazaar where Treasury bonds and blue-chip bank shares changed hands side by side with the shares of dubious companies invented by charlatans. Rules to deter devious traders who fleeced the public could have an unintended impact on Treasury and corporate bond traders who helped finance government and business.

Landis struggled to bring sunlight into this shadowy world, groping for a regulatory approach that would satisfy Congress, pass muster in the courts, and not overwhelm the SEC's resources. He publicly urged OTC dealers to form a self-policing organization of their own, but they were in no hurry to do so. His sole gain by the end of 1935 had been a rule requiring OTC dealers to register with the SEC.

Even that tepid step drew outraged complaints. One of the loudest came from J. Edward Jones, a flamboyant dealer who inflicted more damage on the SEC in 1936 than Landis or anyone else could have predicted.

J. Edward Jones is a character straight out of *The Great Gatsby*. Like the fictional mystery man, Jones had a smile of "eternal reassurance" and spoke in a grandly formal style that "just missed being absurd." Oddly attractive despite an equine face and jug-handle ears, Jones was tall and fair, with thinning hair. He carried himself with an air of aggrieved majesty that seemed to dazzle the journalists of his day.

From a vague start in Kansas, he had left traces in Oil Belt newspapers by the late 1920s—being ousted from one company and forming new companies to buy his older companies. His specialty was the murky world of oil royalties. People who leased land to oil prospectors in those days usually demanded a royalty, a fixed fraction of any future output. Royalty trust certificates—securities issued by trusts that purchased the bits of paperwork documenting these royalty claims—could be bought and sold, and Jones made his fortune selling them. By 1933, he was living in a seven-bedroom mansion in Scarsdale, New York, and his company occupied a suite of offices on Madison Avenue in Manhattan.

Oil royalty frauds aimed at modest investors were costly and chronic in this era, but when the Securities Act of 1933 was passed, oil royalty trust certificates were not put under federal regulation—an omission that Landis quickly regretted. "I doubt if there was a good oil royalty offered anywhere east of the Mississippi," he later said. The most common problem was simple deception. Royalty trust issuers would use misleading accounting tricks to burnish their financial statements. People selling the trust certificates would make false claims about how much investors would be paid in dividends. Some trust operators even used Ponzi tactics, paying dividends to one group of investors not with oil income but with cash raised from the sale of new trust certificates to other investors. In early 1934, when Landis was asked by FDR to draft amendments to the 1933 act, he made sure the oil royalty loophole was closed. That alone would likely have turned Jones's fury against the SEC. An old guard Republican, he had a panoramic hostility toward financial regulation.

But he still had a business to run. In early May 1935, he had filed a prospectus for a new issue of oil royalty trust certificates. The day before the securities could have been sold, the SEC had told Jones it believed the filing contained false and misleading information. The sale had been temporarily blocked and he was sent a subpoena to appear at an SEC hearing on the matter in June.

Rather than comply, Jones had tried to withdraw his allegedly deceptive prospectus. Under SEC rules, that required the agency's consent, which it had refused to give. It had gone to court to enforce its subpoena. Jones had sued, arguing the subpoena was unfair and the agency was unconstitutional. He had claimed publicly he was the target of a vendetta by New Dealers. In a bizarre sideshow, he also had claimed a former SEC staffer had shaken him down for a bribe to "fix" the case against him, charges ultimately thrown out of court.

In August 1935, a federal trial judge had upheld the SEC's subpoena for Jones's records and rejected his claim that the law that created the agency was unconstitutional. In November, the federal court of appeals in New York had affirmed that ruling. Jones had promptly appealed to the Supreme Court. To Landis, the Jones case no doubt seemed a minor nuisance compared to the titanic fight over the holding company act.

But Jones ceased to be a joke on February 3, 1936, when the Supreme Court agreed to hear his appeal. He was represented in this suddenly significant case by two lawyers with the American Liberty League, a new coalition of conservative Democrats like Al Smith and wealthy right-wing Republican businessmen like the Du Pont family. Ostensibly nonpartisan, the group opposed the New Deal and was doing all it could to deny Roosevelt a second term in 1936.

Still, Landis was confident. In a letter to Felix Frankfurter in March, he allowed that the SEC might be defeated "on a procedural point," but added, "I cannot see a sane bench of judges not giving us some freedom in working out our procedural techniques."

He was wrong. On April 6, 1936, the Supreme Court struck down the SEC's subpoena and denounced the agency's refusal to let Jones withdraw his suspicious prospectus. And it did so with language so incendiary that it shocked Washington. The court did not rule that the SEC itself was unconstitutional. But as one magazine noted, the court "might just as well have," given the hostility of its attack.

The SEC's treatment of Jones was "wholly unreasonable and arbitrary," wrote Justice George Sutherland. As the court's majority saw it, the public was not harmed by Jones's refusal to comply with the SEC's subpoena. The SEC's goal had been to stop the sale of the Jones securities; when Jones withdrew his prospectus, the SEC had achieved its goal. Any further inquiry would be an illegitimate "fishing expedition," an outrage on the scale of "those intolerable abuses of the Star Chamber" during the bloody reign of the Stuart kings in England in the seventeenth century.

The ruling's language seems extreme even today, given the minor technical issues under review. The vicious tone led many to interpret the ruling as a grave defeat for the SEC. Even though the constitutionality of the agency was upheld, the fierce tone suggested future challenges to its existence might be successful. Many Wall Street defendants sued by the SEC for misbehavior started adding claims of unconstitutionality to their appeals, just in case the justices were ready to act. John Burns, the agency's general counsel, later complained, "There is hardly a crook in the country whose lawyer does not come in to read juicy extracts from Sutherland's oration."

Justices Brandeis and Harlan Fisk Stone joined in a dissent written by Justice Benjamin Cardozo. He noted that the SEC had valid grounds for investigating Jones—he had, after all, submitted "a false and defective" prospectus. Moreover, the SEC had shown in court that some of his claims "can hardly have been made otherwise than with criminal intent." That was the precise focus of the SEC's ongoing inquiry, so no one could accurately describe it as a fishing expedition. Allowing Jones to block a legitimate inquiry into his practices simply by withdrawing his filing would "invite the cunning and unscrupulous to gamble with detection," daring the SEC to catch them in time to stop them.

In a private letter to Frankfurter, Justice Stone said the majority opinion "was written for morons, and such will no doubt take comfort from it." He added, "I can hardly believe that intelligent people, trained in the law, will swallow such buncombe." Unfortunately, many did.

Of course, Jones was exultant, casting the ruling as "the outstanding one, since the inception of our government, in safeguarding the liberties and freedom of individual citizens . . . from a tyrannical bureaucracy at Washington." He vowed to continue his fight to shut down the agency.

The decision was so poorly understood that Joe Kennedy had to snuff out ill-informed views in his own family. Young Joe Kennedy Jr. wrote his father from college that the ruling "seemed fair enough to me." It looked like John Burns at the SEC wanted to nail Jones "so badly that he wouldn't stop." It was wrong, he continued, that a person might file a prospectus and then find "something wrong which he hadn't known of before" and yet be unable to withdraw the filing.

His father set him straight in his next letter. "It has never been the policy of the Commission to issue a stop order or have an examination made where the error appeared to be anything but a flagrant steal, and in the case of Jones, that is exactly what it was."

Landis wisely saw the ruling as a wake-up call, a warning that the agency needed to refine its rules so that they not only *were* fair in the eyes of agency law experts but *looked fair* to ordinary citizens largely unfamiliar with how the agency worked.

But for Republicans, the Jones ruling was luscious fodder for the 1936 presidential campaign. "Joy and gladness reigned" among Senate Republicans on the day the ruling was released, one columnist reported. "The word had spread that the Supreme Court's decision in the Jones case . . . was made to order for a Republican campaign document." Another pundit said the decision might have been written by the American Liberty League itself, an early contribution to its 1936 campaign against Roosevelt's financial reforms.

BESIDES BEING AN ELECTION year, 1936 also marked the twenty-fifth reunion for the privileged sons of Harvard's Class of 1911—each of whom was etched by name into Richard Whitney's memory. He would be one of the featured speakers and the celebrations loomed large on his calendar as 1936 opened; he had set up an account in his office ledgers for contributions to the festivities.

His first year out of the NYSE presidential office had been eventful, if less newsworthy than the year before.

Whitney may have felt a twinge on New Year's Eve as Charles Gay rang out 1935 in his place. But the mood on the NYSE floor was literally "upbeat." For the first time since the Harlem Hellcats' visit on the last trading day of 1929, the music was back, with two orchestras taking turns from 1:30 P.M. until the closing bell.

Whitney had been reelected to the governing board of the Turf and Field Club and to the treasurer's post at the New York Yacht Club. He served as chairman of the board at a small bank in Apopka, Florida, where he had business interests. (In July, despite Whitney's public attacks on the New Deal, the bank proudly announced its deposits were insured by FDR's new FDIC.) He attended meetings of the NYSE board, where he still sat on the powerful law committee and three lesser panels. Once again outpolling all other candidates for any office, he was elected a trustee of the exchange's long-established Gratuity Fund, the internal insurance plan that collected, invested, and distributed money to pay death benefits to deceased members' families. He was being eyed by New York City leaders to head the committee to sell bonds to finance the 1939 World's Fair. He was a busy man, much in demand.

But nothing would keep him away from Cambridge. In mid-June, Whitney and his wife, Gertrude, were among more than a thousand of his classmates and their relatives who registered in the massive Harvard Union building on Quincy Street. The class was proudly observing its "silver jubilee" just months before Harvard would mark its 300th birthday.

The class also had a more idiosyncratic distinction: it had been put under a microscope by one of its own. John Roberts Tunis, a writer who frequented the Harvard Clubs in various cities, had noticed some of the bleak personal updates sent in by his classmates. "My business is rotten." "I am an utter failure." "I'm a tramp." He decided to dig deeper. He found that fully half the class was disappointed with their careers. One of every eight men was out of work; the class's average annual earnings were less than $4,500 a year, a firmly upper-class paycheck but one which Tunis suggested was a poor return on Harvard's tuition.

A majority of his classmates answered that Harvard nevertheless had been worthwhile. But Tunis had his doubts. In his view, the Class of 1911 was "a group of men whose chief ambition, if their record tells the truth, is to vote the Republican ticket, to keep out of the breadline and to break 100 at golf." When Tunis asked his classmates to name ten among them who "had really achieved something in life," the second name on their list was Dick Whitney.

Whitney upheld the "vote Republican" dictum in a speech in the great hall of Boston's Harvard Club on June 17, when he warned 350 classmates that the nation's economy was at risk of being "ruined by government control." One reporter claimed the boos and cheers greeting his attack on the New Deal were about equal, although Tunis found nearly three-quarters of his class opposed Roosevelt.

Whitney also was a member of Harvard's "visiting committee on economics," chaired by columnist Walter Lippmann, which had just wrapped up a report calling for professors to "take a walk" from campus if they became more engaged with political life than with scholarship. But the report refuted an alumni fear that communist "propaganda" was being taught in economics classes on campus. The study Whitney worked on, and the alarm that inspired it, were likely the by-products of a long public fight over a "teachers loyalty oath" imposed in 1935 by the Massachusetts legislature, where fiercely conservative lawmakers had stoked the fear that communists were infiltrating the state's college faculties and high school classrooms. With rhetoric infused with anti-Semitism and contempt for "crackpot professors," the leaders of this loyalty oath campaign defined "communism" broadly enough to include the entirety of the New Deal. One of the state's most influential anti-communist crusaders at this time was William Cardinal O'Connell, the Boston archbishop who had married Joe Kennedy and Rose Fitzgerald in 1914. Cardinal O'Connell, whose elite social circle included many Harvard men, had largely left the loyalty oath fight to his legislative allies in 1935— but when lawmakers had taken up a ban on child labor the same year, his spokesman denounced the bill as an attack on family and spiritual authority, claiming that "nothing redder ever came out of Red Russia."

The notion of godless communist professors brainwashing their privileged Harvard students into supporting the New Deal was absurd. Only 81 Harvard professors, out of about 1,750, were willing to endorse Roosevelt publicly in 1936. A slim majority of Harvard's student body opposed Roosevelt's reelection, as did more than 70 percent of FDR's own Class of '04.

The 1936 reunion—a crowded schedule of banquets, entertainment events, and sports, including the annual Harvard-Yale baseball rivalry—should have lived up to Whitney's expectations. For the first time in four years, the weather was splendid, with the football field's freshly mown grass scenting the air. To the militant strains of "Onward, Christian Soldiers," Whitney and his classmates marched into the campus stadium just ahead of the graduating Class of 1936. They were uniformly clad in dark blazers, white flannel trousers, and pale straw hats whose bands matched their maroon and orange neckties. That evening, Gertrude Whitney was among the Class of 1911's elegantly gowned wives at the head table in the Hotel Somerset ballroom during a dinner party "for the ladies."

Although she performed at the reunion as Whitney's devoted wife, she and her husband were separated. In late May, the tabloid gossip king Walter Winchell had teased readers by asking if the Whitneys were heading for "a flash." Sometime in June, Gertrude and their daughters moved to the sprawling estate in Far Hills—her son Samuel S. Sands IV was enrolled at Harvard. Whitney remained at the Manhattan townhouse.

Winchell, who loved stock tips and had friends on Wall Street, was more explicit in August: "When the Richard Whitneys of the Stock Exchange are unwound he will wed a bundle of Dupont dividends." He was referring inaccurately to Whitney's romance with Marjorie Pyle Montgomery, a Delaware widow whose sister was Mrs. Eugene du Pont Jr. (She got the stock dividends, not Mrs. Montgomery.) It's not clear when or how they met, although the "slim, vivacious brunette" was an avid horsewoman and, like Whitney, enjoyed the hunt-club society circuit. Whitney began to include her in his social life, but apparently no one told John R. Tunis and the Harvard Class of 1911.

JOE KENNEDY'S EXTENDED TRIP to Europe in September 1935 had been instructive but worrisome. From London, he had sent Roosevelt a cheery telegram about his "amazing" popularity there: "Don't worry about election in America. You could be elected anything in England." But when he returned, he gave FDR a less sunny account. Europe was ugly and unsettled: Hitler was openly rearming and had stripped German Jews of their citizenship. Mussolini was belligerently defending his invasion of Ethiopia. A year after the bloody suppression of a socialist revolt, Spain's government was growing shakier by the day, as parliamentary leaders struggled to form a coalition amid violent protests. English fascists were parading in their distinctive black shirts, bullying Jewish businesses and provoking police. Fierce pockets of fascist support were expanding in the smaller nations all around Germany.

Kennedy's return to Palm Beach did not give him a respite from the vitriol. Republicans and Liberty League Democrats cornered him at church, at golf clubs, at dinner parties, all with the same bitter complaints about the "socialist" Roosevelt. Some of his conservative friends were shocked that he did not turn on FDR. "We thought Joe would help the sane people, but he is going back to the asylum," one wrote.

As always, he stayed in close touch with Roosevelt's inner circle. The openhanded hospitality at Marwood continued. Kennedy found a job at one of his companies for Missy LeHand's brother, and let her use the Palm Beach house for occasional getaways. He sent fresh lobsters to Warm Springs, prompting a joking telegram from FDR that the arrival of live lobsters in the little hamlet was unprecedented: "We are informing [the] Smithsonian." Kennedy had stone crabs sent by air freight to his White House friends, joking with Missy that "the head of the air plane company said he would much rather carry stone crabs than carry one Kennedy, the worst crab he ever knew."

He was making a great deal of money, taking on consulting work for Paramount and RCA that generated fees of $200,000 in just three months. But he was restless out of the public arena, and grew peevish when no new assignment came his way. He threw broad hints about his availability to James Roosevelt and Missy LeHand, but without result.

Finally, he attached himself again to Roosevelt's political campaign. His key role was to answer attacks on the New Deal from businessmen, which he did most visibly and effectively with a small book, *I'm for Roosevelt: A Businessman's Estimate of the New Deal.* The pamphlet had been sketched out with help from Jim Landis and John Burns of the SEC and then secretly expanded and polished by columnist Arthur Krock, who didn't see the unpaid work as a conflict with his day job of impartially covering the national campaign for *The New York Times.* When it was published in September, Kennedy's status as a successful businessman helped lift his comments out of the ping-pong of the political debate.

Kennedy framed FDR's budget deficits not as money wasted but as expenditures that had produced rising incomes, an expanding economy, and more valuable capital assets. In short, he said, the deficit was a smart investment that was paying big returns for everyone—including, of course, those with the biggest stake in the American economy.

He even put an unsentimental businessman's spin on the New Deal relief programs for desperate citizens. "Caring for the needy is social insurance," he said. The premiums for that insurance policy were not small, he acknowledged, "but the property to be protected is so vast as to defy valuation. We have had numerous instances to show how ugly and menacing hungry men may become." Any sensible businessman could see that the relief programs cost far less than repairing the damage of a total breakdown in the social order.

Finally, Kennedy noted how the New Deal was making Wall Street fairer for all investors. With each new law, the old guard had insisted that the reforms would be ruinous and unworkable. Yet the reforms *were* working, and Wall Street was prospering. Investors had access to better information about their investments. Manipulators faced a greater risk of getting caught and punished. Exchanges were being pressed to police themselves more attentively. Soon, when the court battles were over, the labyrinthine utility conglomerates would have to clarify their finances and simplify their structures, to the benefit of both investors and customers.

Kennedy, clearly proud of his young agency, predicted that, "when the economic crisis that began in 1929 is dim in history," these financial reforms would still be seen as among "the most beneficial statutes enacted in years."

By the time the official campaign hit its stride in October 1936, the SEC had fully justified Kennedy's praise.

It had shut down half a dozen smelly stock exchanges, several fraudulent stock "tip sheet" publishers, and a widespread "bucket shop" operated by "old established and trusted" brokers in Chicago, New Orleans, and Atlanta. Rather than backing off after the *Jones* case, Landis set up a separate unit, staffed by experts in the field, to scrutinize all the oil and gas trust prospectuses that came in. The agency sent Congress a full report on the bankruptcy reforms that Bill Douglas recommended.

And Landis, expanding beyond the Meehan stock-rigging case, continued to battle market manipulation. For many investors, that was the crime that had defined the unlevel playing field of the Roaring Twenties market, dividing Wall Street between the clubby insiders rigging the game and the average investors being treated like suckers. It remained an SEC priority.

ONE OF THE ODDITIES of the 1936 presidential campaign was that these financial reforms—still bitterly denounced and resisted by the old guard on Wall Street—were never seriously attacked by Roosevelt's Republican opponent.

Kansas governor Alfred M. Landon, a mild and liberal-leaning oil producer who was the only Republican governor to be reelected when Democrats swept the 1934 midterms, had been the GOP front-runner since early in the year. But the party that convened in Cleveland in early June 1936 was torn between hard-line Hoover loyalists determined to dismantle the New Deal and pragmatic Landon allies who knew Americans would never endorse a return to the callous policies they endured under Hoover. Landon's campaign staff embodied this divide. His chairman was an old guard conservative named John D. M. Hamilton; his biggest national booster was the liberal editor William Allen White.

This tension produced a party platform that reflected both Landon's strength and Hoover's influence. Echoing the fiercest Roosevelt-haters, the platform opened with a dire warning: "America is in peril . . . To a free people, [FDR's] actions are insufferable." But elsewhere, Landon's more moderate voice could be heard. "The necessities of life must be provided for the needy and hope must be restored pending recovery," the platform pledged. "Society has an obligation to promote the security of the people by affording some measure of protection against involuntary unemployment and dependency in old age." The platform vowed to "protect the rights of labor to organize and to bargain collectively" and to support state and interstate efforts to abolish sweatshops and child labor, and to impose maximum hours and minimum wages for workers.

More remarkably, the platform explicitly endorsed the New Deal's key financial reforms—*all of them*. It conceded "the existence of a field within which government regulation [of business] is desirable and salutary." It supported "federal regulation, within the Constitution, of the marketing of securities to protect investors." The final capitulation: "We favor also Federal regulation of the interstate activities of public utilities."

But the galvanizing moment in Cleveland came not from the party's platform but from the party's former leader: Herbert Hoover.

Hoover had not disappeared from the national stage after his defeat in 1932. In 1934, against the advice of his friends, he had published *The Challenge to Liberty,* an impassioned attack on FDR and the New Deal; when Democrats won that year's midterms, Hoover "was dumbfounded" and declared, "Daily the world goes back toward the regimentation of the Middle Ages, whether it be Bolshevism, Hitlerism, Fascism, or the New Deal." According to one biographer, he defiantly "set his sights" on the 1936 nomination "with a courage bordering on delusional." Honing his speeches, he developed "an intransigent critique of the New Deal that defined him more clearly than even his years in the White House," another biographer later noted. As part of this "shadow campaign," Hoover had run a slate of delegates in the California GOP primary and had encouraged his friends to talk up his prospects. But by June, Landon's lead seemed to have erased any chance of a comeback for Hoover.

Landon's allies, however, had underestimated the rage many of the delegates felt toward Roosevelt. When Hoover arrived in Cleveland on June 10, that anger erupted in the form of unbridled, almost hysterical adulation for the former president. About eight thousand people met his train from Chicago, some shouting "Hooray for Hoover." When he arrived in the hall, the fifteen thousand delegates gave him a fifteen-minute ovation; when he was led toward the podium, the convention band struck up "California, Here I Come," his campaign theme in past years. The California delegates chanted "Hoover or His Choice." The Texas delegation rang its loud collection of cowbells. Two state delegations spontaneously paraded through the aisles. Convention programs and any other available scraps of paper were shredded by hand and thrown into the air as impromptu confetti.

When Hoover could finally give his speech, he tore into the Roosevelt administration. Some, he said, thought the New Deal was "sheer opportunism," "a muddle of a spoils systems, of emotional economics, of reckless adventure, of unctuous claims to a monopoly of human sympathy, of greed for power, of a desire for popular acclaim and an aspiration to make the front pages of the newspapers."

That, he said, "is the most charitable view."

Others, he said, saw the New Deal as "a cold-blooded attempt by starry-eyed boys to infect the American people by a mixture of European ideas, flavored with our native predilection to get something for nothing."

Hoover reminded his audience that Europe's fascist and communist dictators had started out by getting elected. The 1932 campaign by FDR "was a pretty good imitation of this first stage of European tactics," he said. "If there are any items in this stage in the march of European collectivism that the New Deal has not imitated it must have been an oversight."

The New Deal, in short, was "poisoning" Americanism. There could be no compromise with it. "Either we shall have a society based upon ordered liberty and the initiative of the individual, or we shall have a planned society that means dictation, no matter what you call it or who does it. There is no half-way ground." He called for "a holy crusade for freedom."

The delegates went wild—journalist Arthur Krock, present in the hall, called it "an ecstatic uproar of approval." Another journalist described it as an "uncontrollable burst of frenzy." Delegates stood on chairs, wept, cheered, applauded, marched, waved banners, and chanted "We want Hoover!" No further business was even attempted that evening. The California delegation slipped out for a caucus, as Hoover waited in a room apart, "wistfully hopeful that the ovation would lead to his renomination," according to one historian. Was a "draft Hoover" movement possible? Could it stop Landon?

Ultimately, no. New York and Pennsylvania delegates gave Landon a first-ballot victory, and Landon quietly rebuffed Hoover's plan to be a prominent voice in his campaign. But to Krock, Hoover's speech helped persuade the crowd "that their cause was so just and so vital that victory must be possible."

Roosevelt dealt deftly with Landon's attempt to juggle the old guard's denunciations of the New Deal and Landon's acceptance of New Deal programs and priorities. Roosevelt joked that Republicans were claiming they would do everything FDR would do, but would do it better. He acknowledged that the New Deal had made mistakes, that not every experiment had been successful. But he also reminded voters of the moral and spiritual differences between his administration and the one that had gone before, and that could return to power again.

"Better the occasional faults of the Government that lives in a spirit of charity than the constant omission of a Government frozen in the ice of its own indifference," he said in his acceptance speech in Philadelphia. Better a warm and humane idealism than a cold and rigid ideology.

———

HINDSIGHT IS A MIRAGE; its shimmer of inevitability distorts events that were actually nail-biting uncertainties for those living through them. This is especially true of the 1936 presidential election.

As the candidates kicked off their campaigns in the fall, the race was widely considered a toss-up. After all, Landon had defeated an array of formidable Republicans to secure the nomination. And while the economy was indisputably better than in early 1933, there were still about 9 million people out of work and the rising cost of living was squeezing those who did have jobs. Most major polls gave the lead to Landon. A landslide for either candidate was "inconceivable," said Dr. George H. Gallup, a dynamic young pollster gaining respect among the pundits. In July, he predicted "one of the closest elections in the political history of the country." The *Literary Digest* poll, with an excellent record for accuracy, showed Landon with a narrowing but still substantial lead right up until Election Day. As late as October 22, Washington pundit Willard M. Kiplinger told the Boston Chamber of Commerce: "The only thing I know for sure is that it's going to be a close election."

Roosevelt wasn't taking victory for granted. After he was renominated at the convention in Philadelphia, he traveled more than 5,000 miles to campaign in defense of the New Deal.

Landon won the endorsements of most of the nation's urban newspapers, with the notable exception of *The New York Times,* and many influential columnists, including Walter Lippmann. Landon also had the support of every prominent Republican and several prominent Democrats, including Al Smith, who grabbed headlines with each fresh attack on his former protégé. A speech Smith made just before the election was reported on the front page of *The New York Times* with the headline: "Smith Links Reds with Roosevelt; President Is Preparing Way for Communist Conquest, He Says in Albany 'Swan Song.'" The few speeches Hoover was allowed to make were equally harsh and got equally rapt attention. Within the newspaper and magazine ecosystem, FDR seemed to be getting a lopsided amount of disapproval.

But among rank-and-file journalists, the private assessment seemed to be that Roosevelt would eke out a victory. Arthur Krock, traveling state by state, noted in mid-October that several solidly Republican states seemed to be leaning toward FDR. Everywhere, enormous crowds lined up to see Roosevelt, even if it was just a glimpse of a passing limousine or railroad car.

The simple fact was that the New Deal had personally touched, and helped, millions of people. Roosevelt's relief programs were putting the jobless to work with a minimum of scandal and an abundance of public investments—libraries, airports, bridges, schools, cultural archives, highways, restored forests. Construction contracts were rebounding, and retail sales were reviving. The Dow Jones index on the eve of the election closed at 176.67 points, more than three times its level on the eve of FDR's inauguration. All this had been done with a level of empathy for "the little fellow" that radiated from Roosevelt at every stop on the campaign trail.

Still, when the national Democratic chairman Jim Farley said publicly in mid-October that FDR would carry every state but two, he was roundly ridiculed. The editors at *The New York Times* said, "Nobody believes this, and it is doubtful if [Farley] does himself." Indeed, the one prediction the editors thought most "political prophets" would endorse was that the 1936 election would be "closer than four years ago," with Landon carrying more states than Hoover did.

Joe Kennedy joined the campaign in late September, overseeing a newsreel special about the Roosevelt family, shot at Hyde Park. He made a number of speeches and a few national radio broadcasts—columnist Drew Pearson kidded him that, on radio, he was a dead ringer for comedian Groucho Marx. He helped organize dinners held simultaneously in several major cities where businessmen heard a personal radio address from Roosevelt. In Boston, he reminded his audience that, over time, "nearly every piece of social legislation passed by the state to protect the laborer" had been smeared by wealthy reactionaries as "entering wedges of socialism and communism." He ridiculed accusations that FDR was a tyrant, joking that the best rebuttal to that was the obvious fact that "my friends in the

Harvard Club can call the president anything they care to, without fear of reprisal."

Roosevelt's own campaign speeches from 1936 still resonate with relevance in the continuing national conversation about the proper relationship between public and private interests.

To the GOP's attacks on his deficits, Roosevelt replied that "to balance our budget in 1933, or 1934, or 1935 would have been a crime against the American people." His listeners surely caught his biblical reference: "When America suffered, we refused to pass by on the other side."

In defending his key financial reforms, he was at his very best on October 14 in Chicago. He recalled conditions in Chicago, and much of the nation, when he had flown in on July 2, 1932, to accept his party's nomination. "I came to a city with its back to the wall, factories closed, markets silent, banks shaky, ships and trains empty," he said. Then he listed the fruits of the New Deal *for American business:* safer banks, fairer markets, cheaper utility bills, lower shipping costs, more affordable credit, and above all, the "precious lifeblood of purchasing power." Relief payments "were spent in the stores and shops of the nation; and spent again to the wholesaler; and spent again to the factory; and spent again to the wage-earner; and then spent again in another store and shop."

But if "the train" of American business was to run smoothly into the future, he warned, "the cars will have to be loaded more evenly" so their axles wouldn't break again. The lopsided train of the past, with so much wealth piled into a few railcars while the vast majority were nearly empty, was the real "menace" to democracy, one that the party of Hoover refused to even acknowledge.

His rich critics had forgotten "how sick they were" in March 1933, Roosevelt said. "But I know how sick they were. I have their fever charts." He continued, "Washington did not look like a dangerous bureaucracy to them then. Oh, no! It looked like an emergency hospital."

With a saucy grin, he added his punch line. "Now most of the patients seem to be doing very nicely. Some of them are even well enough to throw their crutches at the doctor."

———

MEANWHILE, LANDON WAS TRYING to mute the hard-line GOP attacks on the New Deal and amplify his own message that he would address the needs of farmers and small businessmen more efficiently than FDR. As Landon said later: "We had everything set in pretty nice shape, then the Old Guard moved in and took control." His balancing act ultimately failed; by late October, some of his attacks on FDR were as unhinged and vitriolic as Hoover's. The shift left him looking indecisive and inconsistent. When he saw his signature sunflowers waving high across a sea of people at a late campaign rally in New York's Madison Square Garden, "he felt then that he might win," by one account. But his optimism began to fade as he headed home to Topeka to vote.

By Election Day, November 3, 1936, at least a modest Roosevelt victory seemed certain to all but the hardiest Liberty League stalwarts. Even Wall Street's betting rings predicted reelection.

The president was in a jovial mood as he and his family voted at Hyde Park's town hall. After waves and smiles and a few moments in front of the newsreel cameras, the family returned home to await the voters' verdict.

In a big Biltmore Hotel suite in Manhattan, campaign manager Jim Farley had put together a nerve center as modern as the era could provide. In his office, advanced telephone equipment let him "converse with about a dozen persons at once," a reporter admiringly noted. Additional telephones covered a large T-shaped table nearby, where about twenty women were poised to scribble down reports from party officials in more than three thousand counties across the country. Those results were conveyed by teletype to a pressroom elsewhere in the suite. One telephone line remained open to FDR's Hyde Park home throughout the evening.

By nightfall, the stately old mansion was humming. Radios in almost every downstairs room were tuned to the election news. In the dining room at the back of the house, the heavy dark table was cluttered with temporary telephones and vote charts. FDR's sons Franklin and John recorded the tallies conveyed by Farley. An octagonal room off the dining room had been filled with teletype machines, and secretary Missy LeHand moved swiftly between the two rooms to make sure FDR saw the important items.

Eleanor, in a white dinner gown, and Roosevelt's mother, Sara, in somber full-length velvet, circulated through the crowd, encouraging guests to enjoy the sandwiches and doughnuts laid out in the large book-lined living room.

As polls closed and vote totals started flowing in a steady stream, Roosevelt at some point gathered up "a pencil, a pad, and a large voting chart" and rolled his wheelchair into his small study, tucked under a stone loggia at the front of the house. Roosevelt was sure he would win but, like *The New York Times,* he simply didn't believe Farley's outlandish prediction. He estimated he'd get 360 electoral votes to Landon's 171.

When Farley reported that Roosevelt was 15,000 votes ahead of Landon in New Haven, the president was sure it was a mistake. The margin "couldn't be that large" in a Republican stronghold that most pollsters gave to Landon and Gallup said was too close to call. Someone checked to see if the report was accurate. It was. FDR leaned back, took a puff on his cigarette, and "blew a smoke ring into the air." Then he said, softly, "Jesus!"

As exhausted reporters and newsreel cameramen swelled the crowd, Tommy Corcoran carried his accordion through the first-floor rooms, ad-libbing funny parodies of "Oh! Susanna," Landon's campaign tune, and constantly reprising FDR's theme, "Happy Days Are Here Again."

Back at the Biltmore, the news on the teletype machines in the pressroom initially caused skeptical reporters to suspect campaign pranksters were hoaxing them with fake items like "Roosevelt carries Kansas." But Roosevelt had, indeed, carried Landon's home state of Kansas, by more than 16,000 votes.

Pollsters and pundits had been confident it would be a close election. But just as Jim Farley had predicted, FDR carried every single state except Maine and Vermont. He won 523 electoral votes to Landon's 8. The turnout was enormous, with more than 80 percent of eligible voters casting ballots. Roosevelt's total exceeded Landon's by nearly 11 million votes, an historic margin of victory. It was the greatest landslide since 1820, and an extraordinary affirmation of support for Roosevelt's New Deal from rank-and-file Americans.

As Election Day deepened into night, Times Square in New York City was a sea of happy Roosevelt supporters, cheering and celebrating. Among the more somber wealthy diners at the St. Regis Hotel, a small band of New Dealers greeted the news that the race had been called for Roosevelt by rising and proposing a toast to the president. "Not a person stirred," *The Economist* magazine reported. "Not another glass was lifted."

WITHIN DAYS OF THE election, Roosevelt began work on reducing the federal budget. Despite his previous conversations and correspondence with the British economist John Maynard Keynes, who urged FDR to use public spending to support weak private demand, Roosevelt was a man of his time; budget deficits were tolerable only if they were absolutely necessary and he was no longer sure they were.

Another topic at FDR's first postelection cabinet meeting was the Supreme Court. Roosevelt urged his solicitor general to push ahead quickly with any New Deal cases; Harold Ickes told his diary he believed FDR expected to lose those cases and would use the defeat to build public support for a court reform plan.

A month after the election, FDR tapped Joe Kennedy to be the first chairman of the new U.S. Maritime Commission, another difficult task involving another top presidential priority. A war in Europe, looking more likely, would deny America the use of European vessels for shipping, and its own fleet was small and obsolete. Kennedy's job was to get American industry to work building ships again.

Kennedy's return to Washington would mean Marwood again would become a hub of hospitality for his young protégés at the SEC. But one of the most intimate of them was ready to retreat from Washington just as Kennedy returned. During his sixteen months in office, Jim Landis had become a New Dealer to be reckoned with. His speeches were getting attention, notably his warning to investment bankers that "the verdict of November 3" showed the public would not tolerate a return to the unregulated market of the 1920s. There was speculation that he would be one of FDR's first Supreme Court nominations. And on December 21, newspapers listed him among the guests at the Gridiron Club dinner who laughed at the wry jokes by the victorious Roosevelt and the defeated but good-natured Landon.

Landon likened his feelings to those of a Kansas farmer whose house, barn, henhouse, stable, and fences have been wiped out by a tornado. Emerging from the storm cellar, the farmer starts laughing. "What on earth are you laughing at?" his distraught wife demands. Landon's answer: "The *completeness* of it." The crowd roared.

The victor, too, was in jolly form. Noting that Landon's campaign manager, John Hamilton, had gotten a highly paid job with the GOP national organization, FDR told the crowd he had a question. "If John Hamilton is worth twenty-five thousand a year for carrying two states, what salary should Jim Farley get?"

But as Jim Landis laughed along with the raucous crowd, he alone knew this was likely his last Gridiron Club dinner as SEC chairman. He was tired. He felt increasingly bruised by the attacks on him by impatient New Dealers who should be his allies. At one point, he wrote plaintively to Frankfurter that he was "taking it on the chin, psychologically speaking, from the group that hate every effort for general reform" on Wall Street and now found that attacks from liberals were weakening his strength, which "needs not only to be conserved but needs to be built up." He evidently reconsidered and scratched out the complaint before he mailed the letter. But the feelings behind it could not be so easily erased.

The first rumor of his discontent came on New Year's Day 1937, when *The Washington Post* reported that Landis was considering a return to the Harvard law faculty, but had made no final decision.

The law school had grown frustrated by his long "leave of absence." Each year since 1933, the excuses Landis gave for delaying his return had grown more elaborate. Early in 1936, he claimed there were important court cases pending and, besides, he couldn't abandon the president in an election year. But not long after FDR's victory, Harvard president James B. Conant called again, with a slightly different proposal. Yes, he wanted Landis to return to the law school—but as its dean, not as one of its professors. At the young age of thirty-seven, Landis would instantly become one of the most influential law educators in the country. "Without much hesitation, Landis accepted," according to one biographer.

The hesitation came from elsewhere. The first weekday after the *Washington Post* report—a day when Roosevelt had cleared almost everything from his calendar to devote time to his "state of the union" speech—the president summoned Landis to the White House. He listened as Landis explained his concerns—the toll the long hours were taking on his family, his health, his morale. Then the president begged him for more time, and Landis reluctantly agreed to delay his departure until the summer, or maybe a bit longer, or maybe quite a bit longer.

It was very hard for anyone to say no to FDR. Joe Kennedy used to say he had no trouble rejecting the president's demands over the telephone, but once they were face-to-face, he was hooked. For Landis, it was even harder. Like Kennedy and Frankfurter, Roosevelt showered the austere young man with the affection and generous approval that his own father had not been able to offer. Landis's loyalty to the New Deal was embedded in a deep affection for this remarkable president. He later recalled an episode during his SEC years when he had been stricken by influenza and fainted during dinner at Treasury secretary Henry Morgenthau's home. Morgenthau summoned his driver and got Landis safely home. "I was in bed the next morning, and about two dozen roses arrived—from the president," he recalled. "Well, you don't forget a thing like that." Roosevelt personally wrote Conant at Harvard to ask that Landis be allowed to delay his return until September; of course, Conant and Landis agreed.

The delay may have cheered FDR, but it made Bill Douglas quietly furious. Not privy to FDR's role, Douglas assumed Landis was simply trying to thwart his own ambition to be chairman.

As 1937 opened, Douglas's bankruptcy reform proposals were finally bearing fruit and, to his delight, producing even more head-lines than he'd earned in 1936.

Senator Burton Wheeler, digging deeper in Douglas's field, was holding hearings on how the securities of the bankruptcy-bound Alleghany Corporation holding company had been approved for listing on the New York Stock Exchange in 1929 and 1930. On January 15, Dick Whitney was summoned to testify but remarkably disclaimed any knowledge of the "special technical operation" of the listing committee.

Abruptly, Wheeler switched topics. Was it not true that Whitney and his predecessor Harry Simmons had each been allowed by J.P. Morgan to buy a thousand shares of Alleghany for $15 less than the price quoted in the market at that moment?

Whitney flushed with anger. He resented the "unfair implication" that there was anything unethical in the governors' acceptance of this windfall. "I think the implication that the sale to us of these shares affected our judgment is not a fair one," he complained.

"You got the stock for $20 when it was worth $35 and you see nothing wrong in that?" the senator asked.

"No, I certainly do not see anything wrong in it," Whitney replied.

Wheeler then detailed fifteen other NYSE governors who also had gotten bargain-priced Alleghany shares from J.P. Morgan. "I do not think you, or any other official of the New York Stock Exchange, ought to put himself in the position of purchasing stock at less than the market price and, as a member of the governing board, pass on applications for the listing of that stock on the exchange!"

Then Wheeler confronted Whitney with a long memorandum written years earlier by an exchange executive who warned of the dangers of listing the securities of convoluted holding companies like Alleghany—and yet, many such securities had been listed. Whitney denied that he had ever seen the memorandum, or even heard it discussed.

When the hearings resumed on January 26, it was a chastened Dick Whitney who appeared before Senator Wheeler. He said

Charles Gay, Harry Simmons, and he all agreed that it would be wise for the exchange to adopt rules—"after conferences with the Securities and Exchange Commission"—to prevent any governor from voting to list a stock in which he or his firm has a stake.

Douglas was a sort of delighted godfather to these front-page hearings. He was ready to parse them during long evenings at Tommy Corcoran's apartment, which had become a clubhouse for young New Dealers. Douglas knew he could rely on Corcoran to let the president know about his jousts with Wall Street. His speeches in 1936 had been finely tuned to irritate Wall Street and convince Roosevelt's inner circle that he was a forceful reformer—and, indeed, he was. He had made sure copies were sent to the White House. Before 1937 dawned, admirers in the media were citing him as "a strong contender" for the SEC chairmanship.

Douglas clearly believed those reports—and may have planted some of them. The day after the president's second inauguration, a remarkably audacious news item appeared. A national columnist, Raymond Tucker, wrote that "the only objection" to Douglas being named head of the SEC "is Mr. Douglas himself." Douglas would like to crack down on "speculation and similar practices" with a heavier hand than Kennedy or Landis, but he worried about the fallout from "a sharp switch in policy (such as he contemplates) at this time." Douglas "has outlined his predicament to FDR," Tucker warned, "so if the President should name him as the next chairman, it will be the last call to Wall Street to get right with God."

It is hard to imagine how Douglas explained that brazenly inaccurate item to FDR—unless he thought the president would chuckle at such ambitious "bad boy" behavior. More likely, he hoped the item would be lost in the inauguration coverage.

Braving the cold rain and sleet that drenched the intrepid inauguration crowd, Roosevelt again called for a prosperity that was widely shared and not funneled just to the favored few. "We have always known that heedless self-interest was bad morals," he said. "We know now that it is bad economics." He measured how far the nation was from achieving that fair society. "I see one-third of a na-

tion ill-housed, ill-clad, ill-nourished," he said. He nevertheless was
hopeful because he believed the nation was determined to address
this injustice. "The test of our progress," he continued, "is not whether
we add more to the abundance of those who have much; it is whether
we provide enough for those who have too little."

That was the chime that rang through so many of his speeches—
that all Americans, rich and poor, were in the same boat. "In our
personal ambitions we are individualists," he said. "But in our seeking for economic and political progress as a nation, we all go up—or
else we all go down—as one people."

Landis stood bravely through the ceremony but succumbed
within days to a wretched cold. His misery lifted immediately late in
the afternoon of January 29, when he got the call that U.S. District
Judge Julian Mack in Manhattan had sided with the SEC in the
Electric Bond and Share litigation.

It was an enormous, front-page victory for the SEC and for the
young chairman whose strategy was protecting FDR's holding company act from the juggernaut of power industry lawsuits. It wasn't
over, Landis knew. In the Ebasco case, Judge Mack was ruling only
on whether utility holding companies had to register and disclose
their financial structure and operations. The judge rejected Ebasco's
argument that the entire law had to stand or fall in one piece. The
fate of the law's death sentence would be decided another day, in
another case. This was a significant victory, nevertheless, and three
major utility holding companies soon dropped their lawsuits against
the SEC and registered.

But nearly two-thirds of the holding companies remained defi-
ant and refused to register—and the SEC had to stand by its vow
that it wouldn't prosecute the lawbreakers until the law had been
fully upheld by the courts.

That didn't stop Landis from trying to shame the boycotters by
arguing that they were wasting shareholders' money on "the mad
advice of their lawyers—those Liberty League lawyers" who told
them not to register. "To care less about stockholders than the advice
of hired lawyers is a tragedy."

———

BY EXTENDING HIS SEC tenure, Landis was inevitably pulled into the cascading crises that began to hit the New Deal in 1937.

In early February, Roosevelt shocked Washington—and Landis—by proposing a bill that would allow him to appoint an additional Supreme Court justice for each current justice who was old enough to retire but had not. For whatever reason—hubris after his stunning election victory, perhaps—Roosevelt misjudged both his public and congressional support for this initiative, and it cost him a substantial amount of the political capital he had collected with the 1936 vote. By the end of the summer of 1937, the Supreme Court proposal was dead and FDR had settled for far more modest reforms to the appellate courts.

There are acres of contemporary and historical analysis about FDR's "court-packing" plan, but its significance to the fate of his financial reforms is difficult to determine. The SEC had been scorched in the *Jones* case, but it had not been nullified—and it could have been. Its enforcement efforts had been upheld in the trial courts, as had its strategy in the Ebasco test case. Indeed, the Supreme Court had refused to even hear a second constitutional challenge filed against the SEC by J. Edward Jones.

But nearly every minor enforcement case had become a constitutional challenge, thanks to the inflammatory language in the *Jones* ruling. The utility industry's boycott was clearly founded on its belief that the Supreme Court would overturn the holding company law as soon as it had the chance. No one could argue that the SEC did not have any stake in how the court reform battle turned out.

Jim Landis resisted only briefly when he was recruited to help Roosevelt sell the public on the plan to expand the Supreme Court. His speeches won few converts and they cost him a lot of support among the faculty and alumni at Harvard Law School.

But the SEC, arguably at the margin of the court reform fight, was front and center in the next crisis of 1937. By late spring, the economy was quietly cracking, partly because FDR had succumbed too soon to demands for a balanced budget and partly because both his administration and the Fed had taken premature steps to fend off a feared rise in inflation. The deflationary slump would continue for months without attracting much attention in Washington; then it would worsen sharply, putting a desperately large number of people out of work and shaking the nation's confidence in the New Deal's recovery recipe.

There was no question that this "Roosevelt recession," viciously steep although mercifully short, posed significant threats to FDR's financial reforms, and Jim Landis would spend his last weeks in office trying to deal with them—with an increasingly frustrated Bill Douglas kibitzing beside him.

BY MIDSUMMER 1937, THE stock market had been steadily declining since New Year's Day. By the Fourth of July, the market was not only rocky but thin—low volume had plagued the NYSE since May. Reduced trading meant reduced profits for every firm on the Street. New issues had petered out—unsurprisingly, given the growing but unacknowledged weakness in business activity. And tax issues were certainly a factor—investors were still adjusting to new corporate and capital gains taxes aimed at balancing the budget. But by August, Wall Street had come up with its own explanation for the market's problems: government regulation.

"Too many rules, like too many laws, may result in laying unnecessarily restrictive burdens on the many for the sake of disciplining the few," wrote NYSE president Charles Gay in his annual report, released August 18, 1937. He was especially fearful, he said, that "undue restraints" imposed to deal with "what might be called sporadic evils" were damaging the marketplace.

Gay insisted the NYSE was "in sympathy" with the SEC's efforts to promote the public welfare. But he condemned "excessive" regulation that "stifles individual initiative, intimidates and confuses honest men so that they are unable to determine how to act when swift action is essential."

This was not a new theme. Gay had made essentially the same complaint in his annual report the previous year, when market volume was stronger and prices were robust. He repeated his "thin market" complaint in May 1937, when trading volume was still strong and two-million-share days were common; again, the claim was based on questionable analysis and cherry-picked time spans.

Indeed, market research showed that liquidity for the market's dominant stocks had started declining long before Roosevelt, or even Herbert Hoover, had been elected. A study that would soon be reported in *The New York Times* showed that the trend dated back at least to the early 1920s, long before the SEC existed, and seemed to have been caused by "a fundamental change in speculative fashion." Speculators previously focused on a few "market leaders," which could be traded very easily amid that avid interest. But over time, that speculative interest was "buttered more thinly over the list— and the list is much larger than it was," the report noted. The result was less liquidity for the "market leaders," an outcome that had nothing to do with FDR's regulations.

And of course, Gay's assertion that the market suffered only "sporadic evils" inflicted by the few was laughable in view of the record of Wall Street misconduct that both the Pecora hearings and the SEC had assembled.

This fresh attack showed how thoroughly Dick Whitney's old guard still controlled the NYSE. Gay's report "left the clear implication that the Exchange demanded nothing less than repeal of the Securities Exchange Act and abolition of the SEC," one journalist later observed. "The exchange's cards were on the table—and they were Whitney cards."

On September 14, just days before he was due to walk into the dean's office at Harvard Law School, Landis arrived at the White House for an emotional farewell to Roosevelt. "I could not have wished for a richer experience, nor a happier association," he said in the letter he delivered to the president. Roosevelt was equally generous in praising Landis. "You have contributed mightily to a pioneer effort of modern democracy," he wrote. "You have been a leader in a field of financial regulation where most of the supposed experts were sure that government could not intelligently intervene for the protection of the public."

Returning one last time to meet with reporters at his office at the SEC, Landis struck back at Charles Gay with uncharacteristic anger and energy. The attack was condemned even by those who thought Gay had wildly overstated the risks of Roosevelt's reforms. And not everyone did; Wall Street's demands for deregulation grew stronger with each turbulent day in the market.

By mid-September, the stock market had been falling steadily for a month, and Wall Street's leaders had continued to blame the decline on the SEC and the New Deal's financial regulations. They had warned FDR's Commerce secretary that the president needed to make a conciliatory choice to replace Landis. They suggested some prominent business figure like the president of the Sears, Roebuck catalogue house or W. Averell Harriman, the railroad heir and Wall Street titan.

A financial reporter for *The New York Times* in early August noted that Wall Street would see Bill Douglas as an antagonizing choice because of his "reforming tendencies." Thus, "his selection is believed to depend largely on whether President Roosevelt is inclined at this time to make a gracious gesture to the financial community."

It's not hard to imagine a grin lighting up Roosevelt's face when he saw this newspaper punditry over breakfast in bed. He had no intention of making a "gracious gesture" to anyone who opposed the "reforming tendencies" of one of his regulators. Maybe the autocratic forces on Wall Street had already forgotten the lessons of 1929. Roosevelt had not.

Reassured by Joe Kennedy and Tommy Corcoran, Roosevelt affirmed his own commitment to the effort that had begun in those sweltering temporary offices at the FTC in the summer of 1934. He chose the impatient firebrand William O. Douglas, a month shy of his thirty-eighth birthday, to be the third chairman of the Securities and Exchange Commission.

It was, indeed, time for Wall Street to "get right with God."

CHAPTER SIX

DEFENDING AGAINST DEREGULATION

SEPTEMBER 17–NOVEMBER 22, 1937

WHEN REPORTERS CROWDED INTO THE SEC CHAIRMAN'S office on Wednesday, September 22, 1937, the man waiting for them defied every stereotype of an Ivy League law professor. Bill Douglas wore a ten-gallon hat, a stained tie, a rumpled suit, and a crop of fresh freckles from his interrupted vacation on Cape Cod. When he leaned back in his chair and swung his feet up onto his new desk, reporters saw a hole worn through the sole of one of his shoes.

He surveyed his visitors with a steely cheerfulness. To one friend there, Douglas seemed like a western marshal "who took meticulous care of his guns, because it was coming in to High Noon, and he was going to walk down Wall Street for the shootout." There had been a lot of confusion and uncertainty about his views, Douglas said, "so I thought this might be a good opportunity just to have a frank, direct, specific talk with you gentlemen to let you know, as clearly as I can state, what lies ahead."

Not waiting for the reporters to pose their own queries, he rattled off three questions he proposed to answer: What was the proper role of the SEC? What "kind of bird" was he? And what was his attitude toward some of the "specific, live problems that we have before us" at the commission?

What *was* the proper role of the SEC?

Douglas's answer has persisted through history as the SEC's aspirational motto: The SEC should be "the investors' advocate," he said. "We have got brokers' advocates; we have got exchange advocates; we have got investment banker advocates—and we are the *investors'* advocate." That mission, he explained, was "within the framework of the three statutes that we presently administer. That is the one fundamental, underlying philosophy of those three statutes— protection of the investor."

That was the chord he hoped would resonate across Wall Street, marking the end of the patient and accommodating Landis era and the beginning of his own more demanding regime. Douglas made it clear on his first day in office: if Wall Street's old guard and its cherished institutions did not step up to *protect investors,* the SEC would.

William Orville Douglas was a restless man, perhaps because he was so often in the grip of irreconcilable passions. Raised in Yakima, Washington, he loved the western mountains, but he longed for the fame he found only in the concrete canyons of the urban East. His impatience with slower minds could sting without warning, but he sprawled and slouched like a man with all the time in the world. He longed to take risks, but needed financial security.

Douglas portrayed himself to the world as a simple, uncomplicated cowpoke, a tough hombre who could not be pushed around. That surely is who he tried to be in his public life, but his inner reality was far different. In private, he saw himself as having been "launched in life as a package of fears." He had been psychoanalyzed in the 1920s by a doctor who helped him overcome debilitating migraines and intestinal reactions to the phobias that haunted him. Even his remarkable success, for him, was shadowed by regret. He had learned in 1925 that the poverty that dogged his youth was actually the result of his mother's own unwise investment decisions. The funds she squandered could have let him aim higher, work fewer jobs, study more, go further—but "instead of investing in his future, he now knew, [his mother] took a foolish chance on a speculative deal."

Given all that, it was perhaps not surprising that family relationships never seemed to fit easily into his own emotional life. But he almost wistfully admired the closeness and conviviality of Joe Kennedy's clan. A family meal at Kennedy's table "was a seminar. I could not help contrasting those evenings with my own in Yakima, where food was gulped, everyone too busy for dinner-table conversation." By the fall of 1937, he was still too busy. He had been married for thirteen years to the former Mildred Riddle, a shy but loving Latin teacher from Yakima High School, and he was the father of two children. But his ambition-driven schedule and self-absorption, both at Yale and at the SEC, left little time for any of them.

Bill Douglas had campaigned hard for the SEC chairmanship, beset by the shifting politics of the White House. Joe Kennedy's backing might have helped him with Wall Street, but it was less clear whether it helped in Washington. Since early 1937, Kennedy had nagged FDR to balance the budget, publicly opposed FDR's tax proposals, and privately resisted the president's court reform campaign while publicly supporting it. One cabinet official considered Kennedy "a New Dealer merely out of personal loyalty to the President." His support might have fatally tainted Douglas among FDR's more liberal advisors if Douglas himself had not become such an effective scourge of Wall Street during his first eighteen months on the commission.

When NYSE president Charles Gay had first begun to complain in the spring of 1936 that federal regulation was producing "thin markets," Douglas had spoken out to rebut Gay's argument. Conflicts of interest on the NYSE trading floor also affected market quality, he had noted, as did the "normal lassitude" which follows periods of speculative frenzy. Moreover, if regulations against excessive margin trading, abuse of inside information, and price manipulation had reduced market activity, the previous level of market activity obviously had been immoral and unhealthy.

At the U.S. Conference of Mayors in November 1936, he had reprised his brass-knuckle critique of how Wall Street banks mishandled municipal bankruptcies and presciently called for more "sunshine" for municipal bond issues.

And most famously, in an address to the Bond Club of New York in March of 1937, he had fiercely attacked the "financial royalism" that let bankers and insiders control corporations to the detriment of stockholders and called for sweeping reforms in how investment bankers got paid. At a time when many bankers thought it was unethical to lure clients away from a rival bank by offering lower fees, Douglas had urged competitive bidding for most corporate under-writing deals. His audience, which had greeted him with a robust ovation, had been left stunned and nearly silent by the end of his address—"shocked into a state of profound grumpiness," as *Time* magazine had put it.

Even with Douglas's reform credentials freshly buffed, he had heard nothing from the White House as Jim Landis's final days as chairman approached. On September 17, he had flown from Cape Cod to Washington—ostensibly for Landis's valedictory meetings—and immediately telephoned Kennedy, misleading him with a tale that he was going to return to Yale (which may have been true) as its law school dean (which certainly wasn't true) if nothing else was forthcoming, by which he clearly meant the SEC chairmanship. Kennedy, who probably had seen through this ruse, had told him to sit tight and went to work to close the deal. Kennedy likely had re-lied on Tommy Corcoran for the face-to-face lobbying; the presi-dent's calendar for September 17 shows several visits from Corcoran during the day, and none from Kennedy.

In any case, Kennedy had called Douglas early on Saturday, Sep-tember 18, and told him to expect a call from Roosevelt. The call had come after breakfast, with FDR's jovial roar at the other end of the line. At 11 A.M., Douglas had been ushered into the White House, where the president offered to back him as the new SEC chairman. By noon, he was heading back to Cape Cod. On Tuesday, Septem-ber 21, the SEC's three remaining commissioners—Landis, in one of his last official acts, along with Bud Mathews and Judge Healy—had elected him to the post. He returned to Washington that night for his inaugural press conference in his new office.

Warming to the audience of reporters gathered around him, Douglas reminded them the agency also had certain judicial func-tions. He would see that those were carried out in "an objective, disinterested manner, trying to give justice to all parties concerned." But given the way society was organized, he continued, "the great mass of investors, the general investing public, is often without rep-resentation unless we take up their cause." The SEC fielded cases in which "powerful groups have wrestled for control, for power, or for profit, and in each of these cases we must stand between as the investors' advocate," he said, again striking his chosen chime.

With flashes of humor, Douglas explained at some length that it wasn't the SEC's job to keep stock prices high, to boost floor traders' income, or to dispense investment advice. "We can demand full disclosure of the facts; we can insist upon a market free of manipulation; we can fight fraud; but we cannot provide sound business judgment, nor can we save a fool from his folly."

As for "what kind of bird" he was, he said: "To tell you the truth, I think that I am really a pretty conservative sort of a fellow from the old school, perhaps a school too old to be remembered." In that "old school," he said, the overarching rule was "no monkey business."

Douglas sketched out a plainspoken self-portrait. "I'm the kind of a conservative who can't get away from the idea that simple honesty ought to prevail in the financial world. I am the kind of a fellow who can't see why stockholders shouldn't get the same kind of fair treatment they would get if they were big partners instead of little partners in industry. I can't see eye to eye with those whose conscience lets them deal themselves two or three hands to the investor's one." In short, he said, "I don't see why it isn't possible to have a completely honest relationship between finance, industry, and the investors."

He diplomatically added that these standards were merely those "that the best elements in business and in finance adopt for themselves without the intervention of government." Those committed to such standards would get the agency's "fullest cooperation"—but his notion of a healthy relationship between Washington and Wall Street was "industry self-regulation under the close supervision of a government agency," not a timid agency deferring to the traditions of an insular and self-protective industry.

Douglas laid out his to-do list. He hoped to simplify SEC paperwork, clarify audit standards, write new rules for investment trusts and the over-the-counter market, study carefully how to resolve conflicts of interest on the trading floor, and sustain the fight against market manipulation and the abuse of inside information.

The commission staff, he said, was "the swellest gang of fellows" in government and the SEC was "one of the best organizations a government ever set up." He added, "We're going to keep it that way, because we cannot enter a period of action unless we have got talent and brains and imagination and initiative." Clearly, a "period of action" was exactly what he had in mind as chairman.

A wire service reporter had cornered him before the press conference to ask about his agenda, and he had laughed. "Wait a minute," he had said. "I have my own ideas but don't ask me what they are yet. I haven't had breakfast and I need a shave!" But he did explain that, under Joe Kennedy, FDR's reforms to protect investors "were consolidated," and under Jim Landis, "we were taught how to get things done. And we're now going to go ahead and *get them done.*"

Douglas fielded a few more questions at the end of the press conference and then said he had to catch a train in a few minutes to return to his vacationing family and "mull over some of the major problems that lie ahead."

ONE OF DOUGLAS'S CHIEF preoccupations when he returned to Cape Cod to resume his vacation with Mildred and young Millie and Bill Jr. was what to do about the New York Stock Exchange.

Since Joe Kennedy had first released the SEC's "suggested" reforms for the NYSE in January 1935, the exchange had been stalling—perhaps expecting politics or the courts to eventually liberate it from the SEC's oversight. In Dick Whitney's presidency, every suggestion was a battle, fought with sharp words and rigid resistance. After Charles Gay took over in May 1935, the struggle became a quieter charade of public amity and private foot-dragging. New rules were adopted with a bit of fanfare, but were then applied with the same clubby carelessness as always. Gay had persuaded himself that if the NYSE just polished its public image, it could continue to operate pretty much as it pleased. Indeed, that belief had been strengthened by Landis's ineffectual reply to Gay's aggressive attack on the SEC in August. When a reformer on the board confronted Gay over his capitulation to "the old guard," Gay just pointed to Whitney's continued influence and shrugged, "What else can I do? My hands are tied."

Dick Whitney wielded his power most effectively as a member of the exchange's law committee, which served as a presidential cabinet and was a choke point for every rule change and regulatory negotiation. The committee's chairman was Whitney's friend Harry Simmons, the former exchange president who had groomed him for power in 1929 and then returned as Gay's vice president after Whitney was forced out in 1935. The law committee relied on advice from outside counsel Roland Redmond, Whitney's friend and ally in the fight against federal regulation in 1934. Allen L. Lindley, Whitney's vice president while he was in office, was another old guard stalwart on the law committee.

But Whitney also commanded respect on the floor as a trustee of the exchange Gratuity Fund, the NYSE's in-house life insurance plan for its members. While they were not as powerful as the law committee members, the trustees were far more than figureheads. Besides tending roughly $2 million in reserves, they had full discretion to decide which heirs qualified for benefits, when those benefits would be paid, and what role the members' employers and executors could play in the process. The trustees had even dispatched their legal advisor to help a member's heirs argue in court that the death benefit should not be taxable. Thus, every NYSE member had a stake in how well the fund was managed by its seven-member board.

While the exchange's president and treasurer served on the board by virtue of their office, the five other trustees were directly elected by the members. After five years on the board as the exchange's president, Whitney had been elected as a trustee in 1936—and, as when he was "demoted" to the board of governors in 1935, he got more votes than any other candidate for office that year. He was the only bond trader on the board and routinely handled the fund's bond investments at the direction of the full board. Like the law committee, the Gratuity Fund's board of trustees was chaired by Harry Simmons; both were firmly in the grip of Whitney's old guard allies at the exchange.

Whitney still upstaged Gay in the halls of Congress. When Senator Wheeler held his hearings on the NYSE's listing standards in January 1937, it was not Charles Gay who was summoned to testify but Dick Whitney, who had been out of office for nearly two years. Clearly "the Prince of Wall Street" from 1929 remained a powerful element in the stock exchange's resistance to the New Deal's financial reforms.

At some point in early summer 1937, Whitney and his wife, Gertrude, had reconciled after he ended his affair with the Delaware widow. Whitney was hospitalized briefly in June to have his appendix out, just days before his brother, George, underwent the same operation. An appendectomy was no trivial matter in those days, so perhaps the shadow of mortality led Whitney to seek forgiveness on the home front. Or perhaps both he and his wife wanted their family life to look as normal as possible before their younger daughter's society debut in 1938.

Or perhaps the Wilmington connection had just become too messy to manage: on June 30, Franklin Roosevelt's son Franklin Jr. married Ethel du Pont, whose rich relatives had bankrolled the American Liberty League's anti-FDR efforts—and whose aunt had been Whitney's mistress. Indeed, young John Roosevelt's date for his brother's lavish wedding was a Boston debutante who had recently jilted Whitney's stepson Samuel S. Sands IV, whose status as Mrs. Vanderbilt's grandson made him constant gossip fodder. The era's world of wealth and power—the Ivy League classmates and society debutantes who went to the same parties, belonged to the same clubs, and knew the same people—could seem quite small when entanglements like this cropped up. In any case, the couple's 1936 rupture was forgotten gossip by the fall of 1937. When Whitney made news, it usually was for his work as an NYSE governor, an officer or director of the New York Yacht Club or the Jockey Club, or a member of the board planning the 1939 New York World's Fair.

WHEN CHARLES GAY HAD denounced the New Deal's financial reforms in August, his indictment was based on the belief that the underlying American economy was robustly healthy. Given that belief, regulatory overreach was the only logical explanation for the market's erratic behavior.

Of course, Gay was wrong that the economy was healthy—but so was Roosevelt. The president's cuts to federal spending earlier in the year, made in the belief that the economic justification for budget deficits no longer applied, were beginning to kick in and inflict real damage. Relief rolls were trimmed just as payrolls and corporate profits were dwindling. The result was that consumer demand began to shrink before industry was able, or willing, to expand its own spending.

Economists still argue about the precise causes of the 1937 downturn. Certainly, one factor was the Federal Reserve's unwise decision to tighten the money supply between August 1936 and May 1937, while unemployment was still high. The reason was an unfounded fear of inflation; the result was an immediate recessionary drag on bank lending. Other research suggests that the banking crisis that climaxed on the eve of FDR's inauguration, on top of the broad collapse in property values that began in 1925, had done lasting damage to the flow of bank credit to businesses, especially to midsize and small companies.

Whatever the root causes, the economy had silently slipped into a recession in May 1937. Across the country, unsold inventory was piling up, new orders were thin, factory production was slowing down, and unemployment was rising. All these declines were from 1936 metrics that, while stronger than in previous years, were still nothing to wave flags about.

FDR's conservative Treasury secretary, his Hyde Park neighbor Henry Morgenthau Jr., was a decent but limited man with vague economic ideas firmly rooted in the Victorian era. Even as the market slump worsened, he argued that only a balanced budget would provide the big dose of "business confidence" the economy needed. Some younger New Dealers—Bill Douglas among them—quietly argued that the government needed to spend more, not less, to take up the slack in demand. Roosevelt got some version of that advice from Ben Cohen; Tommy Corcoran; Federal Reserve chairman Marriner S. Eccles; Leon Henderson, an economic advisor to FDR's

trusted aide Harry Hopkins; and a few friends in business and publishing.

But FDR's thrifty Dutch soul instinctively felt more comfortable
with the "orthodoxy" of a balanced budget. As the recession deepened and he was pelted with conflicting advice, he seemed to drift
along without a plan, by turns flippant and furious. By September,
the economy's slide had become a headlong plunge that would be
the sharpest and steepest the country had ever seen.

At some level, the troubled markets in the summer of 1937 clearly
had been registering the economy's silent distress. By the time Bill
Douglas returned from Cape Cod to Washington on the first of
October, the markets were experiencing wild gyrations. Traders
blamed "war fears" and a cloudy business outlook, but exchange officials continued to blame the New Deal reforms. After one day's
nosedive, a columnist at *The New York Times* reprised Charles Gay's
August lament almost word for word. And so it went. The market
dropped and rallied and, regardless of those ups and downs, Charles
Gay gravely insisted that "over-regulation" was to blame.

But in private, smiling Wall Street leaders told reporters they
were strongly optimistic that the "debacles" of September would finally force Washington to lift the burdens imposed by the New
Deal. Adolf Berle told his diary—and, quite likely, his friend in the
White House—that what his stock exchange pals really wanted
"was to have the whole national policy reversed." He added, "There
is not a chance of that." But the stock market had dropped 20 percent since Charles Gay's angry attack in August, and would fall
nearly another 20 percent in Douglas's first two weeks in his new
job. Wall Street grew increasingly confident that Roosevelt could
not swim much longer against the cold current of a plunging market.
He would have to deregulate.

As September slid into October and a fragile recovery slid deeper
into recession, it was hard for those around Roosevelt to rekindle the
optimism and exhilaration of his 1936 landslide victory. In hindsight,
some of them may have seen an omen in an incident at the Democratic National Convention at a Philadelphia stadium on June 27,

1936. The small backstage crowd awaiting the president included the snowy-haired poet Edwin Markham. He was the author of "The Man with the Hoe," that profound poetic warning that society must lift up its long-brutalized laborers or risk its own destruction at their hands. In a sense, it was the battle hymn of the New Deal. As Roosevelt moved through the small backstage crowd, gripping his son James's arm, he spotted Markham and reached out to shake his hand. Markham, jostled by someone, bumped into James Roosevelt, who momentarily staggered into his father. Under this added weight, FDR's leg brace came unlocked and Roosevelt pitched forward, the pages of his speech scattering in disorder across the floor. Screened by FDR's entourage, Secret Service agent Michael Reilly instantly stooped and got his shoulder under Roosevelt's armpit; as Reilly rose up, he lifted the president with him, while bodyguard Gus Gennerich deftly locked the offending brace.

There it was: reaching out to a soul in sympathy with his ideals of helping the common man, Roosevelt had relied too much on his accustomed supports, lost his balance, and let his message fall into disarray. The warning was lost in the triumph that followed the incident. FDR deftly reordered the fallen pages while acknowledging the thunderous ovation of the crowd, and went on to deliver a speech inscribed in American history for its prescient call to a generation that had "a rendezvous with destiny." Harold Ickes told his diary it was, simply, "the greatest political speech I have ever heard." And then, of course, Roosevelt had marched steady and upright into that astounding victory in November.

But perhaps the incident seemed more prophetic now that Roosevelt's second term, begun in the soaring confidence of an historic mandate, was becoming an obstacle course, at best, and a minefield at worst. In early 1937, journalist Ernest Lindley had hailed Roosevelt's "demonstration of the capacity of our form of government to act with sufficient energy, imagination, and scope to overcome a grave crisis." But as the recession of 1937 deepened, he found Roosevelt "slow to react. For six months he did almost nothing, clinging to the pleasant hope that there would be an automatic upturn in the

spring of 1938." What had happened to the visionary governor whom
Lindley had known in Albany, the brave national leader who seemed
to light up a rainy day on March 4, 1933?

Historians note that Roosevelt had been deeply affected by the
loss of two trusted companions in 1936. In April, his astute political consigliere Louis McHenry Howe died after a long illness. In
December, the kindly bodyguard Gus Gennerich—Roosevelt called
him his "ambassador to the man in the street"—died suddenly in
Buenos Aires during FDR's postelection cruise to Latin America.
Jimmy Roosevelt, recruited by his father as a confidential assistant
in early 1937, was too unsteady and inexperienced to fill these shoes.
And rather than drawing closer to the lonely and bereaved president,
the First Lady became even more distant, telling her close friend
Lorena Hickok, "I realize more & more that F.D.R. is a great man,
& he is nice to me[,] but as a person, I'm a stranger & I don't want
to be anything else!" In his increasingly lonely life, FDR's instincts
remained sharp, but so did his impulses and his grievances—and
now there were few who could play the role of Louis Howe and say,
"*Mein Gott,* Franklin, that's the stupidest idea I ever heard of!"

The president's ill-fated effort to reform the Supreme Court may
or may not have jolted the justices into being more accepting of the
New Deal—court historians disagree—but it certainly eroded his
authority in Congress. As one New Deal historian put it, "The Court
fracas destroyed the unity of the Democratic Party and greatly
strengthened the bipartisan anti–New Deal coalition. The new
Court might be willing to uphold new laws, but an angry and divided Congress would pass few of them for the justices to consider."

Southern Democrats were joining easily with conservative Republicans, while progressives were struggling to form workable
alliances across party lines. FDR fumed to his close aides about unreliable Democrats. His party, which he still hoped to reshape into a
coherently liberal coalition before 1940, was resisting his leadership.

And almost every business and financial leader who could get his
ear—along with several members of his own cabinet—wanted him
to be vastly less confrontational with business. Wall Street's warning,
echoing Charles Gay in August, was that FDR must dismantle the

New Deal's financial reforms or the Roosevelt recession would become the Roosevelt depression.

It is all the more remarkable, then—and further evidence of how important his financial reforms were to FDR—that Roosevelt had ignored Wall Street's "anyone-but-Douglas" campaign and chosen this ardent young New Dealer to run his cherished SEC, the keystone in his plan to tame an unregulated Wall Street. Roosevelt may not have decided what he *would* do in that sour and stormy season but he clearly had decided by September what he would *not* do: he would not hogtie the SEC.

His vacation over, Bill Douglas arrived at his SEC office on October 4, 1937, for his first meeting as chairman. With Landis back at Harvard and J. D. Ross about to be confirmed as director of the new Bonneville Power Administration, only Judge Healy and Bud Mathews joined him at the conference table abutting his desk. They were hit almost immediately with a rearguard attack from inside the agency. Staff economist Kemper Simpson, the co-author of a report on NYSE conflicts that Landis had rejected as extreme and unworkable, presented his resignation letter to the commission and released it to the press.

It was an angry denunciation of the entire SEC track record, delivered by an unyielding New Dealer who believed the agency had been captured by Wall Street. Simpson accused the agency of being too eager to get new stock and bond issues to market, and claimed its simplified paperwork had eliminated information necessary to protect investors. He attacked Jim Landis, without naming him, for being obsessed with "technical detail and legal phraseology." He said the agency "had not done enough" to curb "undue speculation" in the fall of 1936, or to protect investors in the subsequent decline in 1937, without noting what it could have done differently in either case. Then he attacked Douglas, without naming him, for saying it wasn't the SEC's job to save a fool from his folly; that was just "passing the buck," as he saw it.

Simpson's diatribe, seized on by those in the media who collected the daily conflicts, was typical of the New Deal purists who were unwilling to give an inch to placate Wall Street. Between them and

Wall Street's purists demanding immediate wholesale deregulation, Douglas did not have much common ground on which to stand—a situation that would plague his entire tenure.

His shrunken commission, already divided over how tough to be with Wall Street, would soon have two vacancies. Wall Street was lobbying fiercely to fill one or both of them with its allies. Douglas did not know how long he could command a majority for the reforms he wanted to make—or whether FDR could still command congressional action on any fresh SEC legislation he might need.

Still, as Douglas got to work, he could see a few clear spots where he could make progress. He could encourage the Investment Bankers Conference in its slow but strengthening effort to create some kind of self-regulatory organization for the over-the-counter market, in keeping with his philosophy that the ideal role for the SEC was not to police Wall Street but to make darned sure that Wall Street policed itself. He could keep the pressure on investment trusts through continued hearings into the conflicts of interest that plagued that industry. And he could continue nudging Congress to codify his proposed reforms for the bankruptcy process, despite the protests of a phalanx of corporate lawyers and bank trust departments.

And, right away, he could dust off and resolve a stack of unfinished business. In his first two weeks, the commission issued rules for exemptions to the holding company act. The Supreme Court's recent refusal to let the SEC-Ebasco case skip the appellate review process would further postpone the SEC's effort to enforce that law, but Douglas would be ready when that day came. In deciding a disciplinary case against some so-called "customer's men" who dealt with retail investors, the commission released a stern warning to stock exchanges to crack down on abusive behavior by *any* employee of their member firms, not just floor traders. And it finally produced a long-overdue advisory letter on how the securities laws applied to "pegging" operations, the flurry of purchases Wall Street underwriters made to prop up the prices of new issues in their first few weeks of trading. There was a thin line between what the Street called "legitimate price stabilization" and what the securities laws called "illegal market manipulation," and Douglas was moving the

SEC toward allowing pegging but requiring underwriters to fully disclose their plans to investors.

But Douglas never stopped mulling over ways he could finally persuade the NYSE to trade its private-club traditions for professional management and clear safeguards for public investors. The exchange was best situated to detect and stop market manipulation and trading conflicts, of course. But Douglas doubted it could ever be trusted to do that in an impartial, evenhanded way while it was run by old guard volunteers looking out for their friends. He wanted professional full-time management conducting impartial full-time oversight of NYSE members, under the keen supervision of the SEC.

By the fall of 1937, almost three years since Joe Kennedy's first efforts, Douglas felt the SEC already had waited too long and gotten too little. If his agency was to have any credibility as "the cop on Wall Street," it had to stop accepting the old guard's excuses and start demanding the reforms Roosevelt was elected to deliver.

But every bad day in the stock market seemed to harden Wall Street's determination to be rid of its regulator. The stock market had been dropping steadily since September. After the much-lamented "thin" summer, the number of shares traded had risen sharply in September, but prices had not recovered—and the bond market, Dick Whitney's specialty, had suffered both low volume *and* low prices. There was an unsteady rally in both markets at the beginning of October, but it sputtered out and the downward stagger resumed.

Into that uneasiness stepped Winthrop W. Aldrich, chairman of the Chase National Bank, one of the largest of the Wall Street banks, and a formidable member of a great power dynasty. His father played a role in the creation of the Federal Reserve and made an unseemly fortune as an influential Republican senator in the robber baron days of the late nineteenth century. His favorite sister, Abby, was married to John D. Rockefeller Jr., whose family was his bank's largest shareholder; later, he would groom her son David for a lifelong management role there.

For Bill Douglas and others at the SEC, Aldrich was merely the naïve fellow who sat stunned in a Senate hearing room in October 1933 as his predecessor, Albert H. Wiggin, told Ferdinand Pecora about the stock manipulations he had conducted in the 1920s.

But on October 14, 1937, Aldrich gave a headline-grabbing speech to the Chamber of Commerce in Rochester, New York, in which he endorsed Charles Gay's view that the New Deal was damaging the market. The influential Chase chairman was sure the economy was still robust—a very poor call, in hindsight. And he was confident the market wasn't unduly alarmed by the bloody conflicts in Europe and China—a very poor call, even at the time. Like the NYSE president, Aldrich was certain the market decline was primarily the result of Roosevelt's rules.

Aldrich claimed the market was being hurt by capital gains taxes, high income taxes, and estate taxes—because "to pay such taxes, very large blocks of securities must be liquidated . . . in a thin and inadequate stock market." Further damage, he said, was being done by curbs on trading by corporate insiders—"informed buying," he called it—and "inquisitorial visits" from SEC staffers. "Few men, however innocent their purposes, however legitimate their transactions, welcome governmental inquiry into them," Aldrich declared. Such men "have ceased their activities because they do not wish to invite this kind of attention."

To the editors of *The New York Times*, and to other conservative editorial pages elsewhere, this all made a great deal of sense. After all, Aldrich didn't suggest "that all the regulations adopted since 1933 should be repealed," the *Times* noted. He just pointed out that some regulations were having unintended consequences. It was just a question of amending "internally defective though well-intentioned regulations."

On Friday, October 15, 1937, the president was visited at Hyde Park by Joe Kennedy, whom press wits called FDR's "tame capitalist." He had come for lunch and stayed deep into the afternoon. Both he and FDR denied that Wall Street had been the topic of their long conversation, but that wasn't true. The president was deeply worried about the stock market, Kennedy was deeply attuned to the stock market, and the two men "discussed the ramifications" of recent stock market developments over lunch and well into the afternoon.

On leaving the mansion, Kennedy was asked about Aldrich's attack on the New Deal's financial reforms the previous day and laughed at the notion that the SEC's investigations were affecting the market. Kennedy may have moved on from the SEC—and he had ambitions to move even further—but he remained firmly and fiercely in its corner. After all, he had helped give it birth; it was one of the family. Two days later, another SEC founding father added his voice to Kennedy's. In New York, Judge Ferdinand Pecora told reporters, "The sooner the leaders of the financial community realize the futility of trying to re-create the old happy hunting grounds, the sooner they will attain the stable market they profess so much to want." He itemized the banker's complaints and added: "Mr. Aldrich's theories are not new. This country tried them prior to 1929, and has been recovering from them ever since."

Franklin Roosevelt, as he stewed about the market, had conceived the dark idea that its decline was an "unconscious conspiracy" by bankers to force him to back down on financial regulation. He had nursed the same suspicions in 1934, so an "unconscious conspiracy" wasn't an entirely new idea. Banks were clearly deciding *not* to lend; it was logical to wonder if recession worries were the only reason.

While his suspicions seem strange in retrospect, by late 1937 the nation's wealthiest citizens viewed Franklin Roosevelt with such unrestrained hatred that there's little wonder FDR fretted about how far they would go to undermine him. Such animosity toward someone who did *not* nationalize their banks and utilities or plunder their trust funds or allow grass to grow on Wall Street—predictions every conservative had made since 1932—was a fact of life for the president. One wit, journalist Marquis Childs, found the plutocracy's hatred so outlandish and inexplicable that he wondered if the American rich were faking their rage at FDR "to throw the workers and farmers off their guard" so they would keep electing Roosevelt.

But at least a few cabinet officials believed business leaders resisting FDR were rational and sincere. At a cabinet meeting that fall, Roosevelt bristled when Henry Morgenthau told him, "You must do something to reassure business."

"You want me to turn on the old record," Roosevelt said. He had been playing "the record" of his reassurance for years; he had been rewarded with a chorus of hisses and boos from the wealthy elite who owned the nation's businesses.

"What business wants to know is this," Morgenthau persisted. "Are we headed toward state socialism, or are we going to continue on a capitalistic basis?"

The wonder is that the entire cabinet did not burst out laughing. If FDR had wished to dismantle capitalism, he could easily have done so in the dire days immediately after he took office, when even conservatives like Al Smith were saying it was time to "put the Constitution on the shelf." The actual socialists in the country, in fact, were still deeply disappointed that he *had not* seized the banks or nationalized the power industry. If Morgenthau was conveying genuine concerns from "business," then the nation's businessmen were far more paranoid about FDR than he was about them.

Glaring at Morgenthau across the cabinet table, Roosevelt repeated that he had assured business at least fourteen times that he was committed to capitalism.

"Tell them for the fifteenth time," Morgenthau murmured, looking to one of his fellow cabinet officers like "a spanked child" but not backing down.

Postmaster General Jim Farley backed up the Treasury secretary, urging FDR to "do a little backslapping with business," according to Harold Ickes's account. Then Farley turned to Ickes and whispered, "That's right, isn't it?"

Wise to the depths of the anti-FDR hatred, Ickes whispered back: "I don't think it would make a particle of difference."

THE PRESSURE ON ROOSEVELT increased sharply the Monday after Joe Kennedy's visit to Hyde Park. That day, October 18, was the worst day in the market in six years.

A host of possible reasons were thrown out, including the Supreme Court's surprising refusal that morning to block an SEC subpoena for the private telegrams of a Florida oil royalty trust operation. (Its owner was arrested the next day on state charges of selling unregistered securities.) But it is more likely investors were reacting to reports of a surprisingly large drop in steel shipments, further evidence of the economic slowdown that Charles Gay and Winthrop Aldrich refused to believe was happening.

On the NYSE, steel shares were the first to tumble, but an across-the-board rout followed, and the NYSE was quickly overwhelmed. The ticker fell behind and the specialists and floor traders were beset by chaos. "Brokers were making trades on the fringe of the 'steel crowd' at one price, while others were being made ten feet away at another figure, the ruling pandemonium preventing either from hearing the other," *The New York Times* reported. The drop in bond prices was the worst in three years; at times, trading simply stopped.

Wall Street was swept that day by rumors that the NYSE was on the brink of being shut down by the SEC, or perhaps by the exchange itself. Bill Douglas, meeting that day with his fellow commissioners, immediately told reporters he had ordered the SEC's New York office to track down the sources of these "unfounded rumors."

He could make a good guess about one of them. He later recorded in his memoirs that, on this chaotic day, Charles Gay "called me every hour on the hour" to say "You must close the Exchange."

Douglas was not going to give Gay more ammunition to fire back at him. If he closed the NYSE, he wrote, "the legend would be established that the New Deal was responsible for the market not operating."

He told Gay, "Close it if you want to. I never will."

"But it's going down dangerously fast and will take all of America with it," Gay cried, in Douglas's perhaps fanciful rendition.

"I admit I don't know much about markets, coming as I do from Yakima," Douglas said. "But I always assumed that markets were supposed to go down as well as up."

And go down they did. Tuesday, October 19, was another staggering day—not as numerically damaging as Monday by the end of the day, but still psychologically alarming. Prices plunged at the opening bell, with trading the heaviest since 1933—nearly 7.3 million shares, far more than the exchange typically handled. Lacking any bids to buy, specialists could not start trading some major stocks for as much as thirty minutes. At its noontime nadir, the Dow was nearly 8 percent below the previous day's close, a drop that fully justified comparisons with the dark days of October 1929. Bonds declined all day "with hardly a sign of a rally," by one account. "Most issues closed at their lows for the day." An afternoon rally repaired some of the damage to stock prices, and the Dow index closed up by a single point. (Remarkably, some news accounts said the stock rally had been fed by large buy orders from the very corporate insiders who, according to Gay and Aldrich, had deserted the market because of the SEC's insider trading rules.)

In Washington that day, Henry Morgenthau was deeply shaken; the sell-off looked to him like "hysteria resembling a mob in a theater fire." He renewed his efforts to persuade FDR to embrace and reassure big business. In New York, FDR's former advisor Adolf Berle was also worried. "This looks to me like 1903—a rich man's panic," he told his diary, referring to a slow bear market that had cut the value of stocks almost in half in the early years of Theodore Roosevelt's presidency. "Everybody is watching the Stock Market—the real danger is the freezing of the bond market." No new bonds could be sold in this market; investment bankers announced the withdrawal or postponement of fully $100 million of new corporate bond issues due to be sold that week. With banks not lending and bonds not selling, where was business going to get the money to do the buying and building that the economy so desperately needed?

Indeed, Roosevelt was so concerned about the market maelstrom he had sent his son James to New York on Monday to be his "eyes and ears." From the SEC branch office at 120 Broadway, Jimmy Roosevelt had listened to the reports coming in to the staff about the chaotic trading and plunging prices. He grew increasingly upset; he almost certainly conveyed his alarm to his father. Discretion was not one of Jimmy Roosevelt's gifts, however, so he could easily have been another of the sources for the day's rumors of an imminent shut-down.

That night, Harold Ickes got a phone call from the president and tried to reassure him by quoting a recent column by that old Pecora stalwart John T. Flynn: "We can probably thank the SEC that prices of stocks and commodities did not go as high as they otherwise might and that they could be liquidated at better prices than if the SEC were not in business."

A few people within the NYSE happened to agree with Flynn. They were the oddly assorted figures who had helped deny Richard Whitney reelection as president in 1935. Quietly known around the exchange as the Elders, they were "a sort of Stock Exchange shadow cabinet that met regularly for lunch to grumble" about the Whitney faction's stubborn refusal to work constructively with the SEC, as one journalist put it. Some were FDR donors; some were Liberty League backers. But they all realized the NYSE's resistance to fed-eral regulation was a dead end for Wall Street.

Besides John W. Hanes, who had lost his board seat to a Whitney loyalist in the fevered 1935 election, the leaders of the Elders were Edward A. Pierce and Paul V. Shields.

Ed Pierce was a bluff and unpretentious man, white-haired and a little portly. Raised in Maine, he once claimed he had dropped out of Bowdoin College "because it was the start of the deer season." In 1901, when he was twenty-seven, he gave up a job as a lumber com-pany manager and went to Wall Street. He worked his way up from a clerk's job to the presidency of a prominent brokerage firm that did no investment banking; it was a "wire house," taking orders from its far-flung clients and sending them to market by telegraph and tele-phone. In 1927, the firm changed its name to E. A. Pierce & Co., in "tribute to his stature in the industry." His reputation grew after he steered the firm through the 1929 crash and the Depression. (In 1940, he would steer it into the merger that ultimately produced Merrill Lynch.) Ed Pierce had lost patience with Dick Whitney's royal im-peratives years ago: while the 1934 act was being debated, Whitney had called him at 3 A.M. to deliver a "tongue-lashing" over some friendly gesture he'd made to New Deal negotiators.

Unlike Ed Pierce, Paul V. Shields was a glamour boy on the Street—the society pages noticed whenever he and his wife were seen in the company of her son-in-law, movie idol Gary Cooper. Weathered and silver-haired, with dramatically dark eyebrows, Shields was an intrepid yachtsman, a fierce competitor among the rich and royal sailors on the Atlantic regatta circuit, and a stalwart of the New York Yacht Club. His family's investment bank, Shields & Company, had transformed itself after the 1929 crash into a formidable wire house. Shields had seen early on that Wall Street's business was increasingly coming from investors located far beyond New York; his firm had set up fifteen branches across the country to cater to them. "Unburdened with traditional theories and attitudes, he welcomes government regulation," one reporter noted in 1935. Indeed, he had been on Ray Moley's short list of potential SEC commissioners when the agency was first created. Shields had told a reporter a few years earlier that the new heartland investors his firm dealt with wanted service, not glossy gossip. "A man in Oshkosh with $5,000 to invest isn't sitting around in some customers' room waiting to hear a hot tip." That investor wanted facts—the kind of facts the SEC required companies to provide.

The reform-minded Elders had argued with Whitney and Gay repeatedly over the NYSE's intransigence toward the SEC. They had tried to explain that Main Street investors, who remained suspicious of the Wall Street insiders exposed by Pecora and the SEC, would not fully trust the market until it was better run and better regulated. They had been ignored. Working together in 1935, they had managed to deny Dick Whitney reelection; but now Charles Gay was behaving like Whitney's hand puppet. Gay's annual report in August, with its attack on the SEC and its demand for deregulation, had been a breaking point for Pierce and Shields.

Like a good sailor, Shields had decided to try a different tack. He had called Pierce and suggested they pay a quiet visit to Washington.

Saturday, October 16, had been chilly and blustery in the capital. The SEC offices on Pennsylvania Avenue had been quiet, though not empty. Shields and Pierce had called ahead, so Bill Douglas was there to meet the older men and escort them into his office. He had asked Judge Healy and Bud Mathews to join him.

At some early point, the topic of the NYSE's leadership had come up. Either Pierce or Shields had said, "We think the management is pretty damned bad. What would the SEC think of reorganization of the stock exchange?"

Eight months later, journalists Joseph Alsop and Robert Kintner reconstructed the scene. "Douglas slapped his knee in natural delight. He is a rather puckish fellow, and he leaned forward in his chair, grinning mischievously. 'Would you mind saying that again?' he asked."

They did, telling Douglas, "You can't get anywhere so long as the Exchange is a sort of private club." If the SEC would back them, they would renew their effort to reorganize it.

Douglas had burst out, "Why, damn it, that's just what I want!" He had assured them: "I'm with you one hundred per cent to reorganize the whole outfit, and I'll tell anybody so, whether it's the President or Dick Whitney." Pierce and Shields had flown back to New York and, no doubt, had spent Sunday, October 17, pondering how they could persuade enough exchange governors to support their reform drive.

When the stock market plunged into the turbulent trading of Monday, October 18—the uproar that had terrified young James Roosevelt, worried Adolf Berle, and even unsettled FDR—the plans that Pierce and Shields were making to rally support for reform had to be put on hold, at least briefly, until the crisis eased.

Sometime during that crazy Monday, James Roosevelt arranged for Paul Shields to talk with Joe Kennedy on Wednesday to explore whether Kennedy, and by extension the president, were as supportive of the reform effort as Douglas was.

Shields's meeting with Kennedy was loud and profane, as Kennedy's conversations often were. Kennedy was livid that Gay had blamed the SEC for the market's troubles; he seemed obsessed about the NYSE retracting the accusation. That was not Shields's priority, but he was reassured that Bill Douglas wasn't riding off the New

Deal reservation. When Shields got back to his office on Thursday, he got a call from Gay, asking him to come over to discuss his Washington visit. When Shields arrived, he found Gay had recruited allies from the powerful law committee: Dick Whitney, Harry Simmons, Roland Redmond.

Shields, "a big, fiery fellow," promptly disclosed he had met with Joe Kennedy and repeated Kennedy's demands for management reform and the retraction of Gay's charges. "They were filled with wrath," Alsop and Kintner wrote. Whitney fumed, Redmond argued, Gay agonized, and Shields left.

But the old guard strategists, for all their rage at the reform effort led by the Elders, realized that they, too, needed to tack in this storm before they could resume their preferred course. It was time to make "some gesture of compliance," as they had in the past. They drafted a memorandum for FDR outlining specific reforms they might undertake. Badgered by Whitney, they edited the memo down to a vague statement that management changes, including hiring a full-time paid president, were "under consideration." And they deputized Shields to deliver it to Hyde Park as soon as he could get on FDR's calendar.

On Tuesday, October 26, Bill Douglas was settled in FDR's small office in the Hyde Park mansion at 11 A.M., and their conversation must have included an update on the NYSE negotiations. At 11:45 A.M., Paul Shields joined them, bringing with him the bland commitment letter from the exchange leaders. Alsop and Kintner described FDR discussing the reorganization plan that Douglas envisioned "with the animated interest which the president's enthusiasm always imparts to talk of new plans." At some point, Joe Kennedy joined them. To FDR and Kennedy, wary of Wall Street betrayal, the letter from the exchange was not credible, but Douglas agreed with Shields that the note at least offered a chance to continue the negotiations.

Those talks resumed three days later in Washington. The NYSE delegation included Harry Simmons and Gay's new vice president, Walter L. Johnson, neither of whom was eager for reform, and Paul

Shields, who was. It also included Adolf Berle, who was playing an odd role as an envoy between his current colleagues at the exchange and his former colleagues in the New Deal.

Douglas had invited Kennedy to sit in on the talks, and Kennedy promptly unleashed one of his carefully considered temper tantrums. He warned "that the market crash had put the SEC on the spot, that a congressional investigation threatened, and that the SEC would be certain to blame the exchange" if its members were called to testify. Shields, whose tirade was perhaps more authentic, argued forcefully for a paid president who could run the reorganized exchange in a professional manner, instead of the status quo in which elected officers were reluctant to enforce the rules with any vigor against their longtime friends. Douglas gave the exchange officials a taste of what he would likely say to any congressional committee: "The job of regulation's got to be done. It isn't being done now and, damn it, you're going to do it or we are . . . If you'll produce a program of reorganization, I'll let you run the exchange. But if you just go on horsetrading, I'll step in and run it myself."

The SEC had been patient with the exchange's temporizing for so long that its leaders had perhaps forgotten that Congress had given the SEC the power to deliver on that nuclear threat under the terms of the 1934 act. If so, Douglas had forcibly reminded them. Calm negotiations about reorganization began to look like a good idea. Indeed, Adolf Berle soothingly reminded the group that the exchange had been "working on plans tending toward this end for more than two years." Douglas asked the exchange officials to put its tentative reorganization plan in writing and send it to him.

A plan was made for the negotiators to reconvene at the Yale Club in New York on Saturday, November 13, the day of the Princeton-Yale football game.

Bill Douglas planned to show up at the Yale Club ready to start negotiating an exchange of letters that would commit the NYSE to specific reforms within specific deadlines. Douglas was determined that the NYSE of the future would be run by a professional manager—not by some volunteer nominated by the conflicted board of governors ruled by Dick Whitney and elected by Whitney's equally conflicted cronies on the trading floor.

The stock market continued to sink as November arrived, and Roosevelt must have been keenly aware that the 1938 midterms were then only a year away. New stock and bond issues had vanished. Steel production was still falling; cotton prices were cracking in the face of a record harvest. Factory workers and farmers were in for a tough winter if the economy could not be coaxed out of its doldrums.

But the month brought a slice of good news for the president and the SEC. On November 8, sooner than expected, the appellate court in New York unanimously affirmed Judge Mack's pro-SEC ruling in the Ebasco case. Congress had the right to deny the use of the postal system for "purposes it deems objectionable to sound public policy," the decision noted. It had used that power to deny the use of the mails to any public utility holding company that failed to register with the SEC as required by the holding company act. The majority decision also affirmed Judge Mack's view that the registration rules in the new law could stand on their own even if the so-called "death sentence" clause were to fall. It was a total victory for the SEC's arguments, from one of the most respected appellate courts in the country.

Bill Douglas summoned reporters to his office to express his satisfaction—and answer his critics. Those utility holding companies that had refused to register—fully three-fourths of the industry—had predictably blamed the SEC and the "uncertainties" of the new law for the lack of new utility construction projects. It was the utility industry's version of Charles Gay's lament. Douglas insisted his staff would "go more than half way" to help utility companies to comply with the law so they could raise the capital they needed.

By the morning of Saturday, November 13, Yale was favored to win its sixty-first annual gridiron match with Princeton in New Haven. But no one was giving odds on how Douglas would fare in his negotiations with the NYSE that day. Years of successful opposition were lined up on the side of the exchange. The SEC could call on the will, guile, and intellect that had carried Bill Douglas from

Yakima to its chairmanship. And of course, the agency had FDR as its coach—Douglas had met briefly the previous day with Roosevelt.

Charles Gay had brought the exchange's lawyer William Jackson, Roland Redmond's partner. Douglas had brought an SEC stenographer—and Paul Shields, whom Gay had refused to invite. Douglas dictated a letter of the sort he'd like to get from the stock exchange. Gay insisted that Jackson mark for deletion the phrase about a paid president. "It was on this point that the old guard had decided to fight," according to one account. But that also was the point that Bill Douglas had decided he must win. The day ended with no progress at the Yale Club in Manhattan and with Yale obliterating Princeton, 26–0, in New Haven.

Sometime thereafter, Charles Gay consulted George Whitney and Tom Lamont at J.P. Morgan about the impasse. They endorsed the idea of negotiating, but cautioned Gay against retracting his attack on the New Deal, as Kennedy was demanding. They reminded Gay how lamely the agency, under Landis, had responded to Gay's original complaint about regulation in August and argued that the SEC, under Douglas, would likely back away from this fight, too—if Gay stood firm and refused Kennedy's demands. After all, the market was taking its toll on the New Deal and the Morgan men saw no reason for Gay to let the agency off the hook.

Gay briefly considered whether the exchange could drive a wedge between Kennedy and Douglas by giving Kennedy the retraction he wanted but refusing Douglas's demand for professional management. But Dick Whitney and the NYSE law committee were in full foot-dragging mode. They rejected draft after draft—there would be no retraction of Gay's charge and no promise to hire a paid president if Whitney could help it. And he clearly believed he could: on the Friday after the fruitless Yale Club meeting, the law committee voted to end the negotiations and told Gay to convey the news to Douglas.

Douglas was able to persuade the increasingly dejected NYSE president that everyone should try just once more. Gay pleaded and the law committee members agreed to return to the table—on the condition that John W. Davis, the Morgan firm's powerful lawyer, be given a chair. When Davis had taken his pencil to the exchange's draft for the SEC, the exculpatory paragraph Joe Kennedy had approved in Washington had been altered so much that "it appeared to the SEC that the Exchange really wanted to blame the commission for the market crash."

The members of the law committee approved this amended draft at a morning meeting on Monday, November 22.

The letter was read aloud over the phone to a stenographer at the SEC, and William Jackson caught a flight to Washington to deliver the original in person. Douglas met him with icy anger. He had summoned Judge Healy and Bud Mathews to an official meeting and the SEC already had voted unanimously to reject the law committee's draft and to cease negotiations.

Jackson asked Douglas, "So I suppose you'll go ahead with your own program?"

"You're damned right I will."

Jackson drew himself up and reminded Douglas that the New York Stock Exchange had been in business since 1792 and was now the premier marketplace in the country. "When you take over the exchange . . . there may be some things you will like to ask us," he said.

"There is one thing I'd like to ask," Douglas replied. "Where do you keep the paper and pencils?"

CHAPTER SEVEN

THE NEW DEAL ACTS,
THE OLD GUARD BLINKS

NOVEMBER 23, 1937–MARCH 7, 1938

AFTER STALLING JOE KENNEDY AND JIM LANDIS FOR MORE than three years, Dick Whitney and the old guard at the New York Stock Exchange clearly assumed that Bill Douglas was bluffing in his private ultimatum on Monday afternoon, November 22, 1937.

The continuing bear market—and Wall Street's continuing campaign to blame it on New Deal regulations—should have put the SEC on the defensive. The market had lost more than a third of its value since August. Roosevelt was not dealing effectively with the recession, and he was being pressured to stifle his criticism of business abuses. How could he afford to let a jumped-up law professor with no pedigree in finance run the nation's premier stock exchange?

It was simply unthinkable. Douglas was surely bluffing.

Someone at the exchange felt certain enough about that on Monday night to leak details of the failed negotiations to the *New York Herald Tribune*, falsely portraying Douglas's pressure as an act of petty retaliation for Charles Gay's refusal to absolve the SEC of any responsibility for the market slump. The resulting front-page article on Tuesday, November 23, quoted an unidentified Wall Street source as saying, "We'll not do anything now which might be misunderstood as being prompted by a shotgun."

Ruddy and red-nosed from the unusually cold morning, Douglas arrived at his office in Washington as the story broke in New York. Within hours, he was spooling through stock ticker items that reported other "reliable" Wall Street sources were confirming the misleading report. Douglas, visibly angry, decided it was time to brief the American public on what had really happened.

He sat at his desk and, with help from staff members, began drafting a six-page press release. At an impromptu official session, Judge Healy and Bud Mathews unanimously endorsed Douglas's statement. Secretaries took notes, typed stencils, and cranked out mimeograph copies. Calls were made to summon the press. Douglas watched, "tight-lipped and slightly tense," as reporters filed into his office late that afternoon. He handed out the statement and reporters quickly scanned it, not finding what they expected: an acknowledgment of the *Herald Tribune* account.

One of them asked about the newspaper's allegation.

Douglas abruptly stood up from his deck, punched the air, and forcefully answered: "Hooey!"

Well, it seems likely he used a stronger expletive; in those days, profanity was routinely sanitized by editors. In any case, his outburst shocked the reporters present. As *Fortune* later reported, Douglas generally seemed to them like a "restrained and mild-mannered Scotsman." Some accounts held that Douglas's fury prompted him to go further in his demands than he intended. More likely, Douglas had simply decided to include all his hoped-for reforms in the statement that day, expecting to be forced to compromise in the negotiations to come.

His message to the public was clear: Yes, he had been talking with the stock exchange leaders for two months, but not about "anything so silly as an acknowledgement of blame, from one side or the other, for the state of the stock market . . . Douglas was not interested in face-saving or finger-pointing."

He was interested in getting the New York Stock Exchange to operate less like the gentlemen's fraternity it had long been and more like the public-serving institution it must become to serve the nation's dynamic future. "I am not interested in attacking the New York Stock Exchange," he would tell lawmakers in closed-door testimony the following week. "I am interested in getting a job done." Rules had to be enforced without favoritism or spite; members had to put the public's interests ahead of their own when they conducted business. It was time to change a culture where Dick Whitney could rule from his roost on the law committee and misbehaving members could expect leniency from their pals on the business conduct committee.

The Securities and Exchange Act of 1934 had given the SEC the power to impose its own rules, however drastic, on the NYSE. The patience and priorities of Joe Kennedy and Jim Landis may have let the NYSE leaders forget how potent that law was, *Fortune* noted. "Douglas definitely has not forgotten."

His six-page statement was front-page news across the country on Wednesday morning.

It would be ideal, Douglas wrote, if the nation's stock exchanges could be trusted to regulate themselves. "At the present time, however, I have doubts as to the desirability, from the standpoint of the public interest, of assigning to exchanges such a vital role."

The commission had been patient with the NYSE, Douglas continued. It had not only "invited exchange representatives to the drafting table" but had held back on imposing its own rules on the exchange, as it had the power to do. All the rules that governed the NYSE on that day had been written and adopted by the exchange itself. The question was whether they were subject to "vigilant, vigorous, and full-time" enforcement.

Douglas had already determined to his own satisfaction that they were not. The SEC was investigating several recent instances of stock manipulation that had gone undetected, or at least unpunished, by the stock exchange. In early 1937, Douglas had gone to New York to quiz members of the NYSE's business conduct committee about their gentle handling of these manipulators. By one account, some committee members had told him they didn't like to press members with tough questions because they felt the committee's job was "to *protect* members against incriminating themselves."

"Exchanges have always administered their affairs in much the same manner as private clubs," Douglas wrote in his public statement, providing the phrase that would dominate the next day's headlines. "For a business so vested with the public interest, this traditional method has become archaic." It was no longer adequate for members—with their own financial interests and business affairs to manage—to take on the additional task of running a fair and honest marketplace for public investors. It was time for professional management led by a full-time paid president.

The rest of the lengthy press release laid out the specific reforms the commission believed were necessary and provided the evidence that led the commission to its conclusions. Douglas cited the inevitable conflicts that arose when exchange traders handled public orders and their own trading at the same time. And he raised the long-prickly issue of short selling, reporting on an agency study of short sales during the rocky days of September and October 1937. It found that members, and particularly the specialists for individual stocks, concentrated their speculative trading in the leading stocks, giving them considerable influence over price movements that could drive the market's direction. The data strongly suggested "members of the exchange trading for their own account either create the daily price fluctuations or else contribute materially to their severity," Douglas wrote.

"These problems constitute a challenge to the exchanges and their members as well as to the commission," he concluded. "It is a challenge which can only be met with progressive action." Specifically, he called for "a constitutional revision of the administrative and functional techniques of the exchanges."

This statement stunned Wall Street's old guard. Their fierce and angry objections were collected in "reaction" stories published across the land.

A typical example appeared in *The New York Times* under the headline "Wall Street Sees Retaliation by SEC." In this account, the long-suffering NYSE negotiators had displayed great patience in drafting a statement that said they did not hold the SEC solely responsible for the market slump. But "stronger and stronger terms were demanded." When those demands were rejected, the *Times* claimed, the exchange expected that the whole matter would "be dropped and forgotten. As late as yesterday afternoon there was no suspicion that failure to meet the SEC demand in the matter . . . might lead to retaliation."

This, of course, was ridiculous. If there had been retaliation—as opposed to an exhaustion of the SEC's patience—it had been for the NYSE's failure over several years to commit to any meaningful reforms in the public interest.

How many of these anonymous Wall Street complaints came from Whitney and his allies? He was not quoted directly, but later events showed that he fiercely opposed the constitutional changes the SEC sought.

AS THE RECESSION DEEPENED in late 1937, the pressure on Roosevelt to forswear any further criticism of American business grew more intense. It came from conservatives in Congress, newspaper editorials, chief executives who came to visit, and some cabinet members who had never been comfortable with his combative attitude toward Wall Street and corporate America.

These advisors and critics apparently did not share FDR's impatience with business leaders who refused to negotiate with labor as required by the Wagner Act, or work with the SEC as required by the laws of 1933 and 1934, or comply with the holding company act, or recognize a duty to pay employees a fair wage for a humane amount of work. Such corporate sins were excused or ignored; Roosevelt's criticism of those sins was not.

A national poll released in mid-December 1937 cast an interesting light on the debate. The survey measured the public's level of support for the statement that "the present government was helping rather than hurting business." The headlines looked grim for Roosevelt. "New Deal Hurts Business, Public Opinion Check Shows," blared one Indiana paper. "Opinions of Public on New Deal Shift; Survey Shows More Now Think It Is Hurting Trade Than Thought So in February," a headline in *The New York Times* declared. But a close reading of the stories showed that, when the survey was taken in October, a *majority* of those surveyed still agreed that government was helping. True, the margin of approval was smaller than earlier in the year—70 percent in February versus 58 percent in October—but it was still a very high level of support. More important, the charts showed that approval of FDR's efforts remained strongest among those at the lower end of the wage scale, who made up a majority of those surveyed. The lowest levels of support for FDR were tallied among the survey's "top ten percent" of wealthier families.

Stanley High, a former presidential aide whose tell-all memoir was published in 1937, was critical of FDR for allegedly using such economic divisions for political gain. But he nevertheless observed: "Mr. Roosevelt has served the special interests of certain classes of our citizens. It was undoubtedly high time that somebody served them."

BY LATE 1937, FDR's more enlightened aides were still arguing that the recession called for more federal spending, not less. But Roosevelt had stood by his commitment in the spring to reduce the federal budget. He was essentially running a test to see whether the budget cuts Morgenthau and other conservative advisors demanded actually *would* reassure business, encourage more hiring, and thereby cure the recession. Joe Kennedy, who shared Morgenthau's misguided views, was one of FDR's strongest defenders during this dreary December. At a white-tie debate hosted by the Economic Club on December 6, he bluntly told 1,500 members and guests that business needed to "stop bellyaching" and work constructively with FDR because, "whether you like it or whether you don't, he is going to be there for three years—and he is trying now very definitely to help the situation."

Sometime in early December, Kennedy ushered Joe Alsop and Bob Kintner into his office at the maritime commission and, pounding his desk frequently for emphasis, delivered the same message to the influential columnists. "How on earth can business people hope for any improvement in the present situation if they go on crying bloody murder at every remedy the President proposes," he demanded. "There's nothing the President can do to help matters so long as some of the businessmen in this country are determined to believe that nothing the President does will be beneficial."

The record of these months shows Roosevelt shifting constantly between gestures to placate his wealthy critics in business and demonstrations of his continued commitment to average citizens. He had pressed Douglas in October to accept a Federal Reserve move to liberalize margin rules, and had supported business tax revisions by Congress—but, a month later, he was firmly backing Douglas in his public face-off with the stock exchange.

He was supporting Douglas in other ways, as well. There were two vacancies on the SEC. Wall Street, as ever, was pressing FDR to give at least one of the empty seats to one of its citizens; the ardent New Dealers around Roosevelt were pressing equally hard for him to name commissioners who would back Douglas to the hilt.

Roosevelt appeared to do both.

For one of the seats, he chose John Wesley Hanes II, the Carolina-bred broker who had helped push Dick Whitney out of the NYSE presidency in 1935. Hanes was indisputably a Wall Street man; he was a partner in a major retail brokerage firm and had long been on first-name terms with several Morgan partners. Moreover, his role in installing Charles Gay led some to assume he was Gay's ally. But FDR knew that Hanes shared his own belief that regulated reform was the only way Wall Street could ever regain the public's trust. In early December there were strategic leaks from the White House that John Hanes would get one of the vacant SEC seats. Wall Street applauded, seeing the move as one that could "help smooth the troubled waters that separate the Street and the government today." Those who knew Hanes better were less sure the appointment was a cause for celebration.

For the second seat, FDR's message was bold and clear. He chose the candidate put forward by Bill Douglas: Jerome Frank. A famous jurist once observed that Jerry Frank's life was "a perpetual celebration," and he lived it with "unremitting compassion for the powerless and the poor." Raised in Chicago, Frank was an odd-looking man, with a rubbery grin, a receding chin, and protruding eyes. But he had a beautiful mind and an extraordinary intellect—one admirer declared, "It seems entirely possible that he has read more than anyone alive today." When he joined a New York law firm in 1929, its members "often said, 'It's worth $50,000 a year to us to have Jerry around just to hear him talk.'" It was worth a great deal to Bill Douglas to have a staunch New Deal advocate like Jerry Frank around to back up his tough line at the commission, although Wall Street had labeled Frank as a dangerous radical.

When these SEC choices leaked, Wall Street began to realize that Douglas would not back down and Roosevelt would not rein him in. If the NYSE wanted a say in the rules their members would have to obey, something would have to change.

On Monday, November 29, Charles Gay emerged from days of closed-door conferences with his fellow governors and handed out a statement pushing back against the SEC's criticisms. But buried deep within his protests—so deep that it was missed by almost every reporter who read it—was a single paragraph in which Gay revealed that he was "about to appoint, with the approval of the governing committee, a special committee to study this whole matter and to report as promptly as possible."

It took almost two more weeks for the magnitude of Gay's capitulation to become clear. On December 8, after a meeting with the governors, Gay announced that they had given him permission to appoint a nine-man committee to study "all aspects of a further development of the organization and administration of the exchange." Over Whitney's objections, the reformers had successfully insisted that Gay appoint, as the Associated Press put it, "a committee which would command public confidence."

When the committee's members were announced, alert reporters noticed that none of them were Whitney allies—indeed, only three of them were NYSE members at all. Although one of those, John A. Coleman, was known to be friendly with Whitney, another one, the young William McChesney Martin, seemed more aligned with the reformers' camp. Among the respected investment bankers and other business figures on the committee was Roosevelt's friend and former advisor Adolf Berle, an advisor now to New York Mayor Fiorello La Guardia, a progressive Republican. Berle wryly told his diary that the appointment "will make some of my beloved friends in Washington angry; that is their lookout. The Stock Exchange has quite as much right to the service of liberals as anyone else."

At a meeting on December 16, the committee elected Carle C. Conway, the chairman of the board at Continental Can Company, as its chairman; it would thereafter be known as the Conway committee. Berle's diary shows he initially was not impressed. "I do not think they intend to do very much except to put in a different type of administration, leaving the economic questions unsolved." To the outspoken Paul Shields, who had worked so long for NYSE reform, this conservative panel looked like the "Charles Gay Protective Committee."

Some cynics saw the committee's creation as "a noble piece of window dressing." Others saw more foot-dragging by the old guard, aimed at killing time until a Republican administration could come to power in the next election and put the SEC out of business. As *The New York Times* put it, the logical date for the delivery of the Conway committee's report was shortly after November 5, 1940—Election Day.

Douglas had no intention of waiting that long to engage in this fight. As he put it in closed-door talks on Capitol Hill, he would give the NYSE a chance to put its house in order—but he would keep a shotgun behind the door, "loaded, well-oiled and ready for use" if necessary to see that the job got done.

Dick Whitney was among the first witnesses called before the committee, but his views were kept confidential. The fact that Whitney did not make a public statement about his testimony deepened Douglas's fear that Whitney was working behind the scenes to undermine the reform work.

ON THE SAME DAY that Gay made his announcement about the new study committee, newspapers in Boston and New York revealed that FDR planned to tap Joe Kennedy as the nation's next ambassador to Great Britain—or "to the Court of St. James's," as the prestigious posting in London was officially known. Kennedy himself, of course, was the source of the leak to *The New York Times,* via his friend Arthur Krock. It's a safe bet that the Boston leak came from Kennedy's proud father-in-law, John Fitzgerald.

But Roosevelt was not happy about the leaks; for some days it seemed he would repudiate the rumor. For months, Kennedy had been lobbying his friend and advocate Jimmy Roosevelt to get the post. Young Roosevelt later reported that when he first conveyed the idea to his father, FDR "laughed so hard he almost toppled from his wheelchair." It would be hard to imagine a less diplomatic man in public life: Kennedy had openly criticized aspects of the New Deal, publicly insulted cabinet members and meddled with their departments, and generally made it clear "he thought he was infinitely smarter, certainly about business and the economy, than anyone else who worked for the president." And as an Irish American, he was innately cool toward Britain. Jimmy Roosevelt later said that, once FDR thought about it further, he began to see the appointment as a way of "twisting the lion's tail a little" after British prime minister Neville Chamberlain treated some overtures from FDR with disdain.

Treasury secretary Henry Morgenthau told his diary that FDR was growing mistrustful of Kennedy's loyalty and intended to have Kennedy closely watched in his new post. "The first time he opens his mouth and criticizes me, I will fire him," FDR supposedly told Morgenthau.

Clearly, their relationship—forged in the 1932 campaign, chilled in its aftermath, and rekindled when Kennedy helped bring the SEC to life—was changing. Joe Kennedy was also changing, becoming more certain of his own instincts and less inclined to bow to Roosevelt's judgment on foreign policy, a field in which FDR absolutely insisted on the last word. With the Japanese invading China, fascist-backed rebels gaining ground in Spain, and increasingly violent rhetoric from Berlin and Rome, Roosevelt intended that the only hand on the helm of the American ship of state would be his. By the time Ambassador Kennedy fully understood that, he had squandered much of the goodwill that remained for him in the White House.

Kennedy and FDR would confer regularly, but they never again shared the warmth that brightened their casual evenings at the Marwood estate, when the SEC was a newborn watchdog and Kennedy was a trusted ally. After a round of interviews as the new ambassador-in-waiting, Kennedy flew off to Palm Beach for the Christmas holidays, perhaps not realizing yet what he was leaving behind.

IT WAS A TENSE CHRISTMAS.

Japanese planes had deliberately bombed the *Panay,* an American gunboat on patrol in Chinese waters to protect three unarmed merchant ships, which were also hit. Diplomatic notes were exchanged and apologies extended by the Japanese emperor, but the outrage still simmered—as did isolationist fears that the incident would drag the nation into the Asian war. Labor unrest, on the rise all through 1937, had produced strikes and shutdowns that reached as deep into the economy as New York's taxi fleet and its Automat restaurants. Southern Democrats in Congress were in open defiance of FDR, joining with Republicans and the American Federation of Labor to block his minimum wage bill. And at the last moment, with an elaborate family celebration scheduled for the White House, Eleanor Roosevelt abruptly decided to fly through terrible weather to Seattle on December 23 to spend the holidays with their ailing daughter, Anna.

The gunboat bombing rattled the stock market, but it recovered a bit and stayed steady during the week before Christmas, traditionally observed with sentimental festivity in the financial district.

As it had been since 1923, a fifty-five-foot tree was set up on Broad Street in front of the classic white façade of the stock exchange. At noon and at the end of each day that week, a new public address system installed by the exchange sent seasonal music out along the crowded sidewalks. On the day before Christmas Eve, three thousand singers—"brokers, bankers, clerks and Stock Exchange employees"—gathered at noon around the tree to sing carols, accompanied by a band of trumpeters. Children from a nearby elementary school were ushered to the tree and given gifts. The role of Santa Claus that afternoon was played by a jolly gentleman named Stanley Budd, a clerk at the firm of Richard Whitney & Company.

———

BUT THERE WAS NO holiday respite at the SEC. Douglas had promised he would get things done and, aside from escorting Mildred to one of the formal White House dinners that she found so daunting, he did not slow down.

He met with investment banking groups to hear their views on regulating the OTC market. He paid several confidential visits to Capitol Hill and the White House to field questions about his face-off with the NYSE. And he checked on the cases his investment trust study team planned to explore in public hearings in January.

Some of those cases turned on arcane accounting issues, and Douglas was being pushed by Judge Healy to be much tougher on corporate accountants than he had been. The lanky Vermont judge's passion about the issue was clear. In a speech after Christmas in Atlantic City, he told an accounting group: "These are not mere academic bookkeepers' arguments. They go to the very vitals of investment appraisal and corporate responsibility." Accountancy, he said, "is the heartbeat of modern corporate finance."

Within a year, Douglas would discover just how right Judge Healy was.

Finally, as the year wound down, the SEC enforcement staff sued Gerald M. Loeb, one of the most prominent founding partners of E.F. Hutton & Co., for allegedly helping to manipulate the price of an automaker's stock in March 1936. The papers were filed in court on the last day of 1937.

By then, the brief Christmas market rally had ended and the waning Dow Jones Industrial index closed the year at 120.85 points—down more than 35 percent from its August crest, its lowest point since July 1935. Unsurprisingly, the traditional New Year's Eve trading-floor festivities at the NYSE were not particularly cheerful. There were the usual pranks and music; but when the Army and Navy Band of Englewood, New Jersey, struck up "Happy Days Are Here Again," FDR's campaign anthem, it was met with a loud chorus of booing. A few moments later, one trader threw a punch at another—an infraction of the rules that would earn both men heavy fines and "stern rebukes" from Charles Gay.

IN WASHINGTON, ROOSEVELT DELIVERED an address on January 3, 1938, to "a sullen, divided, and rebellious Congress." The message paid little attention to the continuing recession but was markedly conciliatory toward business. In the prior week, two of FDR's closest allies, Harold Ickes and Robert H. Jackson, had stung business leaders with speeches that fiercely condemned oligarchic and monopolistic business practices. The business community seemed to find FDR's milder tone reassuring, prompting Ickes to tell his diary that his and Jackson's tougher speeches gave Roosevelt the chance, in effect, to play good cop to their bad cop.

Over the next weeks, as the recession inflicted deeper wounds on the country, Roosevelt would meet with some of the most senior business leaders in the country. But despite their relief at his softer tone, many of the executives saw the meetings as little more than political theater. Conservative skepticism seemed warranted when, on January 5, Roosevelt submitted an unbalanced budget to Congress, with a $1 billion deficit earmarked almost entirely for relief for those hit by the recession. It was not a Keynesian epiphany—indeed, a few weeks later John Maynard Keynes himself would chide Roosevelt for not spending more. And the new budget, of course, would not take effect immediately, which was what the economy really needed.

Unfortunately, Roosevelt was still muddled about how to address the recession.

Uncertain of precisely what to do, the president took contradictory steps and put out conflicting messages. But he never hedged on his support for the regulatory work being done by Douglas and the SEC. One historian observed that the SEC, among all the New Deal agencies, "was perhaps the purest single expression of the central purpose, the overall endeavor of the Roosevelt presidency as Roosevelt himself perceived it to be." Roosevelt assured Douglas later that spring, "You are well acquainted with my pride in securities legislation as one of the major accomplishments of my administration. Of course, I could never sanction steps which would in any way weaken the protection which the statutes afford to a nation of investors."

JANUARY 1938 DID BRING a flash of good news for the White House—and from an unexpected source, the Supreme Court.

For three years, private utility companies had been fighting in court to stop Harold Ickes's Public Works Administration from making sixty-one grants to build or improve public power plants. They were furious that their potential competitors were getting government support. Ickes was furious that the litigation had blocked him from pumping more than $109 million into the weakened economy. In a unanimous decision released on Monday, January 3—written, remarkably, by Justice Sutherland—the Supreme Court refused to block the grants, saying the private utilities had no right to sue to protect something they did not possess, "namely a right to be immune from lawful municipal competition."

Two other utility rate cases were returned to the lower courts, which some New Dealers saw as a victory for Roosevelt's efforts to change the way utilities valued the assets on which their rates were based.

But the biggest news for the SEC that day was the announcement that the Supreme Court would review the lower court decisions in the SEC's Electric Bond and Share case. The utility industry was a bit demoralized by the announcement. The issue as presented by the SEC was solely a test of the registration requirements of the holding company act. Thus, the justices seemed to be signaling that they would not weigh the constitutionality of the law as a whole, as Ebasco had urged. But Ebasco's able lawyers still hoped that oral arguments, set for the second week in February, would change some minds on the court.

Two days later, on January 5, Roosevelt got perhaps the best news the Supreme Court could send him: a resignation letter from Justice Sutherland. Roosevelt would quickly appoint, and the Senate would

quickly confirm, Solicitor General Stanley Reed to replace Sutherland. Reed couldn't be a vote for the SEC in the Ebasco case—he
would certainly recuse himself, as his signature may have been on
the government's briefs. But a recusal was surely better than what
might have been a vote against the SEC from Sutherland.

BILL DOUGLAS JUMPED INTO 1938 at top speed, with steps that
would shape the American financial landscape into the next century.
He would finally endorse a regulatory system for the critically important over-the-counter market, where high finance and low frauds
could be found with equal ease. Another of his initiatives would
move the SEC closer to a plan for regulating the American mutual
fund industry so that middle-class investors could safely get the di-
versification, liquidity, and professional management usually available only to the very wealthy. Today's American investors would
scarcely recognize their world if Douglas had sat on his hands during the early months of 1938.

Both issues had been simmering for years. A congressional command to study the role of investment trusts had been included in the
Public Utility Holding Company Act of 1935. A mandate to develop
rules for the OTC market was built into the SEC's birth certificate,
the 1934 act. But as 1938 opened, Douglas used speeches, congressional lobbying, and strategic leaks to influential columnists to put
both topics squarely on the SEC's public agenda. Although success
would ultimately take longer than he hoped, he made remarkable
progress.

The abuses of investment trusts, the closed-end form of mutual funds that soared to popularity in the 1920s, had been well-
documented by the SEC in hearings that began in July 1936. Details
of that misbehavior, both before and after the 1929 crash, would ultimately fill a 5,100-page report.

Before the crash, the most common problems were excessive fees
that promoters and advisors arranged to pay themselves at the fund
investors' expense. After the crash, when the shares of many investment trusts were trading at prices below the per-share value of their

portfolios, new abuses emerged. Scavenger firms would buy control
of undervalued trusts and siphon off the assets that should have been
paid out to preferred shareholders. In both cases, as one historian
noted, "few public shareholders recognized the extent to which they
were being exploited."

Several industry figures had already endorsed the idea that investment trusts should register and follow some basic rules about
disclosure and conflicts of interest. But with such an array of abuses,
the SEC's study was taking much longer than expected. Douglas
believed the agency's investment trust hearings in January 1938
would keep those abuses squarely before the public while the slower
work of drafting legislation continued.

The same month, Douglas put Congress on notice that it would
have to tackle the investment trust issue with new legislation, sooner
or later. Armed with details clearly leaked by Douglas, influential
columnists Joseph Alsop and Robert Kintner proclaimed in a column published in newspapers across the country that the SEC
would soon send its investment trust recommendations to lawmakers. "If Congress heeds the proposals, the management of the
$5,000,000,000 investment-trust business will be brought as com-
pletely under Federal control as have the brokers and investment
bankers." A few weeks later, the SEC lawyer leading the investment
trust study disclosed that the agency was considering bringing investment advisors under whatever regulatory plan it set up for investment trusts.

The second major Douglas initiative of early 1938, a regulatory
scheme for the vast over-the-counter market, had eluded both Joe
Kennedy and Jim Landis. Like Landis, Douglas saw the Investment
Bankers Conference as a natural ally in bringing effective self-
regulation to the OTC market, but unlike Landis, Douglas was
too impatient to wait until thousands of individual dealers finally
reached an agreement on how to move forward.

On Thursday, January 6, Douglas traveled to Hartford, Connecticut, to give his first public speech as SEC chairman. With his
maiden address sure to attract attention, Douglas chose OTC market regulation as his topic. An audience of about 250 brokers, bank-

ers, and insurance executives gathered that evening at the Hartford Club, a Georgian-style mansion that dated from the previous century. Reporters and other spectators filled a gallery around the dinner tables. Douglas was introduced by his longtime friend Senator Francis T. Maloney of Connecticut, a Democrat for whom he had campaigned in past years and the host at whose home he would stay that evening.

Douglas opened with flattery: "If the security business of the country was as well conducted as it is in Connecticut, our headaches would be over." Then he got down to business, pointing out that the over-the-counter market handled ten times as many securities issues as the NYSE and all the nation's other stock exchanges combined.

Douglas did not mention that, in 1937, the SEC had sent out "flying squads" of investigators to examine over-the-counter dealers in Cleveland, Detroit, and the Pacific Northwest. Within a few months, it had obtained criminal convictions of more than a dozen people and indicted sixteen more. Douglas did tell this group that it was glaringly obvious that "the protection of the investor and of the public generally" required OTC regulation—and he thought the best approach would be effective self-regulation.

Then, he read them a classic Douglas catechism: "By self-regulation, I do *not* mean private law-making. By self-regulation, I do *not* imply a private club whereby the few can control the many. By self-regulation, I do *not* mean a guild system operating above the law. By self-regulation, I do *not* mean monopoly nor a monopolistic franchise. I *do* mean, first, self-discipline in conformity to law—voluntary law obedience so complete that there is nothing left for government representatives to do; second, I mean obedience to ethical standards beyond those any law can establish."

He envisioned groups of dealers organized under federal law and operating under federal supervision but with powers over their members that would allow them to both enforce the law and elevate the ethics of the OTC market. His conclusion was hopeful: "I am genuinely convinced that the objectives of the commission and of the rank-and-file of the over-the-counter securities business are fundamentally identical." If he was right, he added, those objectives could be achieved "in the shortest possible space of time and with a minimum of public and private expense."

When Douglas headed north to Hartford, the SEC staff was already at work on a draft to accomplish his goals. Within weeks, their draft had emerged from Senator Maloney's office as a bill to enable self-regulatory groups of dealers to operate with adequate enforcement authority. The result, known simply as the Maloney Bill, was introduced in the Senate on January 17, 1938.

The *New York Herald Tribune* promptly denounced the legislation as an "attempt at Nazification of the private finances of the country." A few days later, the Republican Party's chief policy strategist accused Roosevelt of "Hitlerizing" the nation with all his "fascist" New Deal ideas. Soon, the nation's dealers in municipal bonds, the tax-exempt bonds issued by state and local governments, were demanding an exemption from the new regulatory scheme; lawmakers from their states were quick to obey, over Judge Healy's public objections. A municipal bond dealer, he said, was not "a different kind of man from the fellow across the hall who buys and sells corporate securities . . . They are made of the same clay as you and I."

Douglas was not deterred by the controversy; if compromises had to be made to bring regulatory order to the chaos of the OTC market, he would make them. In a memo to FDR, he said: "Next in importance to my reorganizing the stock exchanges is my desire to obtain some real regulation of over-the-counter brokers and dealers." He laid out two options: direct regulation by a greatly expanded SEC staff or, alternatively, the formation of a self-regulatory dealer group to police the market under federal supervision. Five days later, Roosevelt endorsed the self-regulatory option. It would take months of lobbying and negotiation, but the Maloney Act would be signed into law in June 1938, allowing the creation of the National Association of Securities Dealers. Three decades later, the group would launch the National Association of Securities Dealers Automated Quotation system—still going strong as the NASDAQ market, which gave early technology companies access to American capital and fostered innovation in a host of young industries.

On January 24, 1938, Bill Douglas dropped another depth charge on the NYSE in the form of new limits on short selling. Early in Dick Whitney's regime, as he tried to preserve short selling in the face of President Hoover's implacable opposition, the exchange had imposed a rule that stocks could not be sold short at a price *lower* than the last trade. Douglas wasn't satisfied with that—or, perhaps, he simply wanted to show the NYSE that his threat to impose SEC rules on the exchange wasn't a bluff.

But like Whitney, Douglas knew that short sales could be a significant source of market liquidity, so he moved cautiously. In late 1937, he had sought expert advice from the Street. After being sworn to secrecy about the encounter, Douglas had been invited to a Sunday evening visit with Clarence Dillon.

Douglas had arrived at Dillon's Park Avenue apartment in Manhattan at 9 P.M.; a uniformed butler had ushered him into a handsome room and offered him a drink. A half hour later, Dillon had swept through the door "with the dignity and grace" of a great film star. Douglas had shown Dillon three versions of a short-sale rule the SEC was considering. After several minutes of silent consideration, Dillon had handed the sheet of paper back and said, "If you want to do an effective job, take the first one." Douglas had thanked him and caught a sleeper train back to Washington. The next morning, he had shared Dillon's choice with his fellow commissioners, and it became the basis for their work.

Under this new SEC rule, short sales could only be made at a price an eighth of a point *higher* than the previous trade. Thus, short selling would be more difficult in a declining bear market, but could still function as a brake on an overly exhilarated bull market. This so-called "uptick rule" remained in place into the twenty-first century.

Some small changes would be made to the rule over the next week in response to NYSE comments. But no one missed the fact that this was the first time the SEC had acted first, and consulted the NYSE later.

Meanwhile, Adolf Berle's skepticism about the Conway committee's intentions proved unfounded. It conducted its research and produced its recommendations with remarkable speed. By January 27, its report was finished. Berle, who was in Washington for talks with the State Department, took a lunch break and made the short walk to the SEC's offices. There, he personally presented a copy of the report to Bill Douglas, as a second copy was being handed to Charles Gay in New York.

To Douglas, the Conway report must have looked like a delightful bit of déjà vu. It called for all the major reforms he had demanded in his November 23 statement: a paid president with chief executive duties; public representation on the board of governors; and a reduction in the number and power of the board's committees, most notably the law committee.

AFTER A SPRINGLIKE SUNDAY that had sent New Yorkers scurrying to parks and playgrounds, the morning of Monday, January 31, was wet and cold. Charles Gay's car carried him from his Brooklyn home into the narrow streets of lower Manhattan and delivered him to 11 Wall Street. Today, he would bring the Conway committee report before the board of governors. If he had counted his votes correctly, the report would be approved unanimously and he could get people started drafting the constitutional changes it would require. But with Dick Whitney silent and stubborn, Gay couldn't take anything for granted.

After the closing bell, the governors began to trickle into the magnificent chamber where they met. Charles Gay climbed up onto the podium and called the meeting to order. With good parliamentary order, a resolution was put forward to approve the Conway committee's report and authorize Gay to name a group to draft the constitutional amendments necessary to implement it. Reformers, led by the members from the large retail "wire houses," spoke of the merits of having a professional chief executive, a better relationship with the SEC, and a more progressive public image. Nods and expressions of agreement all around the chamber encouraged Gay to hope for quick and emphatic approval.

Then Dick Whitney rose in opposition, dispassionate and arrogant as ever. Journalist John Brooks, writing later with the benefit of the memories of some of the men in the room, said Whitney urged the board to accept the report "only in a general way, leaving leeway for rear-guard struggles on each individual provision." That was how he had fought in 1933 and 1934; he hadn't killed FDR's laws but he had surely shaped their final form and slowed Wall Street's acceptance of them. The governors could do the same thing again, he told them. "So great was Whitney's eloquence that for a moment it appeared he might still win the day," Brooks wrote.

Charles Gay had heard enough.

Since taking office in May 1935, he had bowed repeatedly to Whitney's forceful style. He had watched Whitney hijack the SEC negotiations in November. Privately, he argued that he could do little in the face of Whitney's broad support on the floor. But support for him in the boardroom had ebbed dramatically; not even old guard stalwarts like former NYSE chairman Harry Simmons rose today to support Whitney's arguments. Gay's hands were no longer tied; this time, he could act.

Gay suddenly put down his gavel and walked down the podium steps. There was a murmur of surprise at this unusual and unexpected move. Was their beleaguered president walking out, bowing once more to Whitney?

No, Gay was simply setting aside his presidential status to address them as an equal. With a warmth Whitney lacked, Gay pleaded with them to reject the delaying games of the past and act, firmly and decisively. The reputation of the NYSE was on the line. This was no time for a display of bad faith. If anyone could not vote for the proposal, he urged, at least just abstain; let the matter move ahead so the full membership could have its say.

The resolution was called. Every governor voted for it except Whitney—who abstained.

Gay promptly appointed three members, including Harry Simmons, to draft the constitutional amendments. Those would come back before the governors for approval and then be put to the members for the decisive vote. It was unlikely the process could be completed before mid-March, but it had at last begun—despite Dick Whitney.

THE DAY AFTER CHARLES Gay faced down Dick Whitney in New York, lawyers for the SEC in Washington sent their final written arguments to the Supreme Court in the Electric Bond and Share case. The brief was blunt and forceful. It compared holding company methods to a criminal swindle and argued that a Constitution that allowed the Congress "to condemn the crude methods of a Ponzi" and take action against prostitution, racketeering, and narcotics trafficking surely did not bar it from regulating "the subtler and more refined methods of holding company finance."

BY TRADITION, LAWYERS APPEARING before the Supreme Court wore formal "morning dress"—striped trousers, a wing-collared shirt under a pale vest, and a cutaway jacket with tails. Ben Cohen had no such costume—he had never argued a Supreme Court case before. Thus, he arrived at his office on Monday morning, February 7, 1938, wearing striped trousers and a double-breasted suit jacket. A little before noon, Cohen and his co-counsel Robert Jackson headed to the new Supreme Court building, an immense Greek temple above an oval plaza. Carved across its frieze were the words, "Equal Justice Under Law." One of Cohen's colleagues, C. David Ginsburg, in a puckish letter to Felix Frankfurter, described hauling "at least 75 pounds of assorted legal literature" up the "70,000 steps to Equal Justice," just in case the references were needed.

This was not the same court that had scalded the SEC in the *Jones* case. Two members of that court had retired and been replaced with FDR appointees, former Democratic senator Hugo Black and FDR's former solicitor general Stanley Reed. But only one of them could vote on this case, and one of the liberals already on the court, Justice Cardozo, was ill.

"The court room was jammed," Ginsburg reported to his former professor. "New Deal Washington was out *en masse*." Old Deal Washington was there as well, ranging from Alice Roosevelt Longworth, President Teddy Roosevelt's acid-tongued adult daughter, to the boisterous Wendell Willkie. Electric Bond and Share was represented by an expensive legal team headed by Thomas D. Thacher, the ruddy court veteran and former judge who had first met Bill Douglas during New York's long-ago bankruptcy scandals. By the time other cases had been disposed of, there were only ten minutes left in the court's day. "Long accustomed to court practices, [Thacher] uttered his final word at precisely 4:30 PM, just as Chief Justice Hughes leaned across the bench" and brought the hearing to a close, according to one account.

The next morning, Ben Cohen and Robert Jackson were back in their places at one of the counsel tables, with Ginsburg and another aide at a smaller table behind them. Virtually the entire SEC legal staff was seated in the crowd.

The utility industry executives were back in force, too, and Thacher raised his voice in their defense as he made his closing argument.

"This is a great industry," he said. "Some of its features should be regulated, but this company is not a gangster, a white slaver, a dope peddler or stealer of automobiles as the government would have you believe."

Thacher left Robert Jackson just twenty minutes to lay out his part of the government's case before the court's lunch break. After a quick and preoccupied lunch in the solicitor general's offices, Jackson continued with clarity and logic. When he was done, Ben Cohen stood to offer his supporting arguments with just seventeen minutes left in that day's hearing. "The room was electric," Ginsburg reported. Cohen "rudely awakened the Court from its customary afternoon doldrums."

Cohen's argument carried over into a third day, when he was much more assured. "He was magnificent," Ginsburg reported. In his conclusion, Cohen argued: "There is no satisfactory legal basis upon which this court can strike down these simple publicity requirements and by such action, bar the only effective approach to the solution of one of our gravest national problems."

The utilities conceded nothing. But their hopes that the court would take on the whole law, and not just its registration provisions, dimmed considerably. Over the next few weeks, several more holding companies dropped their swords and registered with the SEC.

The temperature in the New Deal's heated debate with the utility industry had been dropping steadily since the fall. FDR had held talks in late November with utility operators and told reporters they were making progress. After his victory in the PWA court case, FDR had reassured Wendell Willkie that the government had no intention of putting private utilities out of business; federal power production would remain the same percentage of overall output as it already was, about 10 percent of the total.

But the powerful lawyers and executives engaged in this legal war were determined not to break ranks—as Douglas had discovered, courtesy of Morgan partner George Whitney, Dick Whitney's brother.

Early in January, the elder Whitney brother had phoned Douglas. The SEC chairman had understood Whitney to have said that the United Corporation, the huge Morgan-backed utility holding company on whose board Whitney served, was ready to register with the SEC. Douglas had been exultant; someone had immediately leaked the news to the press. On January 8, 1938, *The New York Times* had duly printed it. On January 14, George Whitney returned to the SEC office in Washington and told Douglas there had been a misunderstanding, that United had *not* decided to register before a final ruling in the Ebasco case.

Douglas had suspected that the Morgan firm was bowing to pressure from important clients in the utility industry. All he could do was accept Whitney's announcement—and tweak his pride a bit.

"This is a great disappointment to me," Douglas had told the austere banker. First, he had said, Morgan was missing a chance to "perform an act of outstanding business statesmanship." Second, United's change of heart would cost Douglas the price of a dinner. "When you phoned that you would register, a friend high in the administration warned me that you Morgan people talk big but act little. I bet him a dinner. He wins."

On Thursday, March 3, 1938, the NYSE board of governors approved the amendments to the exchange constitution recommended by the Conway committee. The changes would now be submitted to the exchange membership for a vote, which would be conducted over a two-week period. Douglas was still mystified by the lack of public opposition from Dick Whitney, and feared he was quietly organizing resistance among his allies on the trading floor.

A little before 3 P.M. the following Monday, March 7, Bill Douglas was in his office when he got a call from Charles Gay—but it was not, as Douglas may have expected, a progress report on the Conway committee reforms. Instead, tense and terse, Gay said he and Howland S. Davis, the conscientious chairman of the exchange's business conduct committee, were about to catch a train to Washington. They needed to meet with Douglas that evening about an urgent matter that could not be discussed over the telephone.

Mystified, Douglas arranged to meet them in the quiet but grandly elegant lobby of the Carlton Hotel, at the corner of Sixteenth and K Streets, well beyond the curious gaze of late-working SEC staffers. Gay and Davis walked into the long, high-ceiling lobby sometime between 7:30 and 8 P.M., and found Douglas waiting alone. They found a quiet spot and broke their news.

That afternoon, Gay said, the board of governors had received a report from Howland Davis's business conduct committee. An emergency audit showed that the firm of Richard Whitney & Company was very likely bankrupt. Worse, it showed that Dick Whitney himself was almost certainly a criminal.

CHAPTER EIGHT

AN ANATOMY OF SELF-DESTRUCTION

"GOOD MORNING, MR. PRESIDENT."

Early Tuesday morning, March 8, Bill Douglas settled his lanky frame into a chair at Roosevelt's bedside.

The president would surely have been shaved and combed, with a silk robe over his pajamas and perhaps a tatty gray sweater or short cape over his shoulders. He had been holding these bedside breakfast conferences for so many years, both as governor and as president, that they had become part of White House routine and Washington folklore.

But this visit was not on his schedule. Douglas himself had not known he would be there until his conversation in the Carlton Hotel lobby the previous evening. He had come early to alert the president to the extraordinary news—to Douglas, extraordinarily *good* news—that would break in a few hours in New York: Dick Whitney was broke and would be suspended immediately from the NYSE, which was investigating him for what sounded like criminal behavior.

"Not Dick Whitney!" Roosevelt exclaimed, rising up from his backrest of pillows.

There was no glee in the president's face.

To Douglas, Whitney was the man who had led Wall Street's war against Roosevelt's financial reforms, the man who insisted Wall Street could police itself in the face of decades of evidence that it could not.

But to Roosevelt, Dick Whitney and his older brother, George, were members of a world that was FDR's birthright. All three of them had attended Groton, gone on to Harvard, and built their careers with the benefit of their gilded family connections. As young men, they had shaken hands in the same sort of receiving lines and attended the same kinds of reunions and sailed in the same annual regattas; even now, they belonged to many of the same clubs and socialized with many of the same people. All three of them were citizens of a society that the young Bill Douglas had encountered only in novels and newsreels.

"Dick Whitney, Dick Whitney. I can't believe it!" the president repeated, shock in every syllable. Douglas thought FDR sounded close to tears.

That Whitney was broke was hard enough to believe, given his ties to the House of Morgan. But that he had been caught in criminal behavior? FDR's face was a picture of disbelief.

After a moment, Roosevelt looked at Douglas. "You'll know what is best to do."

Douglas nodded and stood to leave. He knew exactly what would be best to do: he would use the Whitney debacle to show America that Wall Street simply could not be trusted to police itself without federal oversight. It was imperative that the nation learn exactly what Dick Whitney had done, how he had gotten away with it, and why that mattered to the future of the American market, and thus to the future of American society.

That was not going to be easy. Whitney's downfall had played out in the velvety shadows of gentlemen's clubs, palatial townhouse parlors, and private offices and conference rooms. Its script had been written in a patrician shorthand of euphemisms, unfinished sentences, and mutually understood silences. Its cast consisted largely of wealthy men whose primary professional obligations were to each other.

FOR THE FIRST ACT of this drama, we must return to Monday, November 22, 1937, the day Bill Douglas icily rejected the NYSE's noncommittal response to his demands for reform.

Whitney was among the law committee members who, after whittling the NYSE's response down to banalities, voted that morning to approve their own handiwork. When that was done and the exchange's envoy was on his way to deliver the document to Douglas in Washington, Whitney still had some official business on his calendar: the monthly trustees meeting for the NYSE Gratuity Fund, which had collected dues from members and paid out death benefits to members' widows and orphans for more than sixty years.

Two other weary veterans of the law committee's wrangling, Charles Gay and Harry Simmons, also served on the fund's board of trustees. On this Monday, though, only Harry Simmons, the trustee board's hatchet-faced chairman, found time to attend. It was only the second time that year that Whitney had missed the monthly meeting.

These meetings were clearly casual affairs. The fund's legal structure made it something less than an official trust fund, and its trustees had an elastic view of the fiduciary duties imposed on them. The NYSE constitution explicitly required the fund's treasurer to take "custody of all securities belonging to the Fund." But the current treasurer, like his predecessors, considered that rule to be "a dead letter" and simply ignored it. He rarely checked on the whereabouts of the roughly $2 million in fund assets—the equivalent of about $45 million today. Instead, he relied on the exchange staff and an annual audit to keep track of things. Whitney carried out any buying or selling his fellow trustees decided to do in the bond market, collecting commissions on the trades.

George W. Lutes was the junior employee assigned the part-time task of serving the fund trustees. He prepared the monthly agenda, recorded the minutes, did some basic bookkeeping, and handled the fund's correspondence. Lutes was keenly aware of his lowly status among the trustees. "I am only a clerk," he said later, adding that he was actually a bit afraid of Dick Whitney and the other big men who ran the exchange.

But something had been bothering Lutes since the spring of 1937. The fund trustees had entrusted a foot-tall stack of bonds to Dick Whitney early that year—some to be sold for cash, some to be reinvested in new bond issues. On five separate occasions since March, Lutes had timidly reminded Whitney that he had not yet returned the bonds and cash. Each time, Whitney had replied that he would get to it soon, that he was busy, that his office was shorthanded. Each time, Whitney had failed to return the assets.

Lutes had not dared to take a more forceful tone with Whitney. He knew the former exchange president was sharp-tongued and impatient with underlings. He had feared that raising the question in Whitney's presence would anger and embarrass a man who still had enough influence to endanger the Lutes family's livelihood.

But at that day's meeting, Whitney was not at the table. After the regular business had been conducted, Lutes mentioned to Harry Simmons and a few other trustees that the securities they discussed that day, some Baltimore & Ohio Railroad bonds, were still in Whitney's possession. Nobody seemed particularly concerned—there was no sign of alarm or excitement. Simmons said he would speak to Whitney.

"Well, there is cash and other securities over there, too," Lutes murmured to Simmons. In fact, he admitted, the cash and securities in Whitney's hands totaled just over $1 million, fully half of the fund's assets. And they had been there for many months.

This did surprise Simmons, and he was deeply annoyed—at Lutes. "This system does not seem to be right," he barked. The financial statement handed out that day showed that the fund had $200,000 in cash, and he had assumed it was in the fund's bank account—not in Dick Whitney's office. He complained that Lutes had fallen into "loose practices" and criticized the clerk for not keeping more precise records and not reporting the matter sooner.

Lutes put up a shy defense. "I really couldn't go over Mr. Whitney's head," he said.

Simmons grudgingly agreed that Lutes had been in an awkward spot, but he insisted that future reports to the trustees must show clearly where the fund assets were. Of course, he had no concern about the safety of the bonds and cash; Whitney was a man of unquestioned integrity. It was just a sloppy process that should be changed.

As soon as Simmons got back to his desk that Monday, between 2:30 and 3 P.M., he called Whitney's office at 15 Broad Street. Whitney was out—he had, in fact, just shown up late for the trustees meeting and found the room deserted. Simmons spoke briefly with F. Kingsley Rodewald, who more or less managed the firm's office.

On paper, Rodewald was one of Whitney's partners—along with bond traders Edwin D. Morgan Jr. and Henry D. Mygatt, who each owned a seat on the exchange; Daniel G. Condon, who ran Whitney's seat when he was absent from the floor on exchange business; and John J. McManus, who ran the firm's seat on the Curb Exchange.

They were an odd assortment of men. Ed Morgan, who graduated from Harvard with his own Porcellian charm just two years after Whitney, had been a partner since 1922. Although he was not related to the J. P. Morgan clan, Morgan was a bona fide member of elite New York society, with connections as lofty as Whitney's own. His late father had been a wealthy banker and a famous yachtsman. Ed Morgan himself grew up on two of the most impressive estates in the northeast, Beacon Rock in Newport and Wheatly Hills on Long Island. Through his four siblings, he was related by marriage to a half-dozen socially prominent families. Henry Mygatt joined the firm in 1927. While not in Morgan's league, Mygatt had a very respectable pedigree. But he had lost heavily in the 1929 crash and then landed in a messy scandal of a marriage. Still, his parents' and siblings' connections seemed to keep him in society's good graces. We know little about Rodewald, Condon, and McManus except that they had limited education, had worked their way up from very modest positions, and did not socialize with their better-educated partners.

In reality, none of these men played any role in running the firm. Whitney made all the financial decisions without even consulting them, and none of them ever questioned that arrangement. They just handled their own business on the NYSE floor or on the Curb Exchange, processed paperwork and collected mail at the office, and returned to their various lives and hobbies. One J.P. Morgan partner had privately referred to these hapless fellows as Dick Whitney's "office boys."

Consequently, Rodewald probably had no idea what Harry Simmons was talking about when he said: "The committee has just adjourned here and we decided, in view of the fact that we cannot sell the B&O bonds, that we will call the securities and cash that you have there, and will you please deliver them to us tomorrow?"

Rodewald managed an answer. "There is no reason why we should not."

There was a reason, although none of Whitney's partners knew it. Whitney did not have those Baltimore & Ohio Railroad bonds. He had pledged them, and other bonds belonging to the fund, as collateral for personal bank loans he squandered on reckless investments. As for the cash belonging to the fund, he had already spent much of it.

These were criminal acts. If they were publicly exposed, Whitney would be ruined. But not a hint of that peril was apparent in his manner when, around 3 P.M., he returned Simmons's phone call. He coolly promised—as he had repeatedly promised Lutes—that the securities and cash would be returned the next day, on Tuesday morning.

It was nearly noon on Tuesday, November 23—a day when Washington and Wall Street were buzzing over Douglas's public attack on the exchange's "private club" culture—when Whitney finally visited Simmons's office, empty-handed. He explained that his office was short-staffed, the same excuse he had made repeatedly to Lutes. Would it be okay if he returned the fund's assets the next day?

"As a friend, I wouldn't hesitate," Harry Simmons said after a moment. "But as a trustee of the Gratuity Fund, I just don't feel I have the right to give you that extension of time. You should make every effort to get them in by 3 o'clock."

Whitney answered, "I'll do my utmost."

Something in Simmons's manner must have warned Whitney that his longtime mentor would not grant the open-ended grace period he had counted on. He crossed the street to visit his brother at the House of Morgan. He had nowhere else to turn.

———

WHITNEY SEEMS TO HAVE made no effort to soften the blow—
perhaps because there simply wasn't time. When he arrived at
George's office, he confessed he had been using the Gratuity Fund's
bonds and cash as his own, had suddenly been ordered to return
them immediately, and could not do so.

George Whitney was "terribly disturbed and aghast," his brother
said later. "Thunderstruck, as he had reasons to be."

Of course, George Whitney knew Dick had poor business judgment and had recklessly speculated in various unsuccessful "venture
capital" deals in Florida for years. He knew his brother lived far beyond his means, with his foxhunting and yacht racing and society
parties; at that moment, Dick had more than a hundred bottles of
champagne in his wine cellar! About ten months earlier, in January
1937, George had loaned his brother nearly $1.2 million to pay back
money he had borrowed from various prominent Wall Street figures,
warning that such personal debts could tarnish his good name. Besides borrowing constantly from friends, Dick had been sponging
off his brother's wealth and generosity for nearly two decades.
George had helped pay for Dick's fine townhouse; he'd financed one
of the exchange seats the firm owned.

But he never dreamed that Dick would stoop to this.

Dick Whitney stayed remarkably calm, but his brother could not
stop asking anguished questions. How could Dick have done this?
Why did he do it? George got no satisfactory answer. He could not
comprehend what had pushed Dick to commit this desperate act.

But neither could he comprehend not rescuing his brother from
his shocking folly. "Find out just how much money it will take to
correct the situation," he said. "I will find out what arrangements I
can make here."

Dick Whitney left and immediately walked three blocks south to
the majestic Corn Exchange Bank on William Street. There, he
calmly inquired of an officer, "just in the normal course of business,"
how much it would take to redeem the bonds. Then he checked how
much he would need to add to his checking account to return the

fund's stolen cash. The total came to $1,082,000—more than $22 million in modern terms.

George Whitney's wealth far exceeded that sum but little of it was in cash—and only cash could save his brother. After Dick left for the bank, George left his office and walked down the hall to speak with his close friend and partner, Tom Lamont, who had a sizeable cash balance in his partnership account at that moment.

"Dick is in a very serious jam and is going to need a very substantial amount of money," he told Lamont, giving him a quick sketch of the little he knew about the misuse of the Gratuity Fund assets. As Lamont recalled the conversation, George called his brother's action "illegal" and "improper"—"everything that it should not be."

Tom Lamont, a puckish elderly man with a Dickensian way of expressing himself, was taken aback. "Well, that is a devil of a note, George! Why, Dick Whitney is all right! How could he mishandle securities, even for a moment, no matter what the jam?"

"It's an inexplicable thing," George replied sadly. But despite his private knowledge of his brother's past faults, he felt sure this was "an isolated instance" and told Lamont that he simply had to help his brother.

"I think you are dead right," Lamont told his friend. Like George, Lamont never considered Dick Whitney to be a criminal; he was simply a fellow gentleman who had "gotten in a terrible jam" and illegally used customers' securities. "Certainly, I will help you to help your brother—certainly," Lamont replied. "Count on me." It was what his heart told him to do, he said later.

After Dick Whitney returned and told his brother how much he needed, the efficient clerical engines at the House of Morgan got into gear to save him.

But not even the House of Morgan could stop the clock. The business day was almost over, and Dick Whitney had not yet kept his pledge to Harry Simmons to return the fund's bonds and cash.

Simmons was clearly uneasy, despite his later insistence that he trusted Whitney without reservation. Earlier on that tense Tuesday, in the smoking room just off the trading floor, he came across Blaire S. Williams, a longtime governor and a Gratuity Fund trustee. He confided that Whitney had asked for an extension of time, but he had refused. Williams, also a member of the business conduct committee, agreed Simmons had done the right thing. A bit later, outside the exchange luncheon club, Simmons fell in with Roland Redmond, the exchange's counsel and a good friend to both Simmons and Whitney. In their short chat, he told Redmond about his misgivings about refusing Whitney's request for more time.

"I didn't want to feel mean about the thing," he said. "I did not want to be pushing him or be unreasonable." But Redmond, too, assured him his refusal was "perfectly correct."

Just before 3 P.M., Dick Whitney walked into Simmons's office—still empty-handed.

"I will give you a ring tomorrow morning," he told Simmons with no sign of distress. "I will have everything ready for you, the cash and the securities." Then he added, "I have seen my brother George—if you need that as an extra assurance." Then he left.

Simmons, a bit befuddled by this news, had to hurry upstairs to a 3 P.M. meeting of the law committee, which was still hashing out the escalating public dispute with Bill Douglas. In the elevator lobby, he again met up with Redmond.

"Dick has just been over," he told the lawyer. "He told me that he would have everything delivered tomorrow; that he had been to see his brother George and everything was all right."

Redmond himself had made a loan to Whitney years earlier that had not yet been repaid, but he also insisted later he had no qualms about Whitney's integrity at this point. If so, his instructions to Simmons were extremely odd: "I think as a trustee you just better go across the street and check up with George so there will be no misunderstanding tomorrow."

"That's a good idea." Simmons immediately took the elevator back down and crossed the street to the Morgan corner. "George," he said, "I understand that Dick has been to see you." He made a vague reference to some securities; nothing more needed to be said.

George knew what he meant and promptly replied, "Yes, he discussed the matter with me and you will have nothing to worry about; he will deliver them tomorrow—the cash and securities."

The matter of more than a million dollars stolen from the NYSE was thus settled, without any further discussion. Simmons made a polite inquiry after the banker's health—after an emergency appendectomy early in the summer, Whitney was spending a week away each month to recuperate—and quickly returned to the law committee meeting. The entire expedition took less than fifteen minutes; neither man mentioned the conversation to Dick Whitney.

Tom Lamont, Harry Simmons, Blaire Williams, and Roland Redmond all knew by nightfall on Tuesday, November 23—more than twenty-four hours after Simmons first called Whitney's office—that Dick Whitney could not restore either the fund's bonds or its cash without his brother's help. They had no proof of what Whitney had done with the fund's assets. But the only plausible explanation was that he had used the fund's assets as if they belonged to him. Most likely, he had spent the fund's cash and pledged the bonds to get bank loans for his own use. Those were criminal acts, as George Whitney had immediately realized. But all four men later insisted under oath that, at this time, they never suspected Dick Whitney of any wrongdoing; his brother, after all, was sorting it all out for him.

Some weeks later, George Whitney went to J. P. "Jack" Morgan Jr. for permission to withdraw some of his own partnership funds to repay his debt to Tom Lamont. He told Morgan merely that his brother "had gotten into an awful jam" and Lamont had loaned him the money to deal with the crisis. Jack Morgan was fairly sure the "jam" was a business crisis because the loan was too large for a loss involving "horses or women or anything like that." But he didn't question George Whitney. "It was his lookout; it was his money," Morgan told himself. He authorized the withdrawal and thought no more about it.

The morning of Wednesday, November 24—with the morning papers still quoting Douglas's critique of the NYSE's "private club" culture—George Lutes accompanied Harry Simmons and Dick Whitney to the vault below the exchange and logged in the overdue bonds; shortly afterward, Lutes deposited Whitney's check in the Gratuity Fund's bank account. No questions were asked about why they had not been returned at the beginning of the week—or, in-deed, at the beginning of the year.

As far as the trustees of the Gratuity Fund were concerned, the matter was closed—"completely cured," as exchange lawyer Roland Redmond put it later. As far as the Whitney brothers were con-cerned, there was still a great deal to settle.

ON THANKSGIVING MORNING, NOVEMBER 25, George Whitney welcomed his brother into the study of his redbrick Georgian town-house at 120 East Eightieth Street, a half block east of Park Avenue. At his request, Dick had brought along handwritten and largely fic-tional financial statements that showed his firm was solvent but was burdened with illiquid assets.

The firm held a huge speculative stake in Distilled Liquors Cor-poration, a small New Jersey distillery that was listed, but rarely traded, on the New York Curb Exchange. Its primary product was applejack, a rough apple brandy whose Prohibition-era popularity in the New Jersey hunt country had faded when better liquor became available. There were also smaller stakes in several private Florida agricultural companies, relics of the land boom that went bust in the mid-1920s. The brothers mildly debated whether Dick's estimate of the value of these cash-consuming assets was too high. George de-cided it was, and marked them down.

George believed it was time for Dick to liquidate his firm and leave Wall Street. In his mind, he was not ordering Dick to do that; he did not cite the Gratuity Fund incident as a reason to liquidate, although they discussed it briefly. He merely said he thought it was too difficult for Dick to manage his business interests and his bro-kerage firm at the same time. Dick had little choice but to say he agreed.

We don't know just what was said, but sometime during this meeting, Dick confessed that he had broken all the vows he made when he got that $1.2 million loan from George at the beginning of 1937. He had promised to return the securities he'd borrowed from prominent mutual friends; instead, he had pledged them for fresh bank loans. He had sworn to conduct regular audits, and had not. He had bought more Distilled Liquors stock after pledging that he wouldn't. He could not give his brother any explanation for these failures.

Despite all these broken promises, George apparently still felt certain his brother would never again misuse customer securities, no matter how hard-pressed he was. And he still trusted Dick's estimate that his firm was in the black by about a half-million dollars.

He saw Dick out about 2 P.M., telling him to return later that afternoon because Harry Simmons was going to join them to give his advice about liquidating the firm. Sometime in late afternoon, Dick and Simmons settled in George Whitney's study.

"My brother and I have decided that he had better liquidate his business," George Whitney announced, to Simmons's great surprise. Carrying the liquor business and Florida ventures inside the firm "was a very heavy load, an uphill fight all the time," he explained. It would be better for Dick to leave Wall Street and devote himself to recovering whatever he could from those investments.

The Morgan banker assured Simmons that the Whitney firm had value. But he urged Simmons to go over the numbers himself, both as a trusted friend and as someone more familiar with brokerage finances. Simmons vaguely said he would try to do so, but never did.

Then they fell into a long discussion of whether to liquidate the business or try to sell it as a going concern. No firm conclusion was reached, but George Whitney felt confident enough about a liquidation that he shared the good news the next day with Tom Lamont, just before leaving for a week's rest.

GEORGE WHITNEY AND TOM LAMONT had gone to great lengths to keep the New York Stock Exchange from finding out about Dick Whitney's criminal use of its Gratuity Fund's assets. But both men assumed the New York Stock Exchange was at least keeping track of whether Dick Whitney's firm was solvent. They were wrong.

Given the gaping loopholes in the NYSE's rules and its loose enforcement of what rules it had, exchange officials knew almost nothing about Whitney's finances. Since 1922, the NYSE had required firms that handled margin accounts to file annual unaudited financial reports called "questionnaires." NYSE auditors would routinely check the books of the firms that filed questionnaires, with advance notice; surprise audits were possible, but extremely rare. But under the exchange's honor system, Dick Whitney had always claimed he handled no margin accounts and thus was exempt from filing a questionnaire, and his word had always been sufficient.

But in early December 1937—with Bill Douglas openly on the warpath and the exchange trying to look like it was serious about self-regulation—the board of governors finally decided to close this word-of-honor loophole. Starting in 1938, all member firms would have to file questionnaires and undergo a subsequent NYSE audit, whether or not they carried margin accounts.

Whitney's firm was due to report sometime around Memorial Day. Perhaps Whitney thought he would somehow be out of the woods by then, or believed that his doctored books would fool the auditors. In any case, he made ineffectual efforts to find a buyer for his firm and continued to borrow from any friend who would float him a loan.

This had been Whitney's lifeline for years. He borrowed from one friend, promised to pay the loan back on a certain date, and then asked for numerous extensions; if the lender became insistent—surprisingly few did—Whitney borrowed from another friend to settle that debt. Then, the dance of delay began all over again with a new partner.

In secret and without question, Whitney's generous friends repeatedly loaned him securities and let him pledge them as collateral for bank loans. For Whitney, it was apparently a small step from pledging friends' shares with permission to pledging customers' shares without permission. He had first taken that step more than a dozen years before, and had never stopped.

On December 15, one of the more flamboyant traders on the NYSE finally told Charles Gay about Dick Whitney's precarious finances and boundless borrowing habits. Over lunch, Gay asked

Bernard E. "Ben" Smith, an active pool operator in the pre-SEC days, what he thought about the exchange's effort to achieve peace with its regulators.

Smith was blunt. Nothing would do any good, he told Gay, so long as Dick Whitney and his old guard allies were on the board of governors. "The quicker you get rid of Dick Whitney the better off the exchange would be," he said.

Sounding defensive on his old friend's behalf, Gay asked what Smith had against Whitney. "He is broke and borrowing money all over the Street," Smith told him—although Gay later claimed he could not recall Smith saying Whitney was broke, only that he was borrowing money.

"Well, you know more than I do, if that's the case," Gay said dismissively, deciding in his own mind that Smith was an angry man who "simply didn't like Richard Whitney" and need not be taken seriously.

Gay edged away from the topic. The two men finished lunch in a friendly manner and Gay did not give another thought to Smith's warning. "It made no particular impression on me at the time," he said later.

In early January, Whitney asked Roland Redmond to lend him $25,000 to $50,000. Redmond, whose prior loan to Whitney had finally been repaid just a month earlier, agreed to a fresh $25,000 loan. To Redmond, Whitney seemed like "a man who was pleased and looking forward to an expanding activity." The loan request did not raise any doubts in Redmond's mind about Whitney's circumstances, he said later.

A few weeks later, after lying to his brother once again about his liquidation efforts, Whitney secretly took $900,000 worth of customers' bonds and illegally pledged them to get a new $650,000 bank loan. Toward the end of January, he appealed to Harry Simmons for a loan of $100,000 to $150,000, but Simmons—who knew more about Dick Whitney's financial distress than any other exchange official—gently turned him down and said nothing.

Given the polite reticence of his lenders, who felt such loans among friends should be kept confidential, there's no telling how long Whitney could have continued this game of debtor's tag. But at the end of the first week in January 1938, a specialist on the NYSE floor mistakenly believed he had detected panic selling in Greyhound stock by Whitney's firm. He duly reported his impressions to Herbert "Duke" Wellington, one of Whitney's longtime friends and one of several old guard NYSE governors from whom Whitney had borrowed very large sums of money. Duke Wellington later saw Howland Davis, the chairman of the business conduct committee, in the foyer of the exchange's luncheon club and passed along the rumor.

The formidable business conduct committee was the NYSE's primary overseer of its members' behavior and solvency, so the rumor was clearly relevant to the exchange's official work of self-regulation. Davis listened to Wellington's tip, agreed to keep Wellington's name confidential, and moved away. (Almost immediately after speaking to Davis, Wellington got a message from the floor that Whitney wanted to see him—to ask for another loan, as it turned out. Wellington politely declined.) Dutiful as he was as business conduct chairman, Davis was still wary of confronting such an important colleague with what was, after all, an unverified rumor. He decided he would just quietly exercise his power to move Whitney to the top of the list of firms due to file financial questionnaires.

A day or so later, Davis asked Simmons, whom he knew to be Whitney's mentor and friend, if he had heard any rumors about the financial health of the firm. Protective of his friend's reputation, Simmons's answers were far less than candid. Although he understood that Davis was acting in his official self-regulatory capacity, Simmons did not tell him that George Whitney had to pull his brother out of a $1 million hole in November, or that Dick Whitney had decided to liquidate his firm but was having trouble doing so. Simmons told him instead that the firm's financial condition was "all right," and encouraged Davis to raise any questions he had with Dick Whitney himself. But wary of those assurances, Davis made sure the questionnaire was sent out to Whitney on January 20; it was due back on February 15. Thereafter, an audit would be conducted.

The NYSE had finally asked Whitney to explain himself—not

because of the red flags waving since Thanksgiving week but because of an erroneous rumor on its trading floor.

THE TRAIN TO DESTRUCTION picked up speed after that.

In the following weeks, the Whitney brothers, alone and together, met with various Morgan partners and with Dick Whitney's lawyer, L. Randolph Mason, Roland Redmond's former colleague at Carter Ledyard & Milburn. Randy Mason had first been hired by Dick Whitney to draw up the relatively simple paperwork to document the $1.2 million debt-consolidation loan from his brother in January 1937. Nothing about the rest of Mason's work for Dick Whitney would be simple.

On January 28, 1938, Mason discovered that his client had secretly asked the president of Distilled Liquors if the company would lend him $100,000. The lawyer warned the liquor executive such loans to controlling stockholders were not permitted; the executive made the loan anyway. Mason mentioned this loan during a meeting that day with George Whitney, who made sure it was quickly repaid.

At some point during this meeting, George Whitney told Randy Mason for the first time about his brother's illegal use of the Gratuity Fund's assets in November—news that clearly jolted the lawyer. Shaken, Mason said he now had no hope of getting a reliable audit from his client, who had not disclosed the November incident to him. The sooner the NYSE auditors went in, the better, he said.

"Why don't you speak to Harry Simmons about it?" George Whitney suggested, adding vaguely, "I had some conversations with Simmons on this subject last November." Mason agreed he would do so.

George Whitney soon headed south for some rest at Jekyll Island, and his Morgan partner Francis D. Bartow picked up the burden of saving Richard Whitney.

In his late fifties, Frank Bartow was not as handsome as most Morgan partners—the firm set a high value on good looks and fine tailoring—but he was smart and gregarious. He had been hired by the firm in 1924 after a twenty-two-year career at a major city bank.

At the end of 1926, he became one of the first men ever tapped for a full Morgan partnership after rising through the ranks. He was comfortably wealthy and socially secure, with ties to some of the oldest families in the country—his great-grandfather Francis Scott Key wrote the national anthem.

And he knew Dick Whitney well. Since 1931, they had served together as directors of the Corn Exchange Bank. Indeed, it was Bartow who had initiated one of the early loans the Morgan firm made to Dick Whitney. That $500,000 loan, made soon after Bartow became a Corn Exchange director, was meant to let Whitney pay off an unsecured loan from the bank—although Bartow never confirmed that Whitney had done so. In Bartow's view, the bank's unsecured loan to Whitney was not exactly improper but was somehow "unwise." He struggled later to explain why, finally just shrugging that it "just was not quite done." He had been worried that the Corn Exchange Bank had made the loan as a favor to an influential board member, without having any details about Whitney's finances.

Beyond Wall Street, the public no doubt imagined that the House of Morgan diligently scrutinized the finances of anyone applying for a major loan. Frank Bartow, like all the partners at the firm, was a seasoned banker and a skilled financial analyst. But Bartow's stunning deference to the Whitney brothers was not an aberration; it was simply the way things worked in the back-scratching world of Wall Street. Yes, there were rules at the exchange, just as there were rules at the House of Morgan. But in the culture of Wall Street, those rules simply did not apply to men like George and Dick Whitney.

Dick Whitney was still a Corn Exchange Bank director in 1938 and was still getting loans from the bank—but now, unknown to Bartow or the bank, the loans were secured by collateral stolen from his clients. As for that unsecured $500,000 loan Bartow arranged in 1931, Whitney still had not paid it off.

While George Whitney was away in February 1938, Frank Bartow met several times with Randy Mason, who got the impression Bartow was trying to determine if the Morgan firm could again make a loan to Dick Whitney. But so far, neither Bartow nor Mason could get any financial information at all from Whitney and this time, for the first time, Bartow would not arrange a loan without it.

As February 15 approached, Dick Whitney asked for an additional week to file his NYSE questionnaire, and Howland Davis agreed. Whitney clearly thought he was influential enough to forestall any reckoning. Around this time, he told one of his partners he felt "pretty sure that the questionnaire would never be filed." With the extension granted by Davis, the form was now due on February 21, 1938.

After trying for two weeks to get financial details from Whitney, Randy Mason finally reached out to Harry Simmons, as George Whitney had suggested. Early on Wednesday, February 16, he called Simmons at his home and asked if he could ride downtown with him to discuss an urgent matter. When Mason got into the limousine, he satisfied himself that the chauffeur was out of earshot and, after a few pleasantries, raised the topic at the front of his mind: Dick Whitney.

Mason and Simmons never agreed on what was said during that morning ride from Park Avenue to Wall Street, although Mason's version still seems far more plausible.

Mason testified under oath that he told Simmons he could get no information from his client and therefore had no idea if Whitney's firm was solvent, as NYSE rules required. He feared there was "grave risk" to Whitney in answering the questionnaire, he continued, and he strongly urged that NYSE auditors should examine the firm immediately. Simmons "asked me if I knew of the events in November, and I said that I did." Since Simmons also asked if Mason had spoken with George Whitney, the lawyer assumed Simmons was referring to the misuse of Gratuity Fund assets that George Whitney had recently disclosed to him. Mason recalled that Simmons assured him he would see that an audit was done quickly.

Under oath, Simmons later recalled only that Mason said he was having trouble getting solid financial information from his client, but said he did not recall that the lawyer had questioned the firm's solvency. Then, according to Simmons, Mason merely discussed the prospects for liquidating the firm—although that topic does not seem urgent enough to explain Mason's appeal that morning. Simmons denied promising to speed up an NYSE audit. He conceded he had asked Mason if he knew about "the November situation," but claimed he was referring solely to the delay in the return of the Gratuity Fund assets; he insisted that he had not known, at that moment, about any criminal misbehavior by Whitney. In short, Simmons claimed he had no basis whatsoever on February 16 to suspect that Dick Whitney had committed a crime, that he had confessed that crime to his brother in November, and that his firm might be insolvent at that moment. If Mason got that impression, Simmons said, Mason was mistaken.

Two days later, on February 18, Dick Whitney visited an elderly broker at lunchtime and asked him for a bridge loan so he could arrange some financing for Distilled Liquors. The broker discussed it with a partner and they agreed to lend Whitney $100,000 for two weeks; Whitney "unequivocally" promised the loan would be repaid on March 4 and suggested that he pay a higher rate of interest, since the loan was unsecured. The older broker declined his offer, saying, "I have always been much impressed by the attitude of the elder Mr. Morgan, who held the view that the personal integrity of the borrower was of far greater value than his collateral." Dick Whitney looked the old gentleman in the eye and said, "Mr. Morgan was entirely right." He once again vowed the loan would be repaid on time, and left.

WHITNEY'S QUESTIONNAIRE WAS FILED late in the afternoon of February 21, 1938, signed by himself and his partners, who barely looked at it before adding their signatures under his. A staff auditor at the exchange checked it out and, as Randy Mason had feared, promptly found a major problem. The firm seemed to be carrying some margin accounts and thus, under NYSE rules, it should have had considerably more working capital than it had. The auditor immediately reported these findings to his boss, the exchange's comptroller.

The comptroller seems to have been a remarkably incurious man.

He had known for at least a year that Whitney was borrowing heavily from other NYSE members, but saw no reason to inquire further about that. A fellow auditor told him in late January 1938 about Whitney's delay in returning Gratuity Fund assets; he did not raise any questions about that, either. He got the unnerving results from Whitney's questionnaire on Monday afternoon, February 21, but since the next day was a holiday, he did not convey them to the secretary of the business conduct committee until the morning of Wednesday, February 23.

The secretary promptly informed Howland Davis, who anxiously agreed that a full audit should be conducted immediately—beginning that very day, in fact. After all, with inadequate capital, the Whitney firm posed a continuing risk to every broker doing business with it down on the trading floor. Policing such risks was one of the key duties of the business conduct committee.

Early on Thursday, February 24, Whitney called Davis at his uptown apartment and asked if he could come over. When he arrived, he mentioned that an NYSE accountant was in his office and said he feared the audit "would not be entirely favorable" because of his huge Distilled Liquors stake. Moreover, there were questions about a few client accounts that the auditor considered—wrongly, in Whitney's view—to be margin accounts. He said he was in the process of raising some $700,000 to buy out the liquor shares and improve the firm's working capital levels, and urged Davis to call off the audit to give those negotiations time to bear fruit.

Davis courteously but firmly told Whitney he thought it would be best to just let the auditor complete his work without interruption.

On Monday, February 28, the auditor returned to Whitney's offices at 15 Broad Street. And on that day, he started to see the depths of Whitney's misconduct. He found entries for interest payments on a host of loans—but the loans themselves were not listed on the firm's books. He found the bogus account Whitney had set up to facilitate his use of customers' securities as collateral for those unreported loans. Whitney claimed he had the clients' permission to pledge their securities, but could not produce any written evidence of that. With the full audit still incomplete, it suddenly was no longer a question of whether Whitney was broke; it was a question of whether he had broken the law. Before that Monday ended, the auditor had shared his discoveries with his boss, the comptroller.

It was not until late on Tuesday afternoon, however, that the comptroller told Howland Davis that the routine examination at Whitney's firm was turning up evidence of "possible insolvency and possible misconduct." Horrified by the news, Davis hurried to Charles Gay's office and told him, for the first time, about the Whitney audit and its alarming results. Gay and Davis agreed that the comptroller should direct his auditor to press forward as quickly as possible to nail down exactly what Whitney had done.

Meanwhile, Whitney spent the day getting his most audacious loan yet. With destruction staring him in the face, he arranged for his wife, Gertrude, to cosign a loan for $100,000 from Brown Brothers Harriman, chatting easily with its cofounder and future diplomat Averell Harriman. Here, again, the loan was approved with little scrutiny.

At 9 P.M. on Wednesday, March 2, Charles Gay convened a private meeting at the Metropolitan Club on Fifth Avenue at Sixtieth Street. He invited Roland Redmond; Redmond's law partner, William H. Jackson; and Harry Simmons, who invited Randy Mason. Howland Davis joined them about ninety minutes late, after returning from a day in Washington. With elliptical vagueness, Mason was told that the NYSE auditors were unsure about the accuracy of the Whitney firm's books. Someone suggested that "a strong financial management of Whitney's affairs" might lessen any possible public loss if the firm had problems. It's hard to see this as anything but a veiled plea for Mason to urge Dick Whitney to once again seek help from his brother.

Sometime this same evening, Harry Simmons telephoned George Whitney at home and told him that an auditor was going over his brother's books and that some serious questions were being pursued. He didn't have any other details to share.

The Whitney audit had quickly become the all-consuming focus for top NYSE officials. At noon on Thursday, March 3, Charles Gay held a luncheon meeting in his private dining room with his vice president, Walter L. Johnson, lawyers Redmond and Jackson, and fellow governors Howland Davis and Harry Simmons. The complacent comptroller was summoned to the room and told he should immediately drop whatever he was doing and make the Whitney audit his top priority.

At various points on that nervous Thursday, Dick Whitney called on Howland Davis, Charles Gay, and Harry Simmons, asking each of them to delay the audit or, at least, hold off any action by the business conduct committee. His requests, calmly made, were just as calmly turned down.

Around 4 P.M., Gay met quietly with George Whitney in a private room at Redmond's law offices, housed in a vintage stone building on Wall Street just a few steps west of both the exchange and the Morgan offices. Davis and Simmons joined him; Mason stepped in sometime during the meeting.

Davis told George that the exchange's auditors had "discovered certain irregularities" in his brother's books; if those irregularities were confirmed, the exchange would file formal public charges against Dick Whitney.

George Whitney asked few questions and offered no guidance. He simply told the group his doctor had ordered him to rest, and that he would be leaving the next day for Jekyll Island.

ON FRIDAY AFTERNOON, MARCH 4, the phlegmatic comptroller finally had an answer for the anxious NYSE officials—and it confirmed their worst fears. Gay and Davis, with Redmond and his partner at their sides, listened and learned that the auditors now had "proof, positive proof" of several instances of misconduct by Whitney's firm. The rest of the afternoon was spent discussing whether there was sufficient proof of wrongdoing to take action against Whitney. There was, and Davis immediately called a meeting of the business conduct committee for Monday morning, March 7. Roland

Redmond worked into the evening drafting the accusation that could exile his dear friend from Wall Street. As he sat at his desk writing out the charges, tears slid down his cheeks.

Dick Whitney learned early Saturday morning about the auditor's conclusions and the preparation of formal charges against him and tried once again to get a reprieve. By 4 P.M. that afternoon, after a futile call on Howland Davis, Whitney was sitting in Gay's office at the stock exchange, the room from which he himself had led Wall Street in its fiercest battles with the New Deal.

He freely admitted his misconduct. He could scarcely deny it, with stacks of bonds illegally pledged to banks across town. Instead, for two bizarre hours, he calmly explained to Gay why the NYSE could not possibly bring charges against him, despite what he had done. The publicity would be terrible not only for him, he said, but also for the institution. For millions of people, his name was synonymous with the New York Stock Exchange, he said. "The exchange can't afford to let me go under."

Gay grew increasingly distressed but Whitney seemed to be calm and reasonable, "as if he were discussing someone else than himself." Lying easily, Whitney claimed his firm was only $282,000 in debt—in fact, he had borrowed nearly three times that sum in just the previous six weeks, bringing his debts to $1.8 million. He asked that the business conduct committee meeting be called off and that he be allowed to transfer his seat to someone else and quietly retire. He did not plead for mercy for himself. He simply lobbied, in a strangely disinterested way, for what he said was the wisest course for the NYSE to take.

Uneasy with conflict and contradiction, Gay repeatedly deflected Whitney's proposal, only to have Whitney return to it again and again. Finally, Gay said the exchange simply could not agree to his request and urged Whitney to "seek some man of standing and business experience to act as his advisor."

At that moment, the only "man of standing and business experience" remotely available to advise Whitney was Frank Bartow, the Morgan partner.

Bartow was trying to find any sound basis for Morgan to cover about $450,000 of a $700,000 loan to Whitney, with George Whitney personally covering the rest. Bartow wasn't sure the loan could be made at all, but he was sure it couldn't be made without more financial information from Dick Whitney, which had not yet been provided.

Sometime on that busy Saturday, March 5—most likely after his surreal talk with Charles Gay—Dick Whitney arranged to meet Bartow at the Links Club, an elite Manhattan club on East Sixty-second Street that was devoted to serving golfers at leisure. Whitney was a longtime member, and was currently serving as the club's president. Stepping down from the street into the dimly lit lobby, Whitney asked that Frank Bartow be told he had arrived.

Bartow left his bridge game on an upper floor and trotted down the stairs to meet his friend. As they sat down in a quiet lounge, Whitney pulled some folded papers from his jacket's inner pocket.

"I am in a jam," he said.

"Wait a minute," Bartow said abruptly. "Is your idea in talking to me now to borrow money?"

"Yes."

"Well, in all frankness, I will not agree to that," Bartow replied, with some impatience. He had already told Randy Mason that nothing could be done without the audits he had requested. He assumed Whitney knew that.

Whitney explained, "On Monday at 10:30 my affairs are coming up for examination before the business conduct committee—"

Bartow held up his hand. "Wait a minute, stop right there. I am not the proper person for you to talk to. My advice is that you go and get Randolph Mason and tell him."

With his innate dignity, Whitney folded the papers, returned them to his pocket, and rose to leave. Bartow added, perhaps more gently, "I expect to be here some time longer, if you should want me."

Whitney returned to the club sometime later, accompanied by Randy Mason, and once again asked to talk with Bartow.

"Frank," Whitney said, "we have been talking this over and I want to know if you have any suggestions to offer." Perhaps he still believed in the possibility of a loan from his brother and his brother's firm.

Bartow had nothing to offer, he said.

Whitney again mentioned the upcoming meeting of the business conduct committee. "It is conceivable some embarrassing questions will arise."

"What do you mean 'embarrassing'?"

"Well, for example, the New York Yacht Club has securities with me and I have taken those securities and pledged them in loans."

Bartow was not immediately alarmed. If the yacht club owed a margin debt to Whitney's firm, he was entitled to use its securities to fund his business, up to the limit of the debt. "How much does the New York Yacht Club owe you?" he asked.

"They don't owe me anything," Whitney answered.

Bartow was floored; he could scarcely articulate his next question. "Do you mean that you have taken a client's securities, and pledged them in loans, and taken the proceeds of that and placed it in your business—*when they did not owe you anything*?"

"Yes, I do," Whitney answered calmly.

"That is serious," Bartow said.

"It is criminal," Whitney replied.

Bartow pressed for more details. "Are there any other cases where this has occurred?"

With Randy Mason sitting silently beside him, Whitney calmly told Bartow there were two others: the trust fund set up for his wife and sister-in-law, and the account of Mrs. Martha Stevens Baird, the socially prominent daughter of the founder of Stevens Institute of Technology in Hoboken, New Jersey. (Whitney was lying. He also had misused securities belonging to his own stepson and to the estate of a Homestake Mining Company heiress, Eila Haggin McKee, who had died in August 1936. And he did not mention his misuse of the Gratuity Fund's assets during much of 1937.)

Shaken, Bartow told Whitney he would not discuss the matter with him for a single minute more. "I want now to go to the telephone and call my counsel," he said, rising to leave the room.

Whitney and his lawyer sat and waited as Bartow went to the telephone room and called John W. Davis, the foe of FDR's holding company law and the Morgan firm's longtime legal advisor. They arranged to meet that night at Davis's country home. Bartow rang off and trotted back up the stairs to where Whitney and Mason waited for him. Whitney immediately offered explanations.

"I would like to explain this to you," he said. "I have a loan of $280,000 at the Public National Bank. In that loan are all of the securities taken improperly from the accounts in my office that I have mentioned to you." A $280,000 loan "would enable me to restore all of those improperly used securities," he continued, lying fluently. With the securities restored to the customer accounts, Whitney said, he could "go before the business conduct committee on Monday morning" and "state truthfully there were no irregularities in my office." That, too, was a lie; the $280,000 loan he was seeking would not have come close to curing the "irregularities" at his firm.

As if nothing remarkable had just happened, Bartow invited Whitney and his lawyer to join him for a quick supper in the club's dining room. Then, leaving Whitney to wait at the club, Bartow and Mason left for the nighttime drive to John Davis's twenty-room hilltop estate, Mattapan, near Locust Valley, Long Island. When their car arrived, a butler ushered them inside, most likely to the handsome English-style library.

Davis, silver-haired and long-headed, listened as Bartow repeated as much of Whitney's conversation as he could remember, noting that Whitney said he had misappropriated securities from the yacht club and two other accounts, but that about $280,000 would set them right.

Davis's baritone voice made his message more emphatic.

"You have been put on notice. This man has told you that he used securities improperly," he pointed out. "And from your general statement, you know he is insolvent—at least, you have every reason to believe he is."

Given those facts, Davis continued, neither Bartow nor anyone else at Morgan should do *anything* to help Whitney. The gesture could be "misunderstood and misconstrued" in subsequent bankruptcy actions, he said. Creditors could argue in court that such assistance proved the Morgan firm had assumed responsibility for Whitney's business losses or, even worse, for his business practices.

Bartow asked if he could at least ask Charles Gay for a brief delay of the business conduct committee meeting, just a day or so, to give everyone time to get a clearer sense of Whitney's situation. Perhaps not fully understanding Bartow's plan, Davis said he had no objection, and invited Bartow to use his phone to call Charles Gay. The exchange president agreed to a meeting that night at the Metropolitan Club, and Bartow and Mason motored back to Manhattan.

William Jackson, Redmond's partner, arrived at the club first. Mason immediately asked if the business conduct committee meeting could be held off for just twenty-four hours so that "competent auditors" could go into the Whitney firm and make a report.

"Under no circumstances will there be a single moment's delay in the meeting," Jackson said with great emphasis. The investigation was complete, the report was ready, and the committee was going to hear that report on Monday morning. Charles Gay, who had arrived soon after Jackson, seconded his decree with even greater finality.

Just two blocks north, Dick Whitney was waiting at the Links Club, no doubt looking like any other member enjoying a quiet evening. When Mason and Bartow returned, Bartow delivered the news: nothing whatsoever could be done.

GIVEN JOHN DAVIS'S UNEQUIVOCAL legal advice on Saturday night, Bartow's almost frantic actions on Sunday were very strange.

Starting very early that morning, he made calls inviting two Morgan partners, three staff members at the firm, and lawyer Randy Mason to meet with him at 2:30 P.M. at his townhouse on East Sixty-sixth Street. He asked Mason to bring along Kingsley Rodewald, Whitney's partner, to advise them on how long an audit at the firm would take. Defying the advice from John Davis, Bartow apparently still planned to send the Morgan staffers to Whitney's office so they, "in their expert way," could uncover "the facts which apparently were not obtainable otherwise."

Then Bartow made an appointment to visit his senior partner, J. P. "Jack" Morgan Jr., who had returned just the day before after three weeks away. In late morning, Bartow drove to out to Morgan's baronial Long Island mansion, perched on its own wooded island near Glen Cove with distant views of the Manhattan skyline far to the west.

Frank Bartow, like every Morgan partner, had gotten "the talk" about the Morgan firm's ethical standards. Jack Morgan had always said that "at the first sign of unethical conduct, they should come straight to him." Tom Lamont and George Whitney hadn't done that in November, of course; Frank Bartow would do that today. He was waiting at the mansion when Jack Morgan returned from church.

"I was busy all night on the Dick Whitney matter," Bartow told him.

"What Dick Whitney matter?"

"Dick Whitney is busted higher than a kite," Bartow answered, "and it is much worse than that."

Morgan listened silently as Bartow gave a full report. The elderly banker was "shocked beyond measure," but recognized that there was nothing to be done, and said so. Bartow agreed. There was "no course for us to follow except to abide by the advice that we had received from counsel."

Ultimately, that's what Bartow did. After considering several vague plans for using Morgan staffers to get a reliable audit of Whitney's books, he finally thought to invite Edwin Sunderland, a longtime partner in the Davis law firm, to the afternoon meeting at his townhouse.

When Ed Sunderland arrived, Bartow told him his plan to send Morgan staffers in to check Whitney's books.

Sunderland had known the Whitney brothers for years, and privately felt that Dick had long been consumed by jealousy for his more successful older brother. But this wasn't a matter of sibling rivalry; he had to protect his client, the House of Morgan.

"Under no circumstances, can you or *anyone else* from J.P. Morgan & Company go into the office of Richard Whitney & Company to find out *anything*," Sunderland said.

Finally, Bartow seemed to grasp that not even the House of Morgan could rescue Dick Whitney from ruin and disgrace. He dismissed Rodewald. When the three Morgan staff members arrived, Bartow apologized for interrupting their weekend and sent them away. With his two Morgan partners, he filled Sunderland in on the long, sad story—and then he got up to tackle the most difficult task of all. He called his friend George Whitney, who had arrived at Jekyll Island, Georgia, barely a day earlier. Speaking carefully, aware that there could be listeners along the line, he explained where things stood with his brother.

"My God," said George Whitney. He insisted he would return to New York immediately.

Bartow urged him to stay and rest, promising to call with an update at noon on Monday. But he was still having breakfast on Monday morning when a distraught George Whitney called again to see if there had been any developments.

"He was very disturbed about not being in New York and again wanted to come back that day," Bartow later recalled. "I urged him not to. I reminded him that he was not well, that all was being done that could be done." Whitney asked if he had spoken with his brother's great friend Roland Redmond. Bartow said he would do so, and again promised to call at noon.

Redmond agreed to come to Bartow's office to talk, not as the lawyer advising the stock exchange's business conduct committee on its investigation of Dick Whitney, but as "two friends who are interested in a common friend."

Bartow asked, "Is there anything that anybody can humanly do in this thing, that you know of?"

"Absolutely not," Redmond answered. "I don't know of a solitary thing." He rose and left.

ACROSS THE STREET IN a conference room at the stock exchange, a somber Howland Davis gaveled the Committee on Business Conduct to order at 10:30 that morning. Gay and Redmond were sitting in, but it was not a complicated meeting. The comptroller and his assistant made a verbal report of their findings in the Whitney audit and the committee voted unanimously to ask the NYSE board of governors to authorize a formal investigation.

The governors were summoned to meet at 1:30 that afternoon in their magnificent boardroom. Gay stood at the podium. From this spot, Whitney had steered the exchange through the 1929 crash, the 1931 gold crisis, and the 1933 banking crisis. He had stepped down from this rostrum to accept Gay as his successor in 1935. As Gay watched, twenty-nine governors came in, all of the fifty-man board he could muster on short notice; twenty others couldn't make it, and the fiftieth was Dick Whitney.

The report of the business conduct committee was shared with them, laying out the committee's case against Whitney, Ed Morgan, and Henry Mygatt. Under exchange rules, Morgan and Mygatt were responsible for their partner's misconduct even if their only sin had been to pay too little attention to what Whitney was doing.

The first charge described Whitney's improper use of the New York Yacht Club's securities to get a bank loan; the second, third, and fourth charges described his misuse of the Homestake Mining heiress's shares. The fifth charge revealed his misuse of the Gratuity Fund assets. The final charge was that the firm had filed a false questionnaire, signed by all three men.

This was not a full accounting of Whitney's misconduct. He had been treating his clients' assets as his own for years; he had first stolen from his wife's trust fund in 1926. After 1932, theft became routine. He led the war against FDR's new laws while breaking one of society's oldest laws on an almost daily basis. He had defaulted on countless debts owed to his closest friends and lied repeatedly to them and to the wealthy brother who so often bailed him out.

But for most of the men in that gilded room, this was their first indication that Dick Whitney, once the most powerful voice in their ranks and the voice of Wall Street to the world, was almost certainly a criminal. They were speechless as the charges were read. Howland Davis made a motion for the adoption of his committee's report.

Each man, at his own pace, signaled his support for the motion by standing up from his chair. The minutes reported that the motion passed unanimously "by a rising vote."

The exchange's constitution gave Whitney and his partners ten days to prepare their defense; a final vote on the charges would not be taken until Thursday, March 17, 1938.

After adjourning the meeting, Howland Davis gathered his things as Charles Gay made a telephone call to Bill Douglas at the SEC and asked to see him that night at the Carlton Hotel. By 3 P.M., Davis and Gay were on a Washington-bound train.

CHAPTER NINE

THE GENTLEMAN'S CODE

MARCH 1938–JUNE 1938

A S SOON AS BILL DOUGLAS HAD HEARD THE EXCHANGE OF-
ficials' story Monday night, he dispatched Commissioner John W.
Hanes to New York. Bearing subpoenas for Whitney's records, Hanes
caught the 2 A.M. sleeper, but probably did not sleep much. As a
friend of several Morgan partners and a former NYSE member,
Hanes found it nearly impossible to believe that the case against
Whitney was as clear-cut as Gay and Davis claimed. He would soon
learn that it was.

Shortly after 9 A.M. on Tuesday, the SEC met in Washington and
approved a formal investigative order, giving force to Hanes's subpoenas. Not long afterward, investigators in the SEC's office at
120 Broadway, armed with those subpoenas, raced the two long
blocks to Whitney's offices. They gathered documents from desks
and files, wrapped them in brown paper, tied them with string, and
carried them away before anyone else could.

Hanes arrived at the stock exchange a little before 10 A.M.—just
in time to see Charles Gay climb to the podium above the trading
floor to make an announcement, perhaps the most difficult one he
had ever made from that spot. Gay read a short statement disclosing
that the firm of Richard Whitney & Company had been suspended
for insolvency. But "he could not bring himself to state publicly that
Whitney had been involved in criminal misconduct," one historian
noted.

The whole truth became public just minutes later, with the opening bell still echoing across the subdued trading floor. The NYSE's official public statement revealed that the business conduct committee had found evidence of "conduct apparently contrary to just and equitable principles of trade," a phrase from the exchange constitution. Everyone on the trading floor, everyone on Wall Street, knew that phrase was a euphemism for "wrongdoing." A dead silence was quickly shattered by "a wild babble of voices," according to one account. There was little thought of trading the rest of the day.

Although he was heartsick, Charles Gay no doubt felt proud of how the NYSE had dealt with this case. It had not swept the mess under the rug. It had not bowed to Whitney's repeated requests that the auditors be called off or the committee meetings be postponed. Whitney had been expelled on a unanimous vote, proof that the old guard no longer ruled the boardroom.

But the larger Whitney story, the one that featured unpaid loans and undelivered securities and broken promises, showed a less flattering picture. It revealed Wall Street's unquestioned belief that, whenever possible, a gentleman's crimes should be dealt with privately, among friends and colleagues. At all times, he should be given the benefit of the doubt. Public exposure was a last resort, to be imposed only after every means of covering up the mess had failed.

Whitney's social circle was stunned and saddened by the fall of this much-admired figure, but his professional circle was enraged. A Manhattan society columnist wrote later that Wall Street was showing Whitney "all the ferocity they have hitherto reserved for a certain President and the New Deal." They were not angry about his crimes, she wrote. They were furious because his crimes had delivered Wall Street into the hands of the SEC. That, she concluded, "is what puts him beyond the pale."

The New York *Daily News* observed with relief that Whitney's downfall did not trigger a financial crisis, and gave credit for that to the New Deal's deposit insurance program, the FDIC, which reassured the public. *The New York Times* saw a different lesson: that Whitney's misconduct was so shocking to Wall Street precisely because such behavior was so rare, thanks to "the district's code of fiduciary and business ethics." Judge Ferdinand Pecora was not asked for comment on that highly debatable observation. He knew, better than most, that the rarity was that Whitney was being exposed and punished.

The rest of that dramatic Tuesday was a jumble. John Hanes sat down with Howland Davis's committee and, with Redmond nearby, heard the devastating evidence against Whitney and learned Whitney himself had admitted the charges. At some point, Hanes and Redmond excused themselves to place a call to Douglas in Washington to bring him up to date. Douglas was no doubt also getting updates from John J. Davidson, the New York staff lawyer overseeing the investigation there, but the SEC had no public comment on the case.

IN PRIVATE QUARTERS AND on the public stage, the Whitney case unfolded over the next few weeks as both tragedy and farce.

On Wednesday, March 9, Bill Douglas accompanied President Roosevelt on a drive through Washington's early spring weather and briefed him on the developments in the case, one that FDR still found shocking and sad—he did not gloat or crow about Whitney's vast hypocrisy, or use his crime as a cudgel against the "economic royalists" who continued to denounce the SEC and demand deregulation.

That same Wednesday, a weary and inconsolable George Whitney emerged from his private railroad car and took his limousine back to his Manhattan townhouse. He stood ready to give any help he could to his brother; the ordeal would turn his hair silver within months.

As his brother arrived home, Richard Whitney released a statement exonerating his partners and employees, saying he was solely responsible for his firm's collapse. He acknowledged that "certain of my actions have been wrong" and vowed to do "whatever lies in my power to repair the loss which any one has suffered." And he offered his full cooperation to New York State attorney general John J. Bennett Jr.

The farce emerged in the hyperventilating climate of New York politics.

On Tuesday, as Howland Davis had been briefing the SEC,

an exchange vice president had briefed Bennett's chief assistant, Ambrose V. McCall. McCall, described as "a big, slow-moving, mild-mannered man," almost immediately had convened a closed-door hearing on the case, sending out aides to track down witnesses and assuring reporters he would hold a public hearing in his office the next day.

That hearing on Wednesday, March 9, was an intimate affair. Reporters lined the walls, notebooks in hand. McCall sat at his desk and, one by one, witnesses sat in the wooden armchair beside it, with a stenographer between them scribbling into a pad she balanced on the corner of the desk. One of the first people summoned was Whitney's cashier. McCall asked him for the firm's key records. Before the cashier could answer, John J. Davidson, the SEC lawyer, rose from a side chair and identified himself.

"Just to get the record straight," Davidson said, "I would like it to be understood: all of these records have been subpoenaed by the Securities and Exchange Commission." Douglas's early morning blitzkrieg had put the records into the SEC's hands—they were literally in Davidson's hands at that moment.

"Naturally, you will be given an opportunity to examine them," Davidson added.

"Well, I guess we understand each other then," McCall replied grudgingly. "But I'm not going to be hurried through an examination."

He would, in fact, be hurried—not by the SEC but because, as always, the pace of the investigation in New York would be driven primarily by political calculus.

If Whitney had disputed the charges, making the case more difficult, or if he had been an obscure Wall Street clerk, the case might have languished, as many earlier fraud cases had. But Whitney had confessed, making the case simple, and he was one of the most famous men on Wall Street. Bennett immediately saw that his lieutenant, McCall, would have to sprint or be beaten to the courthouse by the ambitious New York district attorney Thomas E. Dewey.

Politics surely intensified their combat over bragging rights in the Whitney case. At this point, the two men were widely (but wrongly) expected to be rivals in that year's gubernatorial race in

New York—Dewey would get the GOP nomination, but Bennett would bow out when Democratic governor Herbert Lehmann agreed to seek a fourth two-year term.

Bennett held the first hearing, focusing on Whitney's theft from the New York Yacht Club. The president of the club, a peppery commodore who was visibly outraged by Whitney's betrayal, swore out a complaint almost immediately. But to the astonishment of officials at the NYSE and the yacht club, Bennett did not immediately indict or arrest Whitney, apparently hoping to hold daily headline-making hearings until the NYSE acted the following week.

That gave Tom Dewey an opening to act with his characteristic speed on a complaint from a bank that was Whitney's cotrustee for the trust fund set up for Mrs. Whitney and her sister. Dewey hurried both women into his office to ask if Whitney had their permission to use their trust's assets. Gertrude Whitney spoke with Dewey in the privacy of his office. Her sister, the widow of a city judge who had died just ten months earlier, answered Dewey's questions before a grand jury, making "no attempt to hide her indignation." Whitney's improper use of the trust's securities to get personal bank loans was quickly confirmed.

With that evidence, Dewey won the race with Bennett by indicting and arresting Whitney on Thursday, March 10, on charges that he stole $105,000 from the Sheldon family trust fund. Headlines across the country noted this "surprise move by Dewey."

Every detail of Whitney's arrest was captured by the press. His lawyer Charles H. Tuttle was well-known to reporters; he was the former prosecutor who had lost to FDR in the 1930 governor's race. While at Tuttle's office, Whitney posed at some point for a remarkable photograph—as handsome as a studio portrait. His face was grave, but he seemed at ease; the gold pig-shaped fob proclaiming his status as a Harvard Porcellian hung from a glittering watch chain across his vest. With Tom Dewey moving things along, Whitney was quickly arraigned, photographed, fingerprinted, and released on $10,000 bail, with reporters and flash cameras marking each step, each gesture, each casual comment.

According to Bill Douglas, Dewey called him on that Thursday

morning to report that "Whitney would be arraigned that afternoon, plead guilty, and be sentenced." Douglas claimed that Dewey
said he intended to "close this whole nasty business out today."

The remark seems unlikely. Dewey knew that Bennett was still
on the case. Indeed, the state attorney general would indict and arrest Whitney the very next day on the complaint from the New York
Yacht Club. A case could even be made that Dewey would have
preferred a showy criminal trial, not a quick guilty plea. But fairly
or not, Douglas thought Dewey, a fiercely ambitious Republican,
wanted to sweep this embarrassment to Wall Street off the front
pages as quickly as possible.

And Douglas had no intention of letting that happen.

He would hold public hearings. Armed with Whitney's records
and SEC subpoena power, he would put all Whitney's gentlemanly
lenders and exchange allies under oath. Then he would ask them
how one of the most prominent men on Wall Street had broken the
law for so long without any effective oversight from an institution
that still insisted it could police itself. He wanted to know who at
the stock exchange had bailed Whitney out, ignored warning signs,
bent the rules, and kept silent when they should have spoken up.
Whitney claimed no one else played a role in his crimes. Bill Douglas didn't believe that. When his hearings were finished, history
would not believe it, either.

The following week brought Whitney's two court appearances
and his two pleas of "guilty," one uttered on his behalf by Tuttle and
the second given in his own steady voice, familiar to many from his
radio broadcasts, speeches, and testimony. He made no excuses and
assured the court he fully realized "the gravity of what has been done
and that a penalty must be paid."

That penalty was scheduled to be imposed at a sentencing hearing on March 28.

Soon after the closing bell rang on the trading floor on Thursday,
March 17, forty-five somber governors took their seats in the boardroom. The board secretary read the charges against the absent Whitney and his two partners, seated near the front of the room. Witnesses

were called and questioned. Ed Morgan and Henry Mygatt made their plea for mercy.

Finally, a little after 6 P.M., Howland Davis stood and made a series of motions calling for his fellow governors, by a "rising vote," to find Dick Whitney guilty of each of the charges against him.

Whether in sorrow or anger or disgust, every single governor rose from his chair to vote "guilty" on every single charge. There was no mercy in this room for the man who made their long crusade against federal regulation look like the self-serving maneuvers of a common thief. They spent the rest of the evening debating the fate of Mygatt and Morgan, ultimately deciding to suspend the two men for three years.

But there was one more order of business at the NYSE on this day—too apt, almost, to be believed.

This was the final day of voting on the constitutional amendments required to implement the sweeping reforms that were the long-overdue response to the SEC's demand that the NYSE shut down its "private club" and start operating like a grown-up public institution.

The board secretary reported the tally of member ballots. The reform amendments had passed overwhelmingly, 1,013 to 22.

Clearly, Dick Whitney was no longer a force on Wall Street, and Bill Douglas was. But could Douglas be forceful enough to permanently change the way Wall Street worked? He intended to find out.

* * *

IT WAS FRIDAY, APRIL 8, 1938, and Dick Whitney should have been in prison by now. He should have slept last night in a cell, not in his luxury townhouse. He should be wearing a shapeless gray uniform, not one of his four dozen custom-tailored suits, soon to be auctioned off in bankruptcy court with the rest of his princely possessions.

Whitney's sentencing, set for March 28, had been postponed

until Monday, April 11, so that he could testify before the SEC today.

The snow from a freak springtime storm was mostly slush when he arrived at 120 Broadway, where the agency's New York offices were located. By 10 A.M., he was seated with his lawyer in a packed twentieth-floor conference room. He already had testified in various venues—before the state attorney general's chief deputy, before a bankruptcy judge, before the district attorney. Now it was the SEC's turn.

But Dick Whitney was not on trial here; Wall Street was.

Over the next two and a half months, dozens of masters of finance would struggle to explain why they loaned millions to Whitney secured by nothing but his reputation and his Morgan ties. A half-dozen senior NYSE figures would try to defend their dismissal of obvious red flags about Whitney's conduct. Their answers gave America a glimpse of a privileged world whose citizens were so steeped in their own insular, clubby culture that the country's need for a trustworthy, well-behaved marketplace simply never occurred to them.

The trial examiner was Samuel O. Clark Jr., whose brother was the dean at the Yale Law School. Clark's graying temples and old-fashioned glasses made him seem older than his thirty-eight years. He had the rigor of his early training as a civil engineer, and the polish of his service at a Wall Street law firm. He had been the chief attorney on the SEC's grueling protective committee study and Douglas trusted him to craft the final report on these historic hearings.

The chief counsel who would examine this parade of plutocrats was Gerhard Gesell, Douglas's former student at Yale and a star in the SEC general counsel's office. Gerry Gesell, just twenty-seven years old, had a curly mop of dark hair and a broad, sunny face. He was a nephew of SEC commissioner Bud Mathews, but Gesell's extraordinary success as an SEC litigator extinguished any talk of nepotism.

The room was stuffy despite the chilly weather, with Judge Clark and Dick Whitney sharing a little more than 200 square feet of space with a stenographer, eight lawyers, and a pack of photographers, reporters, and spectators that spilled into the hallway.

Gesell's first questions established Whitney as a longtime fixture of NYSE life: a member since 1912, an officer since 1919, president for five years, a trustee of its Gratuity Fund, a director of three of its ancillary corporations, and a governor until the moment of his expulsion on March 17. Then Gesell dissected the slipshod operations and unreliable records of his firm, Richard Whitney & Company, where personal loans and partnership loans were tossed together and rarely disclosed even to his partners, who supposedly owned 49 percent of the firm.

Whitney grew testy with Gesell's effort to make him sort out these muddled personal and partnership debts. "The firm of Richard Whitney & Company was mine at that time and for many years prior," he claimed. "I have always felt that I had a right to do anything I wanted."

Gesell's carefully itemized questions made it clear that Whitney had been routinely breaking the law through at least the last three years of his NYSE presidency. When he voted as a governor to discipline other members, when he defended Wall Street before the Pecora committee, when he denounced FDR's reforms in Congress and across the country, when he stalled Joe Kennedy and ignored Jim Landis and battled Bill Douglas—while demanding that Wall Street be allowed to police itself, he had been a reckless criminal, unable even to police his own behavior.

As the hours passed, Whitney tersely confirmed each loan he had gotten from friends, acknowledged those he had never repaid, admitted stealing customer securities and pledging them for bank loans for himself. He insisted that no one at the stock exchange suspected he was an insolvent criminal until days before his public downfall; even after November, no one at the exchange ever questioned him about why he could not promptly return the Gratuity Fund's assets.

He became less arrogant only when asked about his brother.

Yes, his brother, George, had learned about that Gratuity Fund embezzlement on November 23, 1937, but had believed him when he falsely claimed that it was an isolated case. Well, yes, his brother did learn the next day that Whitney had broken all his previous promises to curb his indiscriminate borrowing and speculation. And yes, despite that evidence of Whitney's faithlessness, his brother had not only bailed him out in November but had made a mighty effort to rescue him in the early months of 1938.

Much of this sorry tale of brotherly betrayal had been told at earlier hearings, of course. But newspapers across the country still paid rapt attention. A Gallup poll days later showed that fully 60 percent of the country knew about the Whitney scandal—and most of those believed it justified giving greater power to the SEC.

Gesell would remember decades later a private exchange he had with Whitney just as he was being led away:

"Mr. Whitney, when did you first realize you were insolvent?"

"I am not insolvent," Whitney answered with stiff pride.

"What do you mean?" Gesell asked in amazement.

"I can still borrow money from my friends."

On Monday morning, April 11, a large burgundy limousine pulled up in front of the Whitney townhouse at 115 East Seventy-third Street; George Whitney had come to bid his brother goodbye. A short time later, a uniformed butler bowed Dick Whitney out the front door for the last time. Impeccably dressed but wearing no jewelry, Whitney calmly stepped down to the sidewalk and got into a waiting car as photographers' cameras clattered. For the rest of the day, a steady parade of limousines would deliver flowers, private notes, and sympathetic callers to the Whitney home.

Lawyer Charles Tuttle was waiting for Whitney at his law office; they took a taxi to the majestic Criminal Courts Building on Centre Street, where a huge crowd was waiting for a glimpse of the gentleman crook.

District Attorney Tom Dewey was at ease in Judge Owen W. Bohan's courtroom. His sentencing recommendation was before the judge. As sober as his signature gray suit, Dewey sat at the prosecutor's table beside Ambrose McCall. McCall's boss, the state attorney general, had agreed that today's sentence could cover both Dewey's case and his own.

Whitney waited on the second row of benches until his case was called and then passed through the bar to stand beside his lawyer, hands clasped behind his back.

Tuttle made a deeply sentimental plea for mercy. "Save for his counsel, he stands here alone," Tuttle said. "He has chosen to drain this bitter cup by himself . . . Even his own brother, who desired most earnestly permission to stand by him at this bar today, shoulder to shoulder, is—at Mr. Whitney's own imperative wish—now with the loyal wife and two daughters upon whom the shadow of grief and desolation today falls."

Whitney had not chosen "the coward's course of flight from the country or from life," Tuttle noted. "He still has courage. He still has character . . . He has faced his friends, which perhaps is the hardest task of all." Surely a prison term was superfluous after such pitiless punishment.

Judge Bohan wasn't moved.

Dewey had asked for a "punitive" sentence, the judge noted, and justice required one. "Were you the ordinary type of cashier or other faithless employee, the Court might be disposed to temper justice with mercy," he continued. But Whitney had "the advantage of the best education in America; you had the fruits of business and financial success . . . [and] were repeatedly chosen as spokesman of one of the largest financial markets in the world. All these you have betrayed."

He sentenced Whitney to five to ten years in prison; with credit for good behavior, he would likely serve less than four. Whitney put his topcoat over his arm and walked quickly through a side door into the bureaucratic warren that courtroom spectators never see. He was handcuffed and taken across the so-called Bridge of Sighs, the enclosed walkway high above the street that connected the court building to the Tombs, the jail where he would spend his first night as a prisoner. He declined the proffered lunch of franks and sauerkraut, but polished off a dinner of spaghetti with meat sauce and strawberry gelatin. In a sharp departure from his manner as NYSE president, he sought no special favors and spoke courteously to everyone, even lowly fellow inmates.

The keenest review of Whitney's final act came later from journalist John Brooks, who described Whitney as "hewing rigidly to the code of his class." For the uninitiated, Brooks explained: "That code, the code of old families and good prep schools and gentlemen's clubs and old guard Wall Street, was equivocal on the matters of ruthless acquisitiveness and even on certain forms of stealing—many of the class's members owed their membership to practices not far removed from stealing—but was explicit and inflexible on the matter of conduct when caught." Stoically calm and uncomplaining, Whitney faced his fate like a gentleman.

His trip up the Hudson to Ossining's Sing Sing prison the next day was a media circus. Wearing his pearl-gray homburg and dark topcoat, Whitney was handcuffed to another felon and marched down an obscure luggage ramp at Grand Central Terminal, cheating a huge crowd of gawkers. He was put on a train with other prisoners. An army of reporters and photographers waited at the prison; they watched as he marched through its gates, standing a full head taller than his fellow inmates.

The day Whitney was sentenced—in what a Brooklyn reporter called "a coincidence of fantastic irony"—the New York Stock Exchange released the slate of candidates for its new board of governors, selected by the terms of the constitutional amendments that had been approved the day Whitney had been expelled. None of the twenty-eight nominees were Whitney allies.

Nominated as chairman and in line to be hired as the exchange's first paid president was William McChesney Martin Jr., a broker with A.G. Edwards & Sons and the son of the president of the St. Louis Federal Reserve Bank. At age thirty-one, he was a full decade younger than Whitney had been in 1930, when he became the youngest NYSE president in history. Martin seemed to have no vices, unless you count a fanatical love of Broadway musicals; he lived frugally at the Yale Club, ate at Automats, and drank nothing richer than hot chocolate. And he was firmly allied with the big retail brokerage firms whose top priority was reassuring a wary public that Wall Street was safe and well regulated. One SEC commis sioner confided to FDR's attorney general that Martin "represents a sort of New Deal in the Exchange."

One of his first acts as president would be to name the dogged Howland S. Davis, who withstood Whitney's pressure to drop the business conduct committee's investigation, as the first paid director of the department of member firms.

To the shock of the surviving veterans of Whitney's old guard, neither Harry Simmons nor Charles Gay was nominated to a seat on the new board. Simmons had lobbied fiercely for a seat and believed, until this moment, that he had gotten one. Gay's friends had fought just as hard, citing his role in moving the recent reforms forward, but Gay declined the honor. (When he rang the closing bell for the last time, on May 16, the entire trading floor gave him a roaring ovation.)

The SEC did not cede the spotlight to Dick Whitney for very long. As he made his train trip to prison on Tuesday, April 12, the SEC's hearings into his downfall resumed in Washington—and they would dominate the financial news for weeks to come.

The first witness was the courtly "Duke" Wellington, the NYSE governor and patient lender to Whitney. He recalled Whitney once asking him for a one-month loan right in the presidential office; he made the loan and, to his partners' growing consternation, waited years for it to be repaid. He also reported telling NYSE lawyer Roland Redmond around 1935 that he "felt that it was unwise" of Whitney to borrow from friends "to finance not only his business but outside interests." His concern, he said, was that Whitney "was using bad judgment and imposing on his friends." Redmond's only response, as he recalled, was to say that he, too, had loaned money to Whitney.

But his most intriguing disclosure was that a Morgan partner, no longer living, had asked him sometime around 1931 to consider merging his firm with Whitney's. He recalled the Morgan partner saying Whitney "uses very bad judgment in his investments but he has got a very good business and he needs a good partner—somebody who isn't just an office boy, as the rest of his partners." The

Morgan man added, "We all love Dick around here, and we would like to help him reorganize his firm."

Notwithstanding all those facts, Wellington insisted he never dreamed Whitney's firm was on the brink of bankruptcy, and therefore did not raise any alarms with the NYSE business conduct committee until he'd gotten the tip from a floor trader that he passed along to Howland Davis in January.

Others in the long parade of NYSE figures told similar tales, with more or less charm and clarity. They had loaned money to Whitney on a handshake and weren't repaid until long after the loan was due—if they got repaid at all, and many didn't. Like Wellington, they all insisted they had never doubted Whitney's integrity and solvency. And like Wellington, they all had felt no duty to report these experiences to the business conduct committee so it could do its critically important self-regulatory job.

Even more infamously, former exchange president and longtime governor Harry Simmons, his fellow governor Blaire S. Williams, and exchange counsel Roland Redmond conceded that they knew Whitney had been unable to restore the Gratuity Fund's assets in November without his brother's help. But even after Howland Davis had begun his inquiry, and once in the face of direct questions from Davis, all three men had remained silent about that episode. To a man, in defiance of common sense, they claimed they had never had the slightest reason to mistrust Dick Whitney until the NYSE's auditors made their shocking discovery on February 28.

Without question, the highlight of these hearings was the testimony from the House of Morgan.

Wellington's testimony showed that some Morgan partners had known that Dick Whitney was a reckless, unskilled speculator as early as 1931 or 1932. It was also clear that Whitney's ties to the Morgan firm had given comfort to many of his friendly lenders; some publicly conceded they had felt sure that, in a pinch, they would be repaid by George Whitney. Dick Whitney himself had documented several occasions when the Morgan firm had loaned him urgently needed cash and restructured the loans without complaint when he didn't repay them. Gesell introduced SEC audits showing that, between 1921 and 1937, George Whitney had loaned his brother $3.2 million, of which only about $300,000 had been repaid. And of course, the world now knew that George Whitney had made the million-dollar loan that allowed Whitney to cover up his crime in November.

How would the men from 23 Wall Street explain all that?

Opening his questions, Gesell asked J. P. "Jack" Morgan, "Do you know Richard Whitney?"

Morgan's answer was "I *knew* him, yes; not well."

Gesell then established that the lofty J.P. Morgan & Company was an NYSE member firm, no different in form than Dick Whitney's firm. One of the two seats it owned was registered in the name of Jack Morgan himself, although his only visit to the trading floor had been a ceremonial one, years earlier. The other was in the name of his son, Junius S. Morgan, who was equally unfamiliar with the exchange's operations.

Gesell questioned what the Morgan partners had known about the Gratuity Fund episode before it became public with Whitney's downfall.

Morgan testified that all he had known about it was that George Whitney sought permission to take a large sum from the partnership because his brother was "in a business jam." He hadn't asked for any details.

Frank Bartow described how he first learned about Whitney's crimes from Whitney himself, on March 5, at the Links Club. But he conceded that, nearly a full day later, he was still trying to find some way that Whitney could be spared through the Morgan firm's efforts.

George Whitney, of course, admitted he'd learned about his brother's crime just before Thanksgiving 1937. When pressed, he conceded that he had told his partner Tom Lamont about it the same day, while arranging to borrow the money to bail out his brother. Tom Lamont confirmed he knew about the embezzlement, but said he helped George Whitney cover it up simply because that was what his heart told him to do.

Indeed, Lamont insisted that when the news of Dick Whitney's public disgrace reached him in Europe, it was "the greatest shock in the world."

"Even though you had known on the 23rd of November, 1937, that Richard Whitney had stolen approximately a million dollars' worth of securities?" Gesell asked.

Lamont groped for words, stumbling over fragments of sentences. He pulled up short when Gesell asked, "You knew it was illegal and unlawful?"

"Sure," Lamont said. "But you used the word 'stealing.' It never occurred to me that Richard Whitney was a thief."

To Lamont, Dick Whitney "had gotten into a jam, had made improper and unlawful use of securities." George Whitney was going to set it right, he added. His only instinct was to help a friend help his brother. (Morgan historian Ron Chernow suggests a more cynical motive for the November cover-up: these conservative Morgan partners "knew the New Dealers would gladly exploit a scandal to impose further reforms on Wall Street. They didn't want to throw Richard to the liberal Democratic wolves" like Bill Douglas at the SEC.)

George Whitney, Tom Lamont, Harry Simmons, and Roland Redmond had also been privy to years of evidence showing that Dick Whitney was a reckless and unreliable speculator with a bottomless appetite for loans he always promised to repay but rarely did; they had good reasons to doubt whether his firm was solvent. But none of them alerted the NYSE about those hazards. None of them warned the exchange in late 1937 that Dick Whitney, conducting business with other members every day on the trading floor, was urgently trying to sell or liquidate his business. At the hearings, George Whitney scoffed angrily at the idea that he should have reported his brother's financial problems. "The stock exchange had just as much opportunity as I of knowing about this," he insisted. "I mean, he was there if they wanted to ask him."

Thus, it became clear that not even the loftiest figures on Wall Street felt any obligation to report misconduct to the NYSE business conduct committee, or to anyone else with a duty to police Wall Street. That sort of "tale-bearing"—as Roland Redmond contemptuously described such disclosures—would have violated their code as gentlemen.

Tom Lamont laid out his tender feelings in a letter to a friend: "Ought we all to forget the principles on which we were trained to help one another, to try to forgive and to try to give the fellow another chance?" Lamont conceded that "as the evidence proved, Dick was a thoroughgoing crook . . . But all this was unknown to George last November at the time that he tried to help Dick undo the wrong that he had done."

None of them—not the Whitney brothers, the House of Morgan, or the entire old guard on Wall Street—could see that the kind of self-regulation they claimed to conduct required exactly the kind of "tale-bearing" disclosures and intrusive scrutiny that they all found so distasteful. Or as Bill Douglas so memorably put it, "It takes a snoop to catch a jiggle."

Thus, the hearings showed history the enduring obstacles to ever letting Wall Street police itself: this code of gentlemanly silence, this contempt for those who report wrongdoing, an eagerness to hide one another's dirty linen behind closed doors, a reluctance to tackle complexity, a myopia that looked at a wellborn thief and saw a good fellow who had gotten into a jam. So long as that culture prevailed— and, given human nature, who could say if it could *ever* be changed?— Wall Street would need a cop on the corner, ready to ask awkward questions and bear tales all the way to the courthouse.

John T. Flynn, the former Pecora staffer who had fought tirelessly for competent regulation, saw Wall Street's trust in Whitney as the act of men "steeped in romanticism" about the noble virtues of the gentlemanly class. "If there is one lesson the world has learned in its several thousand years of civilization," Flynn wrote, "it is that no man who gambles can be trusted with the money or property of other people." He added: "This does not mean that bad men who gamble cannot be trusted. It means that good men cannot."

At the Harvard Law School, Felix Frankfurter was staggered by the testimony coming out of the Whitney hearings. On May 6, 1938, he wrote Bill Douglas urging him to publish the entire transcript— as Douglas ultimately did. "I do not know of any record of hearings that so illuminates the actual conduct of our financial community, that so reveals their processes and their mentality," he said. "It is vital for the present as well as for history that the minutes be made accessible."

Americans in April of 1938 were not slow to see what Douglas had exposed. Reporters across the country focused on the "Wall Street code of silence." At the NYSE, Martin took the unprecedented step of opening the doors of the grand board chamber to the press when he held his inaugural meeting as president. Before leaving office, Charles Gay called on every member firm to make its financial statements available to its clients. For a brief moment, secrecy was no longer the gentlemanly thing.

An incident in St. Louis showed just how well America understood the lessons of the Whitney hearings. On April 20, 1938, a young man came before justice of the peace Louis L. Hicks and admitted stealing two dollars from a gas station.

Justice Hicks said he intended to disprove the idea that "there's one law for the rich and another for the poor" in America. He took out a pencil and some paper and did some quick calculations.

"Richard Whitney got five years for stealing about $225,000 [in cash]. That would be about $45,000 a year, $120 a day, and $5 an hour. You stole $2. That would be 24 minutes, and that is your sentence."

DOUBTS AND DEPARTURES

JUNE 1938–NOVEMBER 1938

THE DENSE FOG THAT BLANKETED PARTS OF THE EAST COAST on Sunday night had lifted by the time the stately *Queen Mary* approached the mouth of the New York harbor on Monday, June 20, 1938, five days after leaving the British port of Southampton.

As usual, a customs office cutter sprinted out to meet her, carrying newspaper reporters and photographers who would seek out prominent passengers while the ship inched toward its berth. But Jimmy Roosevelt, President Roosevelt's son and secretary, had gotten there first, speeding out ahead of the cutter to deliver an urgent warning to one of those prominent passengers: the Honorable Joseph P. Kennedy, United States ambassador to the Court of St. James's.

For months, Kennedy had done little to deter friendly political pundits from predicting that he was laying the groundwork for a presidential run in 1940—an awkward lapse, since Roosevelt had not yet announced his own plans. Kennedy was certain to be questioned about those rumors as soon as the journalists swarmed aboard, Jimmy Roosevelt told him. Young Roosevelt's presence strongly suggested that FDR himself would be listening to the answer.

By the time reporters gathered around him in one of the ship's Art Deco salons, Joe Kennedy was ready.

"I enlisted under President Roosevelt in 1932 to do whatever he wanted me to do. There are many problems at home and abroad, and I happen to be busy at one abroad just now," Kennedy said. "If I had my eye on another job, it would be a complete breach of faith with President Roosevelt." Yes, it would—but that did not mean he was not eying "another job" anyway.

Kennedy was more exuberant on a ship-to-shore telephone chat with a friendly New York *Daily News* reporter.

"I'm just the same," he crowed. "You won't find me changed a bit!"

It was a curious thing to say: Kennedy had only been in his London post for four months. Indeed, it was highly unusual for any diplomat to ask for home leave so early in his tenure. But perhaps the comment reflected Kennedy's sense of how momentous those four months seemed in his own mind.

Joe and Rose Kennedy and their nine children, installed in the thirty-six-room ambassadorial residence once owned by Jack Morgan's father, had made an enormous splash on the diplomatic scene in London. He had made a hole in one at golf, and it was reported everywhere. Equal attention was paid when he had worn long trousers, instead of the traditional knee-length style, while presenting his credentials at court. King George VI and Queen Elizabeth were delighted by the Kennedys; in April, the ambassador and his wife had spent an extremely cordial weekend at Windsor Castle with the royal family. The Kennedys had been invited to dine in the royal enclosure at Ascot; their elder daughters had been presented at court. To her deep delight, Rose Kennedy was being invited everywhere that mattered and entertaining everyone of note; she was universally admired for her vivacious charm and stylish wardrobe.

On the political front, Kennedy had made a good impression on both local and visiting plutocrats. Tom Lamont, returning home to face the Whitney hearings, had assured shipboard reporters that Kennedy was doing a wonderful job in London. Lamont's dear friend Lady Astor added the ambassador to her elite guest list at her country estate of Cliveden. He rekindled his friendships with several dozen British bankers he had met in 1935.

Most significant, Kennedy naïvely was forming a strong, deeply personal bond with Prime Minister Neville Chamberlain.

The two men shared a similar view of the world, a similar set of values. Both were successful men whose status had been earned, not inherited; both saw themselves as brass-tacks businessmen, ready to cut deals without a lot of romantic or chivalrous notions. And both believed that, as a matter of practical politics and economic survival, the Western democracies absolutely had to coexist peacefully with the belligerent fascist powers rising in Europe. Soon, Kennedy seemed to be more in tune with Chamberlain's policies than with Roosevelt's—even in private conversations with German diplomats in London. In a chat with American financier Bernard Baruch, Kennedy overlapped his index and middle finger and said, "I'm just like *that* with Chamberlain. Why, Franklin himself isn't as confidential with me."

These indiscretions proved the wisdom of some disregarded advice Kennedy had gotten from an ally after FDR first offered him the post. Boake Carter, an abrasive radio commentator, had written his friend a letter praising his sincerity, courage, honesty, and the Irish-bred faith that he "can't be licked" at whatever he undertakes. "But the job of Ambassador to London needs not only honesty, sincerity, faith and an abounding courage—it needs skill brought by years of training," Carter had warned. "And that, Joe, you simply don't possess . . . If you don't realize that soon enough, you're going to be hurt as you were never hurt before."

The diplomatic landscape in London in the spring of 1938 was emphatically not a place for amateurs. Chamberlain's foreign minister had resigned in February, in part to protest the prime minister's tacit acceptance of Mussolini's aggression in Africa. Within days of Kennedy's arrival, Germany had forcibly installed a Nazi puppet government in Austria. Chamberlain's response had been to tell Parliament that "nothing could have arrested what actually happened in Austria unless this country and other countries had been prepared to use force." They were not, so Hitler had felt free to extend the bloody reach of the German Reich and his own murderous hatred of the Jews. "For the first few weeks, the behavior of the Vienna Nazis was worse than anything I had seen in Germany," wrote American journalist William L. Shirer. "There was an orgy of sadism" against the city's Jewish citizens.

Kennedy "wholeheartedly concurred" with Chamberlain's view

that it was far more important to preserve the peace than to forcibly protest an outbreak of local Nazi violence against Austrian Jews. Their view was shared by a sizeable majority of British and American voters, who were haunted by the Great War and were determined not to be drawn into another European conflict.

President Roosevelt knew all that; isolationists in both parties had made their views quite clear. But he was not convinced that "conciliating" Hitler, as Chamberlain sometimes called it, would spare the world another war. He had read the dictator's prophetic memoir *Mein Kampf* in the original German, and knew that English translations were not accurately conveying its irrational extremism. FDR suspected Chamberlain's critic Winston Churchill, whom Kennedy dismissed as "a drunken bum," had rightly gauged that Hitler would keep pushing outward until someone stopped him. Roosevelt was walking a very delicate line, weighing the shifting balance between "the growing conviction that America must *at all costs* stay out of war and the growing conviction that Hitler must *at all costs* be stopped." But one thing he was certain about was that his London ambassador should not be spending his time with his arm around Chamberlain's shoulder and his eyes on the 1940 election back home.

Roosevelt knew Kennedy was the longest of long shots in that presidential race, but Kennedy didn't have to run to inflict damage. Given his stature in business and his articulate and unsentimental defense of FDR in 1936, any public attacks he made on the progressive gains of the New Deal in future campaigns would be very damaging—and he seemed, daily, on the brink of making those attacks as he grew frustrated at FDR's unbusinesslike attitude toward the European dictators.

If Kennedy truly didn't dream of running, he was sending very odd signals back to Washington. He had hired his friend Arthur Krock's diplomatic correspondent, journalist Harold Hinton, as his personal press aide in London, paying part of Hinton's salary himself. He told Krock it would be "a very helpful thing if agitation could be started to have me address the Senate and House Foreign Relations Committee in Executive Session," and Krock readily promised to "put it in the works." Most remarkable of all, he had been secretly sending weekly letters, filled with his foreign and domestic policy views and marked "Private and Confidential," to a mailing list of America's most powerful opinion makers: publisher William Randolph Hearst; columnists Walter Lippmann, Frank Kent, Drew Pearson, and Arthur Krock; Senators James Byrnes, Key Pittman, and Burton Wheeler; and elder gadfly and wealthy campaign donor Bernard Baruch.

Conspicuously missing from Kennedy's mailing list was President Roosevelt.

The White House first learned about these letters when Arthur Krock sent a bundle of them to Roosevelt, thinking he was doing Kennedy a good turn by demonstrating the depth of the ambassador's policy analysis. Those in Roosevelt's circle who had never quite trusted Kennedy felt that their doubts had been confirmed. One of them, FDR's press secretary Steve Early, leaked the letters to two "anti-New Deal" journalists, saying "Joe wants to run for President and is dealing behind the Boss's back at the London Embassy."

Meanwhile, the stock market seemed to be welcoming Joe Kennedy home: stock prices on Monday roared upward at the opening bell, flagged a bit at lunch, and then rallied the rest of the day. Trading was surprisingly robust, with more than a million shares trading; there were reports of a heavy flow of foreign orders in the early hours. As prices climbed, short sellers jumped to lock in their profits, which meant buying shares to close out their positions. The Dow Jones Industrial index ended the day at 118.61 points, nearly 5 percentage points above Friday's close. The Wall Street press seemed baffled by the sudden rally, but hindsight suggests it reflected the steady recovery from the steep 1937 recession, which ended this month with an upward surge almost as rapid as its downward plunge had been.

On Tuesday morning, June 21, after a night at the Waldorf-Astoria hotel in Manhattan, Kennedy set out for Hyde Park, where the president was catching up on his work after attending his son John's summery wedding that Sunday in Nahant, Massachusetts. The ceremony had been held in rock-hard Republican country, and

the presidential motorcade had gotten a cheerless reception. A New
York society reporter overheard "some wit" asking presidential aide
Harry Hopkins, "Were you asked here as a friend of the Roosevelts
or to aggravate the community?"

Once upon a time, over martinis at Marwood, Roosevelt had
welcomed Joe Kennedy's confident lectures about the relatively obscure worlds of finance, where Kennedy the speculator was utterly at
home, and commercial shipping, where Kennedy the former shipyard manager had been a quick study. When Kennedy the rookie
diplomat was ushered into the small presidential study at Hyde Park
on this June morning, he stepped back into that familiar tutorial
role. He poured out his insights about the European situation without considering that FDR, who had first dealt with high-level European issues during the Great War, had likely forgotten more about
foreign affairs than Kennedy could possibly have learned in just four
months on the job.

Roosevelt took it with good humor. But he later told Harold
Ickes—who told his diary—that Kennedy had lectured the president about the wisest way to refer to fascism in his speeches. He
urged FDR to "attack Nazism but not Fascism. The president asked
him why," Ickes wrote, "and he said very frankly that he thought that
we would have to come to some form of Fascism here." Kennedy's
idea, Roosevelt told Ickes, was to "organize a small powerful committee under himself as chairman and this committee would run the
country without much reference to Congress."

But Roosevelt's comments to the reporters waiting outside at
Hyde Park gave no hint of any coolness between the two men, and
Kennedy later described a thorough and frank discussion of Chamberlain's policies that did not include any lessons on how to implement or refer to fascism. After chatting with Eleanor Roosevelt over
dishes of fresh local strawberries, he set off to catch the night train
to Boston—or, more accurately, to Harvard.

This was supposedly Kennedy's sole reason for coming home: his
firstborn and namesake Joseph P. Kennedy Jr. was graduating with
honors. But Kennedy thought there would be other honors from his
alma mater, too. For months, friends had encouraged him to think

that he would receive one of the dozen honorary degrees to be handed out at commencement. "Plenty of excitement over here as to whether you are to get a degree," Kennedy's father-in-law wrote from Boston. "The newspapers call me up and I say I do not know but they all believe you deserve it and will get it."

But sometime during his train journey north, Kennedy learned for certain that he was not on the honors list. "It was a terrible blow to him," his wife, Rose, later reported. "After all those expectations had been built up, it was hard to accept that he wasn't really even in the running." Not for the first time, Harvard broke his heart.

When reporters asked about it, Kennedy shrugged it off, noting that his son Joe was graduating with honors and that was "pretty good for one family, I think." Young Joe was the chairman of the Class Day festivities for the graduating class, quite an honor on campus, and Kennedy stayed for every event on Wednesday. But when the day was over, Kennedy decided to continue on to Hyannis Port that night. His son Joe collected his Harvard degree on Thursday, June 23, without a single family member in attendance; later that day, he drove to the Cape to join his father at their beachfront compound.

This heartsore homecoming immediately got worse. On the day of Harvard's commencement, Steve Early's handiwork bore fruit: in Chicago and in Philadelphia, major stories declared that Roosevelt was annoyed with Kennedy, citing both his failure to scotch the presidential rumors and his presumptuous letters from London. While still at Hyannis Port, Kennedy got a letter from Arthur Krock telling him, in strict confidence, that Early had been the source of the two stories.

Kennedy was thoroughly furious, but the record is cloudy about what happened next.

As far as official Washington could see, Kennedy's visit was perfectly normal. He was in Washington on June 24, making his official rounds. He visited his official superior, Secretary of State Cordell Hull, and gave him a tactless report "severely criticizing certain aspects of our foreign service." Then he paid a brief courtesy call on Henry Morgenthau at the Treasury and met with old friends around the city. By then, the stock market had closed its weeklong rally: the Dow had climbed nearly 14 percent, to 129.06 points; more than a million shares traded every day, and more than two million traded on Thursday and Friday. Late on Friday afternoon, Kennedy was honored at a cheerful reception at the Mayflower Hotel "at which former official associates in the Maritime Commission and the SEC and newspaper correspondents greeted him."

Years later, by which point Kennedy was fiercely hostile to the New Deal, he told his friend Jim Landis a different tale of "true Irish anger," as Kennedy put it. He claimed he dined with FDR at the White House after that Friday afternoon reception, and did not learn until the next morning that Early was the one who betrayed him. By then, both Hull and FDR were out of town. When he met with Hull on Monday, June 27, he offered his resignation; Hull told him not to be so upset because FDR "treats me twenty times as badly." Kennedy concluded the tale: "An angry interview with Early brought a half-hearted denial and a further interview with the President, with whom it was not my habit to mince words, brought a denial that he had anything to do with it. In his way, he assuaged my feelings and I left again for London." But Kennedy said he knew "deep within me" that something had changed.

As one biographer later noted, Kennedy had been criticizing FDR behind his back for years but had redeemed himself with his usefulness, most heroically at the SEC. As an unseasoned ambassador and unwelcome presidential aspirant, however, Kennedy stood in a sharply different relationship to Roosevelt.

Kennedy had to endure a few more sticks and stones before he and journalist Arthur Krock, whom Kennedy had invited to travel with him, could make their escape to London with Kennedy's sons Joe Jr. and Jack.

On Wednesday, June 29, they boarded the *Normandie* in New York. As usual, shipboard reporters peppered Kennedy with questions before the "all ashore" order sounded. All they wanted to ask about was a fresh *Saturday Evening Post* feature about Jimmy Roosevelt. The piece claimed the young Roosevelt had been involved in several unsavory business deals and bluntly asserted he had helped

Kennedy "reach the two great positions he now holds—that of Ambassador to London and that of premier Scotch-whiskey salesman in America." Kennedy dismissed the insinuation as "phony" and "a complete unadulterated lie," but when a reporter asked if he would sue for libel, he laughed. "Oh, no! The papers have been too kind to me."

Then, in his last moments at home, he learned that he had been sued for a million dollars; his codefendants were Jim Landis, George "Bud" Mathews, and Judge Healy. The plaintiff was J. Edward Jones, the flamboyant old guard oil royalty marketeer whose litigation had given the Supreme Court an opportunity to blast the SEC's enforcement methods in 1936. Jones claimed the SEC commissioners had "unlawfully planned and conspired" to ruin his business. This baseless lawsuit would go nowhere; Joe Kennedy would, finally, go back to London.

But he was sailing into a fogbank from which his reputation would never fully emerge.

SADLY, THE SEC HAD not escaped Ambassador Kennedy's impulse to meddle, although Bill Douglas did not suffer as much as the State Department did.

The targets of the former chairman's attention were the role of foreign investors in the U.S. market and the role of U.S. investors in foreign markets. With Europe so unsettled, it made sense to study these relationships; as Kennedy's homecoming rally showed, foreign orders flowing into New York could light a spark or, just as easily, douse a rally. And foreign trades raised the nagging worry that investors in New York were steering orders to London to avoid the SEC's rules on short sales, margin accounts, price manipulation, and insider trading—a viewpoint that Wall Street's deregulatory crowd was happy to encourage.

Prodded by Kennedy and aware of the growing significance of foreign capital flowing into the U.S. market, Bill Douglas approved a pair of flawed studies, both conducted out of the London embassy, that ignited a small intellectual mutiny within the agency back home. Commissioner Jerome Frank was among the New Dealers at the SEC who saw the reports from London as amateurish, ill-informed, and fundamentally hostile to market regulation.

Frank complained that the first of these reports "(a) pictures an alarming situation resulting from the fact that dealings in American securities on American exchanges are regulated and that such dealings on the European exchanges are not, and (b) proposes an amazing remedy, namely, that we rid ourselves of virtually all the regulation of our exchanges." The second report did little more than document the differences between British and American practices, with perhaps a modest bias in favor of the London model. What neither report provided was any fresh information about cross-border trading.

Both studies betrayed the authors' failure to grasp the fundamental differences between the markets in London and New York—a difference Joe Kennedy should have known by heart. Even in the late 1930s, the London market was the domain of "gentlemen" investors who relied on the unwritten code of their exclusive fraternity to regulate behavior—a Victorian ideal thoroughly discredited in the United States, where the SEC had just shown how poorly the "gentlemen's code" of Wall Street had served the public in the Whitney case. Kennedy was falling badly out of step with his former New Deal colleagues.

IN AUGUST 1938, WITH Rose and some of the children vacationing in the South of France, Kennedy continued to fumble his diplomatic chores in London. FDR complained to Secretary Hull about Kennedy's credulous support for Chamberlain's efforts to placate Mussolini. Roosevelt also griped about Kennedy's self-promoting media interviews and clumsy meddling in delicate diplomatic matters. But the president repeatedly assigned Hull the hopeless task of curbing Kennedy. "Franklin Roosevelt evidently decided that he could do only one of two things—manage his London ambassador or cope with the hourly changes in Europe," noted historian Michael Beschloss.

As September waned, Kennedy was at Chamberlain's elbow through several nerve-shredding days after Hitler demanded a slice of Czechoslovakia and balked at negotiations. On Wednesday, September 28, Kennedy was squeezed next to the Italian envoy in the gallery at the House of Commons when Chamberlain, just finishing a foreboding speech, received a telegram from Germany inviting him to meet with Hitler the next day in Munich. "The cheers in the House were terrific. Everybody feels tremendously relieved tonight," Kennedy wrote Cordell Hull immediately after he returned to the embassy.

It seemed that a war so imminent that London children were being fitted for gas masks had been avoided, at the eleventh hour. "The only discordant note," Kennedy added, "was that [Czech ambassador Jan] Masaryk riding back with me from Parliament said 'I hope this doesn't mean they are going to cut us up and sell us out.'" After Chamberlain returned from Munich with a deal to do essentially that, Kennedy encountered Jan Masaryk again. According to the Czech leader's account, Kennedy was still exultant about the Munich deal: "Isn't it wonderful? Now I can get to Palm Beach after all!"

Of course, Kennedy was just one of many morally myopic businessmen who could not see the evil madness that was stalking Europe. They were certain Hitler was a rational man who would be content with the deal he cut at Munich. The agreement apparently strengthened Kennedy's convictions that clear-eyed, unsentimental capitalists like the British prime minister and the American ambassador could navigate these troubled European currents better than the fancy-pants diplomats.

On Wednesday, October 19, the British Navy League held its annual dinner to mark Lord Nelson's historic 1805 victory at Trafalgar during the Napoleonic Wars. For the first time in the league's history, it invited the American ambassador to deliver the evening's address. Two days before the event, Kennedy sent a draft of his speech to the State Department to be vetted. By all accounts, that was hastily done by an aide who decided that, since Kennedy was offering only his personal views, there was no reason not to approve the draft verbatim.

Kennedy seemed to be striving for levity, claiming he had considered but—at his wife Rose's suggestion—rejected several topics, including the recent Munich crisis, his nine children, and his hole in one on the golf course.

One of the topics he tried out and then rejected, he said, was "a theory of mine"—he emphasized the phrase—that "democratic and dictator countries" should focus on their common interests and not their "self-apparent" differences. "There is simply no sense, common or otherwise, in letting these differences grow into unrelenting antagonism. After all, we have to live together in the same world, whether we like it or not."

He further warned that the international armaments race "threatens sooner or later to engulf us all in a major disaster" on the military and economic front and called for global treaties to impose "limitations and reduction of armaments."

If the State Department thought no one would pay attention to an ambassador's private theories, it learned its mistake quite soon.

"Kennedy for Amity with Fascist Bloc," was the headline in *The New York Times* the next day. The newspaper's correspondent noted that Kennedy's views were "an excellent summary" of the views of Chamberlain and his cabinet. But those views seemed to put him at sharp odds with Roosevelt.

For one thing, FDR had frequently and forcefully cited the gaping moral differences between democracies and the current dictatorships. "In the circumstances," the *Times* reporter observed, "there is bound to be speculation" that Kennedy's speech meant that Roosevelt was backing away from his policy of criticizing the European tyrants. Moreover, as the newspaper's account noted, Kennedy's call for disarmament came when "the United States is arming at the fastest peace-time pace in its history" as Roosevelt worked to repair the nation's military defenses without igniting isolationist opposition.

Foreign envoys made polite but worried calls to the State Department to inquire about the speech. Officials there desperately denied that Kennedy was "flying a trial balloon" for the president and almost begged reporters to believe that no policy shift was in the works.

To prove that, the White House quickly arranged a fifteen-minute radio address for Roosevelt exactly a week after Kennedy's speech.

The venue wasn't ideal: a forum held by the *New York Herald Tribune* at the Waldorf-Astoria hotel in Manhattan, hosted by columnist Walter Lippmann. Until the White House reached out, the event's top headliner was Herbert Hoover. Addressing the crowd in person, Hoover actually *echoed* Kennedy's "plea for tolerance of the dictator nations of the Old World," as one account put it. "America has always stood and must stand for the right of people to adopt any form of government they like in working out their own destinies," said the former president, gliding over the bloody fact that Hitler had taken that right away from the people of Prague and Vienna. "Militaristic, totalitarian philosophy is not new in the world," Hoover said at another point. "If the world is to have peace, there must be peace between the totalitarian governments and the democracies."

Roosevelt, a master of radio, made the best of a bad spot.

"No one who lived through the grave hours of last month can doubt the longing of most of the people of the world for an enduring peace," he began. "Our business now is to utilize the desire for peace to build principles which are the only basis of permanent peace."

Peace imposed by fear "has no higher or more enduring quality than peace by the sword. There can be no peace if the reign of law is to be replaced by a recurrent sanctification of sheer force." He itemized other barriers to peace raised by the dictators: the deliberate exile of "millions of helpless and persecuted wanderers with no place to lay their heads," the refusal to leave people "free to think their own thoughts, to express their own feelings, to worship God," the use of war threats as an instrument of policy.

"I speak for a United States which has no interest in war," he continued. "We in the United States do not seek to impose on any other people our way of life or our internal form of government." But whatever way of life a people chooses, he said, it "must not threaten the world with the disaster of war."

The speech, filled with the moral intelligence that had been Roosevelt's polestar in his life in politics, firmly rejected the stunted transactional values of his "tame capitalist" Joe Kennedy. The ambassador later said he felt FDR had "stabbed him in the back."

But Kennedy doubled down. Facing Europe in 1938, he concluded that America could avoid war if it would just look at Nazi Germany through the eyes of a businessman, a capitalist, a deal-maker.

As he explained in a letter to a reporter in early November: "I have an idea that maybe if Mr. Hitler enjoyed some good trade with us, he would be so busy trying to protect it [that] he wouldn't have time to think about fighting with everybody."

* * *

A LITTLE BEFORE NOON on Tuesday, November 8, 1938, Franklin and Eleanor Roosevelt and a few other members of the family arrived at the yellow frame town hall in Hyde Park to cast their votes in the midterm elections.

An alert reporter noticed that Roosevelt wasn't wearing his Election Day lucky charm—a gold watch chain once owned by President Andrew Jackson. Roosevelt had worn the chain the day of his extraordinary reelection victory in 1936. Did he have it with him today?

No, the president said. The historic item was "too valuable to wear around and it was home in the safe."

Of course, the old watch chain had not summoned up FDR's victory in 1936—his own political magic had done that—so its absence today mattered only to the superstitious. But if Roosevelt had ever needed a good luck charm on Election Day, he needed it now.

His reservoir of political capital had fallen sharply after his ill-judged effort in 1937 to expand the number of Supreme Court justices; his wavering response to the recession had surely caused additional evaporation. He had done further damage in this campaign year by withholding his support from conservative Democrats who had not supported New Deal legislation.

This so-called political "purge" was, in part, a sign of his frustration with party members who clung to his popular liberal coattails to get elected, and then voted with conservative foes of the New Deal in Congress. But the drive also reflected his belief that these defectors were "blocking the steps that he thought were essential to raise the American standard of living and make the nation strong enough to meet the growing menace from abroad," one of his closest aides later wrote.

The Democratic Party increasingly was a "house divided against itself." Proof of that faced Roosevelt almost daily in the extensive uncritical news coverage of the antics of Congressman Martin Dies of Texas, a fiercely anti–New Deal Democrat and the chairman of the House Un-American Activities Committee. Although the House had expected it would probe radicalism on the Left *and* the Right, the committee devoted itself almost entirely to smearing liberal organizations and New Deal officials as "communists" or as "fellow travelers," a handy catchall label that was wickedly difficult to peel off. In October, Dies had turned his spotlight on Governor Frank Murphy of Michigan, a Democrat and strong New Deal ally, airing baseless claims that the governor was guilty of "treasonable activities" for his efforts to end a sit-down strike without violence.

Roosevelt had defended Murphy as "a profoundly religious, able and law-abiding Governor," and attacked the Dies committee for "permitting itself to be used in a flagrantly unfair and un-American attempt to influence an election." But smears from hostile Democrats were surely a handicap for Murphy and other New Deal candidates.

The Senate race in New Jersey was at risk, too, thanks to another Democratic embarrassment. The political machine ruthlessly run by Mayor Frank Hague of Jersey City had been dragged repeatedly into court for violating the civil liberties of socialist political campaigners and labor organizers, whom Mayor Hague universally condemned as communists. "We hear about constitutional rights, free speech and the free press," he told reporters. "Every time I hear these words, I say to myself, 'that man is a Red, that man is a Communist.' You never hear a real American talk in that manner." His object seemed to be to attract industry to his union-free fiefdom; his effect had been to horrify the liberal voters Roosevelt needed.

The mayor's intemperate language and blatant disregard for the Constitution had produced widespread calls for FDR to repudiate this "Hague-style fascism"—but Hague was a vice chairman of the Democratic National Committee and a power broker across his state. Roosevelt needed more New Dealers in the Senate, but the Democrat in this race was a Hague loyalist who was running against an attractive moderate Republican. Roosevelt hadn't dared go further in repudiating Hague than to offer some emphatic words in support of the First Amendment: "The American people will not be deceived by anyone who attempts to suppress individual liberty under the pretense of patriotism." Obviously, FDR hoped Hague's distasteful machine could elect the Democrat. But even faithful New Dealers would likely find it hard to pull the lever that day for any ally of the autocratic Boss of Jersey City.

It was little comfort that the Republican Party faced its own divisions between die-hard conservatives like Hoover and younger reformers and progressives like Tom Dewey. Roosevelt's hope of building a solidly liberal Democratic Party, one that would protect and extend his legacy into the uncertain future, would be tested today. And he felt pretty sure the verdict would be disappointing.

He had done what he could with a radio address on Friday evening—not an official "fireside chat," but a message delivered from his own fireside at Hyde Park.

In the worldwide struggle with ruthless regimes, he had said, "democracy will save itself with the average man and woman by proving itself *worth* saving." To meet that test, democracy "must become a positive force in the daily lives of its people."

He had spoken about "watching the finishing touches being put on a simple cottage I have recently built," referring to a small stone house that would be his private retreat from "the big house" where his mother reigned. "There was a time not so long ago when I used to think about problems of government as if they were the same kind of problems as building a house—definite and compact and capable of completion within a given time."

He no longer thought the analogy was accurate. Once you build a house, he had said, "you always have it." But "a social or economic gain made by one administration may, and often does, evaporate into thin air under the next one." If liberals did not unify behind the New Deal and embrace its ideals of fairness and empathy, the reforms FDR had delivered could be wiped out.

The next day, Roosevelt had tooled around the village in his new blue Ford convertible, a custom-made model whose gas pedal, brakes, and clutch were manually operated. The president loved the unhindered mobility that came with driving himself. With a Secret Service car at a careful distance behind him, Roosevelt had picked up his neighbor, Treasury secretary Henry Morgenthau, and his son; they had driven around, discussing plans for affordable housing that could be built in the area. Smiling and gracious, with his amber cigarette holder jutting out of his grin at a jaunty angle, he had fielded questions from the reporters and Saturday shoppers who gathered around the open coupe as he idled at the curb.

Had he made his own election-night forecast yet?

Not yet, but he would do it soon, as he always had, and would seal it up in an envelope until the returns were official.

After voting at Hyde Park's town center, the Roosevelts returned home and spent the day with a few close aides. That evening, as other friends gathered at the comfortable mansion, the radios were tuned to catch the returns. As usual, Roosevelt relied on the direct telephone line linking him to National Democratic chairman Jim Farley's nerve center in the Hotel Biltmore in Manhattan.

For most of the nation, the big prizes tonight were the House and Senate. Democrats had held commanding majorities in both chambers since 1932; it would have been an act of blind optimism to believe those majorities would not be trimmed by today's results.

But in New York, this was also a gubernatorial election, and FDR was deeply interested in the outcome. The race pitted incumbent governor Herbert Lehman against New York District Attorney Tom

Dewey, and there was no disputing Dewey's appeal to upstate Republicans—indeed, to Republicans everywhere. Some polls gave Dewey the edge; there was no doubt the race would be close.

Tom Dewey, after his sprint through the Whitney case in the spring, had run a campaign that aimed at putting as much distance as possible between himself and the GOP hard-liners like Hoover and Whitney. "The Old Guard has disappeared," one of his top campaign aides told reporters in mid-October. "During the last two or three years," said another aide, "we've done everything possible to eliminate the charge of [our being] reactionaries," adding, "When I see the party producing a young man with liberal ideas, I'm more than willing to help in the fight."

Alf Landon, of course, had tried the same gambit in 1936, only to have the most conservative voices in his party drown out his "liberal ideas." In this race, Landon himself was preaching the familiar old guard sermon, warning that support for Republicans in the midterm elections and the presidential race in 1940 would determine "whether we are going to be a democracy or a Fascist state."

But Dewey's speech accepting his nomination hailed the "social and labor progress" made in recent years. He called for a democracy that could "feed its hungry, house its homeless, and provide work for its idle." Dewey rested his case on the idea that he could achieve social progress without the taint of the corrupt political machines who supported the state's Democrats. (One editorial writer pointed out that there were corrupt political machines run by upstate Republicans as well, but Dewey made "Tammany Hall" his theme song.)

A week before the election, Roosevelt had told his friend Adolf Berle that he was worried about Lehman's campaign and had urged Berle to ask his friend Fiorello La Guardia, New York's progressive Republican mayor, to endorse the governor. The most that the popular mayor would do was to allow some news photographs of him in cheerful conversation with Lehman after a radio forum on Sunday. It had probably helped, but the polls were still worrisome.

Governor Lehman had been at Roosevelt's side when he first campaigned for governor in 1928. They had fought together for state bank reform and cobbled together the earliest relief programs of the

Great Depression. As a matter of principle, Lehman had broken with FDR over his court expansion plan, but that did not outweigh their long alliance in the liberal fight that brought regulation to Wall Street, gave security to bank depositors, and was taming the great electric power combines—one of their earliest battles in Albany, and now a fight Roosevelt was waging across the nation. Back in his days as governor, facing Morgan-financed utility giants that were protected by GOP legislators, Roosevelt would joke that there were only two things standing between the public's rivers and the power companies: his heartbeat and Herbert Lehman's.

But the New Deal had put the federal government in the way of the power industry's ambitions. The Public Utility Holding Company Act of 1935 was aimed directly at the great utility conglomerates that had grown too big to be regulated or restrained. The law had been fought bitterly by the industry, first in Congress and then, after its passage, in the courts.

The tide in that battle finally had turned sharply in Roosevelt's direction. On Monday, March 28, 1938, the Supreme Court had released its ruling in the Electric Bond and Share case, the landmark test of whether utility holding companies could be required to register with the SEC and comply with the law's disclosure requirements.

Nearly three years had passed since SEC lawyers had raced to Baltimore to confront the sham constitutional challenge filed by John W. Davis, the Morgan advisor who played a cameo role in the recent Whitney drama. When the SEC had filed its own surprise test case against Electric Bond and Share (Ebasco) two months later, Jim Landis had promised to postpone any enforcement efforts until a final ruling came down. Many of the largest utility holding companies had refused to register with the SEC unless, and until, the Supreme Court said they must.

And on that bright spring Monday back in March, while crowds gaped at Washington's annual cherry blossom display, that's exactly what the Supreme Court had done.

Chief Justice Charles Evans Hughes had written the opinion. He noted that the Ebasco defendants had a "highly important relation to interstate commerce and the national economy." Given that, the court has "no reason to doubt" that Congress was "entitled to demand the fullest information as to organization, financial structure and all the activities which could have any bearing upon the exercise of Congressional authority." The ruling, the climax of Ben Cohen's and Robert Jackson's impassioned arguments in February, meant that all major holding companies would now have to furnish data to the public "or suffer the penalties," one front-page report noted.

By Election Day, the Ebasco CEO had already promised that the utility finally would register—and had been cheered at his shareholder meeting for doing so. The legal skirmishing was far from over: Bill Douglas at the SEC wanted to put pressure on all utility holding companies to start drafting the reorganization plans required by the still-disputed "death sentence" section of the law. But the fight to open the ledgers of these economic behemoths to the sunlight of public scrutiny—barely a dream when FDR and Herbert Lehman had fought together in Albany—had been won.

Optimists were predicting Governor Lehman would beat Dewey by 250,000 votes. Roosevelt believed it would be much closer. The early returns from the upstate precincts were overwhelmingly in Dewey's favor. As the big house at Hyde Park emptied out, the president and Jim Farley were still awake, waiting for the later vote counts from New York City. When those finally came in, long past midnight, Lehman had an edge of fewer than 70,000 votes, the narrowest victory margin since FDR's own razor-thin win in 1928. Senator Robert Wagner, one of the most effective and committed New Dealers in Congress, had won his race by almost a million votes, and a Democrat would serve for the two years remaining in the term of Senator Royal Copeland, who had died in June.

That was almost the full extent of the good news that night. Tom Dewey's narrow defeat confirmed his prospects as a GOP contender. The GOP won control of both houses of the state legislature in Albany. Governor Frank Murphy lost his reelection bid in Michigan— indicating, as one historian noted, that "the demagogic reactionary Martin Dies was more persuasive of the Michigan electorate than was the President of the United States." Boss Hague's lapdog was soundly defeated in New Jersey, costing FDR a seat in the Senate.

The Republicans expanded their statehouse control across the country, and trimmed the Democrats' margins in Congress.

In Wednesday morning's newspapers, the election results were predictably being framed as a great victory for the GOP and a major setback for FDR's legislative plans.

But more than a few editorials made a curious observation: that many of the Republicans who won (and some, like Dewey, who narrowly lost) had waged campaigns that largely endorsed the New Deal vision of helping the poor and regulating the powerful.

The Times of London said "nothing in the election, or in the nature of the campaign which led up to it, indicates that the movement toward an enlarged use of regulatory power by the Federal Government would be reversed by the Republicans if they were now to come to office." A Brooklyn paper concluded that "the successful Republican candidates, as a whole, had disassociated themselves from the reactionary leaders of their party." The editors of *The New York Times* pointed out, among the winners, "the great number of Republicans who have pledged themselves this year to defend the essential principles of New Deal legislation" which the Republican party deemed "radical and revolutionary" only a few years ago. Those "essential principles" included accepting a larger role for government "in the policing of financial markets, in the achievement of essential social reforms and in the attainment of a generally higher standard of living for underprivileged people."

The New York Times gave credit for "this quickening of the American conscience" to Franklin Roosevelt. "It has been said of him that he may not have known the right answers to the questions he asked, but that at least he has asked the right questions," the editorial observed.

Not everyone was persuaded that FDR had converted the up-and-coming Republicans to the principles of the New Deal. Some far-seeing editorials saw the same trend and presciently attributed it to "lip service" by cynical Republicans who were simply "afraid of attacking the New Deal directly" while voters were still weighing their options, but wouldn't hesitate to do so once they were in office.

The new Congress would also be more fiercely committed to isolating America from the menacing affairs beyond the Atlantic and the Pacific Oceans. The victor in the Ohio race for the Senate was Robert Taft, an "extreme isolationist" Republican and an implacable foe of "every element of the New Deal." Other new isolationists in Congress would rally to his side. Roosevelt's room to maneuver in foreign affairs would inevitably shrink in the coming year.

To one old friend, Roosevelt cheerily insisted he was "wholly reconciled" to the election results. Many of the losing Democrats had been feuding with other Democrats anyway, he said. He added, "Frankly, I think we will have less trouble with the next Congress than with the last."

That was not a high bar, of course. After his unpopular court fight, Roosevelt had gotten almost nothing *but* trouble from the last Congress. But this, too, would prove a feeble hope; perceiving FDR as a lame duck, "Congress began to handle him more roughly," one historian noted. The conservative bloc hoping in early 1938 merely to hold the line against fresh reforms would soon be "moving aggressively to dismantle the New Deal."

FDR was more candid about the election outcome in his comments to a longtime friend in the diplomatic corps: he wrote that, while the New York races generally turned out well, "we lost in a good many other states because, frankly, our officeholders and candidates had not measured up."

He had not, after all, made much progress in unifying his party behind the idealistic values of the New Deal. But he wrote a friend that he saw signs that anti–New Deal Democrats were finally realizing that, however much power they wielded in the 1940 convention, "they cannot elect their ticket without the support of this administration—and I am sufficiently honest to decline to support any conservative Democrat."

Predictably, some longtime party voices, including ambitious presidential hopefuls like party chairman Jim Farley and Vice President Garner, thought the midterms proved that Democrats must become *more* conservative, not less. The shadow of the turncoat Democrat Al Smith stretched into the future, as onetime Roosevelt allies veered to the right and tried to take FDR's party with them.

Ray Moley, the former brain trust member turned conservative critic, had his own equally predictable take on the election's message: "Government and business met yesterday before a jury of the American people," he said in a speech in Chicago. The people "brought in a verdict [of] 'business not guilty.'" Moley claimed the government's hostility to business was the biggest factor that drove voters into the GOP's arms. Now and for years to come, supporters of the New Deal would struggle to frame a succinct rebuttal to such anti-regulatory rhetoric—which insisted, when times had gotten better, that reforms were no longer needed and, when times had gotten worse, that reforms were to blame.

In any case, Roosevelt now had to place his hopes for a progressive Democratic Party on the maneuvers that would climax at the 1940 convention—and he had to decide what role he himself would play in that fight.

In the week after the election, newspapers gave increasingly prominent front-page attention to stories from Germany about mobs of barely disguised storm troopers rampaging systematically through Berlin, smashing Jewish shops, invading Jewish homes, burning Jewish houses of worship, and terrorizing thousands of Jewish citizens. The frenzy of violence was an officially sanctioned response to a shooting in Paris on Monday, November 7, when a despairing seventeen-year-old Jewish boy had walked into the German embassy there and shot a third-tier diplomat he encountered. His act, he told police after quietly waiting to be arrested, was retribution for Germany's recent expulsion of ten thousand Jews, including his family, who had been dumped into the bleak and unwelcoming fields of neighboring Poland with barely more than the clothes on their backs. "Being a Jew is not a crime," he tearfully told the police officers who questioned him. "I am not a dog. I have a right to live and the Jewish people have a right to live."

History would remember the night of November 9–10, 1938, as "Kristallnacht," the Night of Broken Glass. As more reports poured in from journalists abroad, horrified Americans learned that the German police and firemen had ignored the violence unless non-Jewish property was at risk. At least fifteen thousand Jews had been arrested "for their own protection," and countless others had been beaten or driven to suicide. By Friday, with the Nazi-sanctioned destruction spreading to Vienna, the attacks were front-page news across the United States. Germany fined the Jews $400 million for the damage done by the mobs "provoked" by the young Jewish assassin; it seized insurance payments on the damage claims submitted by Jewish policyholders. Revulsion against Hitler was immediate and widespread, despite the continuing grip of isolationist sentiment.

Back in Washington after his stay in Hyde Park, a grimly angry Roosevelt released an official statement, but then told reporters in obvious anger: "I myself could scarcely believe that such things could occur in a twentieth-century civilization." He summoned the U.S. ambassador home from Berlin for consultations; no American envoy would return to Germany for the duration of the Nazi regime.

World events were steadily carrying Roosevelt's attention further from the work of financial reform that had been so central to his first years in office. But all that he had promised in his campaign in 1932 had, to a large degree, been accomplished. Banks were safer. Securities markets were fairer. The power industry's lawless holding companies were being tamed. Laws were moving through Congress that would give ordinary people a better shake in corporate bankruptcies. It would take a little longer, but the groundwork was already laid for the last of FDR's great gifts to the future middle class, the federal regulation of mutual funds and the people who managed them. For the first time in the nation's history, there was a federal "cop on Wall Street," an advocate to ensure that investors would continue to be protected as the economy grew and the market changed.

But Roosevelt knew that the New Deal was not like his little stone cottage at Hyde Park. When that refuge was finished, it would stand for decades—it stands to this day. Roosevelt's financial reforms, like all his achievements, could never be set in stone; they had to be rebuilt and defended, time and again, from the attacks of those who had never accepted the New Deal and would never stop trying to destroy it.

CHAPTER ELEVEN

THE FIGHT FOR THE FUTURE

DECEMBER 1938–MAY 1939

AT A QUARTER PAST NOON ON FRIDAY, DECEMBER 16, 1938, Bill Douglas and one of his top lieutenants walked into the spacious wood-paneled presidential office at the New York Stock Exchange. The aide was the director of the SEC's Trading and Exchange Division, the arm of the agency that dealt most directly with the NYSE's new management team.

The centerpiece of that new team, William McChesney Martin Jr., greeted them as they arrived. Bill Martin, who would turn thirty-two the next day, had been catnip for the media ever since his installation in May as the first paid chief executive of the exchange. Clean-living, athletic, diligent, and cheerfully competent, Martin was the public-relations evidence that the NYSE was no longer the private club whose old guard had covered up for Dick Whitney for so long.

At Martin's side was retail broker Paul Shields, the intrepid yachtsman who had worked with the SEC for years to reform the exchange. Shields was by several decades the senior statesman in the room. He was a longtime member of the exchange's board of governors and had a reputation for unsparing candor. He also was one of FDR's trusted business advisors; he had visited the White House just days earlier.

This remained a season of unfinished business for Bill Douglas. Part of that work was on the table today—perhaps, for Douglas, the most serious item of SEC business he had ever raised with the New York Stock Exchange.

The SEC's hearings in the spring had clearly shown that Dick Whitney was not, as he claimed, the only one involved in his criminal conduct and scandalous downfall. Two senior Morgan partners, George Whitney and Tom Lamont, had helped Dick Whitney cover up his Gratuity Fund crimes in November 1937, and a "gentlemanly code" of silence had kept NYSE governors Harry Simmons and Blair S. Williams from pursuing Dick Whitney's inability to restore the fund's assets.

On October 28, after months of study, the SEC had described this comprehensive lapse of duty in its formal report on the Whitney affair—a report FDR said was "rather horrifying." Newspapers across the country took note of its key indisputable finding: that "Morgan men" had known Dick Whitney was dishonest long before he was publicly exposed and they had helped him cover up his criminal conduct.

Douglas and Martin had already met several times to discuss the report and the exchange's proposed responses. But Douglas was not satisfied; he wanted accountability.

Right after the Whitney report was finished, Douglas had sent it to the Criminal Division at the Justice Department, highlighting the testimony of George Whitney and Tom Lamont. Douglas felt the two Morgan men could be prosecuted for "misprision of a felony," the failure to report a crime. At the time, this criminal offense was a "rarely prosecuted common law crime," as one legal scholar noted. But it had been part of the nation's criminal code since the Crimes Act of 1790. Even under modern appellate guidance, the facts of the Whitney case seem to fit firmly within the standards for prosecution.

The chief of the Justice Department's Criminal Division, a talented young Connecticut lawyer named Brien McMahon, had rejected complex SEC referrals in the past, and he rejected this one, too. Douglas later complained that "some of the stormiest sessions I had at the SEC" were not with Wall Street executives but with Brien McMahon. In this case, McMahon may have been piqued that the

SEC went ahead with public hearings before his team had decided what it would do. Or he simply may have doubted that there was a solid basis for prosecuting the Morgan men.

Whatever the Justice Department's reasoning, Douglas never suggested that FDR was protecting the Morgan partners—Douglas had tested the president in an earlier sensitive case and had not been disappointed. The SEC enforcement staff had discovered some problems in documents filed by the Transamerica Corporation, the sprawling holding company through which A. P. Giannini controlled the Bank of America in California. Giannini was a prominent and generous Democratic donor who enjoyed a "special relationship" with Roosevelt. In their usual irreverent way, Douglas and the president had discussed the consequences of the SEC investigating the charismatic banker.

"Is the front door of the White House closed when I move in on Transamerica?" Douglas asked.

"Absolutely," the president answered with a grin.

"What about the back door?"

Roosevelt had "roared with laughter," Douglas later recalled, and said, "The back door, too, is closed." But FDR did not lift a finger to deter the SEC's investigation—and neither the front nor the back door of his office was ever closed to Bill Douglas. As Douglas put it, "FDR was usually willing to back us up whenever the SEC really needed it."

But just as it would have been wrong for FDR to quash the Giannini case, it would have been wrong for him to overrule the Justice Department and insist on a prosecution in the Whitney matter. Douglas knew that. But he had one more arrow in his quiver: he sent the hearing transcript to the board of governors of the supposedly reformed New York Stock Exchange, urging that it be reviewed for potential violations of the NYSE's own code of conduct. If Douglas couldn't take the Morgan partners to court, he could at least put them before the same tribunal that had expelled Dick Whitney for the crimes the partners had helped conceal.

By this point, Douglas had an ally on the exchange board. In September, he had persuaded Bill Martin to offer one of the public

seats on the new board to Douglas's longtime friend Robert Maynard Hutchins, who had brought him to Yale and who was now
leading the University of Chicago. Then Douglas sent Hutchins a
telegram urging him to say yes: "The answer is that you must by all
means accept [the seat] and the reason is not only that acceptance
will permit me to see you more often but also that you need a good
fight once in a while to keep you in trim."

On Wednesday, December 14, Hutchins had gotten his "good
fight." At a tense two-hour meeting of the NYSE governors, he had
proposed that the board take action on the SEC's referral—to prove
to the public that no member was powerful enough to be exempt
from the NYSE's rules. He told them he found the vague and publicly disputed testimony by Harry Simmons "incredible." He argued
that Lamont and George Whitney "should not have permitted
Richard Whitney to continue to perpetuate his frauds for almost
four months after they knew of them." He raised the question of
"whether the ties of blood or friendship were [a] sufficient excuse"
for what George Whitney and Tom Lamont had done and left undone.

The board had overwhelmingly disagreed with him, and Hutchins
cast the only vote in favor of pursuing the case. In a day or so, the
news would leak out that Hutchins had walked out of the boardroom in disgust and had submitted his resignation to Martin the
next day to protest the board's inaction.

And that inaction was what Bill Douglas was there to discuss
with the two leading reformers at the New York Stock Exchange.

Douglas sat, restless and twitchy as always, as his colleague took
out a pad and prepared to take notes for the SEC's files. Martin
raised "sundry matters of relatively minor concern," but after a few
moments of this, Paul Shields spoke up.

He suggested Martin show Douglas a letter that the exchange
would soon send to the SEC. Martin handed over the letter and
Douglas read it. He handed it back saying, "Send it to me in Washington."

The letter simply reported that "after due consideration," the
twenty-nine governors present, out of thirty-two, voted overwhelm-

ingly to take no further action on the matters involving George Whitney and Tom Lamont. Only one governor, Hutchins, had dissented from the decision, Martin said.

If Hutchins had not already briefed his old friend about the board meeting, Douglas must have found Paul Shields's candid description of the discussion both disturbing and disappointing.

Shields revealed that about ten members of the supposedly reformed board of governors "felt that there was no element of guilt in the conduct of any of the persons involved." In fact, Shields continued, this group had argued that it would have been far better for the exchange "if the persons involved had been more successful in their attempts at secrecy and [if] the whole matter had been kept from the public and quietly hushed up."

The remaining members, about eighteen of them, generally agreed that "there probably was guilt in the sense of acts having been done that were detrimental to the interest and welfare of the exchange," Shields continued. But they also agreed that "the whole matter had been given such publicity" through the SEC's hearings and its published report that "no further inquisition or discipline" was required.

The SEC aide's assessment, captured in his notes, was that Martin and Shields had sided with the larger group that felt everyone had suffered enough, not with the smaller bloc that wished that Dick Whitney's crimes had been covered up more successfully.

Was the solution to revise the rules? Shields doubted that would help because the board members did not think that they were qualified to make the subjective decisions required to enforce the rules.

Their doubts had been fueled by the Morgan firm's misleading public response to the official Whitney report. The firm claimed that NYSE officials were aware of Whitney's embezzlement in November of 1937, so the partners could not be held to have concealed anything. "The Morgan statement, quite simply, was false; it contradicted earlier sworn testimony by George Whitney and Thomas Lamont," one legal scholar later noted. There was no doubt that the two Morgan partners knew in November that Whitney was a crook—they had admitted as much, under oath. By contrast, although senior ex-

change officials at least should have *suspected* that Whitney was dishonest when he could not return the Gratuity Fund's assets, there
was no clear proof of any criminal behavior before the first days of
March.

Douglas's colleague asked Martin and Shields: Hadn't this action
by the board "virtually written the rule out of the [NYSE] constitution, certainly . . . [with respect to] influential members?"

Yes, Shields conceded, it had—and that was exactly why he
thought this "very dangerous rule" should be literally removed from
the constitution or completely rewritten.

"I disagree," said Bill Martin. He didn't think the rules were at
fault; in his opinion, "no matter how the rules had been phrased," the
board would never have applied them to members with the power
and prominence of the Morgan partners.

Bill Douglas stirred and spoke up. It was not a tolerable situation,
he said, to have a rule "which applied only to the little fellows and
not to the big shots." If it were Shields or Martin or Douglas himself
involved in the facts of the Whitney case, the SEC chairman continued, the board would not have hesitated to act.

Martin and Shields had to agree. Shields, who had stepped on
a lot of old guard toes over the years, was certain that if he had
done what Tom Lamont had done, he would have been punished
for it.

Douglas posed a blunt question: Weren't Shields and Martin actually saying that, in cases like this, "the exchange had to be in a
position to 'pass the buck' to the SEC?"

That unquestionably would have helped, both exchange officials
said.

Douglas, the securities law professor, pointed out to them that
the U.S. Constitution made it extremely difficult for the SEC to
adopt "a rule with any such vague standard" as conduct "inconsistent
with just and equitable principles of trade." Indeed, Douglas pointed
out, the NYSE had long claimed that its status as a private association was precisely what gave it an advantage over government regulators: it could adopt its own constitution and its own rules and was

not bound by "the requirements of legal procedure and constitutional limitations" that governed the SEC.

Shields was not optimistic that this ideal of "self-regulation" could ever work against Wall Street's most powerful players. He pointed out "that the wealthy and influential can escape discipline while the less fortunately placed—the 'little fellow'—will not only invariably be visited with justified action under the rules, but may well be subjected to punishment as a result of whim or prejudice." His point was clear: Dick Whitney's punishment by the NYSE was the exception, not the rule; policing Wall Street's titans would always be a job only the SEC could do.

AS THIS ILLUMINATING DISCUSSION unfolded in the president's office, the stock ticker on the trading floor downstairs delivered the news that another dramatic Wall Street scandal had reached a shocking climax.

This separate drama had begun on Tuesday, December 6, with whispered reports that McKesson & Robbins, one of the largest and most successful drug distribution companies in the country, had been forced into involuntary bankruptcy in Hartford, Connecticut. By that evening, those reports had reached a company director, Goldman Sachs partner Sidney J. Weinberg, while he was attending a formal dinner at the Waldorf-Astoria. Still in his formal wear, he had immediately invited the executive committee of the McKesson & Robbins board and the company's treasurer to his luxury apartment in the Sherry-Netherland hotel.

The treasurer had stunned the directors by reporting that his own confidential investigation strongly suggested that F. Donald Coster, the widely respected president of McKesson & Robbins, was engaged in a massive fraud.

The allegation had sounded absurd. Frank Donald Coster was a European-educated physician with a degree from the University of Heidelberg. He was a yachtsman, a breeder of show dogs, a bank director. A fierce and outspoken critic of Roosevelt's New Deal,

Coster had even been scouted as a Republican candidate for the 1940 presidential race. He was listed in *Who's Who*. His company's health was affirmed by Dun & Bradstreet, its audits were handled by Price Waterhouse, and its shares were listed on the New York Stock Exchange.

When Weinberg had first heard the treasurer's incredible suspicions, he had immediately called Coster at his eighteen-room mansion in Fairfield, Connecticut.

He had described the day's bankruptcy filing. "This is a frightful thing that has happened," he had said. "What is it all about?"

"I know nothing about it," Coster had answered. "Here I am, living in Connecticut. Surely someone would have told me."

"Well, it is a very serious matter," Weinberg had said, "and I think you ought to come down to New York immediately, tomorrow morning, and have a meeting with the executive committee."

Coster had seemed perfectly agreeable. "I've got to go to the Bridgeport office to get my mail and I will come down; I'll be there at 10 o'clock."

After Weinberg hung up, the treasurer had warned the group that Coster was lying, that he had threatened to throw the company into bankruptcy himself if the treasurer didn't drop his investigation into the company's affairs.

Weinberg's next call had been to Bill Douglas at home in Washington. A sleepy SEC chairman had listened as Weinberg laid out the few facts he had; Douglas had promised that his New York staff would check the McKesson filings the next morning. Next, Weinberg had awakened the senior partner of Price Waterhouse and summoned him to the emergency meeting at his apartment. Finally, Weinberg had called the chairman of the NYSE's stock listing committee, reporting the strange bankruptcy filing and asking that the exchange immediately suspend trading in the company's stock "so that all stockholders might be given equal protection." This time, unlike in the Whitney affair, whistles had been blown all over the place; after all, a great deal of money was involved. Unlike Dick Whitney's firm, McKesson & Robbins was a multimillion-dollar company with public shareholders. But perhaps the SEC's warning to Wall Street to mend its clubby habits had also been in the back of everyone's mind.

The distraught treasurer's suspicions of a vast fraud had been well-founded. Despite years of "clean" audits, McKesson & Robbins's entire Canadian division—which supposedly held valuable inventory and cash reserves—was entirely fictional. It consisted of nothing but mail slots in office doors and pigeonholes in office desks, although those details would not emerge for several days.

By Friday, December 9, the SEC had found enough evidence of bad bookkeeping to refer the matter to the Justice Department— and this time, Assistant Attorney General Brien McMahon did not argue. On Wednesday, December 14, warrants had been issued for Coster and three of his senior executives based on an SEC complaint accusing them of filing false statements in violation of the 1933 and 1934 acts. Coster had been arrested, photographed, fingerprinted, arraigned, and released on bail—all without leaving the library of his Spanish-style mansion, thanks to concessions the authorities had made to his claims of ill health. Another company executive who lived nearby had been processed at the same time, in the same library, and two others had been tracked down in their New York apartments.

Then an alert investigator in the New York State attorney general's office had taken a close look at the various photographs of Coster published in the region's newspapers. He knew this man, he had said—but his name wasn't F. Donald Coster. With help from the enterprising head of the SEC's New York office, state investigators had quickly found fingerprint records proving that Coster was actually Philip Musica, a convicted con man from New York's Little Italy who had been a fugitive for years. The three other McKesson executives under arrest were Musica's brothers, his accomplices in several earlier frauds.

This bizarre news screamed out from every New York City newspaper on Friday, December 16, as Bill Douglas and his colleague took a taxi to the New York Stock Exchange to hash out the Whitney matter with Bill Martin and Paul Shields. As the SEC officials arrived outside 11 Wall Street, lawmen in Connecticut with fresh warrants for Musica were driving up the long drive to the front porch of the Fairfield mansion. As Douglas and his aide rode one of the NYSE's high-speed elevators to the president's office and greeted Martin and Shields, the imposter in Fairfield had secluded himself in an upstairs bathroom with a view of his driveway.

And as lawmen rang the doorbell in Fairfield, the imposter took out the gun he had carried in his bathrobe pocket. Facing the medicine-chest mirror, he raised the gun to his head and fired. "The jangle of the bell was lost in the shattering blast of the gunfire," one journalist on the scene reported.

Newsmen and photographers had shown up at the house to cover the arrest. As the door opened to the echo of the fatal shot, they surged into the house on the lawmen's heels. They saw the body, heard the wails of Musica's wife, and raced to report the news to their editors and to the world.

It was the strangest corporate scandal anyone could remember. It would grow to include claims of gunrunning, bootlegging, and blackmail. It would consume the nation's attention for weeks, and rattle every figure in Washington and on Wall Street who had ever spoken to "F. Donald Coster" or vouched for his company.

It would also spotlight another big piece of unfinished business at Bill Douglas's SEC: its chronic reluctance to use the agency's muscle to carve out a clearer role for accountants and auditors in the work of regulating Wall Street and corporate America.

But as Douglas returned to his hotel after his conversation with Martin and Shields, he likely was focused less on the scandal in Fairfield and more on his face-off with what looked like the "old" stock exchange. One historian said his anger over the Morgan incident was "Vesuvian."

IN ONE OF THE little jokes that reality sometimes plays on history, this Friday evening was the first annual running of the "Financial Follies," a Gridiron-like roast of Washington and Wall Street hosted by the New York Financial Writers Association. A parade of gleaming limousines delivered more than seven hundred "leading members of the financial community, industrial leaders and ranking government executives," all in formal dress, to the Hotel Astor on Broadway just north of Times Square. The privileged crowd filled the hotel's gaudy ballroom, perhaps chuckling to find that the evening's programs on their tables had been "printed on worthless stock certificates."

The guests of honor were Bill Douglas and Bill Martin. Prominent among the gathered guests were Tom Lamont, George Whitney, Frank Bartow, and several other Morgan partners.

At one point in the evening, jokey gifts were bestowed. Bill Douglas was given a riding crop; it might have signified his habit of driving Wall Street to speed up its pace of reform, but more likely it was meant to suggest he used Wall Street as his whipping boy.

The fun and games did nothing to cool the white-hot anger Bill Douglas felt over the "Whitney white-wash." On Sunday, December 18, he drafted a blistering rebuttal.

"When persons of outstanding wealth are involved, the Exchange cannot be trusted to do its own house-cleaning," he wrote. "Unhappily we are forced to conclude that discipline by the Exchange authorities" would be imposed "only if the offending person is of relatively little importance." So far as the NYSE was concerned, he continued, there was "one law for the very powerful or wealthy and another for those of little wealth and influence."

The Roosevelt reforms had helped level the playing field for ordinary investors, but the SEC still had a long way to go to hold the most powerful Wall Street players accountable to the public—indeed, as Douglas feared, that would be one of the agency's most difficult tasks throughout its life.

On Monday morning, December 19, cooler heads at the agency prevailed on Douglas not to release his angry statement, which would have cast a cloud over the very real SEC-inspired reforms at the stock exchange. Instead, the commission released a brief observation that the NYSE's decision "does not necessarily indicate that the ideal of self-regulation is impossible. It does, however, suggest the kind of limitations under which even the ablest and most upright management presently functions."

Douglas had clearly had a hand in editing the statement. It concluded with the warning that the necessary balance between government regulation and self-regulation "will not be attained until rules are applied to the little fellow and the big shot alike."

But publicly, Douglas assured columnist Arthur Krock that there was no breach between Martin and himself, or between Wall Street and the SEC. "Mr. Martin and I have worked closely together and we are going to continue to do so," he said. He added that he, Bill Martin, and the "Washington–New York axis" of cooperation were all still young. "Instead of going off its gears, the axis has withstood its first shock perfectly. For the SEC as for the Exchange, the Whitney case is closed. From it we both have learned something."

Douglas later confided to Roosevelt what he had learned: that Wall Street was still unwilling to police its most powerful figures, and that the White House should push to amend the 1934 act to allow the SEC "to take off the hands of the stock exchange cases which they have found 'too hot to handle.' Otherwise, there will be no assurances that discipline will be acted out equally and fairly.'"

ON THURSDAY, DECEMBER 29, the SEC announced that it would hold its own hearings on the McKesson & Robbins scandal.

That initially seemed redundant. By one count, eight different agencies were running in witnesses and gathering evidence in the bizarre case. But as in the Whitney matter, Douglas wanted to harness the power of public outrage and media attention to produce as much positive change as he could.

Until the New Deal, American companies were not legally required to have their books audited, although many of the largest companies did. But the quality of those audits could vary widely. At the time, the culture of the accounting profession bore a strong family resemblance to the culture of Wall Street. Professional "accountancy" societies were proud, self-governed organizations; they had resisted any intrusion of federal regulators into their business. They had opposed the 1933 and 1934 reforms. Their general assumption was that "the ideals of the gentleman" would guide certified public accountants in their conduct; therefore, hard and fast rules were not necessary.

That didn't satisfy Roosevelt's regulators. Companies registered with the SEC were required by law to provide investors with annual *independent* audits. At that time, the codes of the accounting profession didn't even have a definition for "independence." After all, a gentleman of integrity would automatically know if his judgment had been compromised, wouldn't he?

In May 1937, amid grumbling from the accountants, the SEC had laid out its standards for independence; basically, they barred independent auditors from having any other relationship with an audit client or owning shares of an audit client's stock worth more than 1 percent of the auditor's net worth.

Then in April 1938, the SEC had "modestly tightened" a loophole left over from the Kennedy-Landis years by deciding that financial statements using gimmicks that lacked "substantial authoritative support" would "be presumed to be misleading . . . provided the matters are material." It sounded fierce but its impact had been minimal because neither the SEC nor the accounting profession had defined "substantial authoritative support."

Since his earliest days at the SEC, Judge Healy had pressed his fellow commissioners to "take the lead in formulating accounting principles as it was empowered to do under the 1933 Act." But the SEC had been content to let the profession make its own rules. Unfortunately, the accountants were Whitney-class footdraggers, and they had an advantage Whitney couldn't claim: The press and the public did not care even a tiny bit about the obscure but polite battles being waged between the auditors and the SEC. The accounting profession had never faced the public outcry and scrutiny the NYSE confronted after the 1929 crash, and it never expected it would.

The McKesson & Robbins scandal changed that.

Within days, it was common knowledge that Price Waterhouse—one of the foremost audit firms in the country—had examined the books at the company for more than a decade but had failed to detect the fact that fully a fourth of the company's listed assets did not exist.

"Like a torrent of cold water, the wave of publicity . . . has shocked the accountancy profession into breathlessness," wrote one accounting journal editor. "Accustomed to relative obscurity . . . accountants have been startled to find their procedures, their principles, and their professional standards the subject of sensational and generally unsympathetic headlines."

Some of those headlines were courtesy of the SEC and the remarkable hearings that Bill Douglas launched on Thursday, January 5, 1939, in New York. While others focused on the Musica family's fraud, the SEC focused on why the company's first-rate accountants—who had been paid more than a million dollars for their audit work over the years—had failed to detect that fraud.

The questions were obvious: Did Price Waterhouse somehow conduct an audit that fell short of the standards of the profession? Or were the standards of the profession not sufficiently stringent even when they were faithfully applied?

The fault lay in the standards, it turned out. The drug company's auditors—like too many of their colleagues across the profession— had been "entirely too casual" in examining the corporation's internal financial controls. The profession's guidelines did not require auditors to verify the existence of inventory or confirm the validity of "accounts receivable," the payments others owed to the company. And either of those tests, by more diligent auditors more familiar with the drug industry, would have exposed that the accounts receivable were bogus and that the Canadian inventory didn't exist— indeed, some of the inventory *couldn't* exist because the amounts listed exceeded the worldwide supply of those materials.

"In the aftermath of this sensational case," one historian later noted, "the SEC pushed through another reform program, which included a thorough overhaul of the rules of auditing" by the professional accounting associations. These reforms, while they relied too much on the profession's rule-making process, were still significant: "The way auditors were selected changed, the scope of the auditor's work expanded, the audit report more carefully detailed what was actually done, and the cost of audits increased for clients. In particular, the procedures for auditing inventories and accounts receivable were expanded."

As with the bankruptcy study and the investment trust investigation and the Whitney case, Douglas had followed where Ferdinand Pecora had led. He had used compelling headline-making hearings to educate the public and thereby turn a scandal into the impetus for reform. In a way, the "shotgun" he wanted the SEC always to keep behind the door was exactly this: the power of public exposure.

TWO OTHER PIECES OF unfinished business made their way onto Bill Douglas's desk in early 1939.

After the SEC's landmark Supreme Court victory in the Ebasco case in March 1938, Douglas had vowed to enforce the Public Utility Holding Company Act, but that work had been tied in knots by festering personnel problems.

The result, one staff member recalled, was "a disastrous state of affairs." There was anger in Congress from backers of the landmark law; there were newspaper articles about the division's disarray. "Literally nothing had been accomplished," the staffer wrote. "The staff was a shambles, the morale was low, and a bitter split between the top officers hamstrung operations."

Tommy Corcoran was worrying aloud to the president that the SEC mess would be used as a cudgel by utility executive Wendell Willkie, the likely GOP presidential candidate in 1940. Roosevelt, through Corcoran, sent an "urgent request" to Douglas to fix the division so it could do its job. Douglas finally made the necessary staff changes, leaving bruised feelings on all sides.

THE FINAL UNFINISHED FIGHT that rose up in early 1939 came from the same people who had been resisting the SEC since it was born: the leaders of the nation's stock exchanges.

Most exchanges had followed the NYSE's lead in reorganizing their own management. All were pleased at the newfound warmth between Bill Douglas and the new spokesman for Wall Street, Bill Martin. But some of the exchange leaders thought they should be rewarded for helping create this truce—and the reward they wanted was SEC support for their preferred amendments to the Securities Act of 1933 and the Securities Exchange Act of 1934.

With great fanfare, nearly three dozen delegates from the NYSE and at least fifteen regional exchanges arrived on Monday, March 13, 1939, at the brick fortress of the Shoreham Hotel in Washington. The group's informal leader was longtime Lehman Brothers partner John M. Hancock, representing the NYSE.

A financial writer for *The New York Times* was told that the gathering of the Hancock committee was being held with the blessings of the SEC, which for a year had been studying how to improve the securities laws. In fact, the SEC had known nothing about the group until February 23, when news leaks forced Bill Martin to confirm that the committee had been secretly at work for more than a month. According to the newspaper's credulous report, proof of Wall Street's new cordial relationship with its regulator was the fact that the delegates would make "no attack on the philosophy" of the 1933 and 1934 acts, which was the protection of investors. Instead, they "will try to make those laws better instruments for accomplishing their purposes."

But Bill Douglas's idea of revising those foundational laws was to simplify the corporate registration statements and cure a few technical glitches. The Hancock committee's idea of revising the laws was to substantially narrow the ban on market manipulation and completely repeal the limits on trading by insiders. And these, as one well-sourced column put it, "are precisely the policies which the SEC regards as the very heart and soul of effective regulation."

On Tuesday night, March 14, three of the stock exchange delegates met with Bill Douglas at the SEC offices on Pennsylvania Avenue and delivered the Hancock group's proposed amendments.

The cover letter must have sounded familiar: "Today markets are thin, prices [are] erratic," the delegates wrote, in an echo of Charles Gay and Winthrop Aldrich in the late summer of 1937. "We do not intend to attribute the thinness of the present market wholly to regulation," they continued. They just thought "the results of five years of collective experience should be of interest to all."

The next day, the SEC released its unanimous response to the exchange proposals.

The relaxation of market manipulation rules? "Stripped of its legal phraseology, this proposal would bring the pool operator back into the market. This strikes at the very heart of stock market regulation."

The repeal of limits on trading by insiders? "Let us not forget that stock market pools were often the most successful for the manipulator when he worked hand-in-glove with the corporate insider."

The agency warned that "weakening our safeguards against market rigging will not contribute to business recovery. On the contrary, it will serve to destroy whatever investor confidence has been built up through efforts to clean up the stock exchanges."

Or as Bill Douglas put it to reporters gathered in his office, "In terms of a program for business recovery, the [Hancock] report is a phony. Opening things up so that the boys in the Street can have another party isn't going to help recovery." He added, "If you got this program intelligently interpreted to the American public, they would turn it down a hundred to one; there is no question about it—because there is nothing in here for the investor."

The reaction on Wall Street was predictable. Editorials chided the SEC for jerking back the olive branch that it had offered when Bill Martin took charge. Columnists reported that the NYSE was deeply hurt by the way its good-faith proposals had been rejected. Bill Martin said he was sure there had just been some misunderstanding.

Was Bill Douglas punishing the NYSE for its refusal to discipline the Morgan partners? Unlikely, given the unanimity of the SEC's rejection of the proposals. Or was the commission warning FDR out loud that he needed to protect his Wall Street watchdog from fresh efforts to muzzle it? That seems more probable.

But perhaps another factor was also at work.

———

ON MONDAY EVENING, FEBRUARY 13, Bill Douglas had stopped in after work at the Georgetown home of an SEC staffer who "would occasionally open the bar at his house, set out some soggy, stale sandwiches, and see which members of the New Deal came to visit."

That night, journalist Arthur Krock had been among the visitors. He had cornered the SEC chairman about a rumor that Douglas was going back to Yale. Yes, Douglas had been strongly considering it. He had been working himself ragged ever since he signed on with Joe Kennedy in the summer of 1934. Yale was looking very good—or maybe, the University of Chicago. Its president, Robert Maynard Hutchins, had been in town a few weeks earlier, and they had talked about the law school deanship there.

Well, Krock had replied, it was a shame he was leaving town because he'd be a great candidate for the new Supreme Court vacancy.

"What vacancy?" Douglas had asked.

"Brandeis retired today."

IT IS NO PART of this story to follow the political maneuvering that led to Franklin D. Roosevelt's nomination of William O. Douglas to fill Justice Louis Brandeis's seat on the Supreme Court. To be sure, one biographer saw Douglas's rejection of the proposed Hancock amendments as a ploy in those maneuvers, an anti–Wall Street gesture aimed at cementing support from New Dealers in the Senate. But as SEC chairman, Douglas certainly had enough other reasons to react as he did to the Hancock plan, and aides later affirmed that the full commission was genuinely outraged by the proposals, especially by the surprising demand for the repeal of limits on insiders' trading.

The day after his conversation with Krock, Douglas had walked from his office over to the White House to keep a 4:15 P.M. appointment with Roosevelt. "The work of the SEC was largely done," he had told FDR. Soon it would be time for Douglas "to return to private life."

Roosevelt had grinned and said, "We'll see."

A month later, on Sunday, March 19, Bill Douglas returned home from a rare round of golf with some SEC colleagues and found a message to call the White House. He did, and was asked to come to see the president as soon as he could.

At 4:30 P.M., he was shown into Roosevelt's oval study.

"I have a new job for you!" the president boomed. "It's a mean job, a dirty job, a thankless job . . . It's a job you'll detest. This job is something like being in jail."

He smiled at the rangy, restless SEC chairman.

"Tomorrow I am sending your name to the Senate as Louis Brandeis's successor."

THE TWO MEN SPENT several hours talking over the state of the nation, as they had done many times before. Their friendship, the fruit of their mutual commitment to financial reform, would endure for the rest of Roosevelt's life.

With Douglas heading for the Supreme Court, Roosevelt now had to make sure that the SEC, one of the jewels of his legacy, would be secure.

In the weeks after his court appointment, Douglas persuaded FDR to invite the principled Robert Maynard Hutchins to take over at the SEC—a choice that would signal to the world that FDR knew the battle with Wall Street wasn't over. Deeply committed to his educational mission, Hutchins declined the offer. But FDR's second choice, again with the strong support of Douglas, spoke just as clearly to Wall Street about FDR's continued commitment to financial reform. He chose the brilliant and empathetic Jerome Frank, who had served the New Deal almost as long as Roosevelt himself had.

FDR was leaving the SEC in safe hands, even as he placed a young New Deal loyalist on the Supreme Court.

No man who had dedicated his life to the law and his loyalty to Roosevelt would dream of refusing this persuasive president's offer of a Supreme Court appointment. But those close to Douglas re-

called him being ambivalent about leaving the SEC, whether it was
for academia or the judiciary.

Gerhard Gesell, the SEC's able field general during the Whitney
hearings, later recalled Douglas saying, "Dammit, I don't want this
job right now." Douglas joked that he was taking the job because
he "needed the money," and there was a germ of truth in that. Douglas's SEC salary was less than he'd made at Yale, and his wallet was
always thin. But Gesell's impression was that "he didn't like the timing; it cut him off in the middle of his work."

Another young aide, Milton Freeman, remembered that the Supreme Court appointment was announced in the middle of the arm
wrestling over the Hancock committee's proposals. When Freeman
and other staffers heard the news, they went into the chairman's office to congratulate him.

"I shot those boys down," Douglas said of the recent dispute, the
latest but surely not the last battle over the deregulatory demands
from Wall Street. "But there's going to be a war."

"You guys," he said—it was an order, or perhaps a plea—"Hold
the fort."

* * *

THE NEW DEAL'S LAST major financial reforms were already in the
pipeline when Douglas said his farewells at the SEC. He outlined
them in a letter to Roosevelt in mid-April 1939.

Douglas encouraged FDR to support the pending Trust Inden-
ture Act that would "eliminate material conflicts of interest from
corporate trustees." Douglas also urged Roosevelt to support the
SEC's efforts to better regulate the over-the-counter market. Within
a few years, the National Association of Securities Dealers would set
itself up as a "self-regulating" overseer for the OTC market. Its
weaknesses eventually would mirror those of the NYSE under Dick
Whitney and overseeing its work would challenge future SEC regulators. But the organization nevertheless gave investors a far better
regulated OTC marketplace than existed when the SEC was born.

Douglas also wanted to see Congress approve the regulation of investment trusts, that era's mutual funds, which Douglas warned had been among "the most defective and dangerous instrumentalities for investors which the 1920s produced. Drastic legislation is needed if the investment trust is to be preserved at all."

On April 17, 1939, less than a week after he wrote to FDR, William O. Douglas was sworn in as an associate justice on the U.S. Supreme Court. He would serve until 1975, the longest tenure of any justice on the court, and would emerge as a fierce defender of civil liberties—a stance that made him a target of conservative venom for most of his years on the court. In 1965, Douglas wrote the court's landmark ruling in *Griswold v. Connecticut,* which held that a state law against the use of contraceptives violated an inherent constitutional right to privacy. The decision was a forerunner in the line of late-twentieth-century opinions that expanded Americans' personal autonomy over family planning, sexual partners, and marriage choices.

Roosevelt would twice consider Douglas as his running mate, briefly in 1940 and more seriously in 1944; in both cases, the notion died in the face of opposition within the party and Douglas's own ambivalence about resigning from the court. Ailing and weak, he finally stepped down in November 1975, after more than thirty-six years on the bench; he died on January 19, 1980.

DICK WHITNEY WAS A model prisoner at Sing Sing and was treated as a resident dignitary by the warden, the guards, and his fellow prisoners, who addressed him always as "Mr. Whitney." With time off for good behavior, he served three years and four months of his sentence of five to ten years. When he was released on August 11, 1941, he wore a gray double-breasted suit, a white shirt, a bow tie, and a fedora. His brother, George, now the president of J.P. Morgan, met him in a chauffeured limousine.

Dick Whitney lived quietly thereafter, first managing a small Massachusetts dairy farm owned by George Whitney's in-laws and then holding a series of small management jobs in New Jersey and Florida. Whitney's wife and daughters stood by him in these years of Wall Street exile, but there was an understandable coolness in his relationship with his brother. While George Whitney eventually paid all his brother's Wall Street creditors, Mrs. George Whitney "prohibited discussion of Richard in her houses," according to one biographer.

Whitney's beloved Harvard Class of 1911 marked its fiftieth reunion in June 1961. Roughly four hundred of his classmates and their relatives showed up for the celebration, sipping frosty daiquiri cocktails under a canopy in one of the campus courtyards. Dick Whitney was not there—he rarely went out socially—but he did send a short biographical update for inclusion in the class book. "Work harder and longer hours than ever before in my life, but seem to thrive on it, and certainly enjoy it. Still maintain a business of shipping citrus fruit from Florida by express to individual customers."

He lived out his days in Far Hills, New Jersey, in a home on the grounds of a large estate owned by a family friend. He died on December 5, 1974, at the age of eighty-six, outliving both his wife and his older brother.

Whitney's legacy would seem to be one of unadulterated shame. He is, after all, the only president of the New York Stock Exchange to go to prison. He brazenly defrauded his own wife, stepson, and sister-in-law, and he plunged his brother and the House of Morgan into a national scandal. But despite his lifelong opposition to all that Roosevelt fought for, Whitney left his own mark on the New Deal's reforms. Without his persuasive advocacy after the 1929 crash, the practice of short selling might well have been outlawed by the most zealous critics of Wall Street. Thanks at least in part to Whitney's effort to educate Congress and the media, short sellers remain an active and important element of the modern marketplace. Dick Whitney also sensed how critical it was for the nation's financial markets to remain open and functional during a national crisis. Even as he steered his own life down the road to ruin, he kept the NYSE open during the 1929 crash and the 1931 gold crisis, and fought to open it as quickly as possible during the 1933 banking crisis.

Dick Whitney's final gift to the New Deal was his confession. By admitting his crimes, Whitney gave Bill Douglas a star witness at the SEC hearings in the spring of 1938 and helped keep the testimony of Whitney's Wall Street enablers on front pages across the country for weeks. The report of those hearings, like the record of the Pecora hearings five years earlier, remains a riveting assessment of the financial morality of an unregulated Wall Street. Whitney's arrogant candor helped peel away any illusions that the public may have had about the ability of Wall Street to police itself or its most powerful players. At a moment when the New Deal was facing fierce opposition from its conservative foes, Whitney's revelations helped turn the tide of public opinion in the SEC's favor so that Bill Douglas could stand firm in the face of the Hancock committee's demands.

JOE KENNEDY'S NAVY LEAGUE speech and Franklin Roosevelt's immediate repudiation of it damaged their personal relationship beyond repair. In London that autumn of 1938, Kennedy complained privately but ceaselessly about FDR's refusal to admit that the democracies had no choice but to get along with the fascist dictators. "Sticking your tongue out at somebody who is a good deal bigger than you are" made no sense, he told one friend.

But publicly, Kennedy still had a job to do in London—FDR seemed reluctant to bring his ambitious but inept ambassador home until after the 1940 presidential election. So Kennedy stumbled on through the year that remained of Britain's anxious peace—stubborn, rebellious, and nearly hysterical in his outspoken belief that only negotiations with Hitler could avert war.

In April 1939, with Britain shaken by Hitler's march into Czechoslovakia in violation of the Munich agreement, Kennedy arranged a secret dinner meeting in Paris with a top German economist with close ties to Hitler. Kennedy's goal was to try out his own fresh appeasement strategy: he proposed that the democracies should "buy Hitler off by providing him with the means to convert his war economy to a peace economy." When both Roosevelt and the State Department refused to give Kennedy permission to attend the Paris meeting, Kennedy simply invited the German banker to meet him secretly in London and forged ahead—desperately trying but failing to find a way to placate the madman in Berlin.

When the summer of 1939 arrived, Kennedy rented an historic ten-bedroom villa in the hills near Cannes and decamped with his family to the South of France. When Hitler threatened Poland in late August, Kennedy returned to his post. He was in London when Germany sent its tanks and fighter planes across the Polish border on September 1, 1939. On September 3, Britain and France confirmed that they would meet their treaty obligations to defend Poland against aggression.

War had come, but Kennedy still hoped to keep the United States out of it. In a frantic cable sent about a week after war was declared, Kennedy urged FDR to turn his back on Britain and France, two of America's closest allies, by opening his own separate negotiations with Hitler. This "recklessly bizarre" proposal shocked Roosevelt, who told a friend that Kennedy's cable was "the silliest to me I have ever received."

Not long afterward, FDR reached out not to Hitler but to Winston Churchill, Britain's first lord of the admiralty and the likely successor to Chamberlain as prime minister. Their relationship would deepen in the dangerous years ahead.

As the war heated up, Kennedy sent his family home—only his daughter Rosemary stayed behind, happily installed in a rural school where her mental limitations were not a burden. He stayed on for a few months in wartime London, still urging Britain's leaders to seek a negotiated peace rather than face the nation's inevitable destruction by Germany. "England is committing suicide," he insisted.

In December 1939, during a long visit to the United States around Christmas, Kennedy continued to preach his dark prophecies to Roosevelt but the president seemed immune to defeatism of any kind. Kennedy returned to his London post in March 1940, but remained "far out of the policy-making loop" in Washington. He was saddened by Chamberlain's resignation on May 10, 1940, and appalled by the new prime minister: that "drunken bum," Winston Churchill. Inevitably, Kennedy was moved further to the sidelines at the State Department.

As France was falling to German troops in June 1940, Kennedy felt all his dire prophecies of defeat were coming true, and he knew whom to blame. In the wee hours of June 15, he wrote in his diary: "If Roosevelt had followed my advice, we'd have stopped the war."

But angry as he was, Kennedy felt he had no choice but to openly support FDR for a third term—the GOP candidate, utility executive Wendell Willkie, seemed woefully unfit to lead the nation through the trials to come. Despite his public loyalty, Kennedy's relationship with the New Deal was in tatters; FDR accepted his resignation on December 1, 1940.

Sunk in his pessimism, Kennedy feared that American capitalism could not survive the European war, which would wipe out the legacy of his own work at the SEC. He had built better than he knew: capitalism and his cherished SEC would both withstand the pressure of the coming years—arguably, thanks to the reforms Kennedy himself had helped implement. But much else that Joe Kennedy cherished would not survive the war. His firstborn son, Joseph P. Kennedy Jr., a fighter pilot, would be shot down in August 1944; a month later, his newlywed daughter Kathleen's British husband would die in action in France. His daughter Rosemary would never recover from a failed lobotomy he authorized in 1941. In 1948, his toll of grief would rise again when his daughter Kathleen would die in a plane crash in the South of France.

Kennedy remained close to his early SEC protégé, Jim Landis, who served as an advisor to President John F. Kennedy on regulatory reform. But the Landis relationship, too, would end in heartache. Always slipshod about his finances, Landis would be found in early 1961 to have left his income taxes unfiled and unpaid for years. He would be convicted of tax evasion in 1963. In July 1964, he would be found dead in his backyard pool, apparently the victim of a heart attack.

By then, Joe Kennedy would have suffered a debilitating stroke, on December 19, 1961, and would be partially paralyzed and unable to speak—except, oddly, to say the word "no." He would only be able to weep silently when his son Jack, President Kennedy, was murdered in Dallas on November 22, 1963, and again, when his son

Bobby, Senator Robert Kennedy, was fatally shot on June 6, 1968, in Los Angeles. His own death came on November 18, 1969, at age eighty-one, in his beloved compound in Hyannis Port.

ON FRIDAY, AUGUST 23, 1940, Franklin Roosevelt signed the last of the powerful New Deal financial reforms, the Investment Company Act and the Investment Advisors Act.

The SEC and the fund industry had wrestled for more than a year over the legislation. Commonly known as the Forty Acts, the bills were not as "drastic" as Bill Douglas had hoped but they were stronger than the fund industry had wanted, prohibiting the most dangerous conflicts of interest and requiring greater disclosure about investments and operations. The SEC apparently had concluded that it could not get anything stronger enacted that year, or perhaps ever. Since early in the year, Wall Street had been begging Congress to scale back the securities laws of 1933 and 1934; more conservative lawmakers were starting to listen. The GOP's energetic presidential candidate, utility executive Wendell Willkie, was vowing that, if he won, he would "rescue" the country from the New Deal and free business from regulations and red tape. When the Forty Acts passed unanimously in Congress and were promptly signed by the president, the SEC no doubt considered its compromises to have been justified.

Week by week, the domestic New Deal agenda was being eclipsed by the desperate situation in Europe. That August, German guns on the Nazi-occupied coastline of France were bombarding ships in the channel. Air raids on London had been intensifying and Britain, now fighting alone against Hitler's Europe, was braced for an invasion by Nazi troops.

The reporters who crowded into Roosevelt's office for his Friday press conference on August 23—roughly a hundred of them—paid little attention to the new mutual fund laws he had signed that day. They were far more interested in the president's unequivocal and unexpected endorsement of a peacetime draft to rebuild the nation's military forces.

But that day's presidential statement about the Forty Acts showed that FDR saw the new laws as part of the larger architecture of fairness and investor protection he had been working on since 1933—a structure built from the Securities Act of 1933, the Securities Exchange Act of 1934, the Public Utility Holding Company Act of 1935, the Maloney Act regulating the over-the-counter market in 1938, and the bankruptcy and trustee reforms passed in 1938 and 1939.

In his statement, Roosevelt seemed especially proud of the holding company act, which he said had cut down the "corporate monstrosities" that had allowed a few men, with little investment of their own, to control an entire pyramid of local and regional utilities. "Those at the top juggled corporations for selfish purposes," he wrote. "This situation was contrary to the American way of life and, had the holding companies not been checked, they would have threatened the very existence of our democratic process."

The president acknowledged that "the pressure of international affairs" was increasing. But he argued that the nation was ready because his administration was "cleaning house, putting our financial machinery in good order." Defying Joe Kennedy's dark fears, FDR insisted his financial reforms would "enable us to absorb the shock of any crisis."

Citing the SEC's wisdom and essential fairness in handling financial problems, he added: "We have come a long way since the bleak days of 1929, when the market crash swept away the veil which up to then had hidden the 'behind-the-scenes' activity of our high financiers and showed all too clearly the sham and deceit which characterized so many of their actions."

Once it became clear that Roosevelt would accept an unprecedented third term, there was little Democratic opposition to his nomination. The party's convention in Chicago in mid-July 1940 echoed with memories of his victory there in 1932.

The president's campaign was quiet. Roosevelt made fewer than a half-dozen major speeches and rarely even mentioned his rival's name. The vast majority of the nation's newspaper editors were supporting Willkie, and pollsters and pundits in early November expected a close race. But the voting on November 5, 1940, was not close. The nation gave Roosevelt 449 electoral votes, far more than the 266 he needed for victory. Wendell Willkie got 83 electoral votes, nowhere near enough to win but more than Herbert Hoover and Alf Landon had gotten in their battles with Roosevelt. The Democrats increased their hold on the House and kept control of the Senate.

Roosevelt still did not have the unified liberal party he wanted, a party devoted to his ideals of fairness for the vulnerable and accountability for the powerful. But he commanded enough support from the American people to become the first president ever to serve a third term in the White House. In 1944, with the nation in a desperate war against Hitler and his fascist allies in Europe and Japan, Roosevelt would be reelected to an historic fourth term. With Churchill, he would help lead the Allies to victory against the fascist forces in World War II.

On April 12, 1945, just a month before Allied troops would triumph in Europe, Roosevelt would die of a massive cerebral hemorrhage while working at his cottage in Warm Springs, Georgia.

Roosevelt's death would shock the nation, and the world. Every church bell in his home village of Hyde Park would toll; from London to Latin America, the great and the humble would mourn. Bill Douglas and his Supreme Court colleagues would meet the train that brought Roosevelt's body back to Washington, where silent crowds would watch its progress to the White House. "People wept without restraint," Douglas would recall of that day.

Roosevelt's longtime "brain trust" friend Adolf Berle would be serving as the American ambassador in Brazil when FDR died. "Almost immediately afterward," Berle would later recall, "a steady stream of people, high and low, began to come to the Embassy to express sorrow . . . some were little people who had no shoes but merely came up to salute the Embassy and go away in silence." Berle would marvel at the fact that Roosevelt "could make himself as much a personal friend of the little laborer in the Brazilian streets as he did of millions of Americans." That was a tribute to "the tremendous well-spring of vital friendship which he somehow communicated far beyond the borders of his own country."

The morning after Roosevelt's death, before the opening bell at the New York Stock Exchange, traders would observe two minutes of silence before the day's business. On the day of FDR's funeral, the exchange would close to honor the president who, more than any in the nation's history, had insisted that Wall Street practice what it preached so that ordinary Americans could sit at capitalism's table and share in the feast.

* * *

WHAT ROOSEVELT DID TO produce a fairer future for America had been based on what he knew about the predatory past, when the paths to opportunity were tilted steeply against the many and in favor of the few. He had known in his soul that the health of America's democracy depended on the fairness of America's economy.

With the world still at war in 1945 and the national economy humming to equip the war effort, the memorials that would pour forth after Roosevelt's death would pay almost no attention to his long campaign for financial reform. But those reforms must be counted today as a precious part of the legacy he left to his country—and, because his reforms eventually would be adopted widely in other capitalist nations, to investors around the globe.

"The Roosevelt administration did not achieve all it sought in federal securities regulation," one noted scholar concluded. "But what it did achieve fundamentally transformed finance."

And by transforming finance, Franklin Roosevelt—with the loyal energy of Bill Douglas, the short-lived support of Joe Kennedy, and the backhanded help of Dick Whitney—transformed the future and changed the world.

EPILOGUE

THE SECURITIES AND EXCHANGE COMMISSION HAS BEEN AT work for nearly ninety years. Many of those years have been bleak and hard; the years ahead may be worse.

World War II deprived the agency of FDR's empowering attention. To make room for the growing defense bureaucracy in Washington, the entire agency was exiled in early 1942 to Philadelphia, where it set up offices in a remodeled athletic club. When FDR died, President Harry Truman did not get around to calling the SEC back to the nation's capital until 1948, evidence of his own indifference to the Wall Street reforms that had been so central to Roosevelt's New Deal.

Truman's failure to lend any presidential prestige or support to the SEC's mission—he saw the commission primarily as a source of political patronage jobs, which he handed out with scant attention to his appointees' credentials—was followed by President Dwight Eisenhower's reluctance to spend any money on the agency's mission. Even as the strong postwar economy gave rise to "the most widespread pattern of speculative activity and securities fraud to occur since the late 1920s," Eisenhower's priority was cutting the federal budget, not protecting investors. In 1941, the SEC had a staff of 1,723 people; by 1953, after a dozen years of neglect and parsimony, there were only 773 people on staff and the agency faced a substantial backlog of work. The following year, SEC staffing was cut to 699 positions; the agency chairman at that time warned that "people will be defrauded by the hundreds in ways that we could check and would be able to stop if we had the staff we need." The 1955 budget left the SEC with a staff of just 666 people. By that point, even the New York Stock Exchange was appealing to Congress to increase the SEC's resources before the widening swamp of fraud again undermined public trust in the nation's markets, as it had before the New Deal.

The eminent SEC historian Joel Seligman's harsh verdict is that, "during the Eisenhower administration, the Securities and Exchange Commission reached its nadir."

The agency's idealistic and influential staff and well-established reputation helped carry it through these years of fiscal famine, but the damage ran deep. In the 1960s, the agency had trouble keeping up with a sudden explosion of Wall Street activity, which swamped the clerical capacity of the market and was accompanied by a surge in financial fraud. The SEC lacked the staff to address the flagging discipline of the National Association of Securities Dealers, and problems proliferated in the over-the-counter market. A major market manipulation scheme ran unchecked for years on the American Stock Exchange, where self-regulation had completely broken down under weakened SEC supervision.

But through the 1970s, even as it struggled with tight budgets and distracted presidents and ill-informed lawmakers, the agency regularly produced sparks of brilliance and spurts of diligence—enough to show that its regulatory machinery could still protect investors if it had the resources to do the job and could rely on support from Congress, the Justice Department, and the White House.

More recently, despite some valiant commissioners and able staffers, the agency has been caught on a deregulatory seesaw, urged by conservatives to lighten its touch and loosen its rules—and then slapped by those same lawmakers when America's investors suffered from inadequate protection.

Under President Ronald Reagan, the SEC agreed to leave the regulation of financial derivatives to the Commodity Futures Trading Commission, an agency that supposedly governed with a lighter touch. That regulatory default contributed to the shocking market crash on October 19, 1987—Black Monday, the single worst day in

Wall Street history, when the Dow Jones Industrial index fell nearly 23 percent and an avalanche of selling the following day almost crippled the NYSE.

It was part of a broader pattern. Deregulatory enthusiasm led lawmakers in the 1980s to loosen the rules for the nation's savings and loan institutions and underfund their regulators. Again, the result was rising fraud, institutional failures, and investor losses. Similarly, the dubious quality and compromised independence of corporate audits kept slipping through regulatory loopholes until investors were hit by a wave of ruinous corporate frauds, dominated by the 2001 collapse of the Enron conglomerate in Houston. In 2000, deregulatory purists in Congress enacted the Commodities Futures Modernization Act, which actually barred *anyone* from regulating a popular new Wall Street tool called "swaps." The feverish proliferation of those unregulated contracts contributed mightily to the financial crisis of 2008. Lawmakers and regulators dithered for years over whether the SEC, or any other agency, should regulate cryptocurrencies; no one did, and by late 2022, the nation was grappling with bankruptcies, fraud investigations, and enormous investor losses in that technologically tangled and environmentally ruinous field.

A conservative judiciary further threatens the Roosevelt rule book, as it did in the 1930s. In the past several years, targets of SEC enforcement actions have raised sweeping constitutional challenges that already have prevailed in some lower courts; if upheld by the Supreme Court, these challenges will have devastating practical consequences for the agency's ability to carry out its mission of protecting investors.

Meanwhile, America is again afflicted by the ills of the 1920s— stagnant working-class incomes, a widening gap between rich and poor, a staggering enrichment of the top 1 percent—developments that would surprise no one who helped Roosevelt fight for his New Deal. As regulation has grown weaker and less wise, the economy has once again tilted strongly in favor of the richest and most powerful.

———

THE GREAT DEPRESSION POPPED the bubble of lies on which the Jazz Age floated. The magic formula for prosperity—give the rich what they want and they will share their rewards with the rest of us—was exposed as the fraud it had always been. Destructive social unrest seemed to be just one more terrible winter away.

Then a patrician phenomenon named Franklin D. Roosevelt suggested a different recipe for prosperity. Roosevelt said: Let's lift up the great mass of ordinary people—give them a living wage to spend, safe ways to save and invest, a pension for their old age, affordable utility bills—and let *them* fuel a prosperous economy in which the rich can benefit along with everyone else. Let's put some rules in place that will give everyone a fair shake.

In 1932, a desperate nation with little left to lose agreed to try this new recipe of regulation. Voters elected Roosevelt by an enormous margin to do exactly what he promised—to rein in the ruthless and work for a society that was fair to everyone. In 1936, voters reelected him by one of the largest landslides in American history after he had spent four years doing what he said he would—not perfectly, not seamlessly, but with a warm, cheerful heart and general competence. Just two states gave their electoral votes to the candidate whose party was pledged to the plutocratic past. All the other states voted for the man who had said, "Let's help each other; going forward, let's prosper together."

What happened in the decades that followed has become far too familiar: The economy recovered. The rich stopped worrying about social disintegration and pined again for low taxes and no regulation. The rest of the country became complacent, certain that the reforms that helped so many ordinary Americans would surely endure.

But those reforms were always in danger. From the beginning, Roosevelt's foes attacked his supporters as communists, socialists, deviants—calling on the general public to reject and detest those who were working for the general welfare. Down through the years, those who wanted to dismantle the New Deal have continued to slap the same labels on those who wanted to sustain and strengthen Roosevelt's financial and social legacy.

It has taken time for this deregulatory project to gain traction. It has faced setbacks—spurts of generosity, moments of solidarity against injustice, surges of compassion, national calamities that proved we all were, fundamentally, still in the same boat. But decade after decade, more Americans have forgotten their history and accepted the distorted arguments of "free market" purists who are determined to restore the kind of unfettered capitalism that shaped the 1920s.

Decades of deception and distortion don't change the fact that Franklin Roosevelt was right. Taming the predatory instincts and selfish priorities of the most powerful players in our capitalist system still is essential to maintaining a fair society for everyone else.

The bedrock abuses that confront Americans today are fundamentally no different from the abuses FDR confronted in 1932: conflicts of interest, market manipulation, monopoly power, and excessive debt-fueled speculation. Business, especially the financial world of Wall Street, is no more capable of policing itself today than it was when Dick Whitney presided over the NYSE. Behind closed doors, the human impulse is still to cover up, keep quiet, excuse flaws, ignore red flags, and grab whatever can be grabbed while no one is watching. Someone *must be watching*—someone with enough resources and competence and independence to keep the game honest and fair.

Roosevelt was right about this, too: a healthy democracy cannot survive without a fair economy. His wise response to the brazenly lopsided economy of the 1920s protected our democracy for a long time—until his vision was rejected not only by his political foes, whose ideology is little changed since the days of Herbert Hoover, but also by his misguided political heirs, the modern-day Democrats who should know better.

A fairer economy can once again help nurture and strengthen our democratic society—if FDR's reforms are dusted off, modernized, and embraced in Congress, emphasized by the White House, and respected by prosecutors. Some of that work will require bipartisan legislation, and today's poisonous political environment will make that a huge challenge of voter education and public persuasion. Adverse judicial decisions in the next few years could add even tougher challenges to the legislative and administrative to-do list. But much could be accomplished simply by applying FDR's original magic: *presidential attention.* When the head of the SEC has walk-in privileges at the Oval Office, when formidable SEC commissioners command respect in Congress and in the courts, when the SEC's budget is adequate for its mission, and when regulators can communicate effectively and authoritatively with the media and the public, the SEC can reclaim at least some of its founder's legacy.

If today's young adults are to have a fair chance to secure their own financial security, lawmakers—and those who vote them into office—must come to their senses about financial regulation. Deregulating finance is *exactly* like deregulating traffic. In a world without lane markings, stoplights, speed limits, drivers' licenses, and insurance requirements, the roadways of capitalism would serve only the tanks of the richest behemoths and the hot rods of the reckless speculators.

In short, deregulation is the route that would carry today's Americans straight back into the plutocrat's paradise of the unregulated 1920s. In that jungle, the rewards of capitalism would not flow fairly to ordinary Americans whose labor and ideas have always been the fundamental engine for the economy. Life for the powerful few would get easier and more secure; life for the rest of us would not.

Democracy's survival depends on its capacity to secure a hopeful future for the great majority of its citizens. As Roosevelt said in his radio chat on the eve of the 1938 midterm elections, "Democracy will save itself with the average man and woman by proving itself worth saving." To do that, he said, democracy "must become a positive force in the daily lives of its people."

And to do *that,* democracy must adopt and enforce sensible rules that will restrain capitalism's worst predatory impulses and give everyone, across the generations, a realistic chance to build a better life.

CAST OF CHARACTERS

(IN ALPHABETICAL ORDER)

WINTHROP W. ALDRICH—the fiscally conservative president and chairman of Chase National Bank from 1930 to 1953.

JOSEPH W. ALSOP V—prominent journalist and syndicated columnist for five decades, with close family ties to the Roosevelts.

VINCENT ASTOR—the son and heir of John Jacob Astor IV, who died on the *Titanic* in 1912, and a close friend of FDR.

FRANCIS D. BARTOW—a partner in J.P. Morgan from 1926 until his retirement in 1943.

JOHN J. BENNETT JR.—attorney general of New York from 1931 to 1942.

ADOLF A. BERLE JR.—a Columbia law professor who was an original recruit to FDR's brain trust in 1932; he later served as a top aide to New York City mayor Fiorello La Guardia, as a senior State Department official, and as U.S. ambassador to Brazil.

JOSEPH A. BRODERICK—the New York State banking superintendent under FDR and Herbert Lehman and an original proponent of separating commercial and investment banking.

JOHN J. BURNS—the first general counsel for the SEC, appointed after serving on the Harvard law faculty and as a Massachusetts state judge.

NEVILLE CHAMBERLAIN—the prime minister of Great Britain from May 1937 to May 1940; he was a close associate of Joseph P. Kennedy during the latter's tenure as U.S. ambassador to Great Britain.

WINSTON CHURCHILL—prime minister of Great Britain from May 1940 to July 1945, and again from October 1951 to April 1955.

SAMUEL O. CLARK JR.—the trial examiner during the SEC's hearing on the Richard Whitney matter in 1938.

U.S. DISTRICT JUDGE WILLIAM CLARK—the federal judge who allowed William O. Douglas to study the bankruptcy cases on his docket in the late 1920s.

BENJAMIN V. COHEN—a New Deal lawyer who helped draft and defend much of FDR's early securities reforms, including the Securities Act of 1933, the Securities Exchange Act of 1934, and the Public Utility Holding Company Act of 1935.

U.S. DISTRICT JUDGE WILLIAM COLEMAN—the Baltimore federal judge who handled an early industry challenge to the Public Utility Holding Company Act in the fall of 1935.

CARLE C. CONWAY—the president and chairman of Continental Can Company who led the New York Stock Exchange's reorganization study committee in 1937–1938.

CALVIN COOLIDGE—vice president under President Warren Harding and, on Harding's death, the thirtieth president of the United States, serving from August 1923 to March 1929.

THOMAS G. CORCORAN—a New Deal lawyer who, with Benjamin V. Cohen and James M. Landis, helped draft several of FDR's major securities reform laws.

JOHN J. DAVIDSON—a lawyer in the SEC's New York office at the time of the Richard Whitney scandal.

HOWLAND S. DAVIS—a Wall Street broker who was a governor of the New York Stock Exchange and chairman of its powerful business conduct committee in 1938.

JOHN W. DAVIS—the Democratic Party's presidential nominee in 1924 and a prominent securities lawyer whose premier client was J. P. Morgan Jr. and his firm.

THOMAS E. DEWEY—the district attorney of New York County from January 1938 until December 1941, when he became the forty-seventh governor of New York, an office he held until December 1954; he was the GOP presidential candidate in 1944, when he lost to FDR, and again in 1948, when he narrowly lost to incumbent Harry Truman.

CLARENCE DILLON—a founder, with William A. Read, of the Wall Street firm of Dillon, Read & Co., which he helped transform into a leading investment banking house.

WILLIAM O. DOUGLAS—the seventh commissioner named to the Securities and Exchange Commission by FDR, and the agency's third chairman.

MARRINER S. ECCLES—a Republican businessman from Utah tapped by FDR as chairman of the Federal Reserve Board in November 1934; he was chairman until 1948 and a board member until July 1951.

JAMES A. FARLEY—the chairman of the New York State Democratic Party from 1930 to 1944, and Democratic National Committee chairman from 1932 until 1940; he served as FDR's postmaster general from March 1933 until September 1940.

JOHN F. "HONEY FITZ" FITZGERALD—the father of Rose Fitzgerald Kennedy; a Democrat, he was mayor of Boston from 1906 to 1908 and from 1910 to 1914.

JOHN T. FLYNN—a Wall Street critic and prominent financial journalist who was an advisor to the Pecora hearings in the 1930s; an isolationist, he later became a popular conservative radio commentator and a fierce critic of Roosevelt and the New Deal.

ABE FORTAS—a protégé of William O. Douglas at Yale Law School who worked with Douglas at the SEC. He later was appointed to the Supreme Court in 1965, but resigned in 1969, amid a politically charged investigation of alleged ethics violations.

JEROME FRANK—a Yale Law School graduate who became an SEC commissioner in December 1937 and the agency's chairman in 1939. In March 1941, FDR appointed him to the U.S. Court of Appeals for the Second Circuit where he served until his death in 1957.

FELIX FRANKFURTER—a Harvard law professor who advised FDR on utility and securities regulation and recruited able young lawyers to serve in the New Deal; in January 1939, he was sworn in as an associate justice of the U.S. Supreme Court, where he served until August 1962.

GERHARD A. GESELL—a trial lawyer for the SEC from 1935 to 1940 and its lead attorney in the Whitney hearings in 1938; he was appointed in 1967 to the U.S. District Court for the District of Columbia, where he presided over several important cases arising from the Watergate scandal.

C. DAVID GINSBURG—a lawyer for the SEC who later served as executive director of the Kerner Commission, a federal commission that reported on the systemic racism that helped trigger urban riots in the late 1960s.

SENATOR CARTER GLASS—a powerful Democratic senator from Virginia from 1920 until his death in 1946, and co-author of the Glass-Steagall Act, which set up the Federal Deposit Insurance Corporation (FDIC).

JOHN D. M. HAMILTON—a Kansas Republican who was the chairman of Kansas governor Alf Landon's presidential bid in 1936.

JOHN M. HANCOCK—a longtime partner at Lehman Brothers, a member of the NYSE board, and the informal chairman of a committee of delegates from national stock exchanges seeking revisions in the 1933 and 1934 securities laws early in 1938.

JOHN WESLEY HANES II—a Wall Street investment banker who served as a governor of the New York Stock Exchange in 1935; in 1937, he began a brief term as an SEC commissioner but left in May 1938 for a post in the Treasury Department.

ROBERT E. "JUDGE" HEALY—the chief counsel to the Federal Trade Commission from 1928 to 1934, when FDR named him as one of the original members of the SEC; he served until his death in November 1946.

WILLIAM RANDOLPH HEARST—the flamboyant architect of one of America's largest newspaper chains and a force in national politics in the 1930s.

LOUIS MCHENRY HOWE—a New York journalist who signed on in 1912 as FDR's first political strategist; he remained Roosevelt's most trusted advisor until his death in April 1936.

CORDELL HULL—FDR's secretary of state from March 1933 until November 1944, a job that included overseeing Joe Kennedy's service as U.S. ambassador to Great Britain.

ROBERT MAYNARD HUTCHINS—a visionary educator who served as dean of the Yale Law School before being tapped, in 1929, as president of the University of Chicago, where he remained in a leadership role until 1951.

HAROLD L. ICKES—a liberal Chicago lawyer who served FDR as secretary of the Interior from 1933 to 1946; his diaries are a trove of intimate details about FDR and the New Deal.

SAMUEL INSULL—an early assistant to Thomas Edison who built up one of the most complex public utility holding companies in the country; its costly collapse in 1932 helped FDR gain support for the Public Utility Holding Company Act of 1935.

ROBERT H. JACKSON—an immensely talented lawyer who served FDR as solicitor general and attorney general; in 1941, Roosevelt appointed him to the Supreme Court, where he served until his death in 1954. In 1945, he took a leave of absence from the court and served as chief U.S. counsel for the Nuremberg trials of Nazi war criminals.

WILLIAM H. JACKSON—a young Tennessee-born lawyer who became a partner in 1934 at the Wall Street law firm of Carter Ledyard & Milburn, whose most prominent client was the New York Stock Exchange.

WALTER L. JOHNSON—a former president and longtime member of the New York Cotton Exchange, Johnson served as vice president of the New York Stock Exchange from 1924 to 1928, and again from 1937 to 1938.

J. EDWARD JONES—an early marketer of oil trust investments who, after the SEC targeted his marketing methods in 1935, led a long legal fight to have the agency declared unconstitutional.

JOSEPH P. KENNEDY—a Wall Street speculator and film industry mogul who supported FDR's first campaign for president in 1932; he served as the first chairman of the SEC and as U.S. ambassador to Great Britain on the eve of World War II. Married to Rose Fitzgerald Kennedy in 1914, he was the father of nine children, including President John F. Kennedy, Senator Robert F. Kennedy, and Senator Edward M. Kennedy.

ROBERT E. KINTNER—an influential financial and political columnist who, with Joseph Alsop, wrote extensively about the New Deal. He moved to television after World War II, and served as president of ABC from 1950 to 1956, and of NBC from 1957 to 1966.

IVAR KREUGER—a Swedish businessman known as the Match King, whose worldwide conglomerate was based on monopoly franchises to sell wooden matches; his empire, riddled with fraud, collapsed with his suicide in 1932.

ARTHUR KROCK—a prominent and influential reporter and columnist for *The New York Times* who covered Washington for sixty years, starting in 1927.

FIORELLO LA GUARDIA—an exuberant New York lawyer with Italian immigrant roots who served as a progressive Republican congressman for East Harlem from 1922 until March 1933 and as the mayor of New York from 1934 to 1945.

THOMAS W. LAMONT—a prominent partner at J.P. Morgan & Co. from 1911 until his death in 1948; he was a Wall Street envoy to the world, an admirer of Italian fascist Benito Mussolini, and an influential advisor to Japan in the decades before World War II.

JAMES M. LANDIS—a drafter of FDR's securities reforms, an FTC commissioner, one of the five inaugural SEC commissioners, and the second chairman of the agency. He left to become dean of the Harvard Law School in 1937.

ALFRED M. "ALF" LANDON—the GOP presidential candidate who ran for president against FDR in the 1936 election.

HERBERT H. LEHMAN—an heir of the Lehman Brothers dynasty on Wall Street who served as FDR's lieutenant governor in New York, 1929 to 1932; as FDR's successor as New York governor, 1933 to 1942; and as New York's U.S. senator from 1949 until 1957.

MARGUERITE "MISSY" LEHAND—the longtime confidential secretary to Franklin Roosevelt in Albany and in the White House.

WALTER LIPPMANN—a former advisor to President Wilson after World War I who became one of the nation's most influential political commentators from the 1920s to the 1960s.

GEORGE W. LUTES—the clerk for the New York Stock Exchange's Gratuity Fund in November 1937.

U.S. DISTRICT JUDGE JULIAN W. MACK—a longtime federal judge who served in the 1930s on the U.S. Court of Appeals for the Second Circuit in New York.

SENATOR FRANCIS T. MALONEY—a Connecticut politician who served as that state's U.S. senator from 1935 to 1945; William O. Douglas was an early political supporter, and the two worked together on the Maloney Act of 1938, regulating the over-the-counter stock market.

WILLIAM MCCHESNEY MARTIN JR.—the son of one of the original drafters of the Federal Reserve Act of 1913, Martin was a partner in the St. Louis–based brokerage firm of A.G. Edwards & Sons; he became a member of the New York Stock Exchange in 1931, an NYSE governor in 1935, and its first professional chief executive in 1938. In 1951, he was appointed chairman of the Federal Reserve, where he served until 1970.

GEORGE C. "BUD" MATHEWS—an economist by training, Mathews worked as an advisor to the Wisconsin Railroad Commission and was tapped by FDR as one of the five inaugural members of the SEC, where he served until 1940.

L. RANDOLPH "RANDY" MASON—a former partner at Carter Ledyard & Milburn, he represented Richard Whitney in the NYSE's initial investigation of his firm in early 1938.

MICHAEL J. MEEHAN—a longtime member and specialist on the New York Stock Exchange who helped conduct the infamous "pool operation" in RCA stock in 1929; in 1935, the SEC sued him for manipulating an aircraft maker's stock and he was ultimately barred from the securities markets.

ANDREW W. MELLON—a member of the wealthy Mellon dynasty, he was Treasury secretary under Presidents Harding, Coolidge, and Hoover; he was a staunch advocate of low taxes and a minimal government role in the economy.

OGDEN L. MILLS—Andrew Mellon's successor as Treasury secretary under President Hoover; he opposed the New Deal but cooperated with FDR's incoming cabinet during the banking crisis of February and early March 1933.

CHARLES E. MITCHELL—the president of National City Bank, now Citibank, from 1921 to 1929, and its chairman from 1929 until his abrupt resignation during the Pecora hearings in 1933.

RAYMOND MOLEY—a professor of criminal justice at Columbia and one of the organizers of Roosevelt's brain trust in early 1932; he remained a close advisor and speechwriter in FDR's first term, but moved to the right and turned against the New Deal later in the decade.

EDWARD E. MOORE—the longtime confidential assistant to Joseph P. Kennedy, working as Kennedy's aide at the SEC, the maritime commission, and in the American embassy in London.

HENRY MORGENTHAU JR.—the son of a diplomat, he was FDR's Hudson Valley neighbor and served as his Treasury secretary from January 1934 until FDR's death in 1945.

ROBERT MOSES—a young aide to New York governor Al Smith who served as Smith's secretary of state from 1927 to early 1929, when FDR replaced him with Bronx's political leader Ed Flynn. Moses went on to hold a host of public construction positions through which he helped reshape modern New York.

FERDINAND PECORA—a former New York prosecutor whose work as chief counsel to the Senate Banking and Currency Committee's hearings on Wall Street, beginning in 1933, gained national attention; he was tapped by FDR as one of the original members of the SEC but served only a few months before being appointed a state judge in New York.

EDWARD A. PIERCE—a lifelong and highly successful Wall Street broker who supported the SEC's program for reform at the New York Stock Exchange; he was the chief architect of the firm E. A. Pierce & Co., a forerunner of Merrill Lynch, Pierce, Fenner & Smith.

JOHN JACOB RASKOB—a wealthy business executive whose opposition to Prohibition pulled him into national politics; he served from 1928 until July 1932 as chairman of the Democratic National Committee, but later split with FDR and campaigned against him in 1936.

SAM RAYBURN—a Democratic congressman from Texas who helped secure passage for FDR's major financial reforms; in 1940, he was elected Speaker of the House, a post he held during periods of Democratic control until his death in November 1961.

JAMES J. RIORDAN—a self-made financier with real estate interests in Manhattan; in 1929, he was the founder of the County Trust Company.

F. KINGSLEY RODEWALD—one of Richard Whitney's "office boy" partners, and the one most actively involved in the day-to-day management of the firm.

ROLAND L. REDMOND—a family friend of the Roosevelts and longtime partner at Carter Ledyard & Milburn, where FDR first worked after finishing law school; he represented the NYSE during the battle over the Securities Exchange Act of 1934 and the investigation of Richard Whitney in 1938.

ELEANOR ROOSEVELT—the niece of President Theodore Roosevelt, she married FDR in 1905 and, after his death, pursued a long career as a diplomat at the United Nations and a supporter of liberal Democratic causes.

FRANKLIN DELANO ROOSEVELT—the former governor of New York, elected in 1932 as the thirty-second president of the United States, a post he held until his death in April 1945. He led the nation through the Great Depression, building recovery on a foundation of financial reforms, and led America and its allies to victory over Hitler's fascist forces in World War II.

JAMES ROOSEVELT—FDR and Eleanor's eldest son and his father's executive assistant after the death of Louis McHenry Howe in 1936.

SAMUEL I. ROSENMAN—a young lawyer in Governor Al Smith's administration who began working for FDR in 1929 and remained a close advisor until Roosevelt's death.

JAMES DELMAGE "J.D." ROSS—a Seattle utility executive appointed to the SEC by Roosevelt on the heels of congressional passage of the Public Utility Holding Company Act in 1935; he soon left the agency to serve as the first administrator of the Bonneville Power Administration.

PAUL V. SHIELDS—a Wall Street broker who worked with Edward Pierce to support the SEC's reforms at the New York Stock Exchange.

E.H.H. "HARRY" SIMMONS—a member of the New York Stock Exchange from 1900, a member of its board of governors from 1909, its vice president from 1921 to 1924, and its president from 1924 until he handed the gavel to his protégé, Richard Whitney, in 1930.

ALFRED E. SMITH—a personable New York City politician who served four two-year terms as governor of New York and, as the Democratic presidential nominee, lost to Herbert Hoover in 1928; by 1936, he had broken openly with his protégé, Franklin Roosevelt.

HENRY B. STEAGALL—a Democratic congressman from Alabama who helped persuade Senator Carter Glass and FDR to add bank deposit insurance to the banking bill enacted in FDR's "Hundred Days."

GLORIA SWANSON—a star of silent pictures in the 1920s who was able to successfully transition to talking films in 1929; her first talking picture was produced by Joseph P. Kennedy, her business manager and lover before his involvement in FDR's 1932 campaign.

CHARLES H. TUTTLE—a U.S. attorney for the Southern District of New York who lost to FDR in the 1930 governor's race and represented Richard Whitney in 1938.

MAYOR JIMMY WALKER—the flamboyantly corrupt Tammany Hall politician who presided in New York City during FDR's terms as governor.

SIDNEY J. WEINBERG—a onetime janitor's assistant who rose to a partnership at Goldman Sachs in 1927; a staunch ally of FDR and the New Deal, he helped alert the SEC to the McKesson & Robbins scandal in December 1938.

HERBERT "DUKE" WELLINGTON—one of the patrician members of the New York Stock Exchange who quietly loaned funds to Richard Whitney during his presidency at the exchange.

ALBERT H. WIGGIN—a widely respected banker who became Chase National Bank's president in 1911 and its chairman in 1917; he also served as a director of the Federal Reserve Bank of New York. He was forced to cut his ties with both banks after the Pecora hearings in 1933 revealed he had been selling his own bank's shares short during the 1929 crash.

GEORGE WHITNEY—a partner and later president of J.P. Morgan and the elder brother of Richard Whitney, the Morgan firm's bond trader and later the president of the New York Stock Exchange.

RICHARD WHITNEY—a longtime bond trader on the New York Stock Exchange who served as its highly influential president from 1930 to 1935, and remained a force on its board of governors until his downfall in 1938.

BLAIRE S. WILLIAMS—with E.H.H. Simmons, one of the trustees of the New York Stock Exchange Gratuity Fund, which provided benefits to the widows and orphans of members' families.

WENDELL WILLKIE—a young utility industry executive who helped rally the fight against the Public Utility Holding Company Act, FDR's effort to dismantle the complex pyramids that dominated the industry; Willkie was the GOP presidential candidate who lost to FDR in 1940.

WILLIAM H. WOODIN—a railcar manufacturing executive who served briefly, but fortuitously, as FDR's Treasury secretary, helping steer the nation through the banking crisis of early March 1933.

ACKNOWLEDGMENTS

To paraphrase myself, how many people does it take to write a book?

Just one—in theory. As the sportswriter Red Smith supposedly said in the age before computers: "There's nothing to writing. All you do is sit down at a typewriter, open a vein, and bleed."

In reality, writing a book is a collaboration among kindred minds and supportive spirits. I have been blessed with a congregation of such people, without whom this book would not be in your hands.

Gail Ross, my intrepid agent, took on this project at its darkest hour and helped me see daylight ahead for it. I am immensely grateful for her abiding support and her continued friendship.

Mark Warren, my extraordinarily gifted editor at Random House, saw what this book could be more clearly than I did—and then helped me stretch far enough to reach that vision. It was an astonishment to work with him on this project.

Paul Golub, my friend and former editor at Henry Holt, first helped me conceive the rough shape of this tale when it was barely a newborn idea.

Thomas J. Sarentino of MetroTech Systems, my tireless and creative computer guru, was almost singlehandedly responsible for this book getting published now, instead of a year from now. First, he devised a clever way to make a Windows update work with the otherwise incompatible voice-recognition program I rely on. Then, when my computer hard drive crashed on Thanksgiving Eve 2022, Tom rode to the rescue through holiday traffic and managed to salvage the key files that saved me months of footnote reconstruction. Thank you, Tom!

I was so lucky—in pre-pandemic days—to be able to rely on the research skills of the tireless Barbara Oliver, who has been with me through almost every book I've done. She is a treasure!

And when the pandemic derailed my research plans by halting travel and closing archives and libraries, I was rescued by an online world of resources, especially the SEC Historical Society archives, overseen by the steadfast Jane Cobb; the online used bookselling sites where I tracked down dozens of precious references, notably the entire bound record of the SEC's Whitney hearings; the priceless old newsreel footage available through YouTube and elsewhere; and the online treasures from *The New York Times* digital archives, the Newspapers.com service, Marist College's presidential collections, the JSTOR and Hathitrust digital libraries, the Federal Reserve Bank of St. Louis's FRASER database, the SEC's website, and the online offerings of the Franklin D. Roosevelt Presidential Library and Museum in Hyde Park, New York. I owe a huge debt to everyone who labors to make these and other online resources accessible. I hope the pandemic experience will encourage every archive, library, and museum to expand their online offerings.

I am also deeply grateful for the steady support and interest I got from friends in the scholarly community. The deepest bow goes to Dr. Joel Seligman, the legal historian whose two magisterial works on financial regulation were the shoulders on which I stood in this research. I am also deeply in debt to Frank Partnoy, Adam Sterling, and Delia Violante at the UC-Berkeley Law School; Rupert Younger and Liz Smith at the Oxford Fellows program at the University of Oxford; and all the trustees and support staff at the George Washington University, especially Ellen Zane, Grace Speights, Ann Walker Marchant, Peter Kovler, and the ever-enthusiastic Aristide Collins.

I cannot count all the times I was soothed and sustained in this project by the abiding faith of my exceptional friends, especially Beth Hunt, Michael Munzell, Gay Morris, Leslie Eaton, Mark Vamos, Madeleine Jacobs, Sharon Walsh, Floyd Norris, Chris Bockelmann, Jonathan Fuerbringer, Johanna McGeary, David Barstow, Robin Wolfson, and Herb Greenberg.

I am further blessed with a family whose keen minds and kind hearts are a never-failing source of support. I am especially grateful to my sister Peggy van der Swaagh and her husband, Price; my sisters-in-law Noel Brakenhoff and Teakie Welty; all our wonderful nieces and nephews: Alan, Betsy, Bruce, Carolyn, Janice, Sage, Salem, Seth, and Shannon; and cousins Peter and Marlene Henriques.

My beloved husband, Larry Henriques, has stood with me through six books, fifty years of deadline journalism, and a host of orthopedic adventures without ever losing his sunny and patient disposition or his abiding love for his often-distracted wife. I could not have begun this book, much less finished it, without his unfailing support. He also had the brilliant idea of adding to our lives a little joy-producing creature named Sparky, a Havanese puppy whose antics helped me get through the final footnotes and fact-checking. Bless you both!

Finally, I come to my cherished friend Jane Isay, to whom I dedicate this book. Her lucky friends call her "the book whisperer." As an extraordinary veteran editor, she has midwifed more brilliant books that I can count, while somehow finding time to write extraordinary books of her own. For me, she was the lighthouse that kept me on course through stormy setbacks, medical crises, pandemic isolation, discouragement, frustration, and self-doubt. She helped me get this book to port, always cheerfully reminding me to enjoy the journey. For that—and for all the laughter and richness she has added to my life during the years of our friendship—she has my gratitude and, always, my love.

NOTES

PREFACE

xi   **Above all, the era brought America:** Michael Parrish, *Anxious Decades: America in Prosperity and Depression, 1920–1941* (New York: W. W. Norton, 1992), 74–75; Robert S. McElvaine, *The Great Depression: America, 1929–1941,* 25th Anniversary Edition (New York: Three Rivers Press, 2009), 13.

xi   **For them, the Jazz Age:** McElvaine, *Great Depression,* xiii–xxxvi.

xii   **In the 1920s:** Ibid., 15–16.

xii   **I highly recommend:** Eric Rauchway, *Why the New Deal Matters* (New Haven: Yale University Press, 2021), 1–9.

xiv   **"At any given moment":** William E. Leuchtenburg, *The Perils of Prosperity, 1914–1932,* 2nd edition (Chicago: University of Chicago Press, 1993), 193.

xiv   **The prosperity that indisputably emerged:** George Soule, *The Prosperity Decade: From War to Depression, 1917–1929* (Armonk, N.Y.: M.E. Sharpe, 1947, renewed 1975; originally published by Holt, Rinehart and Winston as Volume 3 of *The Economic History of the United States*), 5, 96–99, 114–115, 279.

xiv   **"Cars reduced the demand":** Parrish, *Anxious Decades,* 91–92.

xiv   **"Wages, of course, remained depressed":** Ibid.

xiv   **"Returns to industry as a whole":** Harris Gaylord Warren, *Herbert Hoover and the Great Depression* (New York: W. W. Norton, 1967), 8; similar statistics are in Soule, *Prosperity Decade,* 317.

xiv   **By 1930, the richest 10 percent:** Thomas Piketty, *A Brief History of Equality* (Cambridge, Mass.: Belknap Press/Harvard University Press, 2022), 152–153.

xv   **If reckless lending had not produced:** Soule, *Prosperity Decade,* 278–279.

xv   **In April of 1929:** Parrish, *Anxious Decades,* 92.

xv   **The strikers were attacked:** The Gastonia strike and its aftermath were described in *The New York Times* in dozens of articles over more than two years, beginning with "Troops Guard Mill in North Carolina," April 4, 1929, 2.

xv   **For most industrial leaders:** Harvey O'Connor, *Mellon's Millions: The Biography of a Fortune; The Life and Times of Andrew W. Mellon* (New York: Blue Ribbon Books, 1933), 130–131.

xv   **the destruction of labor unions:** Warren, *Herbert Hoover and the Great Depression,* 14–15.

xvi   **In December 1920:** "Open Shop Here Bethlehem Aim, Grace Admits," *New York Times,* December 12, 1920, 1.

xvi   **Similar corporate-suite cartels:** Soule, *Prosperity Decade,* 145.

xvii   **One way he did that was:** Laton McCartney, *The Teapot Dome Scandal: How Big Oil Bought the Harding White House and Tried to Steal the Country* (New

York: Random House, 2008; Random House Trade Paperback Edition, 2009), 70–71.

xvii **In this case, Doheny and Sinclair:** McCartney's book gives the best in-depth account of all the side-swindles, brazen bribes, and courtroom scams that came to be known as the Teapot Dome scandal.

xvii **Fiercely opposed to organized labor:** O'Connor, *Mellon's Millions*, 187, 217–220.

xvii **In one instance, Harding's new appointees:** Soule, *Prosperity Decade*, 137–138.

xviii **Some of those bonds were used:** McCartney, *Teapot Dome Scandal*, 242–243; O'Connor, *Mellon's Millions*, 117, 266–267.

xviii **When the bond incident later became:** McCartney, *Teapot Dome Scandal*, 278–279; O'Connor, *Mellon's Millions*, 268–269.

xix **"Coolidge's tendency was to resist":** Soule, *Prosperity Decade*, 132.

xix **The budget at Hoover's Commerce Department:** Ibid.

xix **Adding to these benefits:** Parrish, *Anxious Decades*, 55.

xix **"Those on the political":** Ibid., 51.

xix **Parrish credits author and reformer:** Ibid., 66.

xx **One of Hoover's biographers summarized:** Warren, *Herbert Hoover and the Great Depression*, 6.

xx **Herbert Claiborne Pell:** Arthur M. Schlesinger Jr., *The Age of Roosevelt, Volume 1: The Crisis of the Old Order* (Boston: Mariner/Houghton Mifflin, 2002), 397.

CHAPTER ONE: A QUARTET FOR A CALAMITY

4 **For nearly fifteen years:** John Brooks, *Once in Golconda: A True Drama of Wall Street 1920–1938* (New York: Harper & Row, 1969), 113.

4 **When President Hoover had sought:** Ibid.

5 **"Brokers who have passed":** The Trader, "Stocks Toboggan at End in Hysteria of Selling," New York *Daily News*, October 24, 1929, 24.

5 **At the exact point:** Tom Shachtman, *The Day America Crashed: A Narrative Account of the Great Stock Market Crash of October 24, 1929* (New York: G. P. Putnam's Sons, 1979), 88–89. The NYSE trading hours in 1929 were from 10 A.M. to 3 P.M. on weekdays and from 10 A.M. to noon on Saturday. The Saturday session was dropped in 1952, the closing bell was set at 4 P.M. in 1974, and the opening bell was moved to 9:30 A.M. in 1985. See https://www.marketwatch.com/story/a-brief-history-of-trading-hours-on-wall-street-2015-05-29.

6 **George and Richard were:** Malcolm MacKay, *Impeccable Connections: The Rise and Fall of Richard Whitney* (New York: Brick Tower Press, 2013), 13–16, 18.

6 **Dick was his brother's best man:** "Country Wedding for Martha Bacon," *New York Times*, June 3, 1914, 13, was typical. Other accounts can be found in *The Boston Globe:* "Miss Bacon Married to G.W. Whitney," June 3, 1914, 18; and the Washington, D.C., *Evening Star:* "In the World of Society," June 3, 1914, 7.

6 **He had played football and baseball:** Harvard's victory over Yale was front-page news in both *The New York Times* and *The Boston Globe* on July 2, 1909.

7 **Years later, he could astound:** Brooks, *Once in Golconda*, 61; the list of his classmates is from Harvard class records.

7 **Like his brother, Dick relied:** MacKay, *Impeccable Connections*, 16.

7 **Sands's bereaved mother:** Special to *The New York Times*, "S. Stevens Sands Killed under Auto," *New York Times*, July 3, 1913, 1.

7 **Mrs. Vanderbilt sat with her young:** "Mrs. Sands, Bride of Richard Whitney," *New York Times*, May 28, 1916, 17.

7 **By 1920, he was a member:** William A. Schleicher and Susan J. Winter, *In the Somerset Hills: The Landed Gentry* (Charleston, S.C.: Arcadia Publishing, 1997), 100, 108.

7   **In May 1919:** "Election on Exchanges," *New York Times,* May 13, 1919, 26.

8   **In 1928, that golden year:** "Whitney Elected Exchange Vice President," *Wall Street Journal,* May 16, 1928, 8.

9   **Earlier in 1929:** Gordon Thomas and Max Morgan-Witts, *The Day the Bubble Burst: A Short History of the Wall Street Crash* (London: Hamish Hamilton, 1979), 104–106, 114–116, 156, 209–210.

9   **One wealthy speculator:** Special to *The New York Times,* "Raskob Radio Pool Realized $5,000,000," *New York Times,* May 20, 1932, 1; "Named in Chrysler Pool," *New York Times,* May 20, 1932, 15.

9   **In one case:** Brooks, *Once in Golconda,* 144.

10   **Bogus stock trades were done:** All of these abuses were documented in the course of the Senate Banking Committee hearings of 1932–1934, known as the Pecora hearings, and detailed in Donald A. Ritchie, *The U.S. Congress: A Very Short Introduction* (Oxford: Oxford University Press, 2010), hereafter Ritchie, *Congress,* 173–260.

10   **Now, as the clanging:** Barry Eichengreen, *Hall of Mirrors: The Great Depression, the Great Recession, and the Uses—and Misuses—of History* (Oxford/New York: Oxford University Press, 2015), 106.

11   **By 11:30 AM:** These details of stock movements and activities on the floor are drawn from newspaper coverage of the events, primarily in *The New York Times,* the New York *Daily News,* and other large metropolitan newspapers.

11   **Amid this turmoil:** Brooks, *Once in Golconda,* 124–125.

11   **The bankers pledged some undisclosed amount:** Frederick Lewis Allen, *Only Yesterday: An Informal History of the 1920s* (New York: Perennial Library, 1964; originally published by Harper & Brothers, 1931), 273–275.

12   **The day still ended with:** Brooks, *Once in Golconda,* 125.

12   **"There has been a little distress":** "Financiers Ease Tension; Five Wall Street Bankers Hold Two Meetings at Morgan Office," *New York Times,* October 25, 1929, 1, 3.

12   **An image emerged:** Brooks, *Once in Golconda,* 125.

13   **The story of Whitney's glorious march:** Ibid., 286.

13   **He was applauded within the exchange:** Ibid., 124.

13   **"All that he did henceforth":** Matthew Josephson, "'Dick' Whitney Halted a Panic; Must Fight On," *Minneapolis Tribune,* April 14, 1932, 1.

13   **The action, taken without the approval:** Eichengreen, *Hall of Mirrors,* 114.

14   **At his direction, board members slipped:** John Kenneth Galbraith, *The Great Crash, 1929* (Boston: Houghton Mifflin, 1988; original copyright 1954), 113.

14   **The long narrow room:** Ibid., 117–118, crediting the details to Whitney's address to the Boston Association of Stock Exchange Firms on June 10, 1930.

15   **As the board members started filing:** Brooks, *Once in Golconda,* 128.

15   **One journalist later noted:** Josephson, "'Dick' Whitney."

15   **On Black Tuesday alone:** Thomas and Morgan-Witts, *Day the Bubble Burst,* 384.

15   **Normally, the tickers fell silent:** Brooks, *Once in Golconda,* 127.

16   **"Lives were disintegrating":** Ibid.

16   **Several of Kennedy's personal aides:** Mordaunt Hall, "The Screen: Miss Swanson's First Talker," *New York Times,* November 2, 1929, 14; Nancy Randolph, "Social Lion Grins at Wife's Tag," New York *Daily News,* November 2, 1929, 9; Cari Beauchamp, *Joseph P. Kennedy Presents: His Hollywood Years* (New York: Knopf, 2009), 281–282.

16   **They had been lovers:** David Nasaw, *The Patriarch: The Remarkable Life and Turbulent Times of Joseph P. Kennedy* (New York: Penguin Books, 2013; originally published by Penguin Press, 2012), hereafter Nasaw, *Patriarch,* 115–118, 137, 145–148. Axel Madsen, *Gloria and Joe: The Star-Crossed Love Affair of Gloria Swanson and Joe Kennedy* (New York: Open Road Distribution, 2015; original copyright 1988),

206, 213–214, 289–290. Doris Kearns Goodwin, *The Fitzgeralds and the Kennedys* (New York: Simon & Schuster, 1987), 391–397.

17   **Barely a month earlier:** Stuart Rogers, "Rome Is Being Built in a Day," New York *Daily News,* September 19, 1929, 5.

17   **Joe Kennedy had no interest:** Nasaw, *Patriarch,* 134–135.

18   **Boston's anti-Catholic bias:** Goodwin, *Fitzgeralds,* 213–215, quotes Rose Kennedy as saying that Kennedy, unlike Rose herself, was unable to accept "the social divisions at Harvard . . . as elementary facts of life not worth worrying about." As a result, he was deeply hurt and resentful when he was not invited to join any of the final clubs on campus, which accepted few Catholics and almost no Jews.

18   **The Catholic wedding service:** "Ex-Mayor Fitzgerald's Daughter Rose Marries Joseph P. Kennedy," *Boston Globe,* October 7, 1914, 1.

18   **In steady succession:** These nearly annual deliveries stopped with Jean's birth, presumably because of Kennedy's affair with Gloria Swanson. Edward Moore Kennedy, the ninth and last Kennedy child, was not born until 1932, nearly two years after the affair had cooled.

18   **He had made sure:** Nasaw, *Patriarch,* 55–57.

19   **Roosevelt's own papers:** Ibid., 55, discredits this tale entirely. The earliest reference to it is in a *New York Herald Tribune* article on May 9, 1932; it is repeated in a *Boston Sunday Globe* profile by James Wright on September 25, 1932, and, years later, in a *Liberty* magazine article by Ernest Lindley on May 21, 1938. Those sources, which all attributed the tale only to Kennedy himself, were cited in Goodwin, *Fitzgeralds,* 428; Richard J. Whalen, *The Founding Father: The Story of Joseph P. Kennedy* (New York: New American Library of World Literature, 1964); and Joe McCarthy, *The Remarkable Kennedys: The Dramatic Inside Story of John Fitzgerald Kennedy and His Remarkable Family* (New York: Popular Library, August 1960; originally by The Dial Press, February 1960). Michael Beschloss, in *Kennedy and Roosevelt: The Uneasy Alliance* (New York: Perennial Library, 1987), included the tale but his source notes show he doubted its veracity.

19   **"It is easy to make money":** Michael Perino, *The Hellhound of Wall Street: How Ferdinand Pecora's Investigation of the Great Crash Forever Changed American Finance* (New York: Penguin Books, 2011), 199.

19   **He had liquidated:** Goodwin, *Fitzgeralds,* 420–421; Nasaw, *Patriarch,* 155.

20   **Swanson "could talk":** Beauchamp, *Joseph P. Kennedy,* 277.

22   **Roosevelt was the guest of honor:** "Roosevelt Demands End of 'Red Tape' in the Law, Warns of 'Justice for Rich,'" *New York Times,* November 9, 1929, 1–2.

23   **Indeed, he had been getting:** "J.J. Riordan Ends Life with Pistol in His Home; His Bank Declared Sound," *New York Times,* November 11, 1929, 1.

24   **Despite misgivings, the city official agreed:** Frank Dolan, "Riordan a Market Suicide," New York *Daily News,* November 10, 1929, 2. Smith later claimed he had not asked the medical examiner to delay the announcement, but the official stood by his story.

25   **The wedges of ripe melon:** A photograph in the New York *Daily News* on November 10, 1929, showed the luncheon table, with the melon wedges in place, just before the Riordan suicide was announced.

25   **Fellow students at the Groton prep:** Joseph Alsop, *FDR, 1882–1945* (New York: Gramercy Books, 1982), 37–38. Alsop noted that the widowed Sara Roosevelt's decision to move to Boston to be near FDR at Harvard was "just as astonishing at that time as it would be today," and evidence of how far she "was capable of carrying this possessiveness."

25   **He struck them as a little:** James McGregor Burns, *Roosevelt, 1882–1940: The Lion and the Fox* (New York: Harcourt Brace, 1984), 13–14, 17–19; Alsop, *FDR, 1882–1945,*

35–36. Alsop's mother knew FDR in his young bachelor years, and likened him to the handsome young fops depicted on special boxes of handkerchiefs—he was, she said, "handkerchief-boxy."

25 **Those who knew him:** James Tobin, *The Man He Became: How FDR Defied Polio to Win the Presidency* (New York: Simon & Schuster, 2013), 17–18.

25 **To them, one biographer noted:** Terry Golway, *Frank and Al: FDR, Al Smith, and the Unlikely Alliance That Created the Modern Democratic Party* (New York: St. Martin's Press, 2018), 34; Arthur M. Schlesinger Jr., *The Age of Roosevelt, Volume 1: The Crisis of the Old Order* (Boston: Mariner/Houghton Mifflin, 2002), hereafter Schlesinger, Volume 1, 330–331.

25 **Bearing what one early biographer called:** Golway, *Frank and Al,* 34, 40.

25 **He was an engaging campaigner:** Tobin, *Man He Became,* 19; Golway, *Frank and Al,* 53.

26 **"He was like a hothouse plant":** Robert H. Jackson, *That Man: An Insider's Portrait of Franklin D. Roosevelt* (Oxford: Oxford University Press, 2003), 3. "My recollection is of charm more than of strength, of urbanity more than of force, and of idealism more than of practicality," wrote Jackson, who met FDR in 1912 and went on to serve him in the White House before being named to the Supreme Court in 1941; he later helped set up and served on the international tribunal for Nazi war criminals known as the Nuremberg trials.

26 **Within days, this robust father of five:** Tobin provides a complete chronicle of the early stages of FDR's illness, *Man He Became,* 45–51, and Eleanor's faithful care for him at this point, at 52–69.

26 **Only that long-nurtured dream:** Davis W. Houck and Amos Kiewe, *FDR's Body Politics: The Rhetoric of Disability* (College Station: Texas A&M University Press, 2003), 16–17, 22–23. Houck and Kiewe cite studies that showed that those crippled by polio suffered a deeper degree of contempt, as the disease was associated with slums and filth and was believed to infect both body and mind. They quote Hugh G. Gallagher, author of *FDR's Splendid Deception: The Moving Story of Roosevelt's Massive Disability—and the Intense Efforts to Conceal It from the Public* (New York: Vandemere Press, 1999), noting that in the 1920s, "to be handicapped in some visible way [for any reason] carried with it social opprobrium." Some scholars now dispute the idea that FDR fully concealed his paralysis from the public, and my own study of newspaper archives supports that skepticism.

27 **If his public personality seemed:** Schlesinger, Volume 1, 405–406.

27 **It was true, Roosevelt said:** FDR, "Democratic State Convention Keynote Speech," September 27, 1926, 17. All FDR's speeches are available online, listed chronologically, via the FDR Library at: http://www.fdrlibrary.marist.edu/archives/collections /franklin/index.php?p=collections/findingaid&id=582. In this archive, this is File No. 251.

27 **At the 1928 Democratic National Convention:** FDR, "Placing Alfred E. Smith in Nomination," June 27, 1928, 5. File No. 258, FDR Library online archives.

27 **By now, his leg braces were:** Ernest Lindley, *Franklin D. Roosevelt: A Career in Progressive Democracy* (New York: Blue Ribbon Books, 1931), 13.

28 **There were pundits:** Jonathan Alter, *The Defining Moment: FDR's Hundred Days and the Triumph of Hope* (New York: Simon & Schuster, 2006), 80–82.

28 **Both were economic conservatives:** Charles Rappleye, *Herbert Hoover in the White House: The Ordeal of the Presidency* (New York: Simon & Schuster Paperbacks, 2017), 40.

28 **But to have a prayer:** Lindley, *Franklin D. Roosevelt,* 12–13; Robert A. Caro, *The Power Broker: Robert Moses and the Fall of New York* (New York: Vintage Books/ Random House, 1975), 283.

29 **If anyone could remember that:** Kenneth S. Davis, *FDR: The New York Years, 1928–1933* (New York: Random House, 1994), hereafter Davis, Volume 2, 39.

29 **But in the wee hours:** Ibid., 47.

29 **He condemned the glorified selfishness:** FDR, "Inaugural Address," January 1, 1929, 1–2. File No. 300, FDR Library online archives.

30 **When the new governor finally could:** Special to *The New York Times*, "Smith Helps Press to Interview Roosevelt; Confines His Questions to Office Fittings," *New York Times*, March 12, 1929, 10.

30 **Although Roosevelt retained most:** Caro, *Power Broker*, 296.

30 **It went deeper than that:** Ibid., 292.

31 **The City Trust collapse was followed:** "Clarkes Indicted in Federal Inquiry; Face State Charges," *New York Times*, July 11, 1929, 1.

31 **It called for tighter regulation:** "Moses Reports on City Trust Failure, Calls Warder a 'Faithless Official'; He Wants Private Banks Abolished," *New York Times*, July 11, 1929, 1.

31 **Roosevelt praised the prescient report:** Davis, Volume 2, 129, 223–224.

31 **Or perhaps, as one biographer suggested:** Ibid.

31 **At least one state GOP luminary:** Special to *The New York Times*, "Scores Smith on City Trust," *New York Times*, July 22, 1929, 3.

32 **Instead, Jimmy Riordan's friends lined up:** Frank Dolan, "Riordan Bank Ready, but Has No Run," New York *Daily News*, November 12, 1929, 6.

32 **"Probably all of us have":** Melvin I. Urofsky, ed., *The Douglas Letters: Selections from the Private Papers of Justice William O. Douglas* (Bethesda, Md.: Adler & Adler, 1987), hereafter *The Douglas Letters*, 9–10.

33 **After all, Douglas reasoned:** Douglas recounted his arguments to the judge in a letter the next day, December 7, 1929, to Wilbur Clayton Plummer, a professor at the University of Pennsylvania. *The Douglas Letters*, 9–10.

33 **"The notion that law was":** Noah Feldman, *Scorpions: The Battles and Triumphs of FDR's Great Supreme Court Justices* (New York: Twelve/Hachette Book Group, 2011), 63.

33 **As Hutchins saw it:** James F. Simon, *Independent Journey: The Life of William O. Douglas* (New York: Harper & Row, 1980), 101.

33 **After hearing the dean:** William O. Douglas, *Go East, Young Man: The Early Years; The Autobiography of William O. Douglas* (New York: Random House, 1974), hereafter Douglas, *Go East, Young Man*, 160–161; Simon, *Independent Journey*, 101.

34 **As a young associate at Cravath:** Bruce Allen Murphy, *Wild Bill: The Legend and Life of William O. Douglas* (New York: Random House, 2003), 59; Simon, *Independent Journey*, 83–86.

34 **As he wrote decades later:** Douglas, *Go East, Young Man*, 163.

34 **As one biographer put it:** Simon, *Independent Journey*, 103.

34 **Douglas wanted to learn everything:** Douglas's bankruptcy project is described in several Douglas biographies, most extensively in Murphy, *Wild Bill*, 88–91, and Simon, *Independent Journey*, 108–109. Douglas himself describes it briefly in Douglas, *Go East, Young Man*, at page 172, and more fully in "Equity Receiverships in the United States District Court for Connecticut: 1920–1929" (with John H. Weir), *4 Connecticut Bar Journal 1* (1930). It also was reported in many national newspapers. See: "Bankruptcy Study at Yale Is Enlarged," *Hartford Courant*, November 11, 1929; Special to the *Eagle*, "Research in Bankruptcy Field Is Completed," *Brooklyn Daily Eagle*, January 6, 1930, 36; "Study Business Conduct to Avert Failures," *Burlington Free Press*, January 8, 1930, 7; "Why Men Go Broke," *Boston Globe*, April 29, 1930, 18; and E. Pickard Karsten, "The Small Bankrupt," *Minneapolis Tribune*, May 2, 1930, 14.

35   **Courts had handled more than:** Karsten, "Small Bankrupt"; "Wide Reform Urged in Bankruptcy Law," *New York Times,* March 23, 1930, 1.

35   **As that pitiless process ground forward:** Christopher Knowlton, *Bubble in the Sun: The Florida Boom of the 1920s and How It Brought on the Great Depression* (New York: Simon & Schuster Paperbacks, 2020), xvi–xvii.

35   **As his reputation grew:** In a letter to Hoover's Commerce secretary, Robert P. Lamont, on May 21, 1930, Douglas thanked the department for its "great interest in the study of the causes of business failure" and for its "invaluable" cooperation in the past. He also assured Lamont the expanding study would "become more national in scope and importance." *The Douglas Letters,* 11–12.

36   **A high school valedictorian:** These details are broadly repeated in Douglas, *Go East, Young Man,* and in Murphy, *Wild Bill,* 3–42; Simon, *Independent Journey,* 18–36; Feldman, *Scorpions,* 60–62; and Edwin P. Hoyt, *William O. Douglas* (Middlebury, Vt.: Paul S. Eriksson, 1979), 3–21. Hoyt had known Douglas since Hoyt's boyhood and admired his pioneering environmental protectionism.

36   **Douglas was tempted to follow:** Douglas, *Go East, Young Man,* 163.

36   **"It never occurred to us":** Simon, *Independent Journey,* 103–104.

37   **In January 1929:** The details of this sprawling scandal are drawn from coverage in *The New York Times* and the New York *Daily News.* The most helpful are: "Steinhardt's Aide Attempts Suicide," *New York Times,* January 10, 1929; "Grand Jury to Hunt 'Ring' in Bankruptcy Looting; Tuttle Asks City Bar's Aid," *New York Times,* January 12, 1929; "Bankruptcy Reform Long Sought by Bar," *New York Times,* January 15, 1929; George H. Copeland, "Bankruptcy Reforms Started by Scandal," *New York Times,* January 20, 1929; "Court Will Delve into Bankruptcies," *New York Times,* March 8, 1929; Arthur O'Sullivan, "Pinner Tells of Gratuities to Winslow," New York *Daily News,* September 7, 1929; Arthur O'Sullivan, "Fake Burglaries in Bankruptcies Revealed," New York *Daily News,* September 8, 1929.

38   **Indeed, within a few months:** Murphy, *Wild Bill,* 90.

39   **"He picked a hot topic":** Ibid., 91.

CHAPTER TWO: DESCENDING INTO SILENCE

42   **Then, just after the closing bell:** "Topics in Wall Street," *New York Times,* January 1, 1930, 49.

42   **Over the next few weeks:** Barrie A. Wigmore, *The Crash and Its Aftermath: A History of Securities Markets in the United States, 1929–1933* (Westport, Conn.: Greenwood Press, 1985), 24.

42   **Finally, on November 14:** Ibid., 25.

43   **On October 29, a Kansas City:** Associated Press, "Falls Dead at Ticker as Stocks Decline; Providence Merchant Worried over His Holdings—Kansas City Man Shoots Himself," *New York Times,* October 30, 1929, 3.

43   **The next day, a New York:** Special to *The New York Times,* "Merchant's Suicide Laid to Stock Losses; Notes Calling for More Margin in Pocket of Julius Umbach, Found in Hudson River," *New York Times,* October 31, 1929, 4.

43   **One was an obscure cigar maker:** "Ends Life after Stock Losses," *New York Times,* November 13, 1929, 2.

43   **A prominent utility president:** Special to *The New York Times,* "Commits Suicide over Stock Losses," *New York Times,* November 14, 1929, 2.

43   **On November 16, a distraught wholesale:** "G.E. Cutler Dies in Wall St. Leap," *New York Times,* November 17, 1929, 2.

43   **The same day, an engineer:** Associated Press, "Motiska Sets His Clothes Afire and Dies from Burns," *Scranton Times-Tribune,* November 16, 1929, 1; "Suicide's Wife

Also Dies; Burned as Scranton (Pa.) Market Loser Sets Himself Afire," *New York Times,* November 18, 1929, 3.

43   **On November 23, a broker:** "Broker Betts Took Poison out of Pride, Witness Says," *St. Louis Post-Dispatch,* November 25, 1929, 1; Special to *The New York Times,* "St. Louis Broker Suicide over Crash," *New York Times,* November 24, 1929, 15.

43   **On December 11, a ruined investor:** "Loses $30,000, Ends Life," *New York Times,* December 12, 1929, 39.

43   **On Christmas Day, an unemployed broker:** "Ends Life to Leave Insurance to Estate," *New York Times,* December 26, 1929, 17.

43   **Two days later, a prominent Baltimore:** "Sewell Watts, Banker, Commits Suicide; Partner Lays Deed to Nervous Disorder," *Baltimore Sun,* December 27, 1929, 1.

43   **Little is known about the life:** Associated Press, "Suicide's 'Sympathy' Willed to Creditors," *New York Times,* December 8, 1929, 18.

44   **Since relatively few Americans owned:** Davis, Volume 2, 152–153.

44   **As one history of daily life:** David E. Kyvig, *Daily Life in the United States, 1920–1940* (Chicago: Ivan R. Dee, 2004), 211.

45   **Farmers, miners, lumbermen, and factory workers:** Maury Klein, *Rainbow's End: The Crash of 1929* (Oxford: Oxford University Press, 2001), 84–85.

45   **Middle-class families:** Eric Rauchway, *The Great Depression and the New Deal: A Very Short Introduction* (Oxford: Oxford University Press, 2008), 13.

45   **By 1929, the richest 10 percent:** Thomas Piketty, *Capital in the Twenty-First Century* (Cambridge, Mass.: Belknap Press/Harvard University Press, 2014), 292–293; Gabriel Zucman, "Global Wealth Inequality," National Bureau of Economic Research, Cambridge, Mass., Working Paper No. 25462, 2019, 14. Zucman notes that the share of wealth owned by the top one-tenth of 1 percent rose sharply to a peak of 25 percent in 1929; it declined from the 1930s until the 1970s. In the 1980s, it began to climb again, rising to about 20 percent in recent years, on a par with the mid-1920s.

45   **One newspaper editorial:** Unsigned editorial, "A Few 'Prosperity' Facts," *Oklahoma Weekly Leader,* January 4, 1929, 3. In the newspapers.com online archives, the paper is archived as the *American Guardian,* but the masthead on this 1929 issue is as shown.

45   **Those suddenly jobless workers:** Davis, Volume 2, 153.

45   **Yes, people were still ordering milk:** Barry Eichengreen, *Hall of Mirrors: The Great Depression, the Great Recession, and the Uses—and Misuses—of History* (Oxford/New York: Oxford University Press, 2015), 108.

46   **If the boom faltered, he warned:** Special to *The New York Times,* "Work and Moses Reply to Gov. Smith; Deny His Charges," *New York Times,* September 22, 1928, 1; "Smith Charge False, Declares Dr Work," *Boston Globe,* September 22, 1928, 1; Charles Rappleye, *Herbert Hoover in the White House: The Ordeal of the Presidency* (New York: Simon & Schuster Paperbacks, 2017), 42.

46   **At first, President Hoover seemed:** Wigmore, *Crash,* 114.

46   **Hoover's effort fell far short:** Ibid.

46   **He met secretly with Hoover:** Ibid., 116.

46   **We don't know what advice Whitney:** Richard L. Stokes, "Reconstruction of the Crimes of Richard Whitney," *St. Louis Post-Dispatch,* March 27, 1938, 15, 17, quoting a Whitney speech on November 23, 1933.

46   **Banks that had speculated widely:** Wigmore, *Crash,* 121.

46   **Farm prices were falling:** Ibid., 133.

47   **But by spring, Kennedy's restless gaze:** Nasaw, *Patriarch,* 158–159.

47   **Private utilities "must never be":** M. L. Ramsay, *Pyramids of Power: The Story of Roosevelt, Insull and the Utility Wars* (Indianapolis: Bobbs-Merrill Company, 1937), 315.

48 **He intended to be among them:** Doris Kearns Goodwin, *The Fitzgeralds and the Kennedys* (New York: Simon & Schuster, 1987), 427–428.

48 **"I knew that big, drastic changes":** Ibid., 428.

48 **According to his wife Rose's memories:** Michael Beschloss, *Kennedy and Roosevelt: The Uneasy Alliance* (New York: Perennial Library, 1987), 68.

49 **"You're not hearing much about him":** Ibid., 66; Richard J. Whalen, *The Founding Father: The Story of Joseph P. Kennedy* (New York: New American Library of World Literature, 1964), 113; Ronald Kessler, *The Sins of the Father: Joseph P. Kennedy and the Dynasty He Founded* (New York: Warner Books, 1996), 94.

49 **When he got back to his:** Beschloss, *Kennedy*, 69.

49 **As one biographer would later note:** Jonathan Alter, *The Defining Moment: FDR's Hundred Days and the Triumph of Hope* (New York: Simon & Schuster, 2006), 7.

49 **And leftist political organizations were:** Schlesinger, Volume 1, 219–221.

50 **In the spring of 1930:** "Red Riots in Many Cities in America and Europe," *New York Times*, March 7, 1930, 1.

50 **"There probably had never been":** T. H. Watkins, *The Great Depression: America in the 1930s* (Boston: Little, Brown, 1993), 81.

50 **By 1932, thousands of protestors:** Alter, *Defining Moment*, 4.

50 **Grocery stores would be looted:** Watkins, *Great Depression*, 80.

50 **Milo Reno argued:** Milo Reno, President of the National Farmers' Holiday Association, "Farm Holiday Held Old Corn Belt Plan," *New York Times*, August 26, 1932, 6.

51 **From a stream of laudatory American:** Ronald Steel, *Walter Lippmann and the American Century* (Boston: Little, Brown, 1980), 251.

51 **The Morgan managing partner:** For the best analysis of Tom Lamont's embrace of Mussolini, see Edward M. Lamont, *The Ambassador from Wall Street: The Story of Thomas W. Lamont, J.P. Morgan's Chief Executive,* (Lanham, Md.: Madison Books, 1994), 222–224; the author, Lamont's grandson, is kind but candid. See also, for Lamont's tireless effort to soften his friend Walter Lippmann's hostility toward the fascist regime: Steel, *Walter Lippmann,* 251–252.

51 **As early as the mid-1920s:** Charles Higham, *Trading with the Enemy: The Nazi-American Money Plot, 1933–1949* (New York: Barnes & Noble, 1983), 154–155.

51 **Some of America's intellectual fascists:** Arthur M. Schlesinger Jr., *The Age of Roosevelt, Volume 3: The Politics of Upheaval, 1933–1936* (Boston: Mariner/Houghton Mifflin, 2003), hereafter Schlesinger, Volume 3, 70–71, 86–87.

51 **Dennis, who would soon publish:** Ibid., 75.

52 **In contrast to the radical fascist:** Arthur M. Schlesinger Jr., *The Age of Roosevelt, Volume 2: The Coming of the New Deal,* (Boston: Mariner/Houghton Mifflin, 2003), hereafter Schlesinger, Volume 2, 22.

52 **It was a time, Joe Kennedy:** Joseph P. Kennedy, *I'm for Roosevelt* (New York: Reynal & Hitchcock, 1936), 3.

52 **This was "not the easy way":** Herbert Hoover, "Lincoln Day Address," February 12, 1932, in online archives: https://www.presidency.ucsb.edu/documents/radio-address-lincolns-birthday-0.

52 **He once claimed that:** Schlesinger, Volume 1, 241–243.

55 **As early as 1925, he chastised:** Rappleye, *Herbert Hoover,* 48–49.

56 **Few corporations dared to sell:** Wigmore, *Crash,* 143–144.

56 **When Whitney stepped down:** "Business: Stockmarket & Sisto," *Time,* October 13, 1930, online at: https://content.time.com/time/subscriber/article/0,33009,740533,00.html.

57 **But on this Friday, Wall Street:** "Six Indicted in $3,500,000 Loss in Stocks," *Brooklyn Daily Eagle,* October 3, 1930, 1; "Indict 6 for Fraud in Stock Pool Deal," *New York Times*, October 4, 1930, 18.

57   **Prince & Whitely's collapse was front-page news:** "Stock Prices Break; Big Firm Suspended," *New York Times,* October 10, 1930, 1; "Topics in Wall Street," *New York Times,* October 10, 1930, 31.

58   **The cooked books also showed:** "Asks Prosecution of 9 in Stock Firm," *New York Times,* November 2, 1930, 14,

58   **Seabury cited the Prince & Whitely:** "Text of the Seabury Report Recommending Dismissal of the Crain Charges," *New York Times,* September 1, 1931, 14–16.

59   **FDR carried many upstate precincts:** Davis, Volume 2, 189–190.

59   **"I do not see how Mr. Roosevelt":** Ibid., 198.

60   **President Taft's solicitor general:** Matthew P. Fink, *The Unlikely Reformer: Carter Glass and Financial Regulation* (Fairfax, Va.: George Mason University Press, 2019), 75–76, 95.

61   **But banks simply ignored:** Michael Perino, *The Hellhound of Wall Street: How Ferdinand Pecora's Investigation of the Great Crash Forever Changed American Finance* (New York: Penguin Books, 2011), 205–207; Davis, Volume 2, 441.

61   **In 1927, Congress ratified reality:** George G. Kaufman and Larry R. Mote, "Commercial Bank Securities Activities: What Really Happened in 1902," *Journal of Money, Credit and Banking* vol. 24, no. 3 (August 1992), published by The Ohio State University Press, 370–374.

61   **This ignored an inconvenient legal reality:** Wigmore, *Crash,* 125.

61   **Depositors who became shareholders:** Eugene N. White, "Lessons from the Great American Real Estate Boom and Bust of the 1920s," Working Paper No. 15573, the National Bureau of Economic Research, December 2009, 26; and Gary Richardson and Kris James Mitchener, "Does 'Skin in the Game' Reduce Risk Taking? Leverage, Liability and the Long-Run Consequences of New Deal Banking Reforms," National Bureau of Economic Research, Working Paper No. 18895, March 2013, 3–6.

61   **One historian called him:** Allan Nevins, *Herbert H. Lehman and His Era* (New York: Charles Scribner's Sons, 1963), 136. Further details of his career are on the Federal Reserve website; for a casual profile, see Alissa Keir, "Snapshots," New York *Daily News,* October 22, 1931, 43.

62   **His duty, as he saw:** "Laxity Laid to Broderick as He Admits Bank of U.S. Made 'Dishonest' Deals," *New York Times,* March 4, 1931, 1.

62   **By September 1929:** Details of Broderick's dealings with the Bank of United States are from his trial testimony, recounted in *The New York Times* from May 11, 1932, until his acquittal on May 28, 1932. See also R. L. Duffus, "Trial of Broderick Reveals Tense Drama of Bank Failure," June 5, 1932, 152; and Nevins, *Herbert H. Lehman,* 118–119.

62   **Their final conclusion was shocking:** Scholars and economists would later debate whether the bank was illiquid but actually solvent, and thus capable of being rescued, or hopelessly insolvent. For the former, see Anthony Patrick O'Brien and Paul B. Trescott, "The Failure of the Bank of United States, 1930: Note," *Journal of Money, Banking and Credit* vol. 24, no. 3 (August 1992), published by The Ohio State University Press, 384–399. For the latter, see Elmus Wicker, *The Banking Panics of the Great Depression* (Cambridge, U.K.: Cambridge University Press, 1996), 55–56. For the best analysis of why banks in general failed in this period, see Gary Richardson, "The Collapse of the United States Banking System During the Great Depression, 1929–1933, New Archival Evidence," *The Australian Accounting Business and Finance Journal* vol. 1, no. 1 (February 2007), 39–50.

63   **The bank's executives had managed:** "False Rumor Leads to Trouble at Bank," *New York Times,* December 11, 1930, 5.

64   **"More banks failed in this country":** "Bank Failures Set High Records in 1930, Totaling 934, with $908,157,788 Liabilities," *New York Times,* January 11, 1931, 45.

64 **Federal Reserve records show:** Wicker, *Banking Panics,* table on page 26.

65 **Some state bank overseers:** White, "Lessons," 32.

65 **But for Franklin Roosevelt, the collapse:** Davis, Volume 2, 226.

65 **FDR had believed those steps:** Bernard Bellush, *Franklin D. Roosevelt as Governor of New York* (New York: Columbia University Press, 1955), 114.

65 **The failure fueled:** Davis, Volume 2, 226.

65 **So far, he said:** Ibid.

65 **The New York regulator's views:** Fink, *Unlikely Reformer,* 79–80, 82, 86, 89–90. Fink concluded that Broderick's testimony was "perhaps the most important" given during the hearings that ultimately produced the Glass-Steagall Act adopted in the New Deal, because "separation was no longer a theoretical idea, but now was incorporated in proposed statutory language in the most important financial state in the nation."

65 **Broderick was still being politically attacked:** Clinton L. Mosher, "Broderick Fate Political Crisis for Governor," *Brooklyn Daily Eagle,* October 20, 1931, 1.

66 **The statehouse reporter:** "Governor Backing Broderick to Limit," *New York Times,* October 20, 1931, 4.

66 **By winnowing out the worst banks:** Gary Richardson and Patrick Van Horn, "In the Eye of a Storm: Manhattan's Money Center Banks During the International Financial Crisis of 1931," National Bureau of Economic Research, Working Paper No. 17437, July 2017.

67 **Andrew Mellon's family controlled every bank:** Harvey O'Connor, *Mellon's Millions: The Biography of a Fortune; The Life and Times of Andrew W. Mellon* (New York: Blue Ribbon Books, 1933), 342–344.

67 **Hoover was aghast:** Rappleye, *Herbert Hoover,* 278–279.

67 **Europeans began to pull gold out:** Wigmore, *Crash,* 219.

67 **The number of bank failures skyrocketed:** Wicker, *Banking Panics,* 73–74, 77.

67 **The bankers, who included Tom Lamont:** Rappleye, *Herbert Hoover,* 284–285.

68 **Despite his initial opposition:** Gerald D. Nash, "Herbert Hoover and the Origins of the Reconstruction Finance Corporation," *The Mississippi Valley Historical Review* vol. 46, no. 3 (December 1959), 455–468.

68 **Venerable firms had failed:** Wigmore, *Crash,* 237.

68 **With the rise of more complex:** Michael Parrish, *Securities Regulation and the New Deal* (New Haven: Yale University Press, 1970), 33, 39.

69 **The mood was jittery:** John Brooks, *Once in Golconda: A True Drama of Wall Street 1920–1938* (New York: Harper & Row, 1969), 132.

69 **He got the board's approval:** "Stocks Here Rally after Violent Drop," *New York Times,* September 22, 1931, 1.

69 **"Other exchanges were completely disrupted":** Ibid.

70 **In January and February 1932:** Perino, *Hellhound,* 16–18.

70 **Whitney never spoke publicly:** Malcolm MacKay, *Impeccable Connections: The Rise and Fall of Richard Whitney* (New York: Brick Tower Press, 2013), 52.

70 **At the second meeting:** Perino, *Hellhound,* 17.

70 **Every argument boiled down to:** Ibid.

71 **"If you were to be nominated":** Samuel I. Rosenman, *Working with Roosevelt* (New York: Harper & Brothers, 1952), 56–59.

72 **Rosenman promptly recruited Raymond Moley:** Schlesinger, Volume 1, 399.

72 **Well organized, shrewd, pragmatic:** Davis, Volume 2, 265–266.

72 **Moley sat down in March:** Raymond Moley, *After Seven Years* (New York: Harper & Brothers, 1939), 13–14.

72 **The list started with:** Ibid., 15.

73 **Berle had entered Harvard:** Jordan A. Schwarz, *Liberal: Adolf A. Berle and the Vision of an American Era* (New York: The Free Press, 1987), 13.

73 **Within months of joining the brain:** Ibid., viii.

73 **But Moley, Tugwell, Berle, Rosenman:** Schlesinger, Volume 1, 399.

73 **They would develop speeches on everything:** William E. Leuchtenburg, *Franklin D. Roosevelt and the New Deal, 1932–1940* (New York: Harper Perennial, 2009, original copyright 1963), hereafter Leuchtenburg, *FDR and the New Deal*, 32–35.

73 **They were waiting for him:** Special Cable to *The New York Times*, "Ivar Kreuger a Suicide; His Stocks Heavily Sold; Sweden to Protect Trust," *New York Times*, March 13, 1932, 1.

74 **But someone in the know was:** Frank Partnoy, *The Match King: Ivar Kreuger, the Financial Genius Behind a Century of Wall Street Scandals* (New York: Public Affairs, 2009), 199.

74 **Within two weeks, auditors:** Ibid., 203–204.

74 **The verdict was premature:** Ibid., 208.

74 **As one Kreuger biographer would note:** Ibid., 213.

74 **His collapse soon brought down:** Ibid., 207.

74 **In 1932, just eight vast holding:** John F. Wasik, *The Merchant of Power: Sam Insull, Thomas Edison, and the Creation of the Modern Metropolis* (New York: Palgrave Macmillan, 2006), 232.

75 **Roosevelt called out as the reporters:** "Roosevelt Here; for Repeal," *Minneapolis Daily Star*, April 18, 1932, 1, 9.

75 **The ovation for Roosevelt was deafening:** Leif H. Gilstad, "Tariff and Power Regulation Keystone Issue of Roosevelt," *Minneapolis Journal*, April 19, 1932, 1, 14.

76 **The problem of generating and distributing:** "Text of Governor's Appeal for National 'Concert of Interests,'" *New York Times*, April 19, 1932, 16.

76 **"Let us suppose Mr. Whitney":** "La Guardia Charges Pools Paid Writers to 'Ballyhoo' Stocks," *New York Times*, April 27, 1932, 1, 10.

76 **His pool profited handsomely:** Special to *The New York Times*, "Raskob Radio Pool Realized $5,000,000," *New York Times*, May 20, 1932, 1, 15.

77 **Meehan had arranged for his profits:** Ibid.

77 **"I was really worried":** Beschloss, *Kennedy*, 68–69.

77 **By one account, Kennedy gave:** Joe McCarthy, *The Remarkable Kennedys: The Dramatic Inside Story of John Fitzgerald Kennedy and His Remarkable Family* (New York: Popular Library, August 1960; originally by The Dial Press, February 1960), 46.

78 **On May 28:** "Broderick Cleared of Neglect Charge in Bank of US Case," *New York Times*, May 28, 1932, 1.

78 **His notion, he said, was that:** Franklin D. Roosevelt, "Detroit, MI—Campaign Address," October 2, 1932, File No. 549, FDR Library online archives.

78 **"Vague" might apply to FDR's views:** Eric Rauchway, *Winter War: Hoover, Roosevelt, and the First Clash over the New Deal* (New York: Basic Books, 2018), 7–8; Thomas L. Stokes, *Chip off My Shoulder* (Princeton, N.J.: Princeton University Press, 1940), 312; Frederick Lewis Allen, *Since Yesterday: The 1930s in America* (New York: Perennial Library, 1986; originally published by Harper & Brothers, 1939), 94–95.

79 **Before Kennedy headed west:** Raymond Moley, *The First New Deal* (New York: Harcourt, Brace & World, 1966), 379.

80 **Joe Kennedy aided the cause:** Beschloss, *Kennedy*, 72–73.

80 **His Albany guests saw Roosevelt:** Rosenman, *Working*, 72.

81 **Roosevelt won by 945 votes:** Associated Press, "Garner Seen Roosevelt Running Mate," Washington, D.C., *Evening Star*, July 2, 1932, 1.

81 **The flight was slowed by turbulent:** Roseman, *Working*, 73–75.

81 **Joe Kennedy, Jim Farley, and other:** "Roosevelt to Run Campaign at Sea for a Week; Aides to Trail Him in Yacht for Night Talks," *New York Times*, July 8, 1932, 10.

83 **Private charities were exhausted:** Allen, *Since Yesterday*, 66.

83 **A record number of businesses:** Leuchtenburg, *FDR and the New Deal*, 18–19.

83   **At least 25 percent of American:** Allen, *Since Yesterday,* 63. One house-to-house survey in Buffalo in November 1932, for example, showed 46.3 percent of the available labor force was working full-time; 22.5 percent had part-time jobs. Just over 31 percent could not find work.

83   **As the assassin was wrestled:** The assassination attempt is described in numerous FDR biographies, including Schlesinger, Volume 1, 464–465; Davis, Volume 2, 427–424; Conrad Black, *Franklin Delano Roosevelt: Champion of Freedom* (New York: Public Affairs, 2003), 263–264; Jean Edward Smith, *FDR* (New York: Random House Trade Paperbacks, 2007), 296–298; H. W. Brands, *Traitor to His Class: The Privileged Life and Radical Presidency of Franklin Delano Roosevelt* (New York: Anchor Books, 2009), 277–281. One of the best accounts is in Rauchway, *Winter War,* 1–10.

84   **One close aide recalled:** Moley, *After Seven Years,* 139.

84   **A desperate Michigan governor:** Rappleye, *Herbert Hoover,* 434–438.

84   **By the time Roosevelt boarded:** Wicker, *Banking Panics,* 138–139, 144.

84   **Before dawn that morning:** Nevins, *Herbert H. Lehman,* 135–138.

84   **Two days would come and go:** The exchange closed in the Panic of 1873 and when World War I broke out in Europe in 1914.

CHAPTER THREE: CONFIDENCE, COOPERATION, AND CREATION

85   **Democrat Al Smith, just weeks earlier:** "Drastic Step Demanded," *New York Times,* February 8, 1933, 1.

85   **Columnist Walter Lippmann told FDR privately:** Ronald Steel, *Walter Lippmann and the American Century* (Boston: Little, Brown, 1980), 299–300.

85   **Hearst believed the film would be:** Eric Rauchway, *Winter War: Hoover, Roosevelt, and the First Clash over the New Deal* (New York: Basic Books, 2018), 190–192; see also Schlesinger, Volume 2, 3: "Whether revolution was a real possibility or not, faith in a free system was plainly waning. Capitalism, it seemed to many, had spent its force; democracy could not rise to an economic crisis. . . . Some looked enviously on Moscow, others on Berlin and Rome."

86   **Despite a few attempts by Roosevelt:** Eleanor Roosevelt, *This I Remember* (New York: Harper & Brothers, 1949), 77.

86   **Hoover had deep, irreconcilable issues:** Rauchway, *Winter War,* 13–14, 237–238.

86   **He had refused to permit:** Charles Rappleye, *Herbert Hoover in the White House: The Ordeal of the Presidency* (New York: Simon & Schuster Paperbacks, 2017), 426–427.

86   **Hoover was furious because Roosevelt had:** Rauchway, *Winter War,* 215–218; Rappleye, *Herbert Hoover,* 443–447; Davis, Volume 2, 437–438; Raymond Moley, *The First New Deal* (New York: Harcourt, Brace & World, 1966), 140–151.

87   **FDR had one of his aides:** Rexford G. Tugwell, *Roosevelt's Revolution* (New York: Macmillan, 1977), 22–23.

87   **His customary grin was gone:** Details are from newspaper accounts, photographs, and newsreel footage of the inauguration events.

87   **Then Roosevelt began to speak:** Franklin D. Roosevelt, "Inaugural Address," March 4, 1933, File No. 610, FDR Library online archives.

89   **In the ranks behind Roosevelt:** Rauchway, *Winter War,* 194.

89   **Franklin Roosevelt flooded the dark day:** David Michaelis, *Eleanor* (New York: Simon & Schuster, 2020), 286.

89   **He invited congressional leaders to meet:** Ernest K. Lindley, *The Roosevelt Revolution: First Phase* (New York: Viking Press, 1933), 80.

89   **Eleanor, who had attended her uncle:** Grace Robinson, "Mrs. Roosevelt Displays Her Family's New Home," New York *Daily News,* March 8, 1933, 280; Michaelis, *Eleanor,* 295.

90 **Wooden ramps, built in the last:** Rauchway, *Winter War,* 227.

90 **The liveliness dispelled the bitter gloom:** Eleanor Roosevelt, *This I Remember,* 77.

90 **"The hours between Mr. Roosevelt's":** Lindley, *Roosevelt Revolution,* 83.

90 **It *was* ready, and it matched:** Ibid., 81–82; Schlesinger, Volume 1, 480–481; Schlesinger, Volume 2, 4–8.

91 **Dozens of other smaller problems:** Francis G. Awalt, "Recollections of the Banking Crisis in 1933," *The Business History Review* vol. 43 no. 3 (Autumn 1969), published by the President and Fellows of Harvard College, 366–371; Lindley, *Roosevelt Revolution,* 83–86.

91 **Roosevelt's plan to address the banking:** Awalt, "Recollections," 347–371. Awalt provides a priceless eyewitness account of the birth of the emergency banking bill; the process is also detailed in Raymond Moley, *After Seven Years* (New York: Harper & Brothers, 1939), 148–152, and Moley, *The First New Deal,* 171–177; and Kenneth S. Davis, *FDR: The New Deal Years, 1933–1937* (New York: Random House, 1986), hereafter Davis, Volume 3, 49–50.

91 **Will Woodin, a sweet-tempered industrialist:** Awalt, "Recollections," 358–363. Awalt kept remarkably detailed notes of these epic days, recalling even who sat where during a key Oval Office meeting to review FDR's script for his first fireside chat.

92 **These people, Moley wrote:** Moley, *After Seven Years,* 148.

92 **After breakfast on Inauguration Day:** Awalt, "Recollections," 361.

92 **"The president thought it was great":** Ibid., 366.

92 **While Hoover still claimed:** Barrie A. Wigmore, in *The Crash and Its Aftermath: A History of Securities Markets in the United States, 1929–1933* (Westport, Conn.: Greenwood Press, 1985), 445–449, is among those who endorse Hoover's claim, arguing that FDR's "irresponsible semi-public" hints about taking the U.S. off the gold standard were a key cause of the February 1933 crisis. This argument ignores the fact that FDR's fiscal policies had been up for discussion throughout the long campaign, which FDR was widely expected to win, and yet the crisis did not become explosive until February. Other scholars believe, as I do, that the Michigan bank closures were far more influential in increasing public mistrust of banks—what Wicker called "a progressive and continual deterioration of depositor confidence." See Elmus Wicker, *The Banking Panics of the Great Depression* (Cambridge, U.K.: Cambridge University Press, 1996), 156. With each successive crisis from 1930 to 1931, depositors reduced the amount of currency they were willing to entrust to banks. Most persuasive, of course, is the fact that FDR had not repudiated a possible currency devaluation in March 1933, and yet public confidence in the banks was restored almost overnight.

92 **FDR needed a plan concrete:** Moley, in *After Seven Years* (151–152), credits Treasury Secretary Woodin with the final breakthrough in the negotiations: the use of Federal Reserve notes to provide liquidity to reopened banks, instead of scrip, which the bankers favored. The notes, Woodin said, "won't frighten people. It won't look like stage money. It'll be money that looks like money." The anecdote shows FDR's entire team understood the psychological imperatives of the bank rescue plan.

92 **Just hours after Congress passed:** Lindley, *Roosevelt Revolution,* 88.

93 **When the bill passed the House:** Ibid.

93 **He was confident, he said:** Franklin D. Roosevelt, "Fireside Chat #1—The Banking Crisis," File No. 616-1, FDR Library online archives.

94 **In major cities, then in smaller:** Lindley, *Roosevelt Revolution,* 93.

94 **In barely a week:** The bank recovery wasn't seamless, of course, and some isolated problems remained into the summer. But the public's perceptions of the safety of the overall banking system did seem to have been restored very quickly.

94 **The House of Morgan cabled:** Ron Chernow, *The House of Morgan: An American Banking Dynasty and the Rise of Modern Finance* (New York: Touchstone, 1990), 357.

94 **Dick Whitney, called often:** Michael Perino, *The Hellhound of Wall Street: How Ferdinand Pecora's Investigation of the Great Crash Forever Changed American Finance* (New York: Penguin Books, 2011), 48–49.

94 **The committee had immediately summoned:** Ritchie, *Congress,* 176–178.

95 **"The testimony was sufficiently interesting":** Special to *The New York Times,* "Liquidation, Not Shorts, Upset Stocks, Says Whitney; Promises List of Bears," *New York Times,* April 12, 1932, 1.

95 **The committee, with little staff expertise:** Special to *The New York Times,* "Whitney Testified 2-Week Drop Cost Market 6 Billions," *New York Times,* April 13, 1932, 1; Special to *The New York Times,* "Whitney Sees Peril to Market in Tax," *New York Times,* April 16, 1932, 1; Special to *The New York Times,* "Whitney Says Short Sales Saved Market Last Fall; Bears' Names Kept Secret," *New York Times,* April 19, 1932, 1.

95 **Without a chief counsel:** Ritchie, *Congress,* 179; Perino, *Hellhound,* 22–23.

95 **Then on January 22, 1933:** Ibid., 61.

96 **He quit:** Ibid., 24–33, 37–38, 41–43; Ritchie, *Congress,* 179.

96 **He had explained that:** Perino, *Hellhound,* 61–64.

96 **He had hired a handful:** Ibid.

97 **He had managed to wring some:** The banker was Charles G. Dawes, a former U.S. vice president and the winner of the 1925 Nobel Peace Prize for his efforts to restructure European war debts. The previous summer, his Chicago bank had gotten a bailout from the RFC shortly after Dawes resigned as RFC chairman, even as other desperate banks were being turned down.

97 **They also added up to more:** Perino, *Hellhound,* 122–123; Special to *The New York Times,* "Dawes Concedes Bank Abused Law in Insull Loans," *New York Times,* February 17, 1933, 1.

97 **General Electric was one of Insull's:** Owen D. Young led General Electric for seventeen years and was instrumental in the formation of RCA.

97 **Young had added:** David Moss, Cole Bolton, and Eugene Kintgen, "The Pecora Hearings," Harvard Business School Case 711-046, December 2010 (revised June 2018), 6.

97 **But the Insull hearings:** Perino, *Hellhound,* 126–127.

98 **On Tuesday morning, February 21:** Ibid., 137.

98 **One confidential memo described:** "Stock Exchange Practices," Report of the Senate Committee on Currency and Banking, 73rd Cong., 2d Sess., Report No. 1455, hereafter *Pecora Final Report,* 126–132; Special to *The New York Times,* "National City Sold Peru Bond Issues in 'Honest Mistake,'" *New York Times,* February 28, 1933, 1.

99 **What one magazine called:** Moss et. al., "The Pecora Hearings," 7.

99 **President Hoover had told them:** Perino, *Hellhound,* 225.

99 **"These New York bankers haven't any":** Ibid., 226, with quotation confirmed in Lindley, *Roosevelt Revolution,* 75–76.

99 **A few weeks later, Whitney would:** Malcolm MacKay, *Impeccable Connections: The Rise and Fall of Richard Whitney* (New York: Brick Tower Press, 2013), 61; Parrish, *Securities Regulation,* 108–109.

99 **He told them his staff needed:** Perino, in *Hellhound,* 92, quoting Pecora, puts J. P. "Jack" Morgan Jr. at this meeting, as does Ritchie, *Congress,* 182; but Chernow's more plausible account (*House of Morgan,* 360–361) is supported by Edward M. Lamont, *The Ambassador from Wall Street: The Story of Thomas W. Lamont, J.P. Morgan's Chief Executive* (Lanham, Md.: Madison Books, 1994), 335, and I have chosen to rely on that version.

99   **Lamont and Davis pulled every string:** Lamont, *Ambassador,* 337–339.

99   **He and his men trooped:** Ritchie, *Congress,* 182–183.

100   **"He wants me to make a study":** Letter to George E. Bates, April 7, 1933, *The Douglas Letters,* 18–19.

100   **An avid reader:** George E. Bates and William O. Douglas, "Secondary Distribution of Securities: Problems Suggested by *Kinney v. Glenny,*" *Yale Law Journal* vol. 41, no. 7 (May 1932); William O. Douglas and George E. Bates, "Stock 'Brokers' as Agents and Dealers," *Yale Law Journal* vol. 43, no. 1 (November 1933).

100   **He'd polish and practice each one:** Bruce Allen Murphy, *Wild Bill: The Legend and Life of William O. Douglas* (New York: Random House, 2003), 118–119; this unflattering depiction of Douglas is attributed in Murphy's notes to Douglas's first wife and his adult son. In a book published during Douglas's lifetime, James F. Simon, *Independent Journey: The Life of William O. Douglas* (New York: Harper & Row, 1980), 115–116, gives a less hostile account of the Douglas home life, calling Douglas "a fun-loving father, joking and kidding [his children] Millie and Bill junior" while acknowledging that his children felt "there was never enough time for [them]" in their father's busy life. This depiction is also attributed to the first Mrs. Douglas and their son. In any case, the harsher scene clearly shows how important Douglas thought his ostensibly facile storytelling was to his social persona in FDR's circle.

100   **And he had found a mother:** William O. Douglas, "Some Functional Aspects of Bankruptcy," *Yale Law Journal* vol. 41, no. 3 (January 1932), 12–14; the page numbers are from the version of the paper on file with the SECHS. Used with permission of the SEC Historical Society.

101   **Douglas turned Pecora down:** Letter to George E. Bates, April 7, 1933, *The Douglas Letters,* 18.

101   **Pecora forced Jack Morgan:** Chernow, *House of Morgan,* 371.

101   **Pecora produced a letter:** Ibid., 372; the party official was the wealthy Du Pont executive John Jacob Raskob, a onetime National Democratic Committee chairman and Al Smith's ally in his later hostile attacks on FDR and the New Deal.

101   **Even more conclusively, Tom Lamont:** Ibid.

101   **This so-called "preferred list":** Ibid., 370.

102   **"The brightest angel on Wall Street":** Ibid., 375.

102   **"In every instance, Morgan & Company":** Ritchie, *Congress,* 183.

102   **Columnist Walter Lippmann felt personally betrayed:** Steel, *Walter Lippmann,* 289–290.

102   **That mistake over time had:** "Why It Hurts," *New York Times,* May 27, 1933, 12.

102   **"We have passed a lot":** D. B. Hardeman and Donald C. Bacon, *Rayburn: A Biography* (Lanham, Md.: Madison Books, 1987), 150.

102   **"I need help on this thing":** Ibid., 151.

103   **The third was Thomas G. Corcoran:** The recruitment of Landis, Corcoran, and Cohen is described similarly in Schlesinger, Volume 2, 441–442; Joel Seligman, *The Transformation of Wall Street: A History of the Securities and Exchange Commission and Modern Corporate Finance,* Revised Edition (Boston: Northeastern University Press, 1995), hereafter Seligman, *Transformation,* 61–66; Moley, *After Seven Years,* 179–181; and Davis, Volume 3, 85–88. Corcoran's quip about the RFC is from William Lasser, *Benjamin V. Cohen: Architect of the New Deal* (New Haven: Yale University Press, 2002), 74.

103   **In a message to Congress:** Special to *The New York Times,* "The President's Message," *New York Times,* March 30, 1933, 1.

103   **But as FDR preferred:** Seligman, *Transformation,* 63–64, gives this background for the "full disclosure" concept: Huston Thompson, a former FTC chairman, had broached the disclosure idea to FDR during his campaign, and went on to write

the party platform plank on securities regulation, which FDR endorsed. Seligman, *Transformation,* 50–51, 63–64.

103 **As the legislation's coauthor:** Justin O'Brien, *The Triumph, Tragedy and Lost Legacy of James M. Landis: A Life on Fire* (Oxford: Hart Publishing, 2017), 30.

104 **Landis later recalled:** James McCauley Landis, "The Reminiscences of James M. Landis," Columbia University Oral History Research Office, 1964, 172, 175.

104 **Rayburn steered the new full-disclosure bill:** Special to *The New York Times,* "Roosevelt Signs the Securities Bill," *New York Times,* May 28, 1933, 2.

104 **One of their most vociferous champions:** Matthew P. Fink, *The Unlikely Reformer: Carter Glass and Financial Regulation* (Fairfax, Va.: George Mason University Press, 2019), 108.

105 **As a major donor and fundraiser:** Joe McCarthy, *The Remarkable Kennedys: The Dramatic Inside Story of John Fitzgerald Kennedy and His Remarkable Family* (New York: Popular Library, August 1960; originally by The Dial Press, February 1960), 46; Michael Beschloss, *Kennedy and Roosevelt: The Uneasy Alliance* (New York: Perennial Library, 1987), 78, quoting Rose Kennedy.

105 **On December 10, 1932:** Nasaw, *Patriarch,* 186.

105 **There was no response:** Ibid., 187.

106 **But Pecora's work was surely:** Ibid., 188.

106 **Kennedy shared his angry criticism:** David Nasaw, *The Chief: The Life of William Randolph Hearst* (Boston: Houghton Mifflin, 2000), 459–460; Amanda Smith, ed., *Hostage to Fortune: The Letters of Joseph P. Kennedy* (New York: Viking Penguin, 2001), hereafter *Hostage,* 123.

106 **As the silence from the Oval:** Nasaw, *Patriarch,* 188.

106 **The leader of the American delegation:** Beschloss, *Kennedy,* 81; Nasaw, *Patriarch,* 191. The delegation leader was James P. Warburg, of the New York banking dynasty, who would seesaw in his support for FDR in the years ahead.

106 **Although Kennedy denied:** Doris Kearns Goodwin, *The Fitzgeralds and the Kennedys* (New York: Simon & Schuster, 1987), 439–440.

106 **That gave rise to an audacious:** Richard J. Whalen, *The Founding Father: The Story of Joseph P. Kennedy* (New York: New American Library of World Literature, 1964), 132–134.

106 **That idea was born:** Day's status as a Wall Street dealmaker in 1933 showed how little Wall Street weighed the political corruption that had stained the 1920s. Less than a decade earlier, Day had worked as an "international troubleshooter" for Harry F. Sinclair, the oil tycoon who figured in the Teapot Dome scandal. Sinclair was acquitted of bribing Harding's Interior secretary, but both Sinclair and Day were convicted of jury tampering in the course of Sinclair's trial, and both served short sentences in the local jail in Washington, where Sinclair was treated like royalty. See Laton McCartney, *The Teapot Dome Scandal: How Big Oil Bought the Harding White House and Tried to Steal the Country* (New York: Random House, 2008; Random House Trade Paperback Edition, 2009), 166, 263–265, 269, 302.

107 **He invested some of his profits:** Goodwin, *Fitzgeralds,* 440.

107 **There still was no room:** Beschloss, *Kennedy,* 81.

107 **Moley declined the offer:** Moley, *The First New Deal,* 381–382.

107 **Kennedy also courted Missy LeHand:** Kathryn Smith, *The Gatekeeper: Missy LeHand, FDR, and the Untold Story of the Partnership That Defined a Presidency* (New York: Touchstone, 2016), 110–111.

108 **In the summer of 1933:** Ronald Kessler, *The Sins of the Father: Joseph P. Kennedy and the Dynasty He Founded* (New York: Warner Books, 1996), 104–105.

108 **Kennedy had his own agenda:** Accusations that Joe Kennedy was a bootlegger during Prohibition did not surface until the 1960s, when his sons were active in

sharp-elbowed politics; those tales had never surfaced during any of Kennedy's Senate confirmation hearings in 1934–1936, when he faced fierce opponents eager to discredit him and proving he had been a bootlegger would have been a near-fatal blow to the newborn SEC. In any case, the rumors are largely debunked by the historical record. See Daniel Okrent, *Last Call: The Rise and Fall of Prohibition* (New York: Scribners, 2010), 366–371, and Nasaw, *Patriarch,* 71, 79–81. JPK's one foray into illegal liquor deals was buying bootleg gin for his tenth Harvard reunion in 1922, a crime committed on a nearly weekly basis by literally millions of otherwise law-abiding Americans in that era. All his other liquor industry dealings were well within the law at the time.

108   **He hoped the Distillers Company Ltd.:** Kessler, *Sins,* 107.

108   **"He was a brilliant businessman":** Nasaw, *Patriarch,* 192–193.

109   **"Until 1946, when Kennedy sold":** Ibid.

109   **As one legal historian noted:** Seligman, *Transformation,* 66, 72–75.

109   **At Yale, Bill Douglas watched:** Murphy, *Wild Bill,* 106.

109   **He initially defended the law:** William O. Douglas, "New Securities Bill Seen as Meritorious," *New York Times,* April 9, 1933, 63.

109   **He favored a regulatory effort:** O'Brien, *Triumph,* 52.

109   **His mentor replied that Douglas:** Letter from Felix Frankfurter to James M. Landis, March 17, 1934, *The Papers of James M. Landis,* Special Collections Department, Harvard Law School Library, Box 16–7, cited in O'Brien, *Triumph,* 50.

110   **In reality, Douglas was trying to:** O'Brien, *Triumph,* 49.

110   **But the abuses Pecora examined:** Perino, *Hellhound,* 292.

110   **Pecora covered some familiar ground:** Robert C. Perez and Edward F. Willett, *Clarence Dillon: Wall Street Enigma* (Lanham, Md.: Madison Books, 1995), 98; *Pecora Final Report,* 143–147.

111   **In the spring of 1931:** Richard Whitney, "Business Honesty," delivered to the Philadelphia Chamber of Commerce, April 24, 1931, 12; from the archives of the New-York Historical Society Library.

111   **In one case exposed by Pecora:** Ritchie, *Congress,* 189.

111   **One financially savvy senator:** The senator was James Couzens, a wealthy Republican progressive, who represented Michigan in the Senate from 1922 to his death in 1936.

111   **Using one trust's assets:** Perez and Willett, *Clarence Dillon,* 100–101; *Pecora Final Report,* 341.

111   **"That I don't know":** *Pecora Final Report,* 354–358.

111   **Cyrus Eaton, a famous Chicago investor:** Ibid., 358–359.

111   **Samuel Insull, Eaton's rival tycoon:** Ibid., 361–362.

112   **Indeed, Otto H. Kahn:** Ibid., 363.

112   **He was certainly one:** Ritchie, *Congress,* 189–190.

112   **This was a stunning act of malpractice:** Ibid., 190.

113   **"We were all sinners":** Ibid., 188.

113   **By the fall of that year:** Seligman, *Transformation,* 80–83.

114   **The draft, called the Fletcher-Rayburn Bill:** Ibid., 85.

114   **He met personally with the Commerce:** Lasser, *Benjamin V. Cohen,* 87.

115   **A compliant press corps did not:** "Three Tight Rules Added by Exchange," *New York Times,* February 14, 1934, 29.

115   **To drive home the point:** Seligman, *Transformation,* 87–88.

116   **"Congressmen reported receiving vast numbers":** Ibid., 89–90.

116   **By March 5:** Ibid., 93.

116   **Franklin Roosevelt's credibility:** Ibid.

116   **"Republicans never want to do anything":** Landis, "Reminiscences," 183.

116 **Rather than give up:** Seligman, *Transformation*, 93.

116 **He added a warning:** Schlesinger, Volume 2, 466; Ritchie, *Congress*, 325–326.

117 **Weary from the relentless attacks:** Hardeman and Bacon, *Rayburn*, 158.

117 **This time, Roosevelt fobbed Whitney:** Donald A. Ritchie, *James M. Landis: Dean of the Regulators* (Cambridge, Mass.: Harvard University Press, 1980), hereafter Ritchie, *Landis*, 56; as it happened, remodeling work on the West Wing had begun in March, so the president's White House office would have been somewhat disordered.

117 **Encouraged by his opposition:** Parrish, *Securities Regulation*, 131.

117 **Speaking for the bill:** Congressional Record, 78, 73rd Cong., 2d Sess., April 30, 1934, 7693.

118 **The new law:** Seligman, *Transformation*, 99.

118 **But Senator Glass, who favored fragmented:** Fink, *Unlikely Reformer*, 149.

118 **Rayburn ultimately accepted:** Hardeman and Bacon, *Rayburn*, 160.

119 **They felt regulation was the price:** MacKay, *Impeccable Connections*, 64–65.

119 **Jim Landis, so important:** Ritchie, *Landis*, 59; Special to *The New York Times*, "Roosevelt Signs Exchange Curb Bill," *New York Times*, June 7, 1934, 7; Lasser, *Benjamin V. Cohen*, 23, 25–27, 30, 32.

119 **Pecora replied:** Ritchie, *Landis*, 59. In other accounts, the phrase "Mr. President" is omitted. This version seems more likely in the formal setting of a bill signing ceremony.

120 **Most in the media expected:** Ibid., 59.

120 **In Congress, Pecora was seen:** Perino, *Hellhound*, 299; Special to *The New York Times*, "Pecora Is Willing to Rule Exchanges," *New York Times*, June 28, 1934, 1.

121 **Moley recalled that Kennedy responded:** Moley, *After Seven Years*, 288.

121 **To FDR's New Dealers and:** Nasaw, *Patriarch*, 207.

CHAPTER FOUR: POWER TO THE PEOPLE

122 **The Federal Trade Commission was housed:** Shortly after these events, the Federal Reserve Bank would get approval to tear the old FTC building down and use the site for its new headquarters, which still houses the Fed today.

122 **But plug-in fans and open windows:** The heat wave is documented in local newspapers; the source for the internal building temperature is Doris Kearns Goodwin, *The Fitzgeralds and the Kennedys* (New York: Simon & Schuster, 1987), 447.

122 **At age fifty-two, he didn't want:** Michael Perino, *The Hellhound of Wall Street: How Ferdinand Pecora's Investigation of the Great Crash Forever Changed American Finance* (New York: Penguin Books, 2011), 301.

123 **Behind that closed door:** James McCauley Landis, "The Reminiscences of James M. Landis," Columbia University Oral History Research Office, 1964, 192–193.

123 **A few days earlier:** Seligman, *Transformation*, 106; Justin O'Brien, *The Triumph, Tragedy and Lost Legacy of James M. Landis: A Life on Fire* (Oxford: Hart Publishing, 2017), 59, includes Pecora in the White House meeting, but that seems unlikely.

123 **He had made a quick morning:** Goodwin, *Fitzgeralds*, 449.

123 **"Healy and Mathews would have voted":** Landis, "Reminiscences," 192.

123 **In his blunt, breezy way:** Goodwin, *Fitzgeralds*, 449; Ritchie, *Landis*, 60.

123 **Landis had shared his views:** Ritchie, *Landis*, 60.

124 **The stock market rallied:** Barrie A. Wigmore, *The Crash and Its Aftermath: A History of Securities Markets in the United States, 1929–1933* (Westport, Conn.: Greenwood Press, 1985), 540–541.

124 **He added, "If we were":** Associated Press, "Text of President's Speech," *New York Times*, August 19, 1934, 3.

125   **One trusted advisor told FDR:** Michael Parrish, *Securities Regulation and the New Deal* (New Haven: Yale University Press, 1970), 189.

125   **Adolf A. Berle Jr.:** Ibid., 190.

125   **Kennedy calmly explained his refusal:** *Hostage,* 139.

125   **Kennedy and Pecora led the way:** Special to *The New York Times,* "Kennedy in Chair after Long Parley by Exchange Board," *New York Times,* July 3, 1934, 1.

126   **"I will try and do my":** Ibid.; Perino, *Hellhound,* 300–301.

126   **He would later say of Kennedy:** Goodwin, *Fitzgeralds,* 450.

126   **His two colleagues:** Ibid.

126   **"Our ideas have changed":** S. J. Woolf, "Kennedy Sees End of 'Shoestring Era,'" *New York Times,* August 12, 1934, 112; Special to *The New York Times,* "Kennedy Declares Speculation War," *New York Times,* July 4, 1934, 1.

126   **"Boys," he told reporters:** Goodwin, *Fitzgeralds,* 450.

126   **As soon as he accepted:** Letter from Joseph P. Kennedy to Senator Duncan Fletcher, November 22, 1934, used with permission of SEC Historical Society, which credits the permission of the John F. Kennedy Library.

127   **It surely helped that Pecora:** Associated Press, "Pecora Gives Kennedy Proxy; Squelches Rumor of Feud," *Boston Globe,* July 16, 1934, 9; Associated Press, "Assails Kennedy's Pool Activities," *New York Times,* July 16, 1934, 2.

127   **Kennedy was seen as:** Ralph F. de Bedts, *The New Deal's SEC: The Formative Years* (New York: Columbia University Press, 1964), 89.

127   **Over lunch in the tree-shaded garden:** "Mr. Kennedy, the Chairman," *Fortune* vol. 26, no. 3 (September 1937), 57; Richard J. Whalen, *The Founding Father: The Story of Joseph P. Kennedy* (New York: New American Library of World Literature, 1964), 145.

127   **He assured them:** David McKean, *Tommy the Cork: Washington's Ultimate Insider from Roosevelt to Reagan* (South Royalton, Vt.: Steerforth Press, 2004), 56.

128   **He wrangled with Roosevelt's conservative budget:** Joel Seligman, *Misalignment: The New Financial Order and the Failure of Financial Regulation* (New York: Wolters Kluwer, 2020), hereafter Seligman, *Misalignment,* 492–493.

128   **It had fourteen bedrooms and baths:** Goodwin, *Fitzgeralds,* 450–451; Nasaw, *Patriarch,* 213–215.

128   **As he promised, Kennedy assembled:** Landis, "Reminiscences," 228.

129   **Kennedy knew Burns was close:** Seligman, *Transformation,* 110.

129   **As usual, the office next to:** Nasaw, *Patriarch,* 213; Goodwin, *Fitzgeralds,* 334.

129   **But by 1934, Douglas was:** Seligman, *Misalignment,* 493.

129   **He was in debt, as usual:** Bruce Allen Murphy, *Wild Bill: The Legend and Life of William O. Douglas* (New York: Random House, 2003), 107–109.

130   **"Well, what in hell are you":** Douglas, *Go East, Young Man,* 256.

130   **He tapped his former law student:** Laura Kalman, *Abe Fortas: A Biography* (New Haven: Yale University Press, 1990), 18.

130   **At Marwood, Kennedy rose early:** Nasaw, *Patriarch,* 213; Katie Louchheim, ed., *The Making of the New Deal: The Insiders Speak,* with historical notes by Jonathan Dembo (Cambridge, Mass.: Harvard University Press, 1983), hereafter Louchheim, 134.

130   **"We were remaking the world":** Ibid., 142.

131   **When final registration rules were adopted:** Letter from Adolf A. Berle Jr. to Joseph P. Kennedy, December 19, 1934, used with permission of SEC Historical Society.

131   **According to *The New York Times*:** "Topics in Wall Street; Mr. Kennedy's Talk," *New York Times,* July 25, 1934, 23.

131   **Swope told him:** Letter from Herbert Bayard Swope to Joseph P. Kennedy, July 24, 1934, used with permission of SEC Historical Society.

132 **"Whadya mean I done noble":** Telegram from "Joe" to Herbert B. Swope, July 25, 1934, used with permission of SEC Historical Society.

132 **His staff helped the listed firms:** Ritchie, *Landis*, 65.

132 **FDR added:"Perhaps you can help":** Note marked "Personal" from FDR to Adolf A. Berle Jr., August 15, 1934, used with permission of SEC Historical Society.

132 **By one account, Whitney had put:** Malcolm MacKay, *Impeccable Connections: The Rise and Fall of Richard Whitney* (New York: Brick Tower Press, 2013), 68.

133 **The report Kennedy delivered:** Report on the Government of Securities Exchanges, Letter from the Chairman of the Securities and Exchange Commission Transmitting the Commission's Report of the Investigation of Stock Exchanges, Together with Its Recommendations, House of Representatives, 74th Cong., 1st Sess., Document No. 85, 2.

134 **Members were shocked to read instead:** "Whitney Departs for Washington," *New York Times*, January 26, 1935, 29.

134 **"Now I want you to endorse":** Joseph Alsop and Robert Kintner, "The Battle of the Market Place: Richard Whitney Leads the Fight," *Saturday Evening Post*, June 11, 1938, hereafter Alsop and Kintner, Battle Part 1, 76.

135 **In fact, it was about:** Thomas L. Stokes, *Chip off My Shoulder* (Princeton, N.J.: Princeton University Press, 1940), 338–340.

135 **It had therefore become an article:** M. L. Ramsay, *Pyramids of Power: The Story of Roosevelt, Insull and the Utility Wars* (Indianapolis: Bobbs-Merrill Company, 1937), 24, 51, 65.

135 **Where electricity remained expensive:** Ibid., 66, 265–266, 290–300, 315.

135 **Roosevelt knew in his soul:** Ibid., 290. Ramsay, clearly drawing on multiple interviews with Roosevelt and his close aides, wrote that FDR's thinking "runs far beyond electrical conveniences and release from drudgery. It is concerned primarily with democracy, and then secondarily with economics as the means of sustaining and building up democracy."

135 **Senator George W. Norris:** Ibid., 315.

136 **Before FDR, both political parties:** Ibid., 67; Davis, Volume 3, 88–89; Ramsay, *Pyramids*, 65–66; Special to *The New York Times*, "Macy's Attack on 'Invisible Government' in Albany," *New York Times*, December 9, 1933, 2.

136 **Utilities wielded similar power:** Ramsay, *Pyramids*, 67.

137 **"Nevertheless, the use of words":** Special to *The New York Times*, "Trade Board Urges Holding Unit Curbs," *New York Times*, January 28, 1935, 23.

137 **Since 1926, an influential economist:** From 1900 into the late 1920s, Ripley was a prominent advisor to Congress and federal agencies on railroad rate setting, labor relations, and system consolidation, in addition to his important and well-researched public critique of corporate governance and accounting standards in the 1920s. But he also was the author of *The Races of Europe: A Sociological Study*, published in 1899; the work was one of several race-based anthropological studies that were used, and misused, by the advocates of white supremacy and anti-Semitism who influenced public opinion in the early twentieth century, with horrific results for America's response to both domestic racial violence and the murderous attacks on European Jews by German and Italian fascists.

137 **An Investment Bankers Association panel:** William Z. Ripley, *Main Street and Wall Street* (Boston: Little, Brown, 1927), 308.

137 **Some utilities had skimped:** Ibid., 312, 334.

138 **Nothing could have been further:** Ibid., 345–346.

138 **The author of a 1937 book:** Ramsay, *Pyramids*, 175.

138 **Indeed, one utility financier had acknowledged:** Harry M. Addinsell, "Changes in Financing Dictated by Experience," *Electric World*, December 24, 1932, 844–846. Addinsell was the president of Chase Harris Forbes, the securities affiliate of

Chase National Bank. In this essay he defended the general concept of holding companies, but acknowledged the abuses that had come to light.

138 **Since 1919, utility conglomerates:** Carl D. Thompson, *Confessions of the Power Trust* (New York: E. P. Dutton, 1932), 269–282; extensive documentation of specific examples is found in pages 283–486.

139 **The industry, determined to shape public:** Special to *The New York Times*, "Hits Propaganda of Public Utilities," *New York Times*, November 15, 1934, 31; "The Chamber of Commerce of the United States of America, 'Big Brother' of the National Electric Light Association" (report submitted by Senator Norris), Congressional Record—Senate, May 4, 1933, beginning on page 2845; cited quote is in the right-hand column on page 2848.

139 **In November 1934, the FTC:** Summary Report of the FTC to the Senate of the United States, "Efforts by Associations and Agencies of Electric and Gas Utilities to Influence Public Opinion," 70th Cong., 1st Sess., Document 92, Part 71A, 391.

139 **By then, Judge Healy:** William Lasser, *Benjamin V. Cohen: Architect of the New Deal* (New Haven: Yale University Press, 2002), 112–113.

140 **"It is futile," the president answered:** John A. Riggs, *High Tension: FDR's Battle to Power America* (New York: Diversion Books, 2020), Kindle edition, Location 2488, quoting David Lilienthal, *The Journals of David Lilienthal, Volume 1: The TVA Years 1939–1945* (New York: Harper & Row, 1964), 46–47.

140 **On the Far Left, he already:** Schlesinger, Volume 3, 159–161.

140 **On the Far Right, he faced:** Ibid., 69–95, 211.

140 **"To every problem, [business leaders] offered":** Ibid., 142–146; Schlesinger, Volume 2, 501–502.

140 **Impatient progressives cited all this as:** Leuchtenburg, *FDR and the New Deal*, 146–147.

140 **But he had wrestled with unrestrained:** Schlesinger, Volume 3, 302.

140 **His hard-line approach was gaining:** Ibid., 304.

140 **"Although the abuses connected":** Lasser, *Benjamin V. Cohen*, 114.

141 **No fan of holding companies:** Letter from Joseph P. Kennedy to President Roosevelt, July 2, 1935, and letter from Joseph P. Kennedy to Senator Burton K. Wheeler, July 8, 1935, both used with permission of SEC Historical Society, courtesy of the National Archives; Landis, "Reminiscences," 217.

141 **Cohen wryly wrote a friend:** Lasser, *Benjamin V. Cohen*, 119.

141 **On February 6, 1935:** D. B. Hardeman and Donald C. Bacon, *Rayburn: A Biography* (Lanham, Md.: Madison Books, 1987), 171.

142 **As Whitney had claimed about stock:** Schlesinger, Volume 3, 310.

142 **Once again, "flagrant abuses were freely":** Hardeman and Bacon, *Rayburn*, 174.

142 **"I am against [the] *private socialism*":** Franklin D. Roosevelt, "Message transmitting to Congress [the] Report of the National Power Policy Committee," March 12, 1935, Speech File No. 773, FDR Library online archives. (Italics added.)

142 **That same week in March:** MacKay, *Impeccable Connections*, 69.

143 **The advisory panel's members included:** Ibid., 69–70.

143 **"His position was simple":** Ibid.

143 **The New York Times now reported:** De Bedts, *New Deal's SEC*, 146–157.

143 **There is little doubt that Richard:** Alsop and Kintner, Battle Part 1, 78. The two journalists reported that Whitney warned Gay before the election that he might run as an independent and would likely win.

143 **But his brother, George:** MacKay, *Impeccable Connections*, 70. Alsop and Kintner (Battle Part 1) gave a slightly different account, reporting that George Whitney and Tom Lamont dismissed the idea as "too disruptive."

144 **"Mr. Gay has all my good":** "Whitney Pledges Aid to Gay as President, Ending Rumors of Rival Exchange Ticket," *New York Times*, April 10, 1935, 31.

145 **Veteran observers were quick to see:** "E.H.H. Simmons Aide of Gay in Exchange," *New York Times,* May 15, 1935, 31.

145 **Addressing a ballroom crowd:** "Trade 'Blues' Here Infect the Nation, Kennedy Declares," *New York Times,* March 20, 1935, 1.

146 **By one account, he made:** Whalen, *Founding Father,* 174.

146 **These casual gatherings were a carefree:** See "Arthur Krock: Memorandum for the Secret Archives of Joseph P. Kennedy," *Hostage,* 154–157.

146 **At one point:** Michael Beschloss, *Kennedy and Roosevelt: The Uneasy Alliance* (New York: Perennial Library, 1987), 95.

147 **The Supreme Court had struck:** Associated Press, "Supreme Court Wipes Out Codes," Washington, D.C., *Evening Star,* May 27, 1935, 1.

147 **The GOP leader in the House:** Associated Press, "Administration Renews Fight to Attain New Deal Objectives," Washington, D.C., *Evening Star,* May 18, 1935, 1.

147 **While the larger stock market slumped:** "Fear of Deflation Forces a Decline in Stocks after an Early Advance," *New York Times,* May 29, 1935, 10.

147 **A weaker bill without the death:** Hardeman and Bacon, *Rayburn,* 183–185.

148 **As one Rayburn biography noted:** Ibid., 195.

149 **After breaking the news personally:** *Hostage,* 161, footnote number 116.

149 **And within six months:** Ibid., 169–170.

149 **Kennedy was deeply gratified:** Letter from FDR to Joseph P. Kennedy, September 20, 1935, used with permission of SEC Historical Society.

149 **Even the Wall Street scourge:** John T. Flynn, "Other People's Money," *The New Republic,* October 9, 1935, 244, used with permission of SEC Historical Society.

149 **Abe Fortas praised Kennedy:** Letter from Abe Fortas to Joseph P. Kennedy, undated but filed as September 23, 1935, used with permission of SEC Historical Society.

149 **In his aw-shucks tone:** Goodwin, *Fitzgeralds,* 454.

149 **Back at SEC headquarters:** Associated Press, "Landis Takes Kennedy's Job," *Boston Globe,* September 24, 1935, 5.

150 **As Landis stood "speechless":** Ritchie, *Landis,* 68.

150 **An aura of command surrounded Kennedy:** Ibid.

150 **When his father visited him:** Ibid., 13.

150 **He earned "what was reputedly":** Ibid., 18.

151 **But behind both the stern façade:** Ibid., 5.

151 **Indeed, Landis "lived perilously":** Ibid., vii.

151 **At his insistence, Congress had enacted:** Leuchtenburg, *FDR and the New Deal,* 150.

151 **But every victory of that summer:** Schlesinger, Volume 2, 476–479.

152 **No one could seriously argue:** Seligman, *Transformation,* 132–133.

153 **As a financial columnist:** "Topics in Wall Street: Utilities Stand Firm," *New York Times,* September 26, 1935, 33.

153 **The only sincere advocate:** Seligman, *Transformation,* 132–133.

154 **Burns had teased out "testimony from":** Ibid., 133.

154 **The Philadelphia Inquirer said:** "Legal Battle upon Utility Law Opens in Baltimore Today," *Philadelphia Inquirer,* September 27, 1935, 23.

154 **"You should have stayed with us":** Letter from Robert E. Healy to Joseph P. Kennedy, November 27, 1935, used with permission of SEC Historical Society.

154 **Jim Landis was determined:** Lasser, *Benjamin V. Cohen,* 144–146.

154 **The strategy was audacious:** Ibid.

155 **"Let's pick a big one":** O'Brien, *Triumph,* 69.

155 **"Roosevelt liked novel ideas":** Jackson, 15.

155 **The SEC team quietly set up:** McKean, *Tommy the Cork,* 66, although the filing date shown there is incorrect.

155 **Electric Bond and Share:** Thompson, *Confessions,* 109–113.

156 **Thus, it was engaged:** Ibid.; Lasser, *Benjamin V. Cohen,* 144–145.

156   **Moreover, it clearly was committing:** Parrish, *Securities Regulation,* 163.
156   **Best of all, it was based:** O'Brien, *Triumph,* 70.
156   **The staffer was likely:** Landis, "Reminiscences," 222.
156   **The SEC had shown:** Ritchie, *Landis,* 69.
157   **Although Kennedy's last official act:** James F. Simon, *Independent Journey: The Life of William O. Douglas* (New York: Harper & Row, 1980), 152–153.

CHAPTER FIVE: AN OCEAN OF UNFINISHED BUSINESS

159   **The team soon found:** Bruce Allen Murphy, *Wild Bill: The Legend and Life of William O. Douglas* (New York: Random House, 2003), 109.
159   **Then he would rise:** Ibid.
159   **He wanted no kid-glove handling:** Ibid., 108–109.
159   **Journalists, seeing the solid evidence:** Ibid., 110.
159   **These two supposed adversaries:** Laura Kalman, *Abe Fortas: A Biography* (New Haven: Yale University Press, 1990), 56–57.
159   **Questioned by Douglas, Dulles insisted:** James F. Simon, *Independent Journey: The Life of William O. Douglas* (New York: Harper & Row, 1980), 144–146.
160   **He pressed the partners:** Associated Press, "Kennedy to Get $50,000 for Paramount Survey," *Boston Globe,* July 16, 1936, 10.
160   **The backroom dealings of the investment:** "Topics in Wall Street: Paramount Hearing Ends," *New York Times,* July 12, 1935, 27; Murphy, *Wild Bill,* 113.
160   **One banker conceded to Douglas:** "Cuba Cane Records Subpoenaed by SEC," *New York Times,* August 30, 1935, 25; Special to *The New York Times,* "Banks Controlled Cuban Sugar Group," *New York Times,* August 22, 1935, 27.
160   **The firms that sold the bonds:** Simon, *Independent Journey,* 148–149.
160   **Its eight-volume report to Congress:** Ibid.
161   **Douglas was admired within:** Ralph F. de Bedts, *The New Deal's SEC: The Formative Years* (New York: Columbia University Press, 1964), 153.
161   **Adolf Berle, the FDR advisor:** Justin O'Brien, *The Triumph, Tragedy and Lost Legacy of James M. Landis: A Life on Fire* (Oxford: Hart Publishing, 2017), 20.
161   **"I don't mean he wasn't firm":** Kalman, *Abe Fortas,* 60.
161   **Kennedy himself:** Letter from Joseph P. Kennedy to "My dear Colonel Owens," June 5, 1935, used with permission of SEC Historical Society.
161   **He repeated that compliment:** Joseph P. Kennedy, as told to John B. Kennedy, "Shielding the Sheep," *Saturday Evening Post,* January 18, 1936, 23.
161   **Kennedy's support for Douglas:** "Topics in Wall Street; Vacancy on SEC Filled," *New York Times,* January 17, 1936, 27.
161   **"Word is that Douglas":** James McMullin, "Bankers Ponder FDIC," *Asbury Park Press,* January 23, 1936, 11.
161   **But within months, columnists Drew Pearson:** Drew Pearson and Robert S. Allen, "The Daily Washington Merry-Go-Round," *Palladium-Item,* Richmond, Indiana, April 20, 1936, 6.
161   **Another pundit praised Douglas:** Simon, *Independent Journey,* 154.
162   **It *is* clear that Douglas:** Fred Rodell, "Douglas over the Stock Exchange," *Fortune* vol. 17, no. 2 (February 1938), 64; Ritchie, *Landis,* 75.
162   **He wrote FDR:** M. L. Ramsay, *Pyramids of Power: The Story of Roosevelt, Insull and the Utility Wars* (Indianapolis: Bobbs-Merrill Company, 1937), 283–284.
162   **This, he would later say:** James McCauley Landis, "The Reminiscences of James M. Landis," Columbia University Oral History Research Office, 1964, 211.
162   **Many reformers wanted to end:** Seligman, *Transformation,* 146.
162   **With both Douglas and Healy:** Ibid., 146–148; Rodell, "Douglas."

162   **About all Landis could do:** Securities and Exchange Commission, *Annual Report for 1937,* 74.

163   **Congress had ordered the SEC:** Michael Parrish, *Securities Regulation and the New Deal* (New Haven: Yale University Press, 1970), 213.

163   **Landis said later that:** Landis, "Reminiscences," 205.

165   **From a vague start in Kansas:** "Business: Royalist's Revelations," *Time* vol. 26, no. 1 (July 1, 1935), page number unavailable in online archive; Associated Press, "Publisher Lays Paper Failure to J.E. Jones," *Okmulgee* (Oklahoma) *Daily Democrat,* December 18, 1931, 1; "Oil Journal Publisher Asks $60,018 Damages," *Sooner State Press,* January 9, 1932, 2; Associated Press, "Receivership Is Lifted," *Morning Chronicle,* Manhattan, Kansas, April 9, 1932, 6; "Stockholders Meeting," *Iola* (Kansas) *Daily Register,* August 20, 1931, 1; United Press, "Tulsa Corporation under Restraining Order Judge Issues," *Sapulpa* (Oklahoma) *Herald,* November 28, 1931, 5; "Action in Petroleum Royalties Case Delayed," *Parsons* (Kansas) *Sun,* June 19, 1931, 1.

165   **By 1933, he was living:** "Ousted U.S. Agent Seized in Bribe Trap," *Herald Statesman,* Yonkers, New York, June 24, 1935, 1; "Ex-Agent for SEC Seized as 'Fixer' in Broker's Home," *New York Times,* June 24, 1935, 1; "Pleads Not Guilty in SEC Bribe Case," *New York Times,* June 25, 1935, 13.

165   **"I doubt if there was":** Landis, "Reminiscences," 189.

165   **Some trust operators even used Ponzi:** Special to *The New York Times,* "Oil Royalty Curb Is Decreed by SEC," *New York Times,* May 3, 1935, 29; Special to *The New York Times,* "SEC Moves to Halt Oil Security Sale," *New York Times,* October 15, 1935, 31; Special to *The New York Times,* "SEC to Check Up on Oil Royalties," *New York Times,* November 28, 1934, 31.

166   **In a bizarre sideshow:** The details of the legal steps in the Jones case are from an unsigned document titled "Chronology of J.E. Jones v. Securities and Exchange Commission," an SEC document used with permission of SEC Historical Society.

166   **Ostensibly nonpartisan, the group opposed:** Associated Press, "Supreme Court to Decide Securities Act Validity," *Boston Globe,* February 3, 1936, 19; Frederick Rudolph, "The American Liberty League, 1934–1940," *The American Historical Review* vol. 56, no. 1 (October 1950), 19–33.

166   **In a letter to Felix Frankfurter:** A. C. Pritchard and Robert B. Thompson, "Securities Law and the New Deal Justices," *Virginia Law Review* vol. 95 (2009), 32–150.

166   **And it did so with language:** Doris Fleeson, "Capital Stuff: SEC Ruling Hailed as Campaign Thunder," New York *Daily News,* April 7, 1936, 20.

166   **But as one magazine noted:** Jeff Shesol, *Supreme Power: Franklin Roosevelt vs. the Supreme Court* (New York: W. W. Norton, 2010), 211, quoting *The Nation,* April 15, 1936, 465.

167   **Any further inquiry:** Jones v. Securities and Exchange Commission, 298 U.S. 1 (1936), used with permission of SEC Historical Society. Also available at *The New York Times,* April 7, 1936, 16.

167   **John Burns, the agency's general:** Pritchard and Thompson, "Securities Law," 34.

167   **In a private letter to Frankfurter:** Letter from Justice Harlan Fiske Stone to Felix Frankfurter, April 7, 1936, used with permission of SEC Historical Society.

167   **Of course, Jones was exultant:** Special to *The New York Times,* "High Court Rebukes SEC for Bureaucratic Policy; Jones Subpoena Is Voided," *New York Times,* April 7, 1936, 1; "Jones Praises Decision," *New York Times,* April 7, 1936, 17.

168   **"It has never been the policy":** *Hostage,* 180–181.

168   **Landis wisely saw:** Seligman, *Transformation,* 152.

168   **"Joy and gladness reigned":** Fleeson, "Capital Stuff."

169 **For the first time:** "Stock Exchange Bids Noisy Adieu to 1935," *New York Times,* January 1, 1936, 20.

169 **One of every eight men:** "Incomes of Families and Single Persons, 1935–36," *Monthly Labor Review* vol. 47, no. 4 (October 1938), 728.

169 **the class's average annual earnings:** "Education: Class of 1911," *Time* vol. 28, no. 1 (September 14, 1936), page number unavailable in online archive. https://content .time.com/time/subscriber/article/0,33009,756633-1,00.html.

170 **A majority of his classmates:** Otto Fuerbringer, "What Has Happened to 500 College Men Twenty-Five Years after Graduation," *St. Louis Post-Dispatch Sunday Magazine,* October 4, 1936, 4 (Other Editions, page 88, in newspapers.com online archives).

170 **In his view, the Class:** "Education: Class of 1911."

170 **One reporter claimed:** "Free Business, Whitney's Plea; Former Exchange Head Talks to Harvard '11," *Boston Globe,* June 18, 1936, 19; Fuerbringer, "What Has Happened."

170 **But the report refuted:** Special to *The New York Times,* "Harvard Alumni Defend Teaching," *New York Times,* July 2, 1936, 19; "Political Profs Hit in Harvard Report," *Boston Globe,* July 2, 1936, 32.

170 **The study Whitney worked on:** Judith Larrabee Holmes, "The Politics of Anti-communism in Massachusetts, 1930–1960" (PhD diss., UMass Amherst, 1996), 57–74, 77, 80, https://scholarworks.umass.edu/dissertations_1/1229/.

170 **With rhetoric infused with anti-Semitism:** Ibid., 40, 72.

171 **A slim majority of Harvard's student:** Special to *The New York Times,* "81 on Harvard Staff to Back Roosevelt," *New York Times,* October 15, 1936, 16; Special to *The New York Times,* "Landon Wins at Harvard," *New York Times,* October 16, 1936, 18; Special to *The New York Times,* "Harvard, '04, for Landon," *New York Times,* October 22, 1936, 20.

171 **That evening, Gertrude Whitney was:** Details of these reunion events are from the extensive daily coverage in *The Boston Globe* from June 16 to June 19, 1936, including several photographs of the Class of 1911.

171 **Although she performed at the reunion:** "Three Visits to Whitney by Wife Revealed," New York *Daily News,* May 13, 1938, 10.

171 **In late May, the tabloid gossip:** "Walter Winchell's Daily Column," *Tyler* (Texas) *Morning Telegraph,* May 19, 1936, 4.

171 **Whitney remained at the Manhattan townhouse:** "Stock Crook 'Skunk, Scum'— Whitney (1931)," New York *Daily News,* April 12, 1938, 18 (Other Editions, page 130, in newspapers.com online archives).

171 **Winchell, who loved stock tips:** Walter Winchell, "Man about America," *Tyler* (Texas) *Morning Telegraph,* August 6, 1936, 4.

171 **It's not clear when or how:** John Crosson and Warren Hall, "Rich Widow Grilled on Whitney Bubble," New York *Daily News,* March 14, 1938, 1 (2-Star Final Edition, page 46, in newspapers.com online archives).

172 **From London, he had sent Roosevelt:** *Hostage,* 163–164.

172 **Republicans and Liberty League Democrats:** Nasaw, *Patriarch,* 241.

172 **"We thought Joe would help":** Ibid., 246.

172 **As always, he stayed in close:** Ibid., 245.

173 **He was making a great deal:** Doris Kearns Goodwin, *The Fitzgeralds and the Kennedys* (New York: Simon & Schuster, 1987), 494; Michael Beschloss, *Kennedy and Roosevelt: The Uneasy Alliance* (New York: Perennial Library, 1987), 125.

173 **The pamphlet had been sketched:** Nasaw, *Patriarch,* 247; Beschloss, *Kennedy,* 124, reports that Kennedy had offered Krock a $5,000 fee to polish the booklet, but Krock did the work for free.

173 **The premiums for that insurance policy:** Joseph P. Kennedy, *I'm for Roosevelt* (New York: Reynal & Hitchcock, 1936), 49.

174 **Kennedy, clearly proud:** Ibid., 100.

174 **It had shut down half:** Securities and Exchange Commission, "Enforcement Activities," undated report (circa late 1936), used with permission of SEC Historical Society.

174 **Rather than backing off:** Securities and Exchange Commission, *Annual Report for 1937*, 14.

174 **Kansas governor Alfred M. Landon:** Schlesinger, Volume 3, 532; Frederick Lewis Allen, *Since Yesterday: The 1930s in America* (New York: Perennial Library, 1986; originally published by Harper & Brothers, 1939), 235–236; Davis, Volume 3, 623–627.

175 **His chairman was an old guard:** Ibid., 625.

175 **But elsewhere, Landon's more moderate voice:** Felix Belair Jr., "The Platform Is Voted; Containing 14 Planks, It Is Declared Largely a Liberal Victory," *New York Times*, June 12, 1936, 1

175 **"The necessities of life":** Special to *The New York Times*, "Text of the Platform," *New York Times*, June 12, 1936, 1, 14.

175 **The final capitulation:** Ibid.

175 **In 1934, against the advice:** Kenneth Whyte, *Hoover: An Extraordinary Life in Extraordinary Times* (New York: Alfred A. Knopf, 2017), 542.

175 **According to one biographer:** Ibid., 544. According to Whyte, Hoover was "aghast" at FDR's popularity, and "would not hear a word in favor of the president," 543.

176 **Honing his speeches, he developed:** Charles Rappleye, *Herbert Hoover in the White House: The Ordeal of the Presidency* (New York: Simon & Schuster Paperbacks, 2017), 465.

176 **As part of this "shadow campaign":** Whyte, *Hoover*, 545.

176 **About eight thousand people:** Details of Hoover's reception in Cleveland are largely from Turner Catledge, "Hoover Acclaimed in Day of Ovations," *New York Times*, June 11, 1936, 1, 14.

176 **That, he said, "is the most":** Associated Press, "Mr. Hoover's Speech," *New York Times*, June 11, 1936, 1.

177 **The delegates went wild:** Arthur Krock, "Hoover Excoriates New Deal as Fascism, Demanding a 'Holy Crusade for Freedom,'" *New York Times*, June 11, 1936, 1.

177 **Another journalist described:** F. Raymond Daniell, "Ovation to Hoover Draws Twenty State Delegations into Shouting Parade," *New York Times*, June 11, 1936, 15.

177 **Delegates stood on chairs:** Schlesinger, Volume 3, 545.

177 **The California delegation slipped:** Ibid.

177 **But to Krock, Hoover's speech helped:** Krock, "Hoover Excoriates New Deal."

178 **After all, Landon had defeated:** James McGregor Burns, *Roosevelt, 1882–1940: The Lion and the Fox* (New York: Harcourt Brace, 1984), 270.

178 **In July, he predicted:** "Reports Shift Toward Landon," *Boston Globe*, July 8, 1936, 1.

178 **The *Literary Digest* poll:** Associated Press, "Digest Editor Whose Poll Predicted Landon Win 'Astounded' at Result," *Boston Globe*, November 4, 1936, 18. The magazine forecast Landon would win 32 of the 48 states and would defeat FDR by 379 to 161 in the electoral college tally; even its editor, Wilfred J. Funk, acknowledged that he personally thought Roosevelt would win, but thought the race would be very close.

178 **As late as October 22:** "Close Election Sure, C. of C. Members Told," *Boston Globe*, October 23, 1936 (Other Editions, page 15, in newspapers.com online archives). Kiplinger predicted FDR would win the popular vote by 2 million votes and was sure to carry 225 electoral votes; he saw Landon winning roughly 219 electoral votes. "I give the edge very slightly to Roosevelt," he said.

178   **Landon won the endorsements:** Schlesinger, Volume 3, 633.
178   **A speech Smith made:** F. Raymond Daniell, "Smith Links Reds with Roosevelt; President Is Preparing Way for Communist Conquest, He Says in Albany 'Swan Song,'" *New York Times,* November 1, 1936, 1.
178   **Arthur Krock, traveling state by state:** Arthur Krock, "Vote in Michigan Likely to Be Close," *New York Times,* October 13, 1936, 18; Special to *The New York Times,* "Washington Writers by 19–1 Pick Roosevelt; Give Him 374 Electoral Votes to 157," *New York Times,* October 15, 1936, 23.
179   **Indeed, the one prediction:** "Closer Than Four Years Ago," *New York Times,* October 23, 1936, 22.
179   **Joe Kennedy joined the campaign:** Nasaw, *Patriarch,* 250–251. All the direct quotes attributed to Kennedy are from this passage.
180   **His listeners surely caught:** Franklin D. Roosevelt, "Speech at Forbes Field in Pittsburgh," October 1, 1936, File No. 930, FDR Library online archives.
180   **In defending his key financial reforms:** Franklin D. Roosevelt, "Chicago, IL—Western Campaign Trip—Campaign Address," October 14, 1936, File No. 969-A, FDR Library online archives.
181   **Meanwhile, Landon was trying:** Thomas L. Stokes, *Chip off My Shoulder* (Princeton, N.J.: Princeton University Press, 1940), 440.
181   **As Landon said later:** Shesol, *Supreme Power,* 235; Schlesinger, Volume 3, 623–625; H. L. Mencken, "Landon Opens Final Bid for East with Speech in Baltimore This Morning," *Baltimore Sun,* October 26, 1926, 1–2.
181   **But his optimism began:** Stokes, *Chip off My Shoulder,* 447.
181   **By Election Day, November 3:** H. W. Brands, *Traitor to His Class: The Privileged Life and Radical Presidency of Franklin Delano Roosevelt* (New York: Anchor Books, 2009), 454.
181   **In a big Biltmore Hotel:** "Democrats to Get Returns Speedily," *New York Times,* November 3, 1936, 11; "Jubilant Throngs Hail Farley, Idol in Victory," *Brooklyn Times Union,* November 4, 1936, 9.
181   **An octagonal room:** Frederick A. Storm, "Roosevelt Surprised at Sweep; Elated Yet Grave as He Retires," *Brooklyn Times Union,* November 4, 1936, 5; Geoffrey C. Ward, ed., *Closest Companion: The Unknown Story of the Intimate Friendship Between Franklin Roosevelt and Margaret Suckley* (New York: Simon & Schuster Paperbacks, 2009; original copyright 1995 by Wilderstein Preservation, heir to Miss Suckley's personal papers), 88.
182   **Eleanor, in a white dinner gown:** Schlesinger, Volume 3, 641; Samuel I. Rosenman, *Working with Roosevelt* (New York: Harper & Brothers, 1952), 137–138.
182   **but, like *The New York Times*:** Davis, Volume 3, 645.
182   **The margin "couldn't be that large":** "Situation as Nation Goes to the Polls," *New York Times,* November 3, 1936, 18; Davis, Volume 3, 645–646.
182   **FDR leaned back, took a puff:** Schlesinger, Volume 3, 641.
182   **Then he said, softly, "Jesus!":** Shesol, *Supreme Power,* 238, citing the diary of Stanley High, a reporter who had taken leave to work for FDR and who was present that evening. Schlesinger (Volume 3, 641) relies on the account by Rosenman (*Working,* 137) who quoted FDR as saying "Wow!" when he heard about his New Haven victory margin. I am relying on High's version, both because he was a professional journalist keeping a diary for his personal future use and because he was less protective of FDR's image. Also, he was described as being fairly religious, so it seems unlikely that he would have used "Jesus" gratuitously in his private diary.
182   **As exhausted reporters and newsreel cameramen:** Davis, Volume 3, 646; Storm, "Roosevelt Surprised."

183 **As Election Day deepened into night:** "Night Clubs Quiet with Thin Crowds," *New York Times,* November 4, 1936, 21.

183 **Among the more somber wealthy diners:** "All City's Resorts Expect Big Crowds," *New York Times,* November 3, 1936, 16.

183 **"Not a person stirred":** Davis, Volume 3, 650, citing *The Economist,* November 21, 1936.

183 **Despite his previous conversations:** FDR's interactions with Keynes are described in Eric Rauchway, *The Money Makers: How Roosevelt and Keynes Ended the Depression, Defeated Fascism, and Secured a Prosperous Peace* (New York: Basic Books, 2015), 51–52, 98–100, 129; and Zachary D. Carter, *The Price of Peace: Money, Democracy, and the Life of John Maynard Keynes* (New York: Random House, 2020), 291–296.

183 **Roosevelt urged his solicitor general:** Harold L. Ickes, *The Secret Diary of Harold L. Ickes: The First Thousand Days* (New York: Simon & Schuster, 1953), hereafter Ickes, Volume 1, 705.

183 **Kennedy's job was to get American:** Beschloss, *Kennedy,* 128–129.

184 **His speeches were getting attention:** Ralph F. de Bedts, "The First Chairmen of the Securities and Exchange Commission: Successful Ambassadors of the New Deal to Wall Street," *The American Journal of Economics and Sociology* vol. 23, no. 2 (April 1964), 165–178.

184 **If John Hamilton is worth:** Harold L. Ickes, *The Secret Diary of Harold L. Ickes: The Inside Struggle, 1936–1939* (New York: Simon & Schuster, 1954), hereafter Ickes, Volume 2, 22.

184 **But the feelings behind it:** Ritchie, *Landis,* 73–74.

185 **"Without much hesitation, Landis accepted":** Ibid., 75.

185 **"I was in bed the next morning":** Landis, "Reminiscences," 247; Harold Ickes gave a secondhand account of a similar incident but placed it on January 23, 1937 (Ickes, Volume 2, 60). Landis may have confused the timing, but he never forgot the sentiment.

186 **Was it not true that Whitney:** Special to *The New York Times,* "Listing Practices of Stock Exchange Hit in Rail Inquiry," *New York Times,* January 16, 1937, 1; Special to the New York *Daily News,* "Wheeler Raps Rail Deals on N.Y. Exchange," New York *Daily News,* January 16, 1937, 25; Associated Press, "New York Stock Exchange's Policies Hotly Debated," *Boston Globe,* January 16, 1937, 10.

186 **He said Charles Gay:** Special to *The New York Times,* "More Rigid Rules on Listings Likely," *New York Times,* January 27, 1937, 29.

187 **He was ready to parse them:** De Bedts, *The New Deal's SEC,* 134.

187 **Douglas knew he could rely on:** Murphy, *Wild Bill,* 125.

187 **Douglas "has outlined his predicament":** Ray Tucker, "The National Whirligig: The News Behind the News," *Clovis* (New Mexico) *Evening News-Journal,* January 21, 1937, 2. Tucker's column was syndicated by the McClure Newspaper Syndicate and appeared in a host of newspapers nationally.

188 **"The test of our progress":** Franklin D. Roosevelt, "Inaugural Address," January 20, 1937, File No. 1030, FDR Library online archives.

188 **This was a significant victory:** "Utility Loses Fight on Listings by SEC," *New York Times,* January 30, 1937, 1.

188 **"To care less about stockholders":** United Press, "Raps Utilities Lawyers," *Pittsburgh Press,* January 31, 1937, 25; the Associated Press and *The New York Times* gave slightly different versions of these remarks. See Associated Press, "Landis Threatens Holding Concerns," *Baltimore Sun,* January 31, 1937, 1; and Special to *The New York Times,* "Landis Is Elated by Utility Decision," *New York Times,* January 31, 1937, 49.

189 **For whatever reason:** Leuchtenburg, *FDR and the New Deal* , 251.

190 **But he condemned "excessive" regulation:** "Gay Declares Rules Burden Stock Trading," *Brooklyn Daily Eagle,* August 18, 1937, 17.

191 **Gay had made essentially the same:** William O. Douglas, "Margins and Markets," Response to Charles Gay, New York Stock Exchange, July 11, 1936, used with permission of SEC Historical Society.

191 **The result was less liquidity:** Burton Crane, "Thin Markets Held a Gradual Growth," *New York Times,* January 3, 1938, 32. See also Fritz Lehmann, "Thin Markets," *Social Research* vol. 5, no. 1 (February 1938), 55–69.

191 **Gay's report "left the clear implication":** John Brooks, *Once in Golconda: A True Drama of Wall Street 1920–1938* (New York: Harper & Row, 1969), 242.

191 **"You have contributed mightily":** Special to *The New York Times,* "Landis, Resigning, Hits Back at Gay," *New York Times,* September 15, 1937, 33, 37.

192 **The attack was condemned:** "Commissioner Landis," *New York Times,* September 16, 1937, 24. This editorial praised Landis for his stewardship of the SEC but lambasted "what may be called his valedictory remarks."

192 **They had warned FDR's:** Simon, *Independent Journey,* 160.

192 **They suggested some prominent business figure:** Murphy, *Wild Bill,* 132.

192 **Thus, "his selection is believed":** Special to *The New York Times,* "Douglas to Head SEC, Washington Hears, but Wall St. Is Said to Hold Him Radical," *New York Times,* August 10, 1937, 25.

CHAPTER SIX: DEFENDING AGAINST DEREGULATION

193 **When he leaned back in his:** Bruce Allen Murphy, *Wild Bill: The Legend and Life of William O. Douglas* (New York: Random House, 2003), 116–117.

193 **To one friend there, Douglas seemed:** Ibid., 137.

193 **There had been a lot of:** Special to *The New York Times,* "Text of W.O. Douglas's Statement at Press Conference," *New York Times,* September 23, 1937, 45.

194 **In private, he saw himself:** Douglas, *Go East, Young Man,* 179.

194 **He had been psychoanalyzed:** Douglas was a patient of Dr. George Draper, a pioneer in psychosomatic medicine and an unconventional physician who also treated FDR, a childhood friend, after the future president was stricken with polio. Douglas, *Go East, Young Man,* 179.

194 **The funds she squandered could have let him:** Murphy, *Wild Bill,* 57–58.

194 **A family meal at Kennedy's table:** James F. Simon, *Independent Journey: The Life of William O. Douglas* (New York: Harper & Row, 1980), 140–141.

195 **But his ambition-driven schedule:** Ibid., 147, 230–237.

195 **Since early 1937, Kennedy had nagged:** Michael Beschloss, *Kennedy and Roosevelt: The Uneasy Alliance* (New York: Perennial Library, 1987), 151–152.

195 **At the U.S. Conference of Mayors:** Paul W. Ward, "Ickes Calls for Scaling of Works Outlay," *Baltimore Sun,* November 18, 1936, 1.

196 **His audience, which had greeted him:** "Chapter III, Investment Banking," an untitled document describing the "famous 'Bond Club Speech'" by Douglas, posted online with permission of the Yale University Press and used with permission of SEC Historical Society; "End of Banks' Rule in Industry Hinted," *New York Times,* March 25, 1937, 37. In comments to reporters, Douglas also cited Joe Kennedy's belief that "excessive financing, excessive underwriting charges, excessive bonuses, improper loans and a host of other evils" that "would be condemned as graft if occurring in public life, have grown out of the practice of allowing bankers to serve on the boards of industrial companies," as the *Times* put it.

196 **Even with Douglas's reform credentials:** Murphy, *Wild Bill,* 122–123.

196 **On September 17, he had flown:** Ibid., 132–133.

198 **But he did explain that:** United Press, "Douglas Says 'Action' Will Be His Theme," *Brooklyn Daily Eagle,* September 22, 1937, 22 (emphasis added).

198 **One of Douglas's chief preoccupations:** Simon, *Independent Journey,* 165.

198 **Gay had persuaded himself:** Ralph F. de Bedts, *The New Deal's SEC: The Formative Years* (New York: Columbia University Press, 1964), 150.

198 **Indeed, that belief had been strengthened:** Murphy, *Wild Bill,* 142–143.

198 **When a reformer on the board:** Ibid., 139; Simon, *Independent Journey,* 165.

199 **After five years on the board:** "Stock Exchange Picks Officers Tomorrow," *New York Times,* May 12, 1935, 76; "Exchange Elects Gay in Heavy Vote," *New York Times,* May 14, 1935, 29; "Simmons Remains in Exchange Post," *New York Times,* May 13, 1936, 35.

200 **Whitney was hospitalized briefly in June:** "Richard Whitney Improving," *New York Times,* June 10, 1937, 25.

201 **The president's cuts to federal spending:** Kenneth S. Davis, *FDR: Into the Storm 1937–1940* (New York: Random House 1993), hereafter Davis, Volume 4, 9; Kenneth D. Roose, "The Recession of 1937–38," *Journal of Political Economy* vol. 56, no. 3 (June 1938), 245; Jean Edward Smith, *FDR* (New York: Random House Trade Paperbacks, 2007), hereafter Smith, *FDR,* 396–398.

201 **Certainly, one factor was the Federal:** Christina D. Romer and David H. Romer, "Choosing the Federal Reserve Chair: Lessons from History," *Journal of Economic Perspectives* vol. 18, no. 1 (Winter 2004), 132–133.

201 **Other research suggests:** Carmen M. Reinhart and Kenneth S. Rogoff, *This Time Is Different: Eight Centuries of Financial Folly* (Princeton, N.J.: Princeton University Press, 2009), 146–147.

201 **All these declines were from:** Roose, "The Recession," 243–244.

201 **FDR's conservative Treasury secretary:** Herbert Levy, *Henry Morgenthau, Jr.: The Remarkable Life of FDR's Secretary of the Treasury* (New York: Skyhorse Publishing, 2010), 7.

201 **Some younger New Dealers:** Leuchtenburg, *FDR and the New Deal,* 245; H. W. Brands, *Traitor to His Class: The Privileged Life and Radical Presidency of Franklin Delano Roosevelt* (New York: Anchor Books, 2009), 488.

201 **Roosevelt got some version of that:** Conrad Black, *Franklin Delano Roosevelt: Champion of Freedom* (New York: Public Affairs, 2003), 428–429.

202 **As the recession deepened:** Examples can be found in Ickes, Volume 2, 229 and 241–42, and Smith, *FDR,* 397.

202 **By September, the economy's slide:** Roose, "The Recession," 241.

202 **The New York Times reprised:** Burton Crane, "Wall St. Digs Deep to Explain Breaks," *New York Times,* September 12, 1937, 101.

202 **Adolf Berle told his diary:** Beatrice Bishop Berle and Travis Beal Jacobs, eds., *Navigating the Rapids, 1918–1971* (New York: Harcourt Brace Jovanovich, 1973), 136.

203 **Screened by FDR's entourage:** Michael F. Reilly, as told to William J. Slocum, *Reilly of the White House: Behind the Scenes with FDR* (New York: Simon & Schuster, 1947), 70 in the Kindle edition; Schlesinger, Volume 3, 583–584; Smith, *FDR,* 367.

203 **Harold Ickes told his diary:** Ickes, Volume 1, 626.

203 **But as the recession of 1937:** Ernest K. Lindley, "The New Deal Faces 1940," *The Virginia Quarterly Review* vol. 15, no. 3 (Summer 1939), 324.

204 **And rather than drawing closer:** Davis, Volume 4, footnote on page 5.

204 **In his increasingly lonely life:** Ibid., 5–6.

204 **The president's ill-fated effort:** Robert E. Sherwood, *Roosevelt and Hopkins: An Intimate History* (New York: Harper & Brothers, 1948), 90–91; Leuchtenburg, *FDR and the New Deal,* 233–236.

204   **As one New Deal historian put:** Leuchtenburg, *FDR and the New Deal*, 239.

204   **FDR fumed to his close aides:** Samuel I. Rosenman, *Working with Roosevelt* (New York: Harper & Brothers, 1952), 176–177.

205   **Then he attacked Douglas:** Special to *The New York Times*, "Economic Adviser Dropped by SEC," *New York Times*, October 5, 1937, 35

206   **He could encourage the Investment Bankers:** Seligman, *Transformation*, 158.

206   **In deciding a disciplinary case:** Special to *The New York Times*, "SEC Eases Rules on Stock Options," *New York Times*, October 10, 1935, 37; Special to *The New York Times*, "SEC Soon to Adopt Policy on 'Pegging,'" *New York Times*, November 20, 1937, 24.

206   **There was a thin line between:** "To Study New SEC Rules; Bankers Will Consider Moves in Security Distribution," *New York Times*, January 29, 1938, 23.

207   **His father played a role:** Nelson W. Aldrich Jr., *Old Money: The Mythology of America's Upper Class* (New York: Alfred A. Knopf, 1988), 8, 21–24.

207   **His favorite sister, Abby:** David Rockefeller, *Memoirs* (New York: Random House, 2002), 63, 121.

208   **Like the NYSE president:** Special to *The New York Times*, "Break in Market Is Laid by Aldrich to Federal Curbs," *New York Times*, October 15, 1937, 1.

208   **It was just a question:** "Security Regulation," *New York Times*, October 15, 1937, 22.

208   **The president was deeply worried:** Richard J. Whalen, *The Founding Father: The Story of Joseph P. Kennedy* (New York: New American Library of World Literature, 1964), 198; From a Staff Correspondent, "Kennedy Predicts Balanced Budget," *New York Times*, October 16, 1937, 1.

209   **He itemized the banker's complaints:** "Pecora Backs SEC, Chiding Aldrich," *New York Times*, October 18, 1937, 25.

209   **Franklin Roosevelt, as he stewed:** Ickes, Volume 2, 241.

209   **One wit, journalist Marquis Childs:** Marquis W. Childs, *They Hate Roosevelt* (New York: Harper & Brothers, 1936), 5.

210   **At a cabinet meeting that fall:** John Morton Blum, *From the Morgenthau Diaries: Years of Crisis, 1928–1938* (Boston: Houghton Mifflin, 1959), 391–392; Ickes, Volume 2, 241–242.

210   **"Tell them for the fifteenth time":** Blum, *From the Morgenthau Diaries*, 392; Ickes, Volume 2, 241–242.

211   **Its owner was arrested:** Associated Press, "Ryan Arrested on State Charges," *Palm Beach Post*, October 21, 1937, 12.

211   **The drop in bond prices:** "Stocks Off 2 to 15 in Heavy Selling; Bonds Also Break," *New York Times*, October 19, 1937, 1.

211   **He later recorded in his memoirs:** Douglas, *Go East, Young Man*, 281. Douglas is clearly wrong about when this conversation happened. He sets it during the market upheaval on September 7, 1937, before he had become chairman; the first major convulsion after he was sworn in was this one, on October 18, 1937.

211   **Tuesday, October 19, was another staggering:** This occurred exactly fifty years before that date, October 19, entered Wall Street history as "Black Monday" in 1987, still the worst single-day market decline ever.

212   **"Most issues closed at their lows":** "Stock Prices up Sharply after Drop to New Lows; 7,287,990 Shares Traded," *New York Times*, October 20, 1937, 1.

212   **In Washington that day, Henry Morgenthau:** Blum, *From the Morgenthau Diaries*, 386.

212   **"This looks to me like 1903":** Berle and Jacobs, *Navigating the Rapids*, 141–142.

213   **That night, Harold Ickes:** Ickes, Volume 2, 230.

213   **Quietly known around the exchange:** John Brooks, *Once in Golconda: A True Drama of Wall Street 1920–1938* (New York: Harper & Row, 1969), 221.

213   **In 1927, the firm changed:** Robert J. Cole, "Edward A. Pierce Dies at 100," *New York Times,* December 17, 1974, 60.

213   **Ed Pierce had lost patience:** Alsop and Kintner, Battle Part 1, 76.

214   **Weathered and silver-haired:** "Milestones: Jan. 4, 1963; Died: Paul Vincent Shields," *Time,* January 4, 1963.

214   **"Unburdened with traditional theories and attitudes":** Earl Sparling, "The New Wall Street," *Oklahoma News,* April 29, 1935, 3.

214   **Indeed, he had been:** Raymond Moley, *After Seven Years* (New York: Harper & Brothers, 1939), 286.

215   **Pierce and Shields had flown back:** Joseph Alsop and Robert Kintner, "The Battle of the Market Place: Wall Street and Washington Make Peace," *Saturday Evening Post,* June 25, 1938, hereafter Alsop and Kintner, Battle Part 2, 10.

216   **Alsop and Kintner described FDR:** Ibid., 10.

217   **Douglas gave the exchange officials:** Murphy, *Wild Bill,* 140.

218   **It was a total victory:** "Bond & Share Test Is Refused Again," *New York Times,* November 9, 1937, 33.

218   **Douglas insisted his staff would:** Special to *The New York Times,* "Decision Pleases Douglas," November 1937 (Other Editions, page 16, in newspapers.com online archives).

219   **"It was on this point":** Alsop and Kintner, Battle Part 2.

219   **After all, the market was taking:** Ibid.; Murphy, *Wild Bill,* 142–143.

220   **When Davis had taken his pencil:** Alsop and Kintner, Battle Part 2.

220   **"There is one thing I'd like to ask:** Murphy, *Wild Bill,* 143–144.

CHAPTER SEVEN: THE NEW DEAL ACTS, THE OLD GUARD BLINKS

221   **The resulting front-page article:** Fred Rodell, "Douglas over the Stock Exchange," *Fortune* vol. 17, no. 2 (February 1938), 64, 116; Bruce Allen Murphy, *Wild Bill: The Legend and Life of William O. Douglas* (New York: Random House, 2003), 146.

222   **Douglas watched:** Rodell, "Douglas," 116.

222   **As *Fortune* later reported:** Ibid.

222   **Some accounts held that Douglas's fury:** Joseph Alsop and Robert Kintner, "The Capital Parade: Mutual Suspicion over Exchange," *Boston Globe,* November 30, 1937 (Other Editions, page 16, in newspapers.com online archives).

222   **His message to the public:** Rodell, "Douglas," 64, 116.

223   **His six-page statement was front-page news:** Special to *The New York Times,* "Full Text of the Statement by W. O. Douglas," *New York Times,* November 24, 1937, 39.

223   **By one account, some committee members:** Rodell, "Douglas," 119.

226   **The lowest levels of support:** "New Deal Hurts Business, Public Opinion Check Shows," *Palladium-Item,* Richmond, Indiana, December 17, 1937, 5; "Opinions of Public on New Deal Shift," *New York Times,* December 14, 1937, 8.

226   **But he nevertheless observed:** Stanley High, *Roosevelt—And Then?* (Freeport, N.Y.: Books for Libraries Press, 1971; original copyright Harper & Brothers, 1937), 105.

226   **He was essentially running a test:** John Morton Blum, *From the Morgenthau Diaries: Years of Crisis, 1928–1938* (Boston: Houghton Mifflin, 1959), 260–267, 278–283.

226   **At a white-tie debate:** "Role of New Deal in Slump Debated," *New York Times,* December 7, 1937, 22.

226   **"How on earth can business people":** Joseph Alsop and Robert Kintner, "Kennedy in Warning Assails 'Howlers' in Business World," *Boston Globe,* December 13, 1937, 6.

227   **Wall Street applauded:** "Topics in Wall Street: SEC Possibility," *New York Times,* December 2, 1937, 37.

227   **But he had a beautiful mind:** Seligman, *Transformation,* 214.

227 **When he joined a New York:** J. Mitchell Rosenberg, *Jerome Frank: Jurist and Philosopher* (New York: Philosophical Library, 1970), xiii, quoting *Current Biography* (New York, H. W. Wilson, 1941), 301.

228 **It was worth a great deal:** Beatrice Bishop Berle and Travis Beal Jacobs, eds., *Navigating the Rapids, 1918–1971* (New York: Harcourt Brace Jovanovich, 1973), 148.

228 **On Monday, November 29:** Seligman, *Transformation,* 164.

228 **But buried deep within his protests:** "Gay Sees Danger in More SEC Curbs," and "Exchange President's Reply to SEC," *New York Times,* November 30, 1937, 1, 12.

228 **Over Whitney's objections:** Associated Press, "Stock Exchange to Study Revisions in Market Rules," *Democrat and Chronicle,* Rochester, New York, December 9, 1937, 1.

228 **Berle wryly told his diary:** Berle and Jacobs, *Navigating the Rapids,* 150.

229 **"I do not think":** Ibid., 154.

229 **To the outspoken Paul Shields:** Alsop and Kintner, Battle Part 2, 81.

229 **Some cynics saw the committee's creation:** James McMullin, "The Political Whirligig," *Middletown* (New York) *Times Herald,* December 18, 1937, 9.

229 **Dick Whitney was among the first:** Ibid.; "Behind the World News Headlines; Strategy," Port Chester, New York, *Daily Item,* December 24, 1937, 6.

229 **Kennedy himself, of course:** Nasaw, *Patriarch,* 273.

230 **It would be hard to imagine:** Ibid.

230 **Jimmy Roosevelt later said:** Davis, Volume 4, 152.

230 **"The first time he opens":** Nasaw, *Patriarch,* 274.

231 **And at the last moment:** Special to *The New York Times,* "Roosevelts Plan Holiday Parties," *New York Times,* December 23, 1937, 18; Special to *The New York Times,* "First Lady Flies West for Holidays," *New York Times,* December 24, 1937, 15; Davis, Volume 4, 159–160.

231 **The gunboat bombing rattled the stock:** James E. Buck, ed., *The New York Stock Exchange: The First 200 Years* (Essex, Conn.: Greenwich Publishing Group, 1992, for the NYSE), 79.

231 **The role of Santa Claus:** "Yule Spirit Enters Wall St. in Swing Time, with Jazz Accidentally Mixed with Carols," *New York Times,* December 21, 1937, 35; "Yule Tree Parties Draw City Throngs," *New York Times,* December 24, 1937, 10.

232 **Accountancy, he said:** Robert E. Healy, "The Next Step in Accounting" (address before the annual meeting of the American Accounting Association), December 27, 1937, 12, used with permission of SEC Historical Society.

232 **Within a year, Douglas would:** "Memorandum: Atlantic City, N.J., December 27, 1937," signed by John L. Carey, 2, used with permission of SEC Historical Society; Berle and Jacobs, *Navigating the Rapids,* 157.

232 **The papers were filed in court:** Special to *The New York Times,* "Hutton Partners Face SEC Charges," *New York Times,* January 1, 1938, 25. Loeb denied any wrongdoing, but in May 1938, while still denying the charges, Loeb accepted a settlement with the SEC that allowed him to resign from EF Hutton for ten months.

232 **There were the usual pranks:** "Exchange 'Floor' Enjoys Usual Year-End Pranks," *New York Times,* January 1, 1938, 25.

232 **A few moments later:** "'Change Head to Fine 2 Fighters," New York *Daily News,* January 13, 1938 (Other Editions, page 266, in newspapers.com online archives).

233 **The message paid little attention:** Davis, Volume 4, 200.

233 **The business community seemed:** Ickes, Volume 2, 287.

233 **But despite their relief:** Berle and Jacobs, *Navigating the Rapids,* 158, 161–162.

233 **It was not a Keynesian epiphany:** Conrad Black, *Franklin Delano Roosevelt: Champion of Freedom* (New York: Public Affairs, 2003), 432.

233 **One historian observed that the SEC:** Davis, Volume 3, 371.

233 **Roosevelt assured Douglas later that spring:** "Address of William O. Douglas . . . Before the Yale Club of Washington," SEC.gov online archives, April 17, 1938, 3.

234 **In a unanimous decision:** Special to *The New York Times*, "PWA Wins Suits in Supreme Court on Power Issues," *New York Times*, January 4, 1938, 1; Special to *The New York Times*, "Decision of the Supreme Court on PWA Power Financing," *New York Times*, January 4, 1938, 15.

234 **The utility industry was a bit demoralized:** Thomas P. Swift, "Utilities Divided on SEC Regulation," *New York Times*, January 9, 1938, 97.

235 **Before the crash, the most common:** Seligman, *Transformation*, 224.

236 **In both cases, as one historian:** Ibid., 226.

236 **the agency's investment trust hearings:** "SEC Sifts $9,700,000 in 'Good-Will' Item," *New York Times*, January 12, 1938, 29; Associated Press, "Trust Deals Traced in Hearings by SEC," *New York Times*, January 11, 1938, 38. The central figure of these early 1938 hearings was Wallace Groves, who took over the investment trust defrauded by the disgraced NYSE firm Prince & Whitely. Groves would be convicted of federal fraud charges in 1941, and would emerge from prison in 1944 to become a central figure in the development of the casino industry in the Bahamas. In an article published on October 5, 1966, *The Wall Street Journal* alleged that Groves was secretly a front for Miami mobster Meyer Lansky, but he was never charged with organized crime activity.

236 **"If Congress heeds the proposals":** Joseph Alsop and Robert Kintner, "SEC Soon to Urge Reform of Trusts," *New York Times*, January 13, 1938, 29.

236 **A few weeks later, the SEC:** "Market Advisers Studied by SEC," *New York Times*, February 12, 1938, 28.

237 **Douglas was introduced:** "Sen. Maloney Host at His Home Here to Prof. Douglas," *Meriden* (Connecticut) *Record*, January 8, 1938, 1.

237 **Douglas opened with flattery:** "SEC Leader Tells Markets Choice Open," *Hartford Courant*, January 8, 1938, 1; Special to *The New York Times*, "Douglas Outlines Over-Counter Code," *New York Times*, January 8, 1938, 21.

238 **The *New York Herald Tribune* promptly:** Murphy, *Wild Bill*, 156.

238 **A few days later:** Associated Press, "Dr. Frank Declares New Deal 'Fascist,' " *New York Times*, January 30, 1938, 1.

238 **A municipal bond dealer:** "The Maloney Bill," address of Robert E. Healy at the annual dinner of the New York Security Dealers Association, March 10, 1938, 5, used with permission of SEC Historical Society.

238 **He laid out two options:** William O. Douglas, "Memorandum to the President," January 28, 1938, used with permission of SEC Historical Society.

238 **Five days later, Roosevelt endorsed:** William O. Douglas, "Letter to the Honorable Francis T. Maloney," February 4, 1938, used with permission of SEC Historical Society.

239 **Douglas had arrived at Dillon's:** Douglas, *Go East, Young Man*, 286.

239 **The next morning, he had shared:** Ibid., 287; Robert C. Perez and Edward F. Willett, *Clarence Dillon: Wall Street Enigma* (Lanham, Md.: Madison Books, 1995), 102–103.

240 **There, he personally presented a copy:** Berle and Jacobs, *Navigating the Rapids*, 159–162.

241 **"So great was Whitney's eloquence":** John Brooks, *Once in Golconda: A True Drama of Wall Street 1920–1938* (New York: Harper & Row, 1969), 252.

241 **There was a murmur of surprise:** Alsop and Kintner, Battle Part 2.

242 **One of Cohen's colleagues:** Letter from C. David Ginsburg, on letterhead of the National Power Policy Committee, to Felix Frankfurter, February 12, 1938, signed "Dave G.," and used with permission of SEC Historical Society.

242 **But only one of them:** William Lasser, *Benjamin V. Cohen: Architect of the New Deal* (New Haven: Yale University Press, 2002), 148–149.

243 **"Long accustomed to court practices":** Special to *The New York Times*, "Only 7 Justices Hear Utility Case," *New York Times*, February 8, 1938, 35.

244 **Early in January, the elder Whitney:** Drew Pearson and Robert S. Allen, "The Daily Washington Merry-Go-Round," *Tampa Tribune*, February 3, 1938, 20.

244 **"When you phoned that you would":** Drew Pearson and Robert S. Allen, "The Daily Washington Merry-Go-Round," *Bristol* (Tennessee) *Herald Courier*, February 2, 1938, 4. This version, unlike the Tampa version, includes the dinner bet anecdote as its final paragraph, but it also badly garbles both the columnists' names and the name of the column.

245 **Gay and Davis walked into:** Seligman, *Transformation*, 167–168.

CHAPTER EIGHT: AN ANATOMY OF SELF-DESTRUCTION

247 **"You'll know what is best":** Douglas, *Go East, Young Man*, 287.

248 **The fund's legal structure:** The U.S. Securities and Exchange Commission, *In the Matter of Richard Whitney, Edwin D. Morgan, Jr., F. Kingsley Rodewald, Henry D. Mygatt, Daniel G. Condon, John J. McManus, and Estate of John A. Hayes* (Washington: U.S. Government Printing Office, 1938), hereafter *SEC Whitney Report*, vol. 1, 100–101. The original report was issued in three volumes, so my citations will give both volume and page. All the direct quotations, as well as the impressions and emotions described, are based on the witnesses' sworn testimony in the second volume or on documents and other exhibits reproduced in the third volume.

248 **He rarely checked on the whereabouts:** Ibid.

248 **He prepared the monthly agenda:** Ibid.

248 **"I am only a clerk":** *SEC Whitney Report*, vol. 2, 194.

249 **He had feared that raising:** Ibid., 180–181.

249 **"I really couldn't go over":** Ibid., 199–202, 334–335.

250 **As soon as Simmons got back:** Ibid., 335.

250 **Whitney was out:** Ibid., 68.

250 **His late father had been:** "Edwin D. Morgan, Yachtsman, Dies," *Brooklyn Times Union*, June 14, 1933, 18; "Edwin D. Morgan, Noted Yachtsman, Dies at Age of 78," *Brooklyn Daily Eagle*, June 14, 1933, 13; Nancy Randolph, "Suspension of Whitney Firm a Blow to '400,'" New York *Daily News*, March 9, 1938, 39.

250 **Through his four siblings:** "Long Island Society: Mrs. Priscilla B. Preston and T. Archer Morgan Are Married," *Brooklyn Daily Eagle*, October 27, 1934, 4.

250 **Still, his parents' and siblings' connections:** Special to *The New York Times*, "Miss Auchincloss Married at Darien," *New York Times*, August 1, 1937, 75; Special to the New York *Daily News*, "Renos Hubby Again Because of Romance," New York *Daily News*, July 19, 1935, 29.

250 **One J.P. Morgan partner:** Malcolm MacKay, *Impeccable Connections: The Rise and Fall of Richard Whitney* (New York: Brick Tower Press, 2013), 89.

251 **"There is no reason why":** *SEC Whitney Report*, vol. 2, 337.

251 **Whitney answered:** Ibid., 63, 337.

252 **George Whitney was "terribly disturbed":** Ibid., 63–64.

252 **He knew his brother lived far:** MacKay, *Impeccable Connections*, 78.

252 **George had helped pay:** These details of the financial dealings between the Whitney brothers are documented at several points in *SEC Whitney Report*, primarily in their own testimony, vol. 2, 1–80 and 497–528.

253 **The total came to $1,082,000:** Ibid., 522.

253 **"Dick is in a very serious":** Ibid., 525.

253 **As Lamont recalled the conversation:** Ibid., 733–734, 739–743.

254 **But Redmond, too, assured him:** Ibid., 338–339.

254 **Simmons immediately took the elevator:** Ibid., 428.

255 **The entire expedition took less than:** Ibid., 340–342.

255 **Jack Morgan was fairly sure:** Ibid., 838.

256 **As far as the trustees:** Ibid., 432.

256 **Its primary product was applejack:** MacKay, *Impeccable Connections*, 78.

256 **Dick had little choice:** *SEC Whitney Report*, vol. 2, 69.

257 **Despite all these broken promises:** Ibid., 551–552.

257 **And he still trusted Dick's estimate:** John Brooks, *Once in Golconda: A True Drama of Wall Street 1920–1938* (New York: Harper & Row, 1969), 249.

257 **Simmons vaguely said he would try:** *SEC Whitney Report*, vol. 2, 346–350.

259 **"He is broke and borrowing money":** Ibid., 823–825.

259 **"It made no particular impression":** Ibid., 853–860.

259 **The loan request did not raise:** Ibid., 437–438.

259 **A few weeks after that:** Ibid., 351–352.

260 **He decided he would just:** Ibid., 107–110.

260 **Simmons told him instead:** Ibid., 358–360, 395–400.

261 **Randy Mason had first been hired:** Ibid., 878.

261 **Mason agreed he would do so:** Ibid., 883–885.

262 **At the end of 1926, he became:** "3 of Morgan Staff Get Partnerships," *New York Times*, January 1, 1927, 5.

262 **He was comfortably:** The ancestry.com website shows Bartow's mother, Anna Key Steele, was the daughter of Maria Lloyd Key Steele, who was the daughter of Francis Scott Key.

262 **Indeed, it was Bartow:** *SEC Whitney Report*, vol. 2, 563.

262 **He had been worried:** Ibid., 564–566.

263 **Around this time:** *SEC Whitney Report*, vol. 3, 290.

263 **When Mason got into the limousine:** *SEC Whitney Report*, vol. 2, 885–887, 893.

264 **If Mason got that impression:** Ibid., 902–914.

264 **He once again vowed:** Ibid., 620–621. The testimony was given by Walter T. Rosen, a partner with Ladenburg, Thalmann & Co.

265 **He got the unnerving results:** Ibid., 269–314, the testimony of John Dassau, the NYSE comptroller.

265 **He said he was:** Ibid., 401.

266 **Gay and Davis agreed:** Ibid., 402–403.

266 **Here, again, the loan was approved:** Ibid., 40–41; Brooks, *Once in Golconda*, 260–261.

266 **It's hard to see:** *SEC Whitney Report*, vol. 2, 321, 404, 888.

266 **He didn't have any other details:** Ibid., 541–542.

267 **The complacent comptroller:** Ibid., 404–405.

267 **At various points:** *SEC Whitney Report*, vol 1, 45.

267 **He simply told the group:** *SEC Whitney Report*, vol. 2, 541–542.

268 **As he sat at his desk:** *SEC Whitney Report*, vol. 1, 43; MacKay, *Impeccable Connections*, 95; Brooks, *Once in Golconda*, 267.

268 **Dick Whitney learned early Saturday:** *SEC Whitney Report*, vol. 1, 45–46.

268 **"The exchange can't afford":** Alsop and Kintner, Battle Part 2, 82.

268 **He simply lobbied:** *SEC Whitney Report*, vol. 2, 326.

268 **Finally, Gay said the exchange:** Ibid., 323.

269 **Bartow was trying to find:** Ibid., 409.

269 **Whitney was a longtime member:** MacKay, *Impeccable Connections*, 39.

269 **As they sat down:** *SEC Whitney Report*, vol. 2, 590–592. This account of the events ending with Bartow's final conversation with Dick Whitney at the Links Club is drawn from Bartow's testimony.

273 **Jack Morgan had always said:** Ron Chernow, *The House of Morgan: An American*

Banking Dynasty and the Rise of Modern Finance (New York: Touchstone, 1990), 371.

273   **"I was busy all night":** *SEC Whitney Report,* vol. 2, 841–842. J. P. "Jack" Morgan Jr. recited the conversation in his testimony.

273   **Sunderland had known the Whitney brothers:** MacKay, *Impeccable Connections,* 94.

274   **He insisted he would return:** *SEC Whitney Report,* vol. 2, 593.

274   **Bartow said he would do so:** Ibid., 594.

274   **He rose and left:** Ibid.

275   **The comptroller and his assistant:** *SEC Whitney Report,* vol. 3, 297.

275   **They were speechless:** "Topics in Wall Street: The Whitney Affair," *New York Times,* March 9, 1938, 25.

276   **The minutes reported:** *SEC Whitney Report,* vol. 3, 163–166.

CHAPTER NINE: THE GENTLEMAN'S CODE

277   **Bearing subpoenas for Whitney's records:** John Brooks, *Once in Golconda: A True Drama of Wall Street 1920–1938* (New York: Harper & Row, 1969), 268–269.

277   **As a friend of several Morgan:** Louchheim, 133.

277   **But "he could not bring himself":** Seligman, *Misalignment,* 536.

278   **There was little thought of trading:** Ibid.

278   **A Manhattan society columnist:** Nancy Randolph, "Society: Mrs. Byron Foy Shows Portrait by Briton," New York *Daily News,* March 21, 1938, 31.

279   **On Wednesday, March 9, Bill Douglas:** Brooks, *Once in Golconda,* 274.

280   **McCall, described as:** "M'Call, Nemesis of Swindlers, Quits as Attorney General's Aide," *New York Times,* December 18, 1942, 43.

280   **McCall sat at his desk:** These details are based on photographs taken at the hearing and published in the New York *Daily News* and *The New York Times* on March 9 and 10, 1938.

280   **"Well, I guess we understand each other":** "Whitney Assumes Blame in Failure," *New York Times,* March 10, 1938, 1.

280   **At this point, the two men:** Richard L. Stokes, "Brother Saved Whitney Once by Loan of Million," *St. Louis Post-Dispatch,* March 21, 1938, 1. Stokes provided a vivid description of the hearing and its setting.

281   **But to the astonishment of officials:** Richard L. Stokes, "Exchange Trial on Thursday," *St. Louis Post-Dispatch,* March 15, 1938, 1.

281   **That gave Tom Dewey an opening:** Ibid.

281   **Her sister, the widow:** Ibid.; "Daniel F. Murphy, Retired Jurist," *New York Times,* May 24, 1937, 19.

282   **Douglas claimed that Dewey said:** Douglas, *Go East, Young Man,* 287–288.

282   **A case could even be made:** Malcolm MacKay, *Impeccable Connections: The Rise and Fall of Richard Whitney* (New York: Brick Tower Press, 2013), 97.

283   **The reform amendments had passed:** "Exchange Adopts New Constitution," *New York Times,* March 18, 1938, 29.

283   **Whitney's sentencing, set for March 28:** Associated Press, "Asks Delay in Whitney Case," *Boston Globe,* March 22, 1938, 3.

284   **The snow from a freak springtime:** Photo of Richard Whitney with caption, no by-line, "Out—In the Cold and Snow!," New York *Daily News,* April 7, 1938 (Other Editions, page 457, in newspapers.com online archives).

284   **The chief counsel who would examine:** "Brokers' Firm Enjoined by Federal Court after SEC Agent Files Charges," *Detroit Free Press,* May 15, 1936, 1; Joseph Alsop and Robert Kintner, "The Capital Parade: Next Investigation on New Deal List," *Boston Globe,* January 21, 1939, 1.

284   **The room was stuffy:** Associated Press, "Whitney Borrowed for Exchange Seat,"

Boston Globe, April 8, 1938 (Other Editions, page 1, in newspapers.com online archives).

285 **"The firm of Richard Whitney & Company":** *SEC Whitney Report,* vol. 2, 58.

286 **A Gallup poll days later showed:** Dr. George Gallup, "Further S.E.C. Regulation Favored in Gallup Poll on Whitney Case," *Boston Globe,* April 13, 1938, 17.

286 **"I can still borrow money":** Louchheim, 132; Whitney made a similar comment to Gesell in his sworn testimony, *SEC Whitney Report,* vol. 2, 75, explaining that he considered the firm "solvent" so long as he could meet his debts on demand, even if he did so by getting fresh loans to pay off older loans.

286 **For the rest of the day:** Grace Robinson, "Funeral Pall Hangs over Whitney Home," New York *Daily News,* April 12, 1938 (Other Editions, page 377, in newspapers .com online archives); "A Matter of Minutes," New York *Daily News,* April 12, 1938, 84; John Crosson and George Dixon, "Whitney Given 5–10 Yrs.; Under Guard in Tombs," New York *Daily News,* April 12, 1938, 2, 16.

286 **Lawyer Charles Tuttle was waiting:** Crosson and Dixon, "Whitney Given 5–10 Yrs.," 16.

287 **Whitney waited on the second row:** These details are drawn from the cited stories from the New York *Daily News* of April 12, 1938; from Richard L. Stokes, "Ex-Broker to Be Taken to Prison Tomorrow to Begin His Term," *St. Louis Post-Dispatch,* April 11, 1938, 1; and from "Whitney Receives 5 to 10 Year Term," *New York Times,* April 12, 1938, 1.

288 **The keenest review of Whitney's final:** Brooks, *Once in Golconda,* 274.

288 **The day Whitney was sentenced:** "Whitney Group Stunned as 'Liberals' Win All 28 Places in Naming Board of Governors," *Brooklyn Daily Eagle,* April 11, 1938, 1.

288 **Martin seemed to have no vices:** Seligman, *Transformation,* 174–175.

288 **One SEC commissioner confided:** Michael Parrish, *Securities Regulation and the New Deal* (New Haven: Yale University Press, 1970), 218.

289 **One of his first acts:** Leased Wire from New York Bureau of *Globe-Democrat,* "Change Board Holds First Open Meeting," *St. Louis Globe-Democrat,* May 17, 1938, 7.

289 **When he rang the closing bell:** Ibid.

291 **Morgan's answer was:** *SEC Whitney Report,* vol. 2, 833.

292 **"Sure," Lamont said:** Ibid., 742–743.

292 **Morgan historian Ron Chernow suggests:** Ron Chernow, *The House of Morgan: An American Banking Dynasty and the Rise of Modern Finance* (New York: Touchstone, 1990), 425.

292 **"The stock exchange had just":** *SEC Whitney Report,* vol. 2, 535.

292 **That sort of "tale-bearing":** Ibid., 434.

293 **Lamont conceded that:** Chernow, *House of Morgan,* 427.

293 **Or as Bill Douglas so memorably:** Edwin P. Hoyt, *The Tempering Years* (New York: Charles Scribner's Sons, 1963), 36.

293 **"If there is one lesson":** John T. Flynn, "Whitney Case Blamed upon His Speculations," *Cincinnati Post,* March 18, 1938, 5.

293 **"I do not know of any record":** Letter from Felix Frankfurter to William O. Douglas, May 6, 1938, used with permission of SEC Historical Society.

294 **"Richard Whitney got five years":** Associated Press, "'$2 Whitney' Gets 24-Minute Term," New York *Daily News,* April 21, 1938, 4.

CHAPTER TEN: DOUBTS AND DEPARTURES

295 **The dense fog that blanketed parts:** Felix Belair Jr., "Fog at Sea Delays Roosevelt Yacht," and "Fog Delays 2 Liners," *New York Times,* June 20, 1938, 6, 31.

295 **But Jimmy Roosevelt, President Roosevelt's son:** Michael Beschloss, *Kennedy and Roosevelt: The Uneasy Alliance* (New York: Perennial Library, 1987), 170.

295   **"I enlisted under President":** Associated Press, "Kennedy Denies He Has Eye on Presidency," *St. Louis Post-Dispatch*, June 20, 1938, 1; "Kennedy Returns, Bars a 1940 Boom," *New York Times*, June 21, 1938, 6.

296   **Kennedy was more exuberant:** Doris Fleeson, "Not a '40 Candidate, Kennedy Says Flatly," New York *Daily News*, June 21, 1938, 14.

296   **He rekindled his friendships:** Richard J. Whalen, *The Founding Father: The Story of Joseph P. Kennedy* (New York: New American Library of World Literature, 1964), 220.

297   **Soon, Kennedy seemed to be more:** Ibid., 257; Nasaw, *Patriarch*, 310–311.

297   **"But the job of Ambassador":** Doris Kearns Goodwin, *The Fitzgeralds and the Kennedys* (New York: Simon & Schuster, 1987), 510–511.

297   **Chamberlain's foreign minister:** Ferdinand Kuhn Jr., "Britain Is Shocked," *New York Times*, February 21, 1938, 1.

297   **Chamberlain's response had been:** Goodwin, *Fitzgeralds*, 520.

297   **"For the first few weeks":** William L. Shirer, *The Rise and Fall of the Third Reich: A History of Nazi Germany*, 50th Anniversary Edition (New York: Simon & Schuster, 2011), 351.

298   **Their view was shared:** Goodwin, *Fitzgeralds*, 520.

298   **But he was not convinced:** James McGregor Burns, *Roosevelt, 1882–1940: The Lion and the Fox* (New York: Harcourt Brace, 1984), 387–388.

298   **He had read the dictator's prophetic:** The National Archives contains FDR's copy of Hitler's memoir. On the flyleaf, Roosevelt wrote in 1933: "This translation is so expurgated as to give a wholly false view of what Hitler really is or says—The German original would make a different story."

298   **FDR suspected Chamberlain's critic Winston Churchill:** Edward M. Lamont, *The Ambassador from Wall Street: The Story of Thomas W. Lamont, J.P. Morgan's Chief Executive* (Lanham, Md.: Madison Books, 1994), 442.

298   **Roosevelt was walking a very delicate:** Davis, Volume 4, 358.

298   **Given his stature in business:** Whalen, *Founding Father*, 230.

298   **He had hired his friend:** Beschloss, *Kennedy*, 169–170.

298   **He told Krock it would be:** Nasaw, *Patriarch*, 314.

299   **Most remarkable of all:** Beschloss, *Kennedy*, 165–166; Nasaw, *Patriarch*, 317.

299   **Conspicuously missing from Kennedy's mailing list:** Beschloss, *Kennedy*, 171.

299   **The White House first learned:** Ibid.

299   **One of them, FDR's press secretary:** Ibid.

299   **As prices climbed, short sellers jumped:** Todd Wright, "Trading Spurts in Sharp Upturn," New York *Daily News*, June 21, 1938, 39.

300   **A New York society reporter overheard:** Nancy Randolph, "G.O.P. Back Bay Yawns as John and Anne Wed," New York *Daily News*, June 19, 1938, 3.

300   **Kennedy's idea, Roosevelt told Ickes:** Nasaw, *Patriarch*, 315; Beschloss, *Kennedy*, 172.

300   **But Roosevelt's comments to the reporters:** *Hostage*, 265.

301   **"Plenty of excitement over here":** Goodwin, *Fitzgeralds*, 532.

301   **"After all those expectations":** Ibid., 534–535.

301   **When reporters asked about it:** Ibid.

301   **But when the day was over:** "Kennedy May Skip Harvard Exercises," *Boston Globe*, June 23, 1938, 1.

301   **While still at Hyannis Port:** Nasaw, *Patriarch*, 317.

301   **He visited his official superior:** *Hostage*, 265.

302   **Late on Friday afternoon:** Special to *The New York Times*, "Kennedy Visits Capital Offices," *New York Times*, June 25, 1938, 3.

302   **Years later, by which point Kennedy:** *Hostage*, 265–266.

302   **As an unseasoned ambassador:** Nasaw, *Patriarch*, 318–319.

302   **The piece claimed the young Roosevelt:** Beschloss, *Kennedy,* 173; "Ambassador Kennedy Sails for London with His Sons," *New York Times,* June 30, 1938, 18.

303   **"Oh, no! The papers have been":** Associated Press, "Kennedy Raps Story on Aid," *Boston Globe,* June 29, 1938 (Other Editions, page 23, in newspapers.com online archives); "'Premier Scotch Salesman'Title Labeled 'a Phony' by Kennedy," *Brooklyn Daily Eagle,* June 29, 1938, 1.

303   **Jones claimed the SEC commissioners:** Howard Wood, "Oil Man Tells of Persecution by Government," *Chicago Tribune,* June 18, 1938, 21.

303   **This baseless lawsuit:** "$1,000,000 Suit of Scarsdale Man Against S.E.C. Thrown Out by U.S. Court," *Herald Statesman,* Yonkers, New York, October 9, 1939, 9.

303   **With Europe so unsettled:** Memorandum to Chairman Douglas from Paul P. Gourrich, Director, Research Division, February 17, 1937, used with permission of SEC Historical Society.

303   **Prodded by Kennedy and aware:** There is no doubt that Kennedy was deeply involved in initiating and overseeing these studies: see Letter from Joseph P. Kennedy to William O. Douglas, April 28, 1938, used with permission of SEC Historical Society; "SEC Aide Off to Europe to Study Markets There," *New York Times,* April 21, 1938, 29; and Memorandum to Chairman Douglas from Commissioner [John W.] Hanes, March 9, 1938, used with permission of SEC Historical Society.

304   **Commissioner Jerome Frank:** Review by members of the staff of the Trading and Exchange Division of "Report on the London Stock Exchange" and "Report on Foreign Dealings in American Securities," February 21, 1939, used with permission of SEC Historical Society.

304   **Frank complained:** Confidential, to Chairman Douglas from Commissioner [Jerome] Frank, October 13, 1938, used with permission of SEC Historical Society.

304   **The second report did little more:** "S.E.C. Creates Post Abroad," *Montreal Star,* February 2, 1939, 31.

304   **"Franklin Roosevelt evidently decided":** Beschloss, *Kennedy,* 174.

305   **As September waned, Kennedy was:** *Hostage,* 269–293.

305   **"The only discordant note":** Ibid.

305   **According to the Czech leader's account:** Beschloss, *Kennedy,* 177.

305   **The agreement apparently strengthened Kennedy's convictions:** Whalen, *Founding Father,* 223.

305   **By all accounts, that was hastily:** *Hostage,* 294.

306   **"Kennedy for Amity with Fascist Bloc":** Wireless to *The New York Times,* "Kennedy for Amity with Fascist Bloc," *New York Times,* October 20, 1938, 10.

306   **Foreign envoys made polite:** Ronald Kessler, *The Sins of the Father: Joseph P. Kennedy and the Dynasty He Founded* (New York: Warner Books, 1996), 175.

306   **Officials there desperately denied:** Special to *The New York Times,* "No Policy Changes in Kennedy Speech," *New York Times,* October 21, 1938, 8.

307   **To prove that, the White House:** Nasaw, *Patriarch,* 354–355.

307   **"Militaristic, totalitarian philosophy":** "Roosevelt Warns Nation Must Arm in World of Force," *New York Times,* October 27, 1938, 1; "Text of Roosevelt's Talk to Forum," page 15 of the same date.

307   **Roosevelt, a master of radio:** The speech was drafted for FDR by his early brain trust advisor Adolf Berle; Berle's instructions were to "undo the damage done by Kennedy's recent speech [and] make it clear that our foreign policy was unchanged." Nasaw, *Patriarch,* 354–355.

308   **The ambassador later said:** *Hostage,* 228; Whalen, *Founding Father,* 250–251.

308   **As he explained in a letter:** *Hostage,* 298.

308   **The historic item was:** Felix Belair Jr., "Roosevelt 'Grins' over State Results," *New*

York Times, November 9, 1938, 5; United Press, "F.D.R. Cast Vote Without Luck Charm," New York *Daily News,* November 9, 1938, 16.

309   **But the drive also reflected:** Samuel I. Rosenman, *Working with Roosevelt* (New York: Harper & Brothers, 1952), 176–177.

309   **Roosevelt had defended Murphy:** Davis, Volume 4, 360.

309   **"Every time I hear these words":** Ibid., 257.

310   **His object seemed to be:** "I Am the Law," *New York Times,* December 17, 1937, citing Hague's infamous response to a question about which law allowed him to ban labor organizers from his city: "I am the law."

310   **The mayor's intemperate language:** Davis, Volume 4, 257–260.

310   **Roosevelt hadn't dared go further:** Ibid., 256.

311   **But "a social or economic gain":** Associated Press, "Text of President's Address from Hyde Park on Issues in the Coming Election," *New York Times,* November 5, 1938, 5.

312   **"During the last two or three":** "Old Guard Is Gone, Dewey Aides Hold," *New York Times,* October 14, 1938, 1.

312   **In this race, Landon himself:** Associated Press, "Fear of Fascism Voiced by Landon," *New York Times,* November 1, 1938, 7.

312   **The most that the popular mayor would:** Beatrice Bishop Berle and Travis Beal Jacobs, eds., *Navigating the Rapids, 1918–1971* (New York: Harcourt Brace Jovanovich, 1973), 190.

313   **Back in his days as governor:** Conrad Black, *Franklin Delano Roosevelt: Champion of Freedom* (New York: Public Affairs, 2003), 191.

313   **Nearly three years had passed:** Seligman, *Transformation,* 179.

314   **The ruling, the climax of Ben:** Lewis Wood, "Must File with SEC," *New York Times,* March 29, 1938, 1.

314   **Tom Dewey's narrow defeat confirmed:** Richard Norton Smith, *Thomas E. Dewey and His Times* (New York: Simon & Schuster, 1982), 273–274.

314   **Governor Frank Murphy:** Davis, Volume 4, 362–363.

315   **The Times of London said:** Special to *The New York Times,* "London Times Man Analyzes Election," *New York Times,* November 10, 1938, 14.

315   **A Brooklyn paper concluded that:** "Roosevelt and 'Liberalism,'" *Brooklyn Daily Eagle,* November 12, 1938, 10.

315   **The editors of *The New York Times:*** "The Election," *New York Times,* November 10, 1938, 26.

315   **Some far-seeing editorials:** "An Analysis of the Results," *Brooklyn Citizen,* November 10, 1938, 4.

316   **The victor in the Ohio race:** Davis, Volume 4, 363.

316   **To one old friend, Roosevelt:** Letter from Franklin D. Roosevelt to Josephus Daniels, November 14, 1938, in Elliott Roosevelt and Joseph P. Lash, eds., *FDR: His Personal Letters, 1928–1945* (New York: Duell, Sloan and Pearce, 1950), hereafter *FDR Personal Letters,* vol. 2, 827.

316   **The conservative bloc hoping:** Leuchtenburg, *FDR and the New Deal,* 272–273.

316   **FDR was more candid:** *FDR Personal Letters,* vol. 2, 826.

316   **But he wrote a friend:** Ibid., 827.

316   **Predictably, some longtime party voices:** Ibid., 830.

317   **The people "brought in a verdict":** Special to *The New York Times,* "Moley Hails Vote as Gain for Public," *New York Times,* November 10, 1938, 18.

317   **Now and for years to come:** Leuchtenburg, *FDR and the New Deal,* 273.

317   **In any case, Roosevelt now had:** Ickes, Volume 2, 500–501.

317   **"Being a Jew is not a crime":** Davis, Volume 4, 364–365.

318   **Revulsion against Hitler was immediate:** Ibid.

318   **He summoned the U.S. ambassador:** Ibid., 367.

CHAPTER ELEVEN: THE FIGHT FOR THE FUTURE

320   **Even under modern appellate guidance:** Seligman, *Transformation*, 171; see also: https://www.whitecollarbriefly.com/2017/06/07/9th-circuit-clarifies-elements-of-misprision-of-felony/ and https://www.washingtonpost.com/news/volokh-conspiracy/wp/2014/09/29/misprision-of-felony/.

320   **Douglas later complained that:** Douglas, *Go East, Young Man*, 300.

321   **Giannini was a prominent and generous:** James F. Simon, *Independent Journey: The Life of William O. Douglas* (New York: Harper & Row, 1980), 182.

321   **As Douglas put it:** Ibid.; Douglas, *Go East, Young Man*, 295.

322   **Martin raised "sundry matters":** Ganson Purcell, Memorandum of Conference, December 17, 1938, used with permission of SEC Historical Society.

323   **Their doubts had been fueled:** Ron Chernow, *The House of Morgan: An American Banking Dynasty and the Rise of Modern Finance* (New York: Touchstone, 1990), 427.

323   **The firm claimed that NYSE officials:** Special to *The New York Times*, "SEC Holds Silence Let Whitney Go On," *New York Times*, November 2, 1938, 1; the Morgan firm's statement is at the end of the story, on page 18.

323   **"The Morgan statement, quite simply":** Seligman, *Transformation*, 172.

325   **Still in his formal wear:** Charles Keats, *Magnificent Masquerade: The Strange Case of Dr. Coster and Mr. Musica* (New York: Funk & Wagnalls, 1964), 176. Keats covered the Coster/Musica scandal as a reporter and, tipped by a police source, had slipped into the Coster mansion minutes before the suicide occurred. His is the most complete account of the bizarre case.

325   **A fierce and outspoken critic:** Ibid., 3, 125–126.

326   **When Weinberg had first heard:** Securities and Exchange Commission, *In the Matter of McKesson & Robbins, Inc., File No. 1-1435,* Securities Exchange Act of 1934 Release No. 2707, Accounting Series Release No. 19, Section II, 15.

326   **Finally, Weinberg had called the chairman:** Keats, *Magnificent Masquerade,* 178.

327   **Another company executive who lived nearby:** Ibid., 193–196.

327   **With help from the enterprising head:** Ibid., 197–200.

328   **"The jangle of the bell":** Ibid., 206.

328   **One historian said his anger:** Seligman, *Transformation,* 172.

328   **A parade of gleaming limousines:** "'Financial Follies' Given by Writers," *New York Times,* December 17, 1938, 23.

329   **The privileged crowd filled:** John Chapman, "Mainly about Manhattan," New York *Daily News,* December 9, 1938, 60.

329   **Bill Douglas was given:** Felix Belair Jr., "W.O. Douglas Is Nominated for Seat in Supreme Court," *New York Times,* March 21, 1939, 1.

329   **So far as the NYSE:** Seligman, *Transformation,* 172–173.

330   **It concluded with the warning that:** Unsigned "Draft Form," dated December 19, 1938, and attributed to Douglas, used with permission of SEC Historical Society.

330   **" Mr. Martin and I have worked closely":** Arthur Krock, "In the Nation: A Look at the Washington–New York Axis," *New York Times,* December 27, 1938, 16.

330   **Douglas later confided to Roosevelt:** Letter from William O. Douglas to FDR, April 12, 1939, used with permission of SEC Historical Society.

330   **Until the New Deal:** Stephen A. Zeff, "How the U.S. Accounting Profession Got Where It Is Today: Part I," *Accounting Horizons* vol. 17, no. 3 (September 2003), 190.

330   **Their general assumption was that:** Diane H. Roberts, "Changing Legitimacy Narratives about Professional Ethics and Independence in the 1930s 'Journal of Accountancy,'" *The Accounting Historians Journal* vol. 37, no. 2 (December 2010), 96–97, 103.

331   **After all, a gentleman of integrity:** Ibid., 104–105.

331   **In May 1937, amid grumbling:** Ibid., 106–107.

331   **It sounded fierce but its impact:** Seligman, *Misalignment,* 554–556.

331   **But the SEC had been content:** Ibid.

332   **"Like a torrent of cold water":** John L. Carey, "The McKesson & Robbins Case," *Journal of Accountancy* vol. 67, no. 2 (February 1939), 65.

332   **While others focused on the Musica:** "Coster Audit Fees Put at $1,000,000," *New York Times,* January 6, 1939, 2.

332   **The profession's guidelines did not require:** Zeff, "How the U.S. Accounting Profession Got Where It Is Today: Part I," 192.

332   **And either of those tests:** Keats, *Magnificent Masquerade,* 119.

332   **"In the aftermath of this sensational":** Thomas K. McCraw, *Prophets of Regulation* (Cambridge, Mass.: Belknap Press/Harvard University Press, 1984), 350, footnote 69.

332   **These reforms, while they relied:** Sheila Foster and Bruce A. Strauch, "Auditing Cases That Made a Difference: McKesson & Robbins," *Journal of Business Case Studies* vol. 5 no. 4 (July/August 2009), 15.

333   **After the SEC's landmark:** Laura Kalman, *Abe Fortas: A Biography* (New Haven: Yale University Press, 1990), 62.

333   **The result, one staff member:** Seligman, *Transformation,* 182–183.

333   **Tommy Corcoran was worrying aloud:** Unsigned memo attributed to Tommy Corcoran, titled "Securities & Exchange Commission" and dated January 27, 1939, used with permission of SEC Historical Society.

334   **A financial writer for:** "To Debate Revision of Securities Acts," *New York Times,* March 12, 1939, 83; unsigned, undated draft titled "Chapter XI: On Amending the Law," used with permission of SEC Historical Society. This draft incorporates the SEC official response, on March 15, 1939, to exchange officials' proposals.

334   **In fact, the SEC had known:** Unsigned SEC memorandum dated February 23, 1939, and beginning "Lokey of the Stock Exchange phoned," used with permission of SEC Historical Society.

334   **"are precisely the policies":** Joseph Alsop and Robert Kintner, "The Capital Parade: Test of Appeasement Policy," *Atlanta Constitution,* March 13, 1939, 4.

334   **"Today markets are thin":** Burton Crane, "Ask SEC to Repeal Rules on Insiders," *New York Times,* March 15, 1939, 35.

335   **The next day, the SEC released:** Special to *The New York Times,* "SEC Hits Proposals to Loosen Trading," *New York Times,* March 16, 1939, 39.

336   **On Monday evening, February 13:** Bruce Allen Murphy, *Wild Bill: The Legend and Life of William O. Douglas* (New York: Random House, 2003), 165.

336   **Well, Krock had replied:** Douglas recalled (in *Go East, Young Man,* 456–457) that when he arrived at his colleague's home, Krock toasted him openly as "the next Justice of the Supreme Court," but Krock was too jealous of his scoops to make that version believable.

336   **"Brandeis retired today":** Murphy, *Wild Bill,* 165.

336   **But as SEC chairman, Douglas certainly:** Ibid., 169.

336   **Soon it would be time:** Ibid., 166.

337   **"Tomorrow I am sending your name":** Ibid., 172–173.

337   **The two men spent several hours:** Ibid., 171.

337   **Deeply committed to his educational mission:** John Fisher, "Hutchins Asked by Roosevelt to Take SEC Job," *Chicago Tribune,* March 24, 1939, 33.

338   **But Gesell's impression was that:** Louchheim, 136.

338   **"You guys," he said:** Ibid., 143.

338   **The New Deal's last major financial:** Letter from William O. Douglas to "The President," April 12, 1939, used with permission of SEC Historical Society.

339   **The decision was a forerunner:** Noah Feldman, *Scorpions: The Battles and Triumphs of FDR's Great Supreme Court Justices* (New York: Twelve/Hachette Book Group, 2011), 425–427; Simon, *Independent Journey*, 348–349.

339   **Roosevelt would twice consider Douglas:** Simon, *Independent Journey*, 174; William O. Douglas, *The Autobiography of William O. Douglas: The Court Years, 1939–1975* (New York: Random House, 1980), 281–284.

339   **Dick Whitney was a model prisoner:** John Brooks, *Once in Golconda: A True Drama of Wall Street 1920–1938* (New York: Harper & Row, 1969), 286.

340   **While George Whitney eventually paid:** Malcolm MacKay, *Impeccable Connections: The Rise and Fall of Richard Whitney* (New York: Brick Tower Press, 2013), 104–105.

340   **Roughly four hundred:** "Class of 1911 Offers Pusey Classical Cocktail," *Boston Globe*, June 13, 1961, 1.

340   **"Work harder and longer hours":** MacKay, *Impeccable Connections*, 104.

340   **He died on December 5, 1974:** Albin Krebs, "Richard Whitney, 86, Dies, Headed Stock Exchange," *New York Times*, December 6, 1974, 42.

341   **"Sticking your tongue out":** Nasaw, *Patriarch*, 355–356.

341   **But publicly, Kennedy still had:** Doris Kearns Goodwin, *The Fitzgeralds and the Kennedys* (New York: Simon & Schuster, 1987), 610; Davis, Volume 4, 618.

341   **So Kennedy stumbled on:** Nasaw, *Patriarch*, 365–367.

342   **When both Roosevelt:** Ibid., 382–285; Goodwin, *Fitzgeralds*, 572–573.

342   **When the summer of 1939 arrived:** Nasaw, *Patriarch*, 397.

342   **He was in London when Germany sent:** *Hostage*, 365–369.

342   **This "recklessly bizarre" proposal:** Nasaw, *Patriarch*, 413–414.

342   **"England is committing suicide":** Ibid., 427, 429.

342   **Kennedy returned to his London post:** Ibid., 433.

342   **He was saddened by Chamberlain's resignation:** Ibid., 440.

342   **Inevitably, Kennedy was moved:** Ibid., 444–447.

343   **"If Roosevelt had followed my advice":** Ibid., 455.

343   **Sunk in his pessimism:** Ibid., 497.

343   **His daughter Rosemary:** Goodwin, *Fitzgeralds*, 593–595.

343   **In 1948, his toll of grief:** Ibid., 738–740.

343   **Always slipshod about his finances:** Ritchie, *Landis*, 194–195.

343   **In July 1964, he would be:** Special to *The New York Times*, "James M. Landis Found Dead in Swimming Pool at His Home," *New York Times*, July 31, 1964, 1.

343   **By then, Joe Kennedy would have suffered:** Nasaw, *Patriarch*, 780.

344   **On Friday, August 23:** Special to *The New York Times*, "Roosevelt Signs Trust Measure," *New York Times*, August 24, 1940, 17.

344   **The SEC apparently had concluded:** Seligman, *Transformation*, 228–229.

344   **They were far more interested:** Charles Hurd, "Roosevelt Asks Draft Bill Enacted Within Two Weeks; Debate in Senate Continues," *New York Times*, August 24, 1940, 1.

345   **But that day's presidential statement:** Seligman, *Misalignment*, 553; according to Seligman, nearly two-thirds of the corporate bond trustees examined were not required to even complain if a company defaulted unless a certain percentage of bondholders demanded it. "As a general practice," he wrote, trustees often "ignored known defaults," leaving investors no legal protection.

346   **"the tremendous well-spring":** Beatrice Bishop Berle and Travis Beal Jacobs, eds., *Navigating the Rapids, 1918–1971* (New York: Harcourt Brace Jovanovich, 1973), 526–528.

347   **"The Roosevelt administration did not achieve":** Seligman, *Misalignment*, 569.

EPILOGUE

349 **To make room for the growing:** "Topics of Interest in Wall Street Yesterday: The SEC," *New York Times,* January 13, 1942, 29.

349 **When FDR died:** Seligman, *Transformation,* 231.

349 **"the most widespread pattern":** Seligman, *Misalignment,* 903.

349 **The 1955 budget left the SEC:** Ibid., 902–904.

350 **The eminent SEC historian Joel Seligman's harsh verdict:** Ibid., 901.

350 **A major market manipulation scheme:** Ibid., 905–909, 911.

INDEX

DIANA B. HENRIQUES is the author of five previous books, including the *New York Times* bestseller *The Wizard of Lies: Bernie Madoff and the Death of Trust,* which was adapted as an HBO film starring Robert De Niro and was cited in the widely watched Netflix documentary series *Madoff: The Monster of Wall Street.* A staff writer for *The New York Times* from 1989 to 2012, she is a George Polk Award winner and a Pulitzer Prize finalist, and received Harvard's Goldsmith Prize for Investigative Reporting, among other honors. She lives in Hoboken, New Jersey.

This book was set in Caslon, a typeface first designed in 1722 by William Caslon (1692–1766). Its widespread use by most English printers in the early eighteenth century soon supplanted the Dutch typefaces that had formerly prevailed. The roman is considered a "workhorse" typeface due to its pleasant, open appearance, while the italic is exceedingly decorative.